FAIRGROUND FICTION

Detective Stories
of the World's Columbian Exposition

Containing reprints of
Emma Murdoch Van Deventer's
Against Odds: A Detective Story
and
John Harvey Whitson's
Chicago Charlie, the Columbian Detective

**Edited by Donald K. Hartman
Foreword by Carl S. Smith**

Motif Press
1992

Copyright © 1992 by **EPOCH BOOKS, Inc.**

Themes and Settings in Fiction Series, #1

Printed on acid free paper

Cover photo reproduced by permission of the Chicago Historical Society

Library of Congress Card Number: 91-61998

ISBN: 0-962-9586-0-3

Motif Press is an imprint of:

EPOCH BOOKS, Inc.
22 Byron Avenue.
Kenmore, New York 14223

Contents

Foreword vii

Against Odds: A Detective Story 1

Something about the author of *Against Odds* 253

Chicago Charlie: the Columbian Detective 257

Something about the author of *Chicago Charlie* 434

Map of the Fairgrounds 436

Appendix: Fictional Works Using the World's
Columbian Exposition as a Setting 437

Photographs

Administration Building	5
Looking East from the Administration Building	9
Court of Honor, Looking West	10
Golden Door—Transportation Building	16
Nebraska Building	60
New York Building	64
Princess Eulalie	77
South Dakota Building	94
Irish Industrial Village	194
Entrance to German Village	198
Street in Cairo	201
Dancers, Egyptian Theatre	284
Javanese Village	297
Hagenbeck's Animal Show	300
Krupp Building	351
Krupp Gun	353

Foreword

PROBABLY NO EVENT of its kind has had a more profound influence on the American imagination than the World's Columbian Exposition. This is partly because there has been no other event quite like it. Certainly America has hosted other world's fairs, among the most notable being the Centennial in Philadelphia in 1876 and the Century of Progress—once again in Chicago—in 1933–34. But none of them stirred as many different people at the time and since as has the Columbian Exposition, which seemed to materialize out of nowhere on the shores of Lake Michigan for six months from the spring to the fall of 1893, astounding and enchanting visitors from all over America and the world.

The major reason why the Columbian Exposition was so arresting was the physical fact of the fair itself. In a remarkable feat of coordination and cooperation, the nation's leading architects and artists, directing crews of construction workers, designed and built a magnificently landscaped and integrated ground plan centered around a neoclassical Court of Honor composed of monumental exhibition buildings and statuary painted snowy white—hence the popular name, White City. These structures, and the many lesser surrounding ones erected by nations, states, and private enterprise the world over, were filled with seemingly endless displays of every kind. The different buildings were tied together by a remarkably attractive and convenient system of sidewalks and waterways, and in the evenings they were illuminated as if by magic by the modern miracle of electric light.

Having paid a general admission fee, one was free to go anywhere in confident expectation of a transcendent if perhaps ultimately overwhelming and incoherent experience of education and uplift. If this was not enough, abutting the White City was the Midway, a bizarre pay-as-you-go mix of exotic attractions, including "authentic" reconstructions of Aztec, Irish, Javanese, Bedouin and several other cultures, Egyptian belly dancers in the "Streets of Cairo," "Forty Ladies from Forty Nations" at the "World's Congress of Beauties," a menagerie of trained beasts at Hagenbeck's Animal Show, and the first Ferris Wheel, a 264-foot-high mechanical marvel that offered the best view of the whole spectacle. Those still jaded could attend Buffalo Bill's Wild West Show, encamped nearby.

The fair was also a signal event in what is widely seen as a watershed period in American history. In both style and scale, it marked not only the four hundredth anniversary of Columbus's first voyage, but also the declaration of America's imperial ambitions. At the 1893 annual meeting of the American Historical Association, one of several such conclaves held in Chicago in conjunction with the fair, Frederick Jackson Turner pointed out that the American frontier had ceased to exist. The United States had taken over the continent, and the Columbian Exposition announced that it was ready to confront the world. At the same time, the fair was a great coming-out party for Chicago itself, which had burned to the ground twenty-two years earlier and now was the second-largest city in America—and rapidly growing. The so-called "Dream City" and the actual city that hosted it seemed at once to sum up all the achievements of history and to indicate the direction of the future.

It should hardly be surprising, then, that the two novels reprinted in this volume represent just a fraction of the fictional works devoted at least in passing to the Columbian Exposition, and that the fiction of the White City is only a small part of the total body of writing devoted to the fair. This grand occasion inspired dozens of guidebooks of all sorts, from pamphlets on individual exhibits to the first Baedeker travel guide to the United States. Newspapers and periodicals overflowed with special exposition issues and articles of praise and criticism, some questioning the relevance of this snowy fantasy to American life, but most declaring it the outstanding achievement of the age and even the culmination of all human endeavor. Enterprising authors and presses cranked out handsome photographic viewbooks and ponderous multi-volume histories. As years passed the White City also became a milestone in the memoirs of visitors of every background and sensibility, including among American writers of note a range of authors from Theodore

Dreiser (whose eyes were opened "at the sight of this realized dream of beauty, this splendid picture of the world's own hope for itself") to Henry Adams ("since Noah's ark, no such Babel of loose and ill-joined, such vague and ill-defined and unrelated thoughts and experimental outcries as the Exposition, had ever ruffled the surface of the lakes").

With some notable exceptions, most of the fiction of the Columbian Exposition appeared within a few years of the fair and covers the spectrum of realism and fanciful romance that characterizes American literature of the period, though there are far more examples of romance. While Chicago is justifiably associated with the development of realism in America in the late nineteenth century, authors who wished to analyze in detail and depth the new American urban setting best embodied by Chicago itself were not likely to be drawn to the fair as a subject. One exception is Robert Herrick, who was familiar with both the "real" Chicago and the White City since he was a professor at the brand-new University of Chicago, which was located almost in the shadow of the Ferris Wheel. While observing that the Columbian Exposition "in a way was Chicago, its dream, its ideal, its noblest self incarnated," in *The Web of Life* (1900) Herrick concentrated on the ironic juxtaposition of the hopes of the Fair and the distress cast over the city and the country by the depression of 1893, which caused cold and hungry members of the "army of unemployed" to seek shelter in the abandoned grand exhibition buildings (which were largely destroyed in post-closing fires) and soon led to the Chicago-centered Pullman strike of 1894.

The romantic fiction of the fair comes in several different forms ranging from children's stories to more sophisticated literature. In several of these works, the plot is a device to present a more imaginative kind of guidebook to the reader. In others, the situation is reversed, as opportunistic authors exploit the special possibilities of the fair—including the ready-made interest in it—as a setting for an intricately convoluted plot that closely adheres to the conventions of narratives of courtship, mystery, or adventure (frequently all three) familiar to a broad audience of readers. Partly because of their predictability, these books are often intriguing for what they reveal about the the relation of literary form to cultural experience. This is the special interest of both *Against Odds: A Detective Story* and *Chicago Charlie, the Columbian Detective.*

Against Odds is a common hybrid mystery-and-love plot in which the solution of the mystery is closely interwoven with the resolution of a troubled courtship. The marriage of admirable characters follows swiftly upon the undoing of villains, whose crimes usually include some kind of assault on virtue (in this case a wooing of the heroine under false pretenses and the kidnapping of a wealthy and upstanding young man), as well as on the property and persons of honest citizens. Before secret service agent-narrator Carl Masters and his redoubtable colleague Dave Brainerd, on special assignment at the fair, can capture the evildoers and bring the lovers together, however, they must unravel a daunting array of related mysteries including confidence games, counterfeiting, and diamond robbery, not to mention murder. It is not without justification that Masters is struck by the the thought, "I wonder if the world is pouring all its mysteries into this White City of the world." Their task is made all the more difficult by their foes' multiple skills at disguise. Along the way we see many stock characters, from the tall, golden–haired June Jenrys and her kind-hearted but hard-headed Quakeress maiden aunt Miss Ross to the scheming Frenchman Delbras.

What makes this book stand out from others like it is its highly detailed rendering of the fair (including the Midway) and the nearby neighborhood of Hyde Park. In the course of the novel we not only see major attractions like the Ferris Wheel and the Court of Honor, but also many minor ones as well. For example, the narrative sets major action around the Nebraska state exhibit and the fire in the Cold Storage Building, and it takes us into local residences. What *Against Odds* does better than other books of its kind, better even than many guidebooks and memoirs, is communicate an experiential feel for the sights and sounds (including the favorite song of the fair, "After the Ball") of the exposition. Riding the Intramural Railway within the grounds, Masters shares with the reader his delight and awe at the "kaleidoscopic panorama!...such a marvel of glimpses, domes, roofs, the lagoon in the distance, a flashing glimpse of the lake through glittering, airy turrets, trees, statues, flags—beauty and charm everywhere."

Chicago Charlie, the Columbian Detective, resembles *Against Odds* in many respects. It is an elaborately constructed detective story in which the hero of the title solves the puzzle behind the apparent murder of his true love's father while also breaking up a smuggling ring on the lakes. Although this book, too, is rife with multiple mysteries and makes dramatic use of the belly dancers, Hagenbeck's animals, the Ferris Wheel, the Buffalo Bill show, and numerous other features of the fair (in one of many harrowing episodes the hero's newsboy pal Billy Stubbs is perilously trapped in the barrel of the 120-ton Krupp gun), *Chicago Charlie*, if anything, devotes even more attention than *Against Odds* to the twists and turns of a plot that seems nearly as out of control as the inevitable runaway carriage that almost runs Charlie down. There is also a nastier edge to the evil characters in this book, whom we see more up close than we do their counterparts in *Against Odds*.

These features make *Chicago Charlie* typical of the literally thousands of dime novels aimed mainly at boys and young men that were churned out by American publishers in aptly named "fiction factories" in the late nineteenth and early twentieth centuries. By the time this novel was published, these books commonly cost a nickel and were hastily printed on sixteen or thirty-two eight-by-twelve-inch pages of pulp paper laid out in double or triple columns. The conventions of the form were at this point so firmly in place that they dictated the course of the book, and the particular settings in one novel or another were invoked not with the intention of depicting them accurately but to allow the formulaic story line a place to land. Given the interest in the rising city of Chicago, many enterprising publishers ordered their staff writers to set their stories in the Windy City, so that Chicago Charlie found himself righting wrongs along with such stalwarts as Old Cap. Collier, Belle Boyd, Nick Carter (whose exploits in Chicago were translated into French and republished in Paris), Deadwood Dick, Jr., Frank Merriwell, and even Jesse James.

As for *Chicago Charlie*, it is one of a handful of dime novels that took advantage of the fair's celebrity. Old Cap. Collier came to town to find the stolen jewels of the Princess Eulalia, descendant of Ferdinand and Isabella (*The Infanta Eulalia's Jewels; or, Old Cap. Collier Among the Crooks at the World's Fair*). He might well have run into Bob Brooks (*Caught in Chicago; or, Bob Brooks among the World's Fair Crooks*) and Old Search (*Old Search in Chicago; or, 'Piping' a World's Fair Mystery*). Nor was Chicago Charlie's tangle with the Lakeside League in this novel his only "Columbian Adventure." In *Chicago Charlie's Diamond Haul; or Trapping the Tunnel Thieves. A Story of the White City*, like Carl Masters he solves a diamond robbery while the reader encounters an assortment of

World's Fair types from Buffalo Bill to Zulu warriors.

The literary formulas that drive *Against Odds* and *Chicago Charlie* developed and persisted because they derived from and spoke to widely felt beliefs, hopes, fantasies, and fears. These books acknowledge the existence of trouble and evil in human affairs, but insist that intelligence, courage, and persistence in the service of good will win the day. They also assume that the human community depends not only on evildoers being exposed and neutralized, but also on the most virtuous people uniting in marriages that will assure the future. For all their wildness of plot, they are conservative in their emphasis on the protection and preservation of a settled order. In many respects the two novels join a countless number of variations on a theme with a timeless lineage, and their use of the Columbian Exposition as an enchanted setting for love and intrigue has noble antecedents going back to Prospero's island (to which Dreiser compared the fair) and beyond.

Do these works reveal anything in particular about attitudes toward the Columbian Exposition and, perhaps more importantly, about urban culture in America? *Against Odds* and *Chicago Charlie* offer a mainly favorable view of the fair and of the city. The exposition and the Chicago that hosts it are exciting locales full of promise for the future. If they are also places of many dangers and challenges, these perils are vital to their energy and excitement, and in any case the books suggest that there is no obstacle that cannot be overcome by hearts that are brave and true. The two novels and others like them can be read both as a product of and a tentatively hopeful response to the rise of a highly complex and interdependent social order in which the individual's comprehension and control of experience seemed increasingly qualified. In this period of unpredictable and often violent social and economic conflict between capital and labor, rich and poor, city and country, and other large and shifting interests, the assertion made by such works that fearless individual effort in the service of good can surmount all obstacles implies that this underlying social order is sound.

The meanings that these books convey are not entirely positive, however, and for all their fancy and escapism they reflect some of the most unattractive qualities of the times that produced them. Even if these novels assert that virtue will prevail, this comes about only through the extraordinary efforts of special individuals, and even then only just barely. Come to visit the actual or the Dream City, these tales warn, and your money and your life are at risk. In the city you will encounter conniving speculators, weak-willed alcoholics, and child abusers, not to mention murdering conspirators. Seek escape from everyday reality at the fair and you may be kidnapped or killed by an international band of thieves or the evil agents of the Lakeside League. Try to get above it all with a ride on the Ferris Wheel, and you may well find yourself in the middle of a deadly fight. In this context, the simple and natural human act of trusting others can be a dangerous thing. If amidst the shifting currents of strangers on the streets of Chicago and the fair, that newsboy on the corner may turn out to be the long-lost brother of your faultless fiancée and that friendly Columbian guard an English lord, it is also possible that the considerate person who offers to change your money is a counterfeiter, the handsome dashing Frenchman who seeks your hand may be after your fortune, and the petite dark-haired woman who offers you help and companionship may really be a male henchman in a gang plotting against you. In short, these books express some of the darker anxieties of an open society in which, in spite of assurances that we can read goodness or evil in a person's face, finding one's way can be confusing and treacherous.

In addition, for all this society's openness, these novels express the prevailing strains of the sometimes virulent racism and xenophobia in America in the 1890s. We have to wait only to the third page of *Against Odds* before we hear the word "nigger" from the lips of a character we are supposed to like. Chicago and the fair, which causes "the great lakeside city" to "swarm" with foreigners, are places where "good" characters risk contact with the dark "other" who wishes to undo them, whether in the form of the duplicitous Maurice Voisin with his "soft, insincere ways" or the immoral gypsy Zel Magruder, whose voice reminds Billy Stubbs of "the squeal of a rat." In one of the most important scenes in *Against Odds*, June Jenrys meets Carl Masters by being thrown into his arms when a group of reckless Turkish palanquin-bearers practically run her down. Our righteous hero contemptuously calls one of the bearers "Mr. Morocco" and tells him to give way to "free American citizens," following which "the glowering sons of Allah" continue on, but not without "darting black glances from under their heavy brows." In both books the Midway in particular is a sinister bazaar of aliens that makes it "veritable sanctuary for the fleeing criminal," and as such it becomes the concentrated expression of the problem of a mixed population that the heroes and heroines of these books, and presumably those who read about them, must encounter and overcome.

There is perhaps some danger in reading too much into these two novels and of confusing their timeless elements with the timely ones. It is important to keep in mind that they were unabashedly created to entertain, to reflect an audience's views and satisfy its expectations, and what readers were most looking for was excitement, mystery, and the fulfillment of true love. If these novels also reveal some more subtle and sometimes unappealing dimensions of those views and expectations, this makes them and the entire body of fiction of the fair all the more interesting as one of the unofficial "exhibits" of the World's Columbian Exposition.

> Carl S. Smith
> Associate Professor of English and American Culture
> Northwestern University

AGAINST ODDS

A Detective Story

BY

LAWRENCE L. LYNCH
(E. MURDOCH VAN DEVENTER),

AUTHOR OF
'SHADOWED BY THREE,' 'A SLENDER CLUE,' 'A DEAD MAN'S STEP,'
'MOINA,' ETC.

COPYRIGHT.

LONDON:
WARD, LOCK & BOWDEN, LIMITED,
WARWICK HOUSE, SALISBURY SQUARE, E.C.
NEW YORK AND MELBOURNE.
1894.
[*All rights reserved.*]

AGAINST ODDS:
A DETECTIVE STORY OF THE WORLD'S FAIR

CHAPTER I.

"CHICAGO GITS MY MONEY."

"EUREKA!"

It was I, Carl Masters, of the secret service, so called, who uttered this exclamation, although not a person of the exclamatory school; and small wonder, for I was standing beneath the dome of the Administration Building, and I had but that hour arrived at the World's Fair.

I was not there as a sight-seer, not on pleasure bent, and even those first moments of arrival, I knew well, were not to be wasted.

I had come hither straight from the Terminal Station, seeking this stately keystone to the great Fair, not to steep my senses and fill my eyes with beauty in myriad forms, but to seek out the great man whose masterful hand was to create for me the Passport which was to be my "open sesame" to all within this fair White City's walls; but when I stood beneath that lofty double dome and looked about me, I forgot all but the beauty all around and gazed upon the noble rotunda through the western entrance, where "Earth," majestic but untamed, a masterpiece of giant statuary, guards one massive pillar; and the same "Earth," yet not the same, conquered yet conquering, adds her beauty to the strength of the column opposite—to the east, where Neptune sports, classic as of old, around about the octagonal interior with its splendid arches, its frescoes and gilding, its medallions and plates of bronze, wherein gleamed, golden and fair, the names of the world's greatest countries at its gilded panels, supported by winged figures, and bearing engraven upon each shining surface the record of some great event. Its medallions and graceful groups, allegorical or symbolic, all mounting high, and higher, until illuminated by the opal-like circle of light at the summit, Dodge's great picture crowns the whole, with its circling procession of arts and sciences, gods and muses, nymphs and graces, and Apollos radiant in the midst.

Small wonder that, forgetting all but the scene before me, my lips shot out the single word "Eureka!" and smaller wonder that, having vented my admiration in sound, I became aware of the fact at once, and remembered not only who I was, but what I was, and why I was there.

It was scarcely ten a.m., but there were people all about me, and my exclamation caused more than one eye, inquiring, amused, cynical, or simply stupid, to turn toward me where I stood, near the centre of the great rotunda.

"Big thing, ain't it?"

I turned my head, a little rattled at the notice I had thus brought upon myself, and saw standing close beside me a man whose garb, no less than his nasal utterance, proclaimed him a Yankee, and a son of the soil. I had seen him upon my entrance, standing beneath the dome, with his head thrown back at a painful angle in an effort to read one of the brazen plates above him, one hand tightly grasping a half-inflated umbrella—long past its palmy days—and the other fiercely gripped about the handle of a shawl-strap drawn tight around a handleless basket, by no means small, and bristling at the top with knobby protuberances which told but too plainly of the luncheon under the pictorial newspaper tied down with abundant lashings of blue "Shaker" yarn.

"Big thing, indeed!" Evidently my burst of enthusiasm had brought upon me this overture, no doubt meant to pave the way to further conversation; and I answered, after a single quick glance at my neighbour, as blandly as Ah Sin himself.

"Yes, sir," resumed the man, with a brisk nod, "it's a big thing! When 'twas first talked up I was a good deal sot on havin' it in Noo York State. I'd been there, ye see, twenty years ago on my weddin' trip; I was livin' in Pennsylvany then. But, Lor! Noo York couldn't 'a' done this here! No, sir, she couldn't. Chicargo

Against Odds

Administration Building.

gits my money—not that I've got much on it," with a nervous start and a shrugging movement as if he were trying to draw in his pockets and obliterate all traces of them. "I don't never believe in carryin' money to sech places." Then, as if anxious to get away from a dangerous subject, he asked, "Been here long, stranger?"

"About half an hour."

"M—um! I've done better than that; been here two hull hours. Come in on one of them Village Grove cable cars, and come plum through Middleway Pleasants. M—um! but they're some, them furren fellers; only it seems to me they ain't no need of so many of them niggers of all shades, dressed up like Callathumpians on Fourth of July, and standin' round in everybody's way."

I was not there to impart information, and I let the honest soul babble on. He had brawny shoulders and an ingenuous face, but I felt sure he had brought with him more money than was wise or needful, and that he would come to grief if he continued to deny the possession of money, with his tell-tale face flatly contradicting his words.

But I was now recalled to myself and my own affairs; and dropping a few politely meaningless words, I left my first acquaintance and made my way toward the pavilion at the corner, where I had been told I should find the "man in authority" whom I sought.

Putting my question to a guard in the ante-room, I was told that the man in authority was absent—would be absent two hours, perhaps; and, not much loth to pass a little time in that splendid rotunda, stood gazing about the beautiful Court of Honour, with its fountains, statues, glittering and fair facades, rippling lagoons, and snowy and superb peristyle, statue-crowned and gleaming, with blue Lake Michigan, sun-kissed and breeze-tossed, stretching away to the horizon in pulsating perspective.

Fairer than any dream it looked that fair May day, with Justice, golden and glorious, rising from out the waves, splendid as a sun goddess, and dominating all the rest.

As I turned away, having looked and looked again, I saw my first White City acquaintance seated upon a settle in the shadow of one of the mammoth arches, his basket between his knees and his umbrella between his two clasped hands. He was talking just as amiably and frankly as before, and this time he had for audience a dapper man with a thin face that might have been old or young, and which I disliked at sight. He was exceedingly well dressed; he looked very respectable, but he also looked smug and sophisticated—too sophisticated, I thought, to be really so well entertained as he seemed to be with my rustic friend's confidences.

For a few moments I watched the two, to the exclusion of the golden Justice, the peristyle, everything; and then, the settle being long, and the two being its sole occupants, I moved around, going in and out unobserved among the crowd, and seated myself upon the end of the bench, unseen by my friend, who sat with his broad shoulders and back squarely toward me, and affording an ample screen between myself and his companion.

I have wondered since just what actuated me to do what I did; but I only recall now a vague remembrance of a small black book, seen in memory as in a vision, and a fluttering page which seemed to blazon forth the question, "Am I my brother's keeper?" The book?—it was buried in dead hands long ago; and the words?—they had not been printed in the book more indelibly than upon my memory.

Why should the sight of this homely, honest rustic bring back these things? I did not know; but I seated myself in the shelter of his broad back, and affected to be absorbed in a notebook and the bronzed plates upon the walls about me, keeping meanwhile, with one ear, sufficiently close note upon their conversation, and letting my mind wander.

What a strange scene! Out upon the lagoon swift electric launches swept by, and gondolas, slower, but graceful and picturesque, glided to and fro, their lithe boatmen swaying to the sweep of the single oar.

Why did the sharp-eyed little woman opposite, on the bench in the shadow of the goddess of Air, eye me so keenly and so long, dividing her attention, in fact, between myself and a young mother with two tired children, scarce more than infants both?

Yonder went two Turks, bearing between them, swaying betwixt two long poles, a genuine Turkish palanquin, and crying, "Hi! hi!" to those who obstructed their direct line of march.

Where was the man of authority? I looked at my watch, and my thoughts came back to myself and my own affairs.

"An hour and a half to wait! I wonder if Brainerd is on the ground, and what he will say of our joint undertaking when we meet; for you can by no means establish a precedent by which to judge of Brainerd's thoughts and deeds to come. How will our work prosper—Shall we find it easy? and shall we succeed?"

For Dave Brainerd and I, both professional detectives, "man-hunters," if you will, were sent to this White City on a twofold mission.

It was not our first work together, and at first we did not enter into it with enthusiasm.

"Masters, Brainerd," our chief said to us one morning, "they are going to want a lot of good men at that World's Fair; I think I'd better put you both on the list." And this was all that was said then, but when we were out of his presence Dave exploded.

"Wants to send us to watch little boys, look after ladies' kerchiefs, and hunt up lost babies, does he?" he began, in a fume. It's not meself that'll do it; d'ye hear, Masters? I'll go like the biggest gentleman of all, or like the sleuth I am, but no child-rescuing and kid-copping for me! Let his honour give us," with a theatrical gesture, "a foeman worthy of our steel."

Nothing came of this whimsical tirade, and a week had passed before the chief spoke again upon the subject. Then we were both called into his private office, and he said:

"Boys, we have just found out to a certainty that Greenback Bob and his pals are going to operate at the World's Fair. I've already promised them more good men than I like to spare, but we can't let Bob and his crowd slip. I did not really mean to send you, either of you, with the others; but this is something worth while."

"I should say!" broke in Dave, who was no respecter of persons, unless perhaps it might have been of Dave Brainerd "Do you mean to tell us, Cap, that the dandy Frenchman is in it?"

"He is very much in it. He crossed from Calais on the last boat in hot haste, and I'm much mistaken if the whole gang is not already on its way to the White City, though he only reached this side the night before last; and there's another party who may give us some trouble. We don't know him, but he is said to be an all-round bad one, just come over from Calais with this Delbras. I wish I could give you even a description of him."

Greenback Bob was a counterfeiter, or so it was believed, for he was so bold, so shrewd, and so generally successful, that no one as yet had been able to entangle him in the meshes of the law; though samples of what was believed to be his handiwork had been passed from hand to hand, and travelled far before they had been challenged, and their journeys summarily ended in the cabinet of our chief. Bob was known as a gambler, too, and more than once had he been watched and shadowed because of some ill deed connected with his name; we had seen his face, and his

Against Odds

Looking East from Administration Building.

Court of Honor, Looking West.

picture adorned the rogues' gallery. Delbras, however, was likely to give us some trouble; we had seen him, it is true, but it was only a fleeting glimpse, with the possibility that he was at the moment cleverly disguised.

Of Delbras we knew, first, that he was and had been for years the occasional partner or confederate of the counterfeiter, and presumably a counterfeiter also; next, that he was set down in the records of the London police as "dangerous"; and last, that he had crossed the ocean, leaving Paris, which had grown "too hot to hold him," and was avowedly *en route* for the World's Fair, it was thought upon mischief intent.

This last item came to our chief direct from the French police, together with the information that two or three diamond robberies which had occurred in the French capital during the previous winter were laid at his door, although it had been thus far impossible to bring the thefts home to him.

Concerning Greenback Bob—the fellow was known to us by no other name—we felt quite sanguine; we had seen him, we had his photograph and his full description according to the Bertillon system, and, once seen, he would hardly be lost to sight again, or so we flattered ourselves. Delbras we must identify through Bob, or as we best could; and the third member of the "gang"—well, a great deal must be left to chance, as usual.

This much we knew of Delbras: he was "handsome, educated, familiar with the ways of good society, and not an easy bird to catch." This from the French police *commissaire*.

"A pinchbeck gentleman, eh!" had been Dave Brainerd's scornful comment upon hearing this. "The worst set to deal with; I'd rather tackle a straight out-and-outer any day."

Recalling this speech of Dave's brought my thoughts back to the old question, "Where was he?" And then the dialogue at my elbow aroused my flagging attention, and brought it back to my rustic acquaintance and the smug personage at his side.

"Wal, now, I hadn't thought of that, but now 't you mention it, 'twas a good idee; and they wouldn't change it to the eatin'-house?"

"Not there." The smug man's tones were low and cautious. "Pardon me, but—don't speak too loud, my friend—the mere mention of money is likely to attract some sharper to you. No, they refused me there. You see, I anticipated some difficulty inside the gates, so I had tried just before entering; but the man at the desk refused, and very curtly, too. I wanted to enter at once in order to meet half a dozen young men from my town who are sort of under my care."

"Orphans?"

"Not quite. They belong to my Bible class, you see," Mr. Smug explained modestly; "and I had promised to be at the Terminal Station in case they arrived by the early train."

"Whar from, d'ye say?" with awakening interest. "I'm a Sunday-school teacher myself, when I'm to hum."

"Indeed! It's a very interesting and useful work—labouring for souls. Ah, they come from Marshall, in Iowa."

"Don't say! Why, I—"

"But they did not arrive; their train had been delayed. But, as I was about to tell you, if I had not chanced to have in my possession a roll of bills, put in my care by the father of one of the younger lads, I might have been kept outside for some time longer."

"How's that?"

I had been a little puzzled at this dialogue, and was losing my interest somewhat when it reached this point, and I pricked up my ears anew, while I continued to copy inscriptions and jot down memoranda.

"It seems almost like confessing to a breach of trust; but there seemed no other way, and so, stepping to one side, I took out the package of money belonging to my young friend. I had counted it in his father's presence, and knew that it contained on the very outside of the roll a two dollar bill. I took this and procured my ticket. Of course I shall explain to him and replace it at once."

"In course! but—you was a-saying—"

"I began to tell you how I learned where to go to get money changed. I had entered, you must know, at the Cottage Grove gate opening upon Midway, and walking toward the east I soon met a guard." He had drawn a cigar from his pocket while speaking, and he now turned toward me. I had lighted a weed upon seating myself near them, and as he uttered a polite "Pardon me, sir," I smoked calmly on, while I copied upon a fresh page of my notebook the legend, "Jenner discovered the principle of vaccination in 1796," putting an elaborate final flourish after the date.

"Sir! Your pardon; may I trouble you for a light?" A light touch of his hand accompanied the words, and I turned slowly, favoured him with a look of as well-managed stupidity and inquiry as I could muster, drew from my pocket a little ear-tube, and, adjust-

Against Odds

ing it to my right ear, said, "Hey?"

Again the fellow made known his want, and then, apparently convinced that I had not been a listener, he resumed, somewhat hurriedly, I thought:

"As I was saying, I met a guard and asked him where to go to get a bill exchanged; he mentioned one or two places a long way off, and then, happening to think of the arrangement made for the accommodation of foreigners, he courteously directed me to one of the agents quite near at hand." He allowed a big puff of smoke to escape his lips very slowly, and added, as if it were the final word, "Those agencies for home and foreign exchange are a great convenience to travellers."

"What air they?" demanded my rustic. "Never heerd on 'em."

"Really! Why, the administration has arranged a system of agencies which are supplied with a certain sum in small banknotes, greenbacks, which they are authorized to exchange for foreign currency; and, for the convenience of Midway Plaisance, one of these agents is established in Midway, near the Turkish Village. One may know him by a small blue badge with a silver stamp in the form of a half-dollar souvenir upon his coat."

"Oh!"

"He proved very affable—the guard assured me I would find him so; and as the other agencies were so far away, I took advantage of his good nature, and instead of exchanging ten dollars, I got him to put a hundred-dollar bill into fifty crisp new two-dollar bills, fresh, like all this exchange money from the Government treasury—a part, in fact, of that great output of two-dollar greenbacks issued by the Government at the same time as the souvenir coins, as you no doubt remember."

No, the rustic did not remember, but neither did he doubt. He was full of exclamations of wonder and admiration at the workings of so wonderful and generous a Government; and then came the climax. Would Mr. Smug direct him to this affable agent upon Midway? etc.

"As I was saying at first, I don't lug much money around with me to sech places as this here, but what little I've got ain't quite divided up enough to be handy; I don't mind gettin' a fifty into new Gover'ment greenbacks myself. My wife 'n' me are countin' on stayin' on here a consid'able of a spell, maybe, an' small change is handiest."

"It's positively necessary," declared Smug, getting up quickly. "I'll show you the place, and the man; and then I must be looking for my young men again."

I had not looked for this conclusion, but as the rustic arose I closed my notebook and made ready to follow them. I was all agog to see this amiable dealer in brand new Government notes.

As the countryman turned toward his guide, the small sharp faced woman, who had eyed us so long and often from her bench almost opposite, arose with a movement suggestive of steel springs, and made her way toward us, waving her umbrella to attract attention. I moved rapidly aside, in anticipation of the sweeping gesture of arm and umbrella, which dislodged a tall man's hat and sent it rolling to the feet of a frisky maiden, from whence it was rescued by Smug, who restored it, with a placating word, and so averted an unpleasantness. Meanwhile the woman had reached her husband's side, and a few quick words had passed between the two. Then a gesture, and another word or two, evidently meant for an introduction, brought the smug stranger to her notice, and the three turned their faces toward the Plaisance; but not until I had heard her say to her better-half as she clung to his arm, while Smug opened a way ahead, "I tell you he's a confidence man, and I know it. I've been a-watchin' him!"

Following the three at a little distance, and discreetly, I smiled at the woman's rustic cleverness; and never did man smile more mistakenly.

CHAPTER II.

"TOLD MY TALE OF WOE."

I FOLLOWED the trio as they went rapidly past the Terminal Station, and halted, laughing inwardly, while Mr. Smug, as I had mentally named the man whose game I was watching so intently, stood fidgeting before the great golden door of the Transportation Building waiting for the sharp-eyed woman to exhaust her ecstasies, and for her more stolid husband to close his wide-opened mouth and remember his errand to Midway Plaisance.

As for myself, I could have gazed at this marvel of doorways and have forgotten all else; and I was not sorry that the small farmeress had a will of her own, and that this will elected to stay.

Against Odds

Oh, that superb eastern facade! Never before has its like been seen. Never in such a setting and in such gigantic proportions will we see it again.

But we left it at last and made a slow and halting progress past Horticultural Hall on one side and the sunlit lagoon on the other; and here, overcome by the grandeur of it all, the woman of the party sat down, with her face toward the water.

"'Tain't no kind of use, pa!" she declared loudly. "I'm goin' to set down by the lake for a minit; I guess there'll be some two-dollar bills left in Midway yet when we get there. I've heard tell of them lovely laggoonses till I'm achin' to see one; and I'm jest goin' to set right here till one goes by. Land! just see them stone anymals, and all them old-fashioned stone figgers of folks! 'Pears to me they's people enough alive and frisky, 'thout stickin' all them stone men around so dretful lib'ral; though they look well 'nough, fur's I know." She cast her eyes all about her, and then beckoned to Smug, standing uneasily in the rear: "Say, can't you show me one single laggoon?"

Smug came nearer, and waved his hand comprehensively toward the shining waters below them, and southward where a red-sailed Chinese junk lay at anchor opposite the Transportation Building.

"That is a lagoon, madam," he said, affably but low.

"Umph! It's no better-lookin' than our old mud scow! Come on, father." And they resumed their line of march, but not until in turning to take a last look at the belittled "laggoon" her snapping small eyes encountered mine frowningly, and I said to myself, "She saw me in the rotunda; can she suspect that I am following them?"

Contrary to my expectation, she did not call a halt upon entering Midway, but went straight on, still clutching her spouse by the arm, while the smug one walked sedately at her farther side; she passed the divers' exhibit, the beauty congress, the glass displays, and paced steadily on, her eyes riveted upon a palanquin borne by two waddling Turks; and when this ancient conveyance had paused before the Turkish Bazaar, then, and only then, did she pause or take further heed.

As the bearers gently lowered the chair, and stood beside it at ease, she snatched her hand from her husband's arm, and hurrying towards the front, peered within the curtained box.

"Land of gracious!" she ejaculated, "and I s'posed they was carrying one of them harums, no less, in the outlandish thing!"

Golden Door—Transportation Building.

Against Odds

Then, stooping to read with near-sighted eyes the legend, "One hour 75 cents, one-half hour 50 cents, ten minutes 15 cents," she turned again to her better-half: "Come, pa, let's get that change right quick; I'm goin' to ride in that thing if I drop out through the bottom."

There was a crowd in the Turkish Bazaar, but our smug friend led the way to an angle of the building where the hawkers were unusually busy, and I drew near enough to see that he was now looking covertly all about him, and for a little seemed at a loss.

"Kum-all-ong! Kume-mol-o-ng! Ku-m-m-m!"

The shrill long-drawn-out cry caused him to turn suddenly, and to elbow his way, with his prey at his heels, toward a small railed-in space, wherein, seated on a Turkish ottoman, a little higher than the genuine, was a swarthy man with beetling brows, big rolling black eyes, and a fierce moustache bristling underneath a hooked nose. He wore a red fez, much askew, and his American trousers and waistcoat were enlivened by a tennis-sash of orange and red and a smoking coat faced with vivid green. He was smoking a decorated Turkish pipe—"Toor-kaish," he called it—and a low table and sundry decorated boxes and packages were his sole stock-in-trade.

"Kum-all-ong!" he reiterated. "Kum-e see-e me-e-e smoke! Easy—so—no noise; so! Soo-vy-nee-yra; Toorkaish soo-vy-nee-yr matches!" At every pause a "soo-vy nee-yr match" was struck, deftly and without noise, and a big puff of smoke was sent circling above his head.

"Bah!" exclaimed Mrs. Rustic, turning away, "if you've brought me here just to see a Turkey man smoke a big pipe, Adam Camp, you may jest take me home ag'in."

A shout of laughter followed this sally, and as she turned away I fancied that I saw a quick look exchanged between the man of the pipe and our smug guide. Whether this were true or not, I observed that Smug no longer seemed eager to hasten them onward, and I saw another thing— the woman, in turning from the man of the souvenir matches, had once more fixed her eye, through a sudden opening in the crowd, upon myself; and immediately after she had whispered something in the ear of her spouse, which something he soon after repeated, or so I fancied, to his kind friend Smug.

I had followed them, trusting to the crowd and my skill as an "artful dodger," up to this moment quite closely; but I now fell back, and withdrew myself a little distance from the aisle where all three were now loitering, the woman examining with wondering eyes marvellous Turkish slippers with turned-up toes, and olive-wood beads and bracelets, proffered by fierce Mohammedans in baggy trousers and tasselled fez, or by swarthy, oily-skinned girls with bushy hair and garments of Oriental colouring, or in tailor-made gowns, and with the ubiquitous fez as a badge of their office —or servitude; rugs and draperies, attar of roses in gilded vials, souvenir spoons, filigree in gilt and silver, toys of unknown form and name, cloying Turkish sweets, foreign stamps, coins, relics, all came under her unsophisticated eyes, while her spouse gazed upon Moorish daggers, swords of strange workmanship, saddles and stirrups of singular form, and much strange gear and gay trappings, the use of which he could never have guessed but for the learned explanations of his now carelessly amiable guide.

They had gazed so long that I had begun to grow impatient and to wonder how this tame chase would end, when the trio drew up at a point where the long arcade turns sharply to right and left, and where at one of the intersections a vendor of singularly-carved canes and sticks was mounted upon a stool draped with Oriental rugs, and so high and slender that one looked to see the occupant topple and fall from moment to moment. He was a brown-faced fellow of small stature and as lithe as an Indian, and he was juggling recklessly with a pair of grotesque carven sticks, crying the while:

"He-ur you-ur ur! He-ur you-ur-ur! Soo-vy-neer! Soo-vy-neer! Gen-oo-ine Teer-keesh—gen-oo-ine! Come-mon! come-mon! Teerkeesh—genooine; only tree dollyeer!"

A smart young man, breathing of opulence in air and attire, came briskly forward and held up his hand to receive both sticks, with a harlequin bow from the dark-eyed Oriental, who wore a spruce black broadcloth suit, in honour of America, and a red fez, in loyalty, doubtless, to the land of the Sultan and then my interest became suddenly and widely awake.

The youth chose between the two canes, and handed up in payment a worn five-dollar bill, and after a feint at searching for the correct amount the man of the fez bent down and placed in his hand a crisp new two-dollar banknote; at the same moment, almost, friend Smug touched the arm of Farmer Camp, and I saw the two turn their heads toward the southern wing. I had made my way so near them that I could hear the words of the farmer, who evidently had no subdued tones, and after a long look

Against Odds

toward the south entrance I heard him say:

"That him? Why, he looks like one of these fellers!"

And then I saw his guide's lips moving, and caught the final words, "an educated Oriental." In another moment he had moved hurriedly forward and put out his hand to stop the man who, with head very erect, and crowned with a black and gold embroidered fez, was coming toward him, but with eyes levelled upon the active young man upon the lofty stool. He wore a severe suit of black, relieved upon the breast of the close-buttoned Prince Albert coat by a blue satin badge, bearing upon its upper half a silver-gilt souvenir half-dollar, and upon the lower portion a tiny facsimile of a Government banknote.

He paused as the smug young man addressed him, and looked into his face, at first with indifference, almost amounting to annoyance, then with growing recognition, and finally with a bland and condescending smile. He wore a long and flowing beard, and the black cloth fez, unlike the red one, was not rakishly set on; but I recognised him at once.

It was the man with the "soo-vy–neer matches," quickly and deftly metamorphosed to escape the unobservant or untrained eye, but the same, notwithstanding. And now my interest grew apace. I knew that at last we were in the presence of that powerful official who dispensed virgin two-dollar notes to the unwitting foreigner or native; and Adam Camp was about to be mulcted.

I had formed no plan of action. I had been interested, first, in the welfare of Adam Camp, and then the mention of these new Government two-dollar bills had aroused in me the desire, stronger for the moment than any other, to see this "agent" whose duty it was to make easy the path of the stranger and alien in our midst.

And now our smug friend demonstrated his ability to do quick work when occasion required.

Throwing caution to the winds, I drew close behind the woman, and heard the introduction of Camp and the case stated briefly.

Smug had ventured to bring this chance acquaintance, etc., who desired a like favour to that conferred upon himself not long since. Mr. Camp desired to exchange a banknote, say ten or twenty dollars, perhaps, for smaller bills, for convenience at the Fair, etc.

The man of the badge looked closely at Farmer Camp, who was bowing like a mandarin, and then back at his spouse.

"You can vouch for this person?" he asked with a touch of severity, and in excellent English.

"Pardon me; we are mere passing acquaintances, but I should think—"

He of the badge drew himself up with a stately gesture.

"We are not permitted to judge for ourselves," he said "our Government require some sort of voucher, as, for instance, a bank certificate, cheque-book, even a receipt or letter."

Before Farmer Camp could pull himself together and reply, his wife interfered, taking a swift step forward.

"If you want dockyments, mister," she said tartly, "I guess I kin supply 'em. I've brought our weddin' stiffykit, and our letters from the church to Neeponsit, and our fire insurance papers." She laid a suggestive satin-gloved hand upon her bosom and tossed her head. "I didn't count on nobody's takin' us to be anybody else when I brung 'em, but I didn't want 'em lost, case of fire or anything."

The "agent" put up a remonstrant hand, and Camp hastened to produce a letter from his brother in Nebraska, which was gracefully accepted; and so overpowered was Camp at so much condescension that he opened a plump wallet—carried in a breast pocket high up, and evidently of home manufacture—and drew from it, after some deliberation and a whispered word with his wife, a one hundred dollar bill.

"I guess we might jest as well break that." He was extending the bill, and the hand of the now eager agent was outstretched to grasp it, when I stepped quickly to his side.

"Pardon me, sir," I said, with my best air. "Could you tell me where the bank is located? I am told that there is one on the grounds." The four pairs of eyes were full upon me, and I knew that by three of them I was recognised. "I am anxious to get some money changed," I went on glibly, but with a meaning glance at the "agent," "to buy some souvenir matches down here, and I'm told there's counterfeit money circulating here."

I was playing a bluff game, and I knew it, for as yet I had not secured my credentials; but when I saw the swart face of the sham agent change to a sickly yellow, and Smug begin to draw back and look anxiously from left to right, I was inwardly triumphant; but, alack! it is only in fiction that the clever detective always has the best of it, and at this moment there came an unexpected diversion.

Camp still stood with the bill in his hand, open mouthed and evidently puzzled; and now his wife, who had drawn closer and was peering into my face, turned upon him quickly.

"Adam Camp, put up that money!" she cried. "I know this feller; I seen him talkin' to you back there by the Administration Buildin' and he's been watchin' and follerin' us ever sence. I know him! In another minute he would 'a' grabbed your money and run for it."

There was a sudden movement, a shifting of positions, a mingling of exclamations and accusations, with the woman's tongue still wagging shrilly, and heard through all. People crowded about us and a brace of Columbian guards came hurrying up.

"What is it?"

"Anyone been robbed?"

Instantly the hands of Smug and his confederate began to slap and dig into their pockets, while the woman answered eagerly:

"All of us, like enough! He's a pickpocket or a confidence man. I seen him follerin' us. I've kep' an eye on him." And then came a cry from Smug.

"My wallet!"

He turned upon me, calling wildly to the guards, "Search him!"

Into my nearest pocket went a gloved hand, and when it came out, there, sure enough, was a brown leather wallet.

"Here it is !" cried one.

"Lord-a-massy!"

"I told you so!"

"Run him in!"

I was the centre of a small bedlam, and I shut my lips tightly and inwardly cursed my interest in all rustics, and particularly the Camps. I was fairly trapped. I saw my position, and held my peace, while the two rascals told their tale, making sure by their volubility that the Camps did not tell theirs. Only as the two guards, one on either side, turned to lead me away, I said to Smug, "We shall meet again, my fine decoy;" and to the sham agent as I passed him, "Better stick to your matches, my friend."

Inwardly chafing, I marched through the crowd between my two captors, bringing them to a momentary halt as we came abreast of the place where the souvenir matches were hawked, and seeing there, as I had anticipated, a new face beneath the red fez.

Then I spoke to my captors:

"Men, you have made a mistake for which I can't blame you. Take me before your chief at once, and I will not only prove this, but make it worth your while to be civil."

For answer the two merely exchanged glances, and hurried me on, and, convinced of the uselessness of further remonstrance until I had reached someone in authority, I strode on silently.

At the entrance to the great animal show there was a dense crowd, and for a moment we were brought to a halt. Standing upon the edge of the mass of bobbing bonnets and heaving shoulders, I could see in the midst of the throng two Turkish-fezzed heads wildly dodging and struggling toward us, and a moment later a full bass voice called impatiently:

"Go ahead! Get out of this, can't you?"

I started at the sound of the big, impatient voice, and stood with my eyes riveted upon the spot from whence it seemed to come. A moment later the two red heads had emerged from the crowd, and with them a sedan-chair, which, evidently, they found no easy load. As they shuffled past me I started again, so violently that my two captors caught at me with restraining hands.

At the same instant there was a quick exclamation from the swinging chair and a peremptory order to halt.

"Masters, I say! Stop, you infernal heathens! Stop, I say! Open this old chicken-coop and let me out!"

As the astonished Turks slowly and with seeming reluctance set down their chair and liberated their prisoner, my guards made a forward movement.

"Stop, you fellows!" called the newcomer, in the same peremptory tone. "Where are you going with that man?"

As he flung himself from the chair he tossed a coin to the bearers, and promptly placed himself squarely in the way of my two guards.

"Masters," he began, "what in the name of wonder—"

"He's our prisoner," broke in one of my captors; and at the word Dave Brainerd threw back his head and laughed as only Dave could, seeing which my indignant escort made another forward movement.

"Stop, you young—donkeys!" Dave threw back his coat, and at sight of the symbol upon his inner lapel the two young men became suddenly and respectfully stationary. "Now," panted Dave, still shaken with merriment, "what has he done?"

Against Odds

I stood silent, enjoying somewhat my guards' evident doubt, and willing to let Dave enjoy to the full this joke at my expense, and after a moment's hesitation one of the guards replied:

"He picked a pocket, they say."

"Oh, they do? Well, my young friends, I can't blame you much; he is a suspicious-looking chap, but really he's quite harmless. You can turn him over to me with a clear conscience. I'll run him in." And he laughed again, and tapped his coat-lapel. "Really, boys, you've made a regular blunder. This pal of mine is entitled to wear this same badge of aristocracy, only he seems to have wandered out for once without his credentials. How did it happen, Carl?"

But now my impatience broke out afresh, and I turned to the guards.

"Look here," I said hurriedly, "those two fellows who called you up and pretended to be robbed are fine workers, and I believe counterfeiters. I was watching them while they were roping that old countryman. If you want to repair a blunder, go back, see if you can trace the men, or the old man and his wife, and report to your chief."

They were very willing to go; and when we were free from them, my friend indulged in another long and hearty laugh at my expense.

"Jove! Carl, but it's the richest thing out—that you, a crack detective, coming here with extraordinary rights and privileges, should be nabbed by a couple of these young college lads at the very beginning; it's too funny. How did it happen? Who caused your arrest?"

"An old woman," said I shortly, feeling that the fun was quite too one-sided. But seeing the absurdity of it all, and knowing that Dave would have it all out of me sooner or later, I drew him out of the crowd, and under the shadow of the viaduct just behind us, and standing as much as possible aloof from the throng, I told my "tale of woe."

Before I had reached the end Dave was his serious self once more—a detective alert and keen.

"You are sure," he began eagerly, "that the old farmer was not one of them?"

I smiled, thinking of Mrs. Camp and the "laggoons."

"Perfectly sure. It was the old woman's quick eyes that did for me," I replied; "she had seen me once too often, and her suspicions were on the alert. I dare say she saw a 'confidence man' in every person who came suspiciously near them, but a woman pal could not have played one whit better into their hands."

Dave made a sudden start. "Look here," he said, "I'm going to try for a look at those fellows! I've got a sort of feeling that they may belong to our gang, some of them—that match-vender now; the other, your smug friend, is too short, as you describe him, to be either of our men; but the agent, and that fellow with the canes—describe them a little more in detail, but be quick, too; and the old folks—of course they're taken in and done for before now; but I'd like to meet that old woman, just on your account. I'm going straight to that Turkish village; and you?" He began to laugh again.

"Oh, I'm going back to the Administration Building," I said with a grimace, "as soon as I've described your men for you. I don't feel inclined to wander about this mysterious and dangerous White City any more until I am fitted out with a trade-mark. It is not safe—for me."

Five minutes later Dave was on his way to the scene of my absurd escapade, and I was hastening back to the place which I never should have left until I had made my bow before the "man in authority," and had been duly provided with the voucher which would open for me all doors and command the aid or obedience of guards, guides, etc.; until, in fact, I had been duly enrolled, and had taken rank as one of the "specials," who went and came at will and reported at pleasure or at need.

On my way I soundly berated myself for my folly in venturing so recklessly and without authority to interfere in behalf of a sheep, when besieged by wolves, and in danger of losing no more than his fleece.

I had lost all interest in Farmer Camp, and felt not a spark of philanthropy in my whole being.

But the White City was a place of surprises, and Farmer Camp and I were destined to meet again.

As I approached the viaduct which separated the Midway Plaisance from the World's Fair proper, with my mind thus out of tune, and was about to pass under, a sharp guttural cry close beside me caused me to turn quickly about.

"Ta-ka ca-ar-h! La-dee, la-dee!"

"Ah—h—h!"

The first cry, or warning, came from the throat of a grinning Turk, one of a number of palanquin-bearers, and the last from the lips of a tall golden-haired girl who had been walking somewhat

Against Odds

slowly, and quite alone, just before them, in the path she had chosen to take and to keep without swerving. There were half a dozen of them pattering along in line between their vacant swinging palanquins, and they had evidently learned that, being a "part of the show," they might claim and keep the right of way.

The rascally Turk had uttered his cry of warning without in the least slackening his shuffling trot, and as the lady uttered the single frightened syllable, I saw that one of the poles in the bearer's hands had struck her with such force as to send her reeling toward me.

Throwing out one hand for her support, I thrust back the now surly bearer with the other with such force as to throw him back upon his poles and bring the whole cavalcade to a momentary halt. At the same time a guard came up and ordered a turn to the right.

"You fellows are not running in a tramway, Mr. Morocco, and you'll find yourselves switched on to a side-track if you try the monopoly business on free American citizens—see!" The last word, emphasized with a sharp shove to the right, was easily comprehended by the glowering sons of Allah, and they moved on, silent, but darting black glances from under their heavy brows.

Meanwhile the fair one had recovered her poise and dignity, and thanked me, in the sweetest of voices, for my slight assistance, and I had found time to note that she was more than a merely pretty blonde.

At that moment I was sure that I had never seen a more charming face, though she gave me only a glimpse of it; and when she turned away, and the crowd about us, attracted for the moment, separated again into its various elements, I stood gazing after her for a moment as stupidly as the veriest schoolboy smitten at sight of his first love, and then, turning to go my way, and letting my eyes fall to the ground, I saw just at my feet a small leather bag, or what is called by the ladies a "reticule." It lay upon the very spot where the young lady had been so rudely jostled, and I picked it up and turned to look after her. She had disappeared in the crowd, and after following the way she had taken for two or three blocks, and finding the crowd more dense and the trail hopelessly lost, I turned at last and went back, bestowing the little reticule in my largest pocket, and gradually bringing my thoughts back to my own affairs, and those of Greenback Bob and the rascal Delbras.

CHAPTER III.

A CONUNDRUM.

I HAD not gone far on my way after deciding that the lovely blonde had quite escaped me—in fact, I was once more about to pass under the viaduct opposite the Woman's Building and which separated Midway from the grounds proper—when a tall figure in blue appeared at my elbow, and fell easily into my somewhat hasty stride while saying:

"You will pardon me, I hope, for intruding, and let me say how much I appreciated and enjoyed the sudden way in which you halted that Turk just now. It was scientifically done."

I turned to look at the speaker. His words were courteously uttered, and I knew him at once by his blue uniform for one of those college-bred guards who have helped so much to make the great Fair a success to question-asking visitors. He was a tall, handsome fellow, with an eye as brown as his hair, and as honest and direct as the sun's rays at that very moment, and I recognised him almost at once as the guard who had hastened to lend his aid, and had sent the Turks to the right-about, there being nothing else to do. A churl could not have resisted that pleasant half-smile.

"It was nothing," I said carelessly; "the fellow was wantonly heedless."

"It was a very pretty and scientific turn of the wrist," he insisted, "and—yes, those fellows at first were obsequious enough; now, some of them, having found out how ill-mannered the Americans dare be without being beaten, are aping our manners. I—I trust the young lady was not hurt?"

The big brown eyes turned from me as he put the question, for that it was, and I saw a dull-red flush rise from his throat and dye his face to the very tip of his jaunty visor. I detected, too, a note of anxiety in the mellow voice that he could not quite suppress.

"I don't know, but fancy not—not much, at any rate." We had come out from the shadow of the viaduct, and he halted as I spoke. I checked my steps also, and I checked my speech too. The anxiety in the voice was reflected now in the face. I was smiling slightly, and through my mind flitted a fragment of doggerel:

> "Oh, there's nothing so flirtatious
> As the bowld soldier boy!"

Suddenly the brown eyes came back to my face, open and clear as day.

"I owe it to myself," he said, with sudden dignity, "to explain. At the moment when she turned away, I recognised the young lady as an acquaintance, and was naturally interested to know if she had received any hurt—the blow seemed a severe one. I saw you pick up her bag and start in pursuit, and when you came back I ventured to address you. I could not follow far; this is my beat."

"I see!" I was quite won by the young fellow's frank and manly air and his handsome face; "and I'm sorry I can't enlighten you. I did not find the lady."

"Oh!" There was a world of disappointment in this one syllable, and before he could utter another a new voice broke into the dialogue.

"Pardon me, please! But"—a little pant—"but I saw you pick up my friend's bag, and—and she was so fatigued after the shock that I ran back."

The speaker stopped here, and for several seconds seemed occupied in recovering her breath. She was a small and plump brunette, well dressed, and wearing a dashing sailorhat of black, wide-brimmed and adorned with two aggressive-looking scarlet wings; this and the red veil dotted with black which partially concealed the face was all that I had time to note before she spoke again, coming closer to me and altogether ignoring the good-looking guard.

"She was so startled and nervous after the shock that she sat down near the Java Village, and I came back the moment I could leave her." She shot a glance over her shoulder, and turned her look squarely upon the guard, who had drawn back a pace. "A chair-boy," she hurried on, "waiting near the Libbey Glass Works saw you pick up the bag, and told us the way you had gone. Will you please give me the bag?"

I had been studying the little brunette while she talked, and I now said:

"I am very sorry your friend did not come in person. She did not seem much hurt."

"She was not, and she would have come with me, only—" Again she cast her eyes in the direction of the guard, who still stood looking both anxious and ill at ease, and for a moment she seemed to hesitate. In that moment the guard's fine face flushed again, and then set itself in cold, resolute lines. He lifted his hand in salute to me, and, without a second glance at the little brunette, strode back toward the viaduct.

The face of the girl showed instant relief, and she put out her hand.

"The bag, please!"

"Excuse me," I answered, "but really I can't let the lady's property out of my hands without something to prove your right to it. Since the lady is so near, if you will permit, I will go back with you."

"How dare"— she threw back her head, and her black eyes darted annihilation—"how dare you, sir! Because I condescend to address you, to oblige an acquaintance, do you fancy I will accept your escort and pocket your insult? Not for ten thousand leather bags!" She turned upon her heel and went swiftly back towards Midway, and after watching her for a moment I resumed my often-interrupted march, smiling as I went to think how the clever little brunette had been thwarted. That she was an adventuress I did not for a moment doubt. She had seen the dropped bag, of course, and had noted my pursuit of its owner, and its failure, and she had counted upon making me an easy dupe with that assured little demand of hers. But I was not quite a stranger to her kind. Perhaps if the good-looking guard had not been so suddenly put to rout I might have turned the young lady over to him; such offenders were his legitimate care. But as I thought of her easy, self-possessed, good society air, and the black eyes so keen and sophisticated, and then of his frank, ingenuous face, I almost laughed aloud. She would have laughed at his authority, and slipped through his fingers easily.

How quickly he had turned away at the first hint that she found his presence at our brief interview undesirable, flushing like a boy, too!

Of course I readily saw why she should prefer to make her little attempt without witnesses, especially those clothed with a measure of authority; and yet he had seemed to go away reluctantly.

And then I remembered his explanation or excuse in having followed and addressed me. He had known the young lady-owner of the bag. Why, of course—he wanted to hear of her further, from the lips of this supposed girl friend.

"Poor fellow!" I thought, beginning to imagine a little romance there in the White City; and then I turned myself about with a sudden jerk.

Truly, my wits were woolgathering. Confound that little adventuress! He had turned away so suddenly, and he knew the owner of the bag. I would find him at once—he was not far away—and I would wash my hands of that little black bag.

But it was not to be. I had expected to find my handsome guard easily, and I did not find him at all. After a half-hour spent in prowling up and down, I encountered a file of guards marching briskly. I caught at my watch, and then scoffed at myself. Of course my guard had gone to dinner; I would do likewise, and then, when my other and more personal duties had been discharged, I would look up the guard. It would be quite easy.

The arrangements for our comfort during our stay in the White City had been completed in advance of our coming, and Dave and I had been quartered together in a cosy little apartment, which we could reach easily and as quietly as if it were an isolated dwelling, instead of being in the very centre of all the beauty and bustle of the Fair.

Having paid my respects to the "man in authority," and after he had made me familiar with the inner workings of the splendid system by which the White City was to be watched over and protected, and acquainted with some of my co-workers, I was ready for a hearty luncheon, and then I found myself my own master for the remainder of the day, or until four o'clock, when Dave and I were to meet by appointment at the Ferris Wheel and tempt its dangers together.

Of course my first attempt, after luncheon, was to find my handsome guard; but while good-looking young fellows and polite young fellows in blue uniforms were to be seen on every hand, the one face for which I looked was nowhere visible. I still had the lost bag in my outer pocket, which I watched jealously, for its bulk could be but too plainly seen; and when Dave and I found ourselves moving slowly upward at the tip of one of those giant spokes of the big wheel, he fixed his eye upon this pocket, and asked with a grin:

"Got an extra luncheon in case we are stranded in midair until past the Christian dinner-hour?"

Of course I told him the story of the find—but briefly, for my eyes were busy watching the people in the grounds below grow less and less in size, until they seemed like flies moving about eccentrically, the legs of the men seeming to jerk about convulsively, and looking automatic from that height.

There was much to amuse us in Midway, or on it; for at first the street, with its strange population, was spectacle enough, and we did not think of the black bag again until we found ourselves occupying isolated places upon the lofty seats in Hagenbeck's great animal show, and being serenaded by an excellent band, while we watched the entry of the happy family.

We had entered at a time midway between the closing of one performance and the beginning of another, and we found it a comfortable place in which to exchange experiences and compare notes.

My first question had been of the Camps and their swindling friends, but Dave's report was scant. He had seen the man of the canes, but the seller of 'soo-vy-neer' matches was no longer he of the big moustache and goodly height, but a small elderly Turk, who piped weakly and plied his calling listlessly. The Camps, Smug, the gentlemanly agent, all had disappeared from off Midway. I was not surprised at this, neither was I disappointed; and having said as much, I took up the parable of my latest adventure upon Midway, telling of my encounter with the guard and the little brunette, and letting my fun-loving friend enjoy another good laugh at my expense.

"I must say, Carl, old fellow, that so far as I have traced your career this first day at the Fair, you have not shone out brilliantly. But never mind, partner: 'a bad beginning'—you know the rest. Oh, are we to have a look at the bag?"

I had drawn it forth and placed it upon my knee. It was a small receptacle of finest alligator-skin, with an outside pocket, and having attached to it the tiny chain and hook by which it had been secured to the young lady's girdle. It closed with a silver clasp, and in the open outside pocket was a fine white handkerchief with some initials embroidered in one corner.

"J. J.," read Dave slowly. "That don't tell us much, does it, old man?"

I looked about me. There was no one near us, and on the opposite side of the big pavilion the band was playing "After the Ball." I pressed the silver clasp, and the bag lay open in my hand.

"Gad!" exclaimed Dave. "The woman who owns that is as dainty as a princess."

Against Odds

He was quite right. The little bag contained only a small silver-handled penknife, a dainty tablet and pencil, a glove buttoner, a second little handkerchief, fine and smoothly folded, and two letters.

When I had taken out these articles one by one and laid them on my knee, Dave took the bag from my hand and turned it upside down.

"Nothing more," he said, shaking his head sagely. "Not a bit of candy; not a powder-puff or perfume sachet. Well, well! Carl, the owner of this little article, whoever she is, besides being dainty and without vanity, is a very clever little woman, and I'll wager she's pretty, too."

This outbreak was so like Dave that I only smiled, while I unfolded the handkerchief and shook it out over my unoccupied knee. In one corner, in exquisitely dainty embroidery, were the two initials "J. J.," and when Dave had shut the bag and looked again at the closed clasp, he discovered, finely cut on the metal, the same initials.

"J. J." mused Dave; that suggests any number of charming personalities—Juliet, Juno, Jessica."

"Jane, or Jemima," I supplemented, taking up one of the letters.

It was post-marked Boston, and bore date three days before, but it gave us no further information.

Through the name, across the middle of the square envelope, half a dozen heavy lines had been pencilled, and these in turn checked through with little vertical dashes; below were the sketchily-drawn supports, which indicated a bridge, and upon this bridge a procession of people vaguely outlined as to body, but elaborated as to face to such a degree of artistic cleverness that Dave uttered an exclamation of delight.

"An artist, upon my soul! Look at those faces! Gad! but that is well done! There are types for you, and hardly more than thumb-nail portraits at that. But it's spoiled the address; we can't get J. J.'s name out of that."

It was quite true; under the crossed lines forming the platform of a bridge, evidently a sketch of one of the structures spanning the lagoons, the name was quite concealed, but below, through the waving water-lines and the curves of the arch, we could read and guess the remainder of the address, thus:

'___ ___ ___ ___ ___ ___,

'Chicago,
'Illinois.
'Massachusetts Building, World's Fair.'

I put this letter down and took up the other envelope. Upon this was written a woman's name, nothing more, neither town, county, nor state.

"Conundrum?" commented Dave over my shoulder. Just then there was a sudden blare from the band, and a roar that almost startled my sophisticated nerves.

I turned my eyes toward the arena, where a splendid white horse now stood, caparisoned in a sort of armour upon back and neck, and pawing impatiently, while he waited opposite a sort of portable platform higher than the horse's back, and gaily cushioned and decorated. A great tawny male lion was in the act of leaping from the ground to this high perch. I had seen many exhibitions of animal intelligence and training, but when this king of lions, uttering a second mighty roar, leaped to the back of the waiting horse and rode about the ring like a trained rider, leaped through a hoop held in the mouth of a big spotted boarhound, and otherwise acquitted himself like an accomplished rider, I forgot the conundrum of the little black bag, and my mission at the World's Fair, and looked and applauded, and was simply one of five hundred sightseers.

It was useless to contend; the charm was upon us; the first day at the Fair had us at last in thrall, and we watched the trained lions, tigers, bears, and pumas, admired the ponies, applauded the dogs, and wondered at the plucky woman trainer, without a thought beyond the passing moment.

The fever lasted until night had fallen, until we had trundled from end to end of Midway in a pair of wheeled chairs, visited the Dahomey Village, the Ostrich Farm, the Chinese Theatre, and the little community of quaint, shy, industrious Javanese, leaving it still in the spirit of adventure, and sauntering, after a dinner in Old Vienna, here and there through a veritable fairyland, glittering, glistening, shining, radiant from the splendid dome of the Administration Building, with its girdles of fire, its great statues shining under the golden glow, and the lagoons with their lights and shadows, their gondolas gliding to and fro between flowering banks or illuminated facades, with fountains playing, music filling the air, and everywhere laughter, merry voices, and gay throngs of enchanted pleasure-seekers. What wonder that we lingered long, and that it was only when we were shut between four walls, the lights out, the White City asleep, that I thought again of J. J. and her lost letters; and now, as I thought, the fair blond face seemed to rise before me, and I saw again the slim figure flit past me on Midway.

Brainerd lay sleeping near me, and I thought of his comment, "A conundrum?" Why not search for the answer in these white billets, and, finding it, take the little black bag to the bureau of the "lost or found?"

I took up the bag, opened it, hesitated, and put it down. Why should I read those letters from a stranger, and to a stranger? I leaned out of the window and drank in the loveliness all about me, illuminated by a faint young moon.

"A conundrum?" I took up the letter postmarked Boston, and slowly drew out—ah, it was more than a mere letter that my hand touched that night. I had put my finger upon a thread in the web of fate!

CHAPTER IV.

"I CAN'T MAKE MYSELF LIKE HIM."

I AM not superstitious, and I certainly had no intimation then of the part these letters would soon play in my World's Fair adventures, nor of the use I should make of them; but I opened that letter with an uncomfortable feeling of curiosity and interest, and without even pausing to look again at the tiny grotesque faces of that little bridge procession so artistically sketched upon the envelope.

The letter, like its cover, was dated from Boston, and was just four days old.

"Just received," I said to myself, as I took up the wrapper to look at the Chicago postmark. "Yes, came last night. She must have read it this very morning, sitting upon some one of those shaded seats on Wooded Island, and after reading it she must have amused herself by copying the people passing over the nearest bridge. Ergo, she must have been alone." My detective instincts were rousing themselves; already I was half unconsciously handling that unread letter as if it were a "feature" in a "case."

She was alone, too, when we met on Midway, that is, I saw no companion. Could it be possible that the young lady was really alone in this densely populated place? How absurd! I looked at the letter again.

It was written in a beautiful flowing hand, and I said, after a moment's scrutiny, "Written in haste and under excitement." There were eight closely written pages, and having begun their perusal, I read to the end without a pause. The letter was signed "Hilda O'Neil," and there was no street number nor post-office box, only the name of the city from whence it came, Boston.

Hilda O'Neil was the name written on the second letter, this and nothing more; but this no longer surprised me. Miss O'Neil was a New York girl, and a guest, at the time of writing, of the sister of her affianced, in Boston. This young man was already in Chicago, making arrangements for his family, who were to come as soon as informed by him that apartments in the already crowded city were in waiting. They were "all ready for the flitting," and were now wondering why "Gerry" did not wire them. He had written that his plans "were near completion," and that he should telegraph them in two or three days at the latest, at the time of writing. The three days were just about to expire, hence the excitement visible in the penmanship of Miss O'Neil. Betwixt impatience and anxiety she confessed herself "growing really fidgety," especially as "Gerry" was always so prompt, "and then—"don't think me silly, dear—but, really, Chicago is such a wicked, dangerous place, especially now."

I smiled as I read this paragraph, and thought of Master "Gerry" doubtless giving himself a last day or two of freedom from escort duty, and of fun, perhaps, on Midway. Decidedly, detectives are not seers.

And the second letter. Since the first did not tell me how or where to find the owner of the little bag, this letter must. And her name—would that be revealed? I opened the missive and read it through, with some surprise and a great deal of admiration.

I had been right in my conjectures of the writer. I found her name signed in full at the bottom of her last thick sheet of creamy note-paper; she had penned the letter in her own room that very morning, and had held it unsealed and only half addressed until she had applied at her State post-office for the expected letter from her friend, and this having been received, she had thrust the newly-written missive into the little bag, hoping, doubtless, soon to meet her correspondent, who might now be on the way, and to tell her story—for the letter contained a story—which, doubtless, she would much prefer to do.

And now, so much can a few written pages do, I almost felt that I knew June Jenrys, for that was her name, and her friend Hilda O'Neil.

Miss O'Neil's letter had told me first something about herself: that she was a petted and somewhat spoiled only daughter; something of an heiress, too, if one might judge from her prattle about charming and costly costumes and a rather reckless expenditure of pin-money; and that she was betrothed to Gerald Trent, of the great Boston firm of Trent and Sons, with the full consent and approval of all concerned. What life could be more serene? Young, fair, rich; a lover and many friends; and now *en route* for the World's Fair, to enjoy it in her lover's society. Happy girl! the only little speck upon her fair horizon when she penned that letter was the fact that her dearest friend and schoolmate was not quite so happy.

And June Jenrys? The two letters taken together had told me this: She was an orphan, and wealthy, left in her teens to the guardianship of an aunt, her father's widowed sister, a woman of fashion *par excellence*. During her niece's minority this lady had tyrannized all she would, and now, Miss Jenrys having recently come of age, she yet tyrannized all she could. The aunt was eager to mate her niece to a man of her own selection and a heavy purse. The niece until recently had looked with some favour upon a young man, handsome enough—even Miss O'Neil admitted that— and a gentleman beyond question; but with no visible fortune. A short time before—but I will let Miss Jenrys tell this much of her own story, quoting from the fourth page of her letter:

"I did not mean it so, really, Hilda dear, although it has seemed so to you. You see, I expected to meet you in Boston ere this, and that is so much better than writing; and now I must write after all, and instead of its being from me in Boston to you in New York, it is from me here in the 'White City'—such a city, Hilda!—to you in Boston, and at Nellie Trent's.

"Well, you must know this, that it was just after Aunt Charl had 'washed her hands of me,' matrimonially speaking, for the— well, for the last time; and I was feeling very high and mighty, and Aunt Charl quite subdued, for her, that we gave a reception, the last before Lent. Of course he was there, and I had made up my mind that day that I would be honest with my own heart in spite of Aunt Charl. 'I'm sure he cares for me,' I said to myself, and—well, I knew I liked him a little. I knew he only waited for the opportunity to speak, and while I would have died rather than help him make it, I said, 'If he does find the chance—if he does speak, or when he does—well!'

"I shall never forget that night! Aunt was good enough to say that I was looking my very best. I am sure I felt so. But of course aunt spoiled it all—her pretty speech, I mean.

'June,' she wheedled, 'that handsome Maurice Voisin will be here, and I happen to know that he admires you very much. Charlie Wiltby says he is no end of a swell in Paris, and that he is really a rich man, who prefers to be modest, and avoids fortune-hunting girls. You are old enough to settle down, and with your fortune and his you might be a leader in Parisian society. There's no place in the world where money and good looks together will do so much for one as they will in Paris.' Think of it, Hilda! If I had not felt so at peace with all the world just then, there would have been an—occurrence then and there. But I held my tongue, and was even inclined to be a little sorry that aunt's silly talk was making me feel a genuine antipathy for M. Maurice Voisin of Paris renown; and really at that time I hardly knew the man. He is certainly rather good-looking, in a dark, Spanish fashion, and he is taller and somehow more muscular-looking than the typical Frenchman. He is certainly polished, shines almost too much for my liking; but that may be, really, Aunt Charl's fault rather thin Mr. V.'s. That night, at least before supper, I had no word or thought against him.

"But I must get on about him, and I'll make it very short. You know how our conservatory is arranged, and that little nook just at the entrance to the library, where the palms are grouped? Well, I had danced with them both, and he had just asked me to go with him into the conservatory, to 'sit out a waltz,' when M. Voisin came to claim it. I had for the moment forgotten it, and he had only time to say just one word—'after.'

"Well, I'll be candid, if it does humiliate me; after that waltz I eluded M. Voisin, leaving him with Aunt Charl, and went into the conservatory.

"It was so early, and the dancers still so fresh, that no one was there as yet. I had been stopped once or twice on my way, and when I entered the conservatory by way of the drawing-room, I fancied for a moment that someone was standing in the shadow of the palms, just inside the library door; but I went on, and reached the nook without being observed. I sat down, quite out of sight, thinking that if he entered from the ball-room the most direct way I should see him first. Imagine my surprise, then, when almost instantly I heard a movement on the other side of the mound of fairy palms, and then at the very first word came my own name. There! I will not repeat the shameful words, but it was his voice that owned to an intention to 'honour' me with a proposal, because his finances were getting low, and he must choose matrimony as the least of two evils, etc. While I sat there, unable to move, and half stunned by this awful insult, suddenly there was a quick rustling, a half-stifled laugh, some whispered words, and then another voice which I did not at first recognise, said, very near me, 'Ah, good-evening, Mr.—a—Lossing! Charming spot, really.' Then there was another movement, some low muttered words, and the sound of footsteps going across the marble toward the library. Then suddenly, right before me, appeared M. Voisin. I could not conceal my agitation, and gave the same old hackneyed reason—heat, fatigue, sudden faintness. M. Voisin hastened in search of water, and I dropped my face upon my hands, to be aroused the next moment by *his* voice, agitated, hurried, making me a proposal. Then something seemed to nerve me to fury. I sprang up, and, standing erect before him, said:

"Mr. Lossing, as I am unfortunately not in the matrimonial market, I fear I cannot be of assistance to you, much as I regret that the low state of your finances is driving you to so painful a step. Allow me to pass!" Before he could reply I had swept past him, and meeting M. Voisin just beyond the palms, I took his arm and went back to the ball-room. Hilda, pride and anger held me up then, for I fully believed him the most perfidious of men. But since, much as I hate myself for it, there are times when I doubt the evidence of my own senses, and cannot believe that he ever said those words. The next morning, while my anger still blazed, he sent me a letter, which I returned unopened. That is all, Hilda. He left town the same day, I have been told.

"And now you understand, doubtless, why I am here. M. Voisin, of course, was not to blame, but I could not disconnect him from the rest of the hateful experience; and so at the beginning of Lent I packed my trunks and set out for the country and Aunt Ann's at Greenwood. Dear Aunt Ann, who is so unlike Aunt Charl!"

Then followed some details of their arrival at the World's Fair and an amusing account of the good lady's first impressions, which were so large and so astounding that she was obliged to "'remain at home and take the entire day to think things over in. Think of it, Hilda, shut up like a hermit just two blocks from the gate! Is not that like nobody on earth but sweet, slow, obstinate, countrified Aunt Ann?—of whom, thank heaven, I am not one bit ashamed, in spite of her Shaker bonnet. But I can't lose a day of this wonder, and fortunately dear Aunt Ann never dreams of tabooing my sight-seeing. When I proposed to come alone this morning, the dear soul said:

"'Well, I should hope thee could. Only two straight blocks between here and the gate at Fifty-seventh Street, and if thee can manage to get lost with all those guards and guides, to say nothing of the maps and pictures, thee is a stupid niece, and thee may just go back to thy Aunt Charlotte Havermeyer.' If Aunt Charl could only hear that! Well, dear, I have promised myself a happy time here with Aunt Ann when she is not occupied with her meditations, and yourself soon, and without Aunt C.; but, alas! everybody will visit the Fair; and yesterday, upon Midway, whom should I see but M. Voisin! He was attired as I have never seen him before, quite *negligee*, you know, and wearing a Turkish fez. It was very becoming. He did not see me, and for this I was thankful. I did not come to the World's Fair to see M. Voisin, and even to please Aunt Charl I can't make myself like him."

I put down this letter and smiled over its sweet ingenuousness, and singularly enough I joined the fair writer in heartily disliking M. Voisin.

"He was altogether too conveniently near at the scene of that unlucky proposal," I muttered to myself, and then I turned to the other letter. I wanted to see what I could make, between the two, out of young Lossing.

"I have asked you twice," Miss O'Neil wrote, "about your affair with young Mr. Lossing. Your aunt is entirely at a loss, only she declares she is sure that you have refused him, and that in some way he has offended you; and I thought him almost perfect, a knight *sans reproche*, etc.; and he is so handsome, and frank, and manly. What happened, dear? It is so strange that he should vanish so utterly from society where he was made so much of; and no one seems to know where he went, or when, or why, or how. Gerry says he was a perfect companion, 'and as honourable as the sun.' There, I'll say no more."

My reading was broken in upon at this point by a prolonged

Against Odds

chuckle, and I looked up to see Brainerd wideawake and staring at me.

"Well," he queried promptly, "have you found out her name?"

"Yes; it is June Jenrys." As I spoke I returned Miss O'Neil's letter to its decorated envelope, and replaced the two in the bag. "I'll tell you about them," I said, as I put it aside. Somehow I felt a sudden reluctance at the thought of seeing those two letters in the hands and under the eyes of an inveterate joker like Dave. "I'm no wiser in the matter of address, however." And then I told him the purport of the letters in the fewest words possible.

"Do you know," said Dave, when I had finished my recital, "I don't like that Voisin, not even a little bit. I think he's a bad lot."

I smiled at this. There was not a jot of romance in Dave Brainerd's make-up, and not a great depth of imagination; but he was the keenest man on a trail, and the clearest reasoner among a large number of picked and tried detectives. It amused me to think that both had been similarly impressed by this man as he had been set before us; but I made no comment, and to draw away from a subject which I felt it beyond our province to discuss I asked:

"Dave, what did you mean this afternoon, when we opened that bag, by saying that the owner was a clever woman? Upon what did you found that remark?"

"Why, upon the fact that she did not put her purse in that convenient, but conspicuous, little bag; in consequence of which she is, or was, only slightly annoyed, instead of being seriously troubled at its loss. By the way, or rather to go out of the way, do you know that they have in the French Government Building a very fine and complete exhibition of the Bertillon identification system? I want to get to it bright and early in the morning."

I moved to his side and sat down upon the bed. We were both admirers of this fine system, and for some moments we discussed it eagerly, as we had done more than once before; and when I put my head upon my pillow at last, it was with J. J. and her interests consigned to a secondary place in my mind, the first being given over to this wonderful French system, the pride of the Paris police and terror of the French criminal.

But we little know what a day, or a night, may bring forth.

Someone rapped at our door at an unpleasantly early hour, and the summons brought Dave out of bed with a bound, and in another moment had put all thought of the previous night out of our heads.

"Will you come to the captain's office at once, gentlemen?" said a voice outside, and I caught a glimpse of a guard's blue uniform through the half-opened door. "There's been a big diamond robbery right under our noses, and they're calling out the whole force."

CHAPTER V.

"IT'S ALL A MIRACLE."

IT WAS even as the summoning guard had said, and the Secret Service Bureau was in a very active condition when Brainerd and myself arrived.

Already telephone messages were flying, or had flown, to the various districts, and at every gate, thanks to the almost perfect system instituted by Superintendent Bonfield, shrewd and keen-eyed men were on the alert for any and all suspicious personages, and woe to those whose descriptions were written down in the books of the secret service men. They must be able to give good account of themselves, or their liberty would be brief.

It was not difficult to guess why my friend and myself had been so promptly summoned, in spite of the fact that already more than three hundred men, trained detectives, from our own large cities and from abroad, were upon duty here.

It was because they were on duty, every man at his post, whatever that might be, and because Brainerd and myself—having newly arrived and being for the moment unoccupied—were both near and available. Because, too, we were specials, that is, not subject to routine orders.

The robbery had really been a large one, and a bold one.

A collection of gems, cut and uncut, belonging to a foreign exhibit, and placed almost in the centre of one of those great well-guarded buildings, must be, one would think, proof against attack. Carefully secured in their trays and boxes, shut and locked behind heavy plates of glass in bronzed iron frames, guarded by day by trusted employees always under the eye of manager or exhibitor, and by night by a guard of drilled watchmen, what collection could be safer?

Against Odds

Nevertheless, at night there sparkled in those crystal prisms a little silver leaf with slightly curved edges, holding what looked like a tiny heap of water-drops, congealed and sparkling, shot through by a winter sunbeam; several larger diamonds, uncut, but brilliant and of great value; some exquisite specimens of pink topaz, and one great limpid, gleaming emerald, the pride of the fine collection. This at night. In the morning—they were not.

We sat down, a small group, for we did not hold council in the outer office, nor with one superfluous member, and began to find or make for ourselves a starting-point.

The work had been done very deftly. One of the glass plates had been cut out close to the bronze frame, and the gems removed; but that was not the strange part of the affair. In their places counterfeit gems had been put, careful imitations of the originals, and the glass plate had been deftly put in its place again.

"Ah!" said the fussy and half-distracted little man who represented the great foreign house so neatly defrauded, "Ah! if I had not come down this morning, not one othair would haf know. I am the one only expairt. See! I am praisant wen the plaice is uncloase. I stant near, wen soomsing make a beeg chock"—he meant shock or jar—"ant richt town falls out the klass. Wen I haf zeen it, I go queek ant look at doze shems. Ach! I know it awal—'tis fawlze awal—effery stonzes!"

That was the story. They had found the glass cut, and false gems in place of the true.

When we had stemmed the tide of this foreign eloquence, which was not for some time, I asked:

"How many know of this?"

"Nopotty at all onlee—"

"Not more than half a dozen," broke in the chief of the bureau. "Of course it wouldn't do! These are not the things that we like to let the public into. It wouldn't harmonize."

"Ah-h-h!" aspirated the little man. "It would trive away awal the tiamont mershants togetheer! U-u-og!"

"Right you are," murmured Dave; and then in a louder tone, "Can you trust your people to keep silent?"

"Ah! neffear fe-ur; tay know it is for tare goo-et."

"Where are they?"

"The attendants?" queried the captain. "Two are in charge of the pavilion, which remains closed. Lausch here was very clever; he sent for me at once, meantime keeping everything under cover; and when I saw how the land lay, I ordered close mouths all around, and put up a card, 'Closed for repairs.' Then I sent for you, and we came back here. Of course you will want to see the place."

"The place and the people," I said, somewhat impatiently; and "we can't get it over too quick."

We spent three of the long morning hours in viewing, first the case where the real gems had been, and next the shams that had taken their place; then the surroundings, and last, and one by one, the people engaged about the Lausch pavilion. They were all Viennese, speaking the English language fairly well, far better than Mr. Lausch himself; and after we had questioned them closely and carefully, we closeted ourselves together and discussed the few "points" so far gathered, if points, upon investigation, they proved to be.

"Carl," chuckled my friend when we were at last alone, "one of our missions here at the great Columbian Exposition was to hunt diamond thieves—eh!"

Of course his meaning was plain to me, but I chose to differ with him; there was no better way of rousing his wits.

"Of all the expert thieves on the two continents, the only ones who will not come here will be those whose faces are in every rogues' gallery in the land," I replied. "It would be too much good luck to find Bob and Delbras mixed up in this deal."

"And yet," declared he, "I am willing to wager that it's the work of Delbras *et al*. Who but he would have prepared himself with a full assortment of paste jewels. Honestly, old man, don't you agree with me?"

"Yesterday," I replied, "I was ready to swear that Greenback Bob and his friend Delbras were circulating, perhaps issuing, those two-dollar Government notes."

"And what's to hinder you thinking so still, eh?"

"Only that it would be too much of a fairy story to find our work cut out for us in such a way."

Dave threw one sturdy leg across the chair nearest him, and settled himself in his favourite attitude for an argumentative discourse.

"Young man," he began, "if you can find anything connected with this White City that has sprung out of the lake and the prairie that has not a touch of the Arabian Nights about it, I want to know where it is. Can you show me anything more fairylike than this fairy city, built, as it has been, in the teeth of time?"

Against Odds

"Oh—"

"I tell you it's all a miracle, a nineteenth-century miracle! To come down to facts, now, you and I came here expecting to find Greenback Bob, didn't we?"

"Yes, of course."

"And we have good reason to believe that Delbras is also here. Not much miracle about that, you'll admit."

"No," I assented, knowing that he must reach his climax in his own way.

"No; I should say so! But here is a miracle, a regular White City miracle. I wonder if Delbras and company know that—leaving a couple of thousand of blue-coated Columbian guards out of the question, and they're bright fellows, let me tell you—there are here three hundred and odd picked detectives, a squad at every gate, and every gate and every district connected by telephone with the main office here. Let a suspicious character appear, click goes the nearest telephone, sending the man's description to headquarters, and then, click, click, click, to every district, every gate, every man, goes this same description. Oh, the crooks whose faces are known will find a warm welcome here! It's only the fine workers, who have been so successful that they are not well known, who can make hay in this place."

"All the same," I here submitted, "for such fellows as Delbras and his ilk, who know the world on both continents, this is a promising field, in spite of the telephone system and the detectives in plain clothes at every gate."

"As how ?"

"To the man who can speak several tongues, and is an adept at disguise, this Fair, with its citizens from every clime, will be a better place for concealment than London, Paris, and New York rolled into one."

Dave gave utterance to a long, low whistle, and jerked himself to an upright position.

"You're right again!" he cried. "Come, let's get down to business. What's your idea about this robbery?"

"About the same as yours, I fancy."

"And what's that?"

I took out my notebook, wherein I had jotted down the most important items of testimony elicited from the Lausch attendants, saying:

"Get out your notes, Dave; let's see how they agree."

Dave produced his own briefer notes, and I began running my

finger slowly down the pages.

"It was done during the day."

"Of course!" impatiently.

"And slowly—that is, a little at a time."

"How slowly?"

"Well, for instance, Lausch himself told of a young woman who was much taken with the pink topaz display—you remember?"

"Yes;" beginning to smile behind his book.

"He said that she wore a coat with a deep cape, and that she rested one arm upon the case."

"Well, I did wonder what the woman's dress had to do with it. Gad, but you questioned those people until I began to feel sorry for them. What figure, now, is the dress likely to cut?"

I laughed.

"In this case let us suppose that the young woman is one of the gang."

"Oh!"

"And let us fancy that while she peered at the pink topaz—you remember Lausch told us that she excused her nearness by saying that she was very near-sighted?"

"That's so."

"Well, while looking at the gems, with her face bent over the case, one arm upon the edge, and with the voluminous cape outspread, what is to prevent her using the other hand and arm to draw a diamond point slowly and heavily along the glass, close to the metal?"

"By Jove! what indeed?"

"And why may not this act be repeated, three or four times, say, by the same woman, slightly changed as to dress, as she could have been? Lausch, you recall, accosted her."

"Yes."

When Dave grew laconic I knew him to be almost convinced.

"You will recall how each of the attendants remembered one or more instances of persons lingering long near the gems, or crowding so close as to attract the attention of some of them."

"Umph!"

"And Lausch distinctly remembered how a good-natured guard came to his aid just as he was about to close his exhibits, and stood with his back to the case, and his arms carelessly outspread upon the edge chaffing with a group of late sightseers, and keeping them from annoying him (Lausch) while he

Against Odds

made things secure. Now I don't say that it was done, but I can see how that guard might have played into the hands of the gang, who might have been at hand three or four strong. Observe, the cases were high at the inner sides and shallow at the front, and while the top sheet of glass, for purposes of display, was a large one, those forming the outer side were small and set into stout bronzed squares not to exceed seven inches in depth and ten in length. Now, we will note that the back of the case, besides being higher than the front, is not of glass, but of wood, to admit of the use of a mirror for lining, and to double the show and glitter of the gems."

"Upon—my—word!"

"Now let us suppose our guard as standing before the case and directly in front of the diamonds. He is facing outward, and before him, hovering close, are some others, two or three, or more. On the other sides of the octagonal pavilion the other assistants are busy 'closing up.' Lausch in person presides at the small safe in the centre of the place. Now, while he is busy, with his eyes averted for a moment, a hand thrust under the outstretched arm of the guard may gently press something adhesive against the already cut glass and pull it out, and soon, when Lausch bends down to open the safe, or to place some article therein, the hand draws out the little tray of gems; it was small, and could have been concealed under one of those wraps thrown conveniently across the arm. Now, a little ruse to substitute the false gems and replace the glass under the guard's concealing arm, and the thing is done. If it all happened at the closing hour, when the big building was shadowy and one could see clearly only a short distance, when every exhibitor was occupied with his own, and visitors, for the most part, were intent upon reaching the nearest exit—it was bound to succeed. Of course this is all theory, but—"

"It's the explanation of that theft, or I'm a sinner!" cried Dave, jumping up and beginning to pace the floor nervously. "Carl, old man, I'll never chaff your 'bump of imagination,' after to-day. I'm ready to begin work on just that theory."

"Steady, steady, Dave."

"All right, sir; at least we can make a beginning—we can find that guard."

"How?"

"Take his description from Lausch—find out who was detailed here—"

I put up my hand, and he stopped—staring.

"Dave, there is not a Columbian guard on the force who would, or could, have played that part—if it was played. It was simply one of the band wearing a guard's uniform."

My friend sat down opposite me, and for some time not a word passed between us. Then he took up his notebook, and, drawing a small table toward us, said:

"Let's go over the ground slowly, and see if there is anything here to corroborate your theory, or to point to any other conclusion."

And now I knew that Dave was fixed, so far as his opinions were concerned, and that while he might declare himself convinced by my wisdom, he had been all the time simply establishing his own convictions, and that he was now ready for earnest work.

It was some time before we came out from the superintendent's little inner sanctum, but we were now quite ready to begin our campaign; and when we were given *carte blanche* as to methods, and were promised as many men as we might need for the work, we could ask for nothing more, or better.

Our first demand was peremptory. There must be no publicity; no word of the robbery must reach the vigilant reporters who were everywhere in search of news.

Next, we caused an accurate description of Greenback Bob to be sent to all the gates and different districts, with orders for an instant report of the fact should he be seen, and that once seen he must be constantly shadowed.

Before we left the place we had arranged with Lausch to put a man of our own choosing into the pavilion, whose business it would be to keep constant watch over his people. For while he was ready to vouch for their honesty, we were not; rather, we were not willing to let any possibility of a clue escape us. A second man was placed where he could cultivate these people, and as much as possible outside of business hours. Not that we expected much from this, for we had seen no slightest sign of dishonesty among these people, who seemed to shun all society and to have no acquaintances outside their own pavilion.

After considering long, we decided not to bring the name of Delbras into the case, or to attempt to set any watch upon him in the regular way. To "locate" Delbras should be our own especial work, and to freshen our memories we reviewed the information furnished our chief by the French commissaire.

Against Odds

So far as was known there was no picture of him extant, and the French report described him about as follows:

"Nationality, French; age, probably about thirty to thirty-three years; height, six feet, or nearly; weight, one hundred and seventy-five pounds, approximate; figure good; square shoulders, military air; features, regular; thin-lipped; chin sharply pointed; wears at times heavy beard, at others moustache and goatee; eyes dark, called black; hair same, heavy, and sometimes worn quite long; hands well kept, with long slender fingers; speaks English perfectly, accomplished, etc.; a small triangular scar upon temple close to roots of hair. Known to have been in Paris and London in early winter, and to have crossed to New York about January 1st. Returned to Paris some time in March, and crossed last to New York in early May by steamer *Normandie*."

"Well," had been Dave's comment as we reperused this summary of M. Delbras, "he may disguise himself in many ways, but he can't change his height very much, nor the colour of his eyes, nor his 'regular features' "—Dave's features were not strictly regular, and it was a weakness of his always to resent this descriptive phrase—"nor his slim fingers, nor the scar on his temple close to the roots of the hair."

We had spent a long morning in the rooms of the Secret Service Bureau, and as we were about to take leave, with but a step between us and the outer door, it was hastily opened and a guard entered, followed by two people whom I recognized as Farmer and Mrs. Camp. With a backward step and a quick glance at Dave, I turned and deliberately seated myself.

The only occupants of the outer office at the moment of their entry were the officer in command, who had just accompanied us from the inner office, and the subordinate who was in charge of this outer office, where complaints were received and first hearings granted.

I had drawn back quickly, but the eye of Mrs. Camp was still keen, though she looked a trifle subdued.

"The good land!" she ejaculated, catching at her husband's arm. "Here's one of 'em now, Camp! They've caught him, anyhow!"

The words furnished Dave with a clue to the situation, and he dropped into a chair beside me, and, after one droll look in my direction, gave himself up to a fit of silent mirth.

Meantime the guard had advanced with dignity and announced to the officer at the desk:

"This man has a complaint to bring, sir."

"Wait!" It was Mrs. Camp, standing determinedly near the door of entrance, who spoke. "Afore you make a complaint, Adam Camp, about a raskil that ain't here, s'pose you jest make sure that this here one that is here in our midst don't git away."

CHAPTER VI.

A CRIMINAL HUNT.

NOW, I had told the officer in command my belief and suspicions concerning the counterfeit business which I believed was going on about us, and had been told that two of the counterfeit bills had already been brought to his notice and captured within the week; and Dave had insisted upon his hearing the story of my absurd arrest by the guards, and now it only needed a look from me, and the sight of Dave's convulsed face, to make the situation plain to him. He stepped forward, but before he could speak a new thought had darted into Dame Camp's active mind.

"La!" she finished, "I s'pose, come to think, he's been brought here now to be tried, ain't he?"

With the shadow of a smile upon his face, the officer turned toward the farmer.

"What is your complaint?" he asked courteously; and he shot me a glance which I knew meant, "Let him tell his own story." And now, being authorized to speak, Farmer Camp began to tell, in his own homely way, the story of the "greenback swindle," as he termed it. When he had reached the point in the narrative where I made my unlucky attempt to rout the swindlers, he turned toward me.

"I've had an idee sence, though my wife didn't agree with me much"—here came an audible sniff from Mrs. Camp—"that this here young man might 'a' meant well, after all, and we wus a little mite hasty; but, ye see, he'd been a-lookin' at us so long, an' my wife'd been a-noticin' it, havin' her mind kind o' sot like on confidence people and sech, that she felt kind o' oneasy at his sharp looks—they wus so keen, she said, an' so quick to look

Against Odds

away, she got nervous, and said she felt as if he wus a-lookin' right inter my pockets."

"There now, Camp, you needn't be a-excusin' me! I stick ter my idee. Anyone can see that the young feller ain't innocent, else somebody'd 'a' spoke fur him, fust off—"

Here Dave exploded audibly, and the officer checked her with a motion of his hand.

"Let me settle this point at once by telling you, madam, that the gentleman you have accused is an officer high in his profession, and sent here to protect the public and look after criminals. He had but just arrived, and it was because of this that he was without his officer's badge, which would at once have put those men to rout had it been worn and displayed to them. Let me tell you now, to prevent further mistakes, that the detectives upon whom we rely in greatest emergencies are always to be found in citizen's clothes, and they are not likely to display a badge, except when necessary."

Long before the end of this speech consternation was written all over the face of Adam Camp, but his wife was made of sterner stuff, and when her better half had stuttered and floundered half through a sufficiently humble apology, directed, of course, toward myself, she broke in upon his effort, no whit abashed:

"There, Camp, it's easy enough ter see how we came ter make sech a mistake, and I'm sure the young man will bear no malice to'ard a couple of folks old enough ter be his parients. Twas them sharp-lookin' eyes that set me ter noticin' ye, when you was lookin' over Camp fust off, down to the Administration Building, and when you went an' sot down on the settee by him, an' then got up an' followed us so fur, what was I to think? You was a-watchin' us sure enough, only you meant well by it. But, land sakes! in sech a place, where everybody is tryin' to look out fur number one, I did what looked my dooty. I'm willin' to ask yer pardon, though, and I ain't goin' ter bear no malice."

Overwhelmed by this magnanimity, I murmured my thanks and complete satisfaction with her *amende honor able*, and tried to turn the occasion to such profit as might be by questioning the man a little.

"You were saying that you changed a bill, or were about to do so. Did the man make any difficulty after I left?"

"No, sir. He seemed in a kind of a hurry, and made out to be onsartin whether he could spare so much small money, as he called it. But finally he counted out a roll of bills, and had me count them after him."

"There—in the crowd where you stood?"

"Wal, no. He took us to one side a little—right in behind the place where the little man was a-sellin' canes—sort of up ag'inst a partition, and there we made the dicker."

"And he left you right away?" queried the officer in charge.

"Yes—jest about as quick as he could."

"And the other," I asked, "the man who took you to this agent—the man with the large Sabbath-school class?"

"Oh! he asked us to go to the terminus station with him and see his young men; but my wife wanted to see things, and we jest went as fur as the door, out of perliteness."

"And when did you discover that you had been swindled?"

"Wal, M'riar wanted to ride in one of them coopy things with a man-hoss behind and before; and when she got ready to get out, which was purty soon, I give one of them fellers a two-dollar soovyneer bill, but they made a great jabbering about it, and M'riar says, says she, 'I guess they ain't got the change;' so I fished out some pennies, and a dime and two postage stamps, and after a bit they tuk 'em and waddled off. Then we got to lookin' up and down, and we didn't have no more 'casion to use money—M'riar was so busy seein' the folks and their clo's—till we got hungry, and then come the rumpus. When I come to pay the bill, they was a reg'lar howl, an' we come mighty near bein' marched off to the calaboose, same's you was. They said the bill I offered 'em first off, an' all the rest, was counterfeit."

Until now Brainerd had taken no part in the dialogue; but now, with a quick glance in my direction, he asked:

"Will you describe the man who gave you the money—the supposed agent?"

Camp pondered. "Wal," he began, "he was tall, 's much as six foot, I should say, an' his eyes were black an' big. His hair was consid'able long, and he had a good deal of it on his face in a big bushy moustache. He had a slim nose—and he wore a big di'mond on his little finger."

"Did you notice his hands?"

"M—no."

"Wal, I did!" interposed his wife. "I seen the di'mond, ef 'twas a di'mond. His hands was white—real white, 'long side of his face, and they looked like reg'lar claws; sech long fingers and pointed nails."

"Ah!" Dave shot me a glance full of meaning. "Now, Mrs.

Against Odds

Camp, you seem a very observing woman. Will you describe the other man—the gentleman with the Sabbath-school class?"

The woman's head became even more erect, and her look more firm and confident than before. "Yes," she said at once; "I can." She cast her eyes about her, and, seeing a vacant chair near her interlocutor—the one lately vacated by myself—she seated herself deliberately, and began:

"He wasn't much to look at; about as big as you, mebbe, and about the same complected as that gentleman," pointing to the sergeant at the desk, "only his nose was longer, and sort of big and nobby at the end, and a leetle red. I remember he had bigger ears than common, too; they sort of set straight out. His eyes were little, and a sort of watery gray, and his hair was kind of thin and sandy-like. He had some little mutton-chop whiskers, and a little hair, a'most tan-colour, on his upper lip. His mouth was quite big, and I noticed he had two front teeth with gold fillin' into 'em. He had gloves on his hands when we see him first, but when we met him afterward they was off."

"Afterward, you say—did you meet him after you had discovered that you had been swindled?" I broke in.

"Yes—we—"

"You see," broke in Adam Camp, "it was this way: we was comin' out of Midway, for we'd been out a'most to the end a-seein' the sights, an' when we got hungry we went into a place a blue-coat said was good, the Vienny Caffy, he called it. Well, it was there we had the fuss about the money, and they told us to come here right away and make a complaint. We started, and was jest comin' past that menagerie place, when M'riar wanted to stop jest afore the place and look at the big lion over the door."

"A live one," interpolated M'riar.

"Yes, a live one. Well, standin' there, all to once I see that Sunday-school feller come out o' the door a pickin' his teeth. He was right in front of me, and at first he seemed not to see me, and was hurryin' off dretful fast, but I caught on to his arm and says, quick-like: 'Look here; I want to tell you somethin' fer your own good and to swap favers.' Then he sort of slowed up, and axed me to pardin him—he was in haste, an gettin' orful anxious about them boys. Then I says right out, 'My friend, I'm anxious too, and you've got cause to be: you an' me's been swindled'; and then he most jumped, and asked, 'How swindled ?' 'Hev you broke one of them two-dollar bills yit?' says I. 'No,' says he; an' then I up an' told him the hull story."

"Did you tell him you were coming here?" I asked, as he paused a moment.

"No, because he got so excited and talked so fast; I declare, he put it all out of my head."

Again he stopped, as if loth to continue, but again Mrs. Camp took up the parable.

"Now, father, yer may jest as well out with it! Ye see, this chap flew all to pieces, so to speak, an' he was goin' to have a officer right away. He had a letter of interducshun from his minister to home to the capt'in of the Columbine perleecee—they was related somehow—and he would jest have them men arrested; an' then he happened ter think that 'twas gittin' late and time a'most for that train with them Sunday-school children to come, and it put him out awfully; but he said that he'd make it his bizness to see to that, and then he made a 'p'intment with Camp to meet him at half-past ten terday, an' they'd go tergether ter see the Columbine perleeceman." She paused, and uttered a cackling laugh. "Wal," she concluded, "Camp see that 'twas gittin' purty late, so he 'greed to it an' I didn't say nothin', but after he'd gone ter meet them boys ag'in I put my foot down ter come here fust, an' not to wait till mebbe the feller'd git away, and finally Camp reckoned 'twould be best, and so we came. Someway that feller sort o' went ag'in' me, to'rds the last. I don't want to be hasty ag'in, but I sort o' feel as if he might be kind o' tricky, 's well's the rest."

It did not take us long to convince the Camps that they had been duped all round, and while we had little faith in their ever seeing the 'Sunday-school feller' again, we obtained their promise to keep their appointment with him and here Dave Brainerd suddenly muttered an excuse to the two officers, and said in my ear, "If I am not back in fifteen minutes meet me at the Administration at four sharp." And with a nod to the Camps he went hastily out. I felt very sure of his errand. He had fancied, like myself, that "Smug," fearing lest the Camps might prove too clever for his wiles—perhaps suspecting the keen-eyed old woman—had followed them in order to assure himself whether it would be safe to keep his latest appointment with them, and this indeed proved to be the case.

Before the Camps left the place we had easily convinced them that their "Sunday-school friend," and not I, had been the "confidence man," and that if he kept this last appointment with them it would only be to lure them into another trap, and a worse

Against Odds

one, for it would have for its aim the suppression of any and all evidence they might have been inclined to give to the "perleece."

In convincing the gentle old man, and shattering his faith in my friend Smug, I could see that we had dealt his simple, kindly nature a real blow, but Mother Camp was of sterner stuff.

"You needn't worrit about me, not now," she assured me, with a vigorous nod. "After gitten' into one trap I ain't a-goin' to tumble into any more, an' I ain't goin' ter let him, neither, not when I'm on hand. I've told that man, more times 'n I've got fingers an' toes, that he was too softhearted; allus feedin' tramps 'n' stray dawgs, an' swallerin' all the beggars' yarns."

"I guess ye needn't worrit, M'riar," the old man said, with a faint show of spirit. "Things might 'a' been worst. I didn't aim ter squander a hundred dollars to one lick, but I've got 'n-nuff left yit ter see the Fair an' git home on, so I guess we may as well be a-seein' it; a body hes to live, live an' larn."

And with this sentiment the pair took their departure, a little the wiser, and more wary, perhaps, for the words of warning and advice given them by the officer in charge, who had taken their names and address, and made a memorandum of their complaint.

He had smiled slightly when told their street and number, and had remarked that at least Stony Island Avenue had the merit of nearness, adding the friendly caution, "Don't make boarding-house acquaintances, good people, and keep on the bright side of the way in going home late." Whereupon I made a mental note to investigate this same hardly-named avenue.

Long before the end of the Fair I had cause to thank myself for this mental note, and that it was held in remembrance.

Brainerd did not appear at the stipulated time, and I was too eager to be out in full sight of that wonder city to remain at the bureau; so taking the Intramural Railway at the nearest station I began to circle in and out among those marvels of genius, skill, and nineteenth century enterprise which, combined, had placed, in a time so short as to seem a miracle, this city of beauty beside the blue Lake Michigan.

And now I began to ask myself why the visitor who had nothing to do but to see this wonder of wonders, and had no need to keep one eye upon the passing faces, did not see it, at least until it grew familiar from that point of view, from a seat in an Intramural.

What a kaleidoscopic panorama! In taking my place I had not

even noticed the direction in which I was moving. I had been seeing such a marvel of glimpses, domes, roofs, the lagoon in the distance, a flashing glimpse of the lake through glittering, airy turrets, trees, statues, flags—beauty and charm everywhere. I had taken a round-trip ticket, and I whirled on and on, until somehow I saw the great glass dome of the Horticultural Building, and a moment later a fleeting view of Midway recalled to my mind my own personality and interests. As I gazed at it, stretching away westward, a veritable Joseph's coat of a street, it was gone, and I saw the tall dome of Illinois, the Art Gallery in the distance, with the lagoon again gleaming through trees, to be lost again, while roofs, windows, vistas of streets surrounded me, and I could peep in at the windows we were passing; and then I heard the cry of the guard, and noted the name as we slacked speed at Mount Vernon Station, almost upon the roof of the Old Virginia Building. I peered out as we drew up to this station in the air, and drew back a little as a second train, moving in the opposite direction, dashed by. I am in the rear car, and as we move away from Mount Vernon, suddenly I have a vision of someone who must have flung himself from the forward car at the last moment, and who is running along the platform, and in the direction of the passing train, in breathless haste, his head bare, his hat clutched in his swinging hand.

It is Dave Brainerd, and as we tear around a curve and he is lost to my sight, I am brought back to thoughts of business. Dave has evidently "struck a trail." Wondering much, I stop at the north loop, and standing with the Government Building to my right and the Fisheries with its curving colonnades on my left, I gaze off upon the blue and shining waters of the lake, and realize fully for the first time the awful incongruity between all this stateliness and beauty and our mission in its midst—a criminal hunt!

CHAPTER VII.

"IT WAS GREENBACK BOB."

OUR CHIEF had arranged for us, and in advance of our arrival, that our letters should be received at the bureau, where a desk was always at our disposal; and a little before four o'clock I dropped in once more to look for letters and ask if Dave had made a second appearance. The letters were in waiting for both of us, but there was no news of Dave, and, stowing the letters in my pocket, I sought once more the Court of Honour; seating myself near the great MacMonnies Fountain, in the shade of the Administration Building, where Dave could not fail to find me, to read my letters and wait for him.

I was in no haste, with that magnificent court spread out before me, and the blue dancing waves of Lake Michigan in the distance, Nature's background for the great Peristyle, surmounted by that novel and beautiful Columbus quadriga, in itself a work of art such as is seldom seen, and with golden Justice, dominant and serene, commanding and overlooking all.

Forgetting my letters, I let my eyes wander slowly from point to point of beauty, letting the moments pass unheeded.

"Fine figure of a woman, eh?"

I started, and came suddenly down to earth, at the sound of one of my friend's characteristic speeches. He was standing beside me, as imperturbable of countenance as usual, but looking somewhat blown; and he dropped upon the bench, and stretched his legs, and pulled off his hat, like a weary man who means to enjoy a little well-earned rest.

I knew him too well to display any curiosity, and I merely sorted out from the bundle of letters still unopened in my hand those bearing his name, and laid them upon his knee, and with merely a nod and smile, by way of greeting, addressed myself to my own.

The first was a brief business document; the next a schoolboy's letter, short, of course, from a young brother, my sole living tie and charge. The third was from our chief, and I saw, upon opening it, that it was addressed, within, to both of us.

"Dave," I ventured, "may I interrupt?"

"You can't," he replied. "I've done. They're of no consequence," and he thrust the two missives I had given him into his loose side-pocket. "Blaze away, boy."

The letter was not long, and, after some minor instructions and some suggestions, came this passage:

"'I wonder if either of you remembers the case of the Englishman who wrote us at much length some six months ago concerning his son, 'lost or missing'—we did not succeed in finding him in New York—'"

"And small wonder," chuckled Dave, whose memory was a storehouse. "We hadn't even the skeleton of a description."

"'In New York, you remember,'" I read on, "'and it has seemed to me that you may as well look out for him in your intervals of leisure, if there are such.'"

"Old man's growing sarcastic," grumbled my friend.

"'It's a good thing, if successful,'" I continued; "'and the Fair is the best place in the world for a 'hide out.' If the young fellow's above-ground I'll wager something he's in Chicago now; that is, if he really did come to America a year ago, as his fond father (?) writes. I enclose for your further information his letter; and I would be proud of the fact if you two fellows could unearth him at the Columbian City. I give you *carte blanche* for the case.'"

"Umph! That means roll up your sleeves and go in."

I took up the copy of the Englishman's letter. "Shall I read it?" I asked, "or is it—"

"Don't say 'engraven on your memory,'" implored Dave. "Yes—go ahead."

"'Dundalk House,
"'January 3, 1893.

"'MESSRS. ——————.

"'GENTLEMEN,—On November 6th, in the year 1892, Carroll L. Rae, Esq., of Dundalk House, left his home, ostensibly for a few days in London. He was never seen again at Dundalk, and we have been accurately informed that he sailed for America in that same month. Being of age, he drew from his bankers while in London one thousand pounds, the full amount deposited to his credit; since that time no trace of him has been found.

"'Carroll L. Rae is twenty-six years of age, and tall, lacking one-half inch of being six feet in height. He is slender, broad-shouldered, upright; fair skin, blue eyes, brown hair; features regular and refined; hair worn very short, but inclined to curl close to skull; strong in athletic sports; a graduate of Queen's College; has small, aristocratic feet and hands; a skilled horseman; sings a fine and unusually high tenor; has a singularly strong control over all animals. We have no portrait of him since childhood. Has strong leaning toward military life and somewhat literary tendencies. Am prepared to send blank cheque for the payment of expenses of thorough search, and add as reward when found two thousand pounds. Address all correspondence to

>"'SIR HUGO RAE,
>"'Dundalk House, Egham,
>"'Surrey.'"

"Umph!" broke out Brainerd, when I had read the last word. "Typical old English paterfamilias! Tyrannical, I'll be bound. I'll bet something the young fellow ran away from parental tyranny. How did the thing come out at the first attempt? I don't seem to recall it."

"And for a good reason. You were in Canada, and I was occupied with that Rockville murder. I think they put Sturgis on the case. English himself, you know."

"Yes—well?"

"Well, as nearly as I remember, Sturgis advertised, to begin, 'something to his advantage,' etc."

"Of course!" contemptuously.

"This failed, and he made the tour of the hotels, swell places first, then going down in the scale, hunted the registers; haunted the places most affected by the English tourist; halted good-looking, or English-looking, blond young men until they turned on him. In fact, tried all the dodges—and failed."

"Of course! It's one thing to find a person who has been hidden, and quite another to search for one who hides himself. What do you think has set the chief to looking this lost son up here, and through us?"

"Why, you know his ways—he seldom stops to explain; but I fancy he may have heard again from Sir Hugo Rae."

I took up the two sheets, and was about to thrust them into their envelope, when Brainerd suddenly said:

"Hold on, boy! there's something written across the back of that copied letter."

I turned it over and read the half-dozen lines written thereon:

"'Carroll Rae, if found, is to be told at once that his brother, Sir Hugo, is dead.'"

"Oh!" ejaculated Brainerd; "so it's not his father. Well, that alters things. We may be able to find a Sir Carroll Rae, especially as he must have about exhausted that thousand pounds if he has been doing the States in true English style."

"At any rate," I added, "it's on our books. I suppose one may keep an eye out for a swell young Englishman here as well as elsewhere. It's only one more face in the crowd."

"And that reminds me," said my friend. "This business almost put it out of my head. I took a turn on that Intramural road this afternoon."

"Yes?" I knew better than to interrupt at this point.

"And I saw, I am sure I saw—whom do you think?"

"Dave, that's like a woman! I'm surprised at you. You saw Delbras."

"Wrong! I saw, I'm certain of it, Greenback Bob."

"Good!"

"He was dressed very swell—you might have mistaken him for one of the board of directors; but it was Bob."

"And you piped him home, of course?" I queried.

"Of course I didn't. He was going one way, and I the other, each on an Intramural car."

"Oh! and you were running to stop the car, and Bob, when I saw you at Mount Vernon Station," I said wickedly, "did you overtake it?"

"I did—just."

"And Bob?" eagerly.

"Well," with a grin, "I'm sorry to disappoint you, but when I jumped on board, at the last moment, I found that Bob had got off while I got on. In fact, I saw him going downstairs as I was borne away to Fifty-seventh Street. There, boy, don't look so mournful; it's all in the game. I couldn't find a trace of him; but we know he's here."

*   *   *   *   *

I had decided on the night of my arrival, after pondering late the adventure of the black bag, or, as I now described it to myself, Miss Jenrys' bag, upon my course of action concerning it.

In her letter to her friend she had mentioned the entrance at Fifty-seventh Street as being near their place of abode, and I had promised myself that I would be early at that gate to watch for the coming of Miss Jenrys, and to restore her property—what else?

But I had not counted upon a diamond robbery at the very beginning of my World's Fair adventures, and as I wished to go unaccompanied, I did not attempt to stand guard at evening.

But the second morning saw me at an early hour alone, and so near the gate at Fifty-seventh Street that I could in no possible way miss the lady should she appear.

I had not needed to avoid Dave. He had been prompt to tell me that he meant to put in the day looking for Greenback Bob, and that he should "do his looking" upon Midway.

"And why Midway?" I had asked him.

"Because, if there's a place that is better than all other places in which to hide one's self, that place is the Midway."

It was quite true; and as I made my way toward the northern entrance, I turned over in my mind an idea suggested, or revived, by Dave's last words.

As I passed toward the entrance between the unique little house of South Dakota on one side and hospitable and home-like Nebraska State Building on the other, my gaze was caught by the restfulness and charm of the western facade of the latter, with its broad portico and the little lawn lying between the broad steps facing the western boundary of the grounds, the little stream flowing under overhanging trees of nature's own planting, and past the little natural arbour of climbing vines draping themselves among the branches, making shade and coolness for the groups loitering underneath upon the rustic seats scattered freely and inviting all.

While I gazed, a voice close behind me said, in a wheedling drawl:

"Dew come in! You never saw sech a place! Why, upstairs beats this all out of sight. Sech parlours, with velvet chairs, and sofys, and a pianer; I tell ye Nebrasky beats some o' them stuck-up Eastern States!"

I turned, to see a fat, rosy-faced and eager woman, in the defiant bonnet I have learned to know as from "out west," piloting a lean and reluctant woman, quite as typical as a rural New Englander, through the gate of the inclosure; and, prompted doubtless by the words I had just heard, I took another and more extended survey of the building so justly extolled, this time lifting my eyes to the upper window and the balcony overhanging the stream.

Was it a mere passing resemblance, or a fancied one, or was the face I saw for just an instant at one of those upper windows the face of the little brunette adventuress who had laid claim to Miss Jenrys' bag? If so, she had been scanning the increasing crowd through an opera-glass, and had dropped this in seeming haste, and vanished, before I could prolong my glance.

Nebraska Building.

Against Odds

"It's hardly likely," I said to myself, and turned toward the bridge spanning the little stream, and lying between me and the entrance I sought.

As I stepped upon the bridge I saw, on the other side, just coming out from the shadow of the elevated tracks above the entrance, the lithe form and rare blond face, not to be mistaken anywhere, with its fine clear contour, its dark eyes, and fine healthful pallor.

She came forward leisurely, and stopped by the railing at the edge of the platform to look down at the white-hooded Laplander who constantly paddled up and down in the little stream, between the bridge and the Lapland Village behind the inclosure, a few rods to the north.

Just then there was a cry from beyond the gates, followed by the rat-tat-tat of a drum, and one of those perpetually arriving "processions" came filing down the platform and across the bridge. I was in no haste to accost Miss Jenrys at the very entrance, and possibly in the face of one or more of my everpresent brethren of the watchful eye, and so, while she waited unhurried upon one side the bridge, I stopped also, looking down upon the little stream and feigning interest in the whiterobed canoeist paddling, and doubtless perspiring, in the mild June air. The procession was not a long one, and was formed of boys, half-grown, and wholly effervescent, wearing what was evidently an extemporized uniform, and carrying a banner which informed me that it was a boys' school, sent from an outlying town through the liberality of an "Honorable" somebody whose name I did not hear; for the fact of the sending was not emblazoned upon the red-silk banner they carried, but was announced, often and willingly, in reply to queries along the line.

They were a healthy and wholesome lot of fellows, and while I gazed at them, not without a feeling of interest in and sympathy with their day's pleasure, a little figure flitted past me, through the tiniest of spaces between the marching lads and myself, pressed close against the rail, and I saw again the little brunette hastening toward the platform at the gate. Wondering a little, I kept my post.

There was the usual rabble of all sorts and conditions swelling the ranks in the rear, and when these had crowded across the bridge, there was another throng of more leisurely moving visitors. But Miss Jenrys was not in this throng; and when they had passed and the stream of travel had somewhat thinned I moved forward, only a few steps, however, for just beyond me, advancing slowly, with a smile upon her lips, and her eyes turned toward a companion, came Miss Jenrys.

She had entered the grounds alone—of that I had been ocularly convinced; and that she should find a companion so soon had never entered my thoughts.

But she had a companion, and I almost gnashed my teeth as I saw tripping along at her side the little brunette.

She was talking volubly, in the low, quiet manner that I knew, and if she saw me in passing she disguised the fact skilfully.

I waited until they were a few paces ahead, and then followed them slowly, chewing the cud of bitter reflection.

Could it be that I was losing my skill in reading and judging faces—I upon whom the men of our force relied for a rapid, and usually correct, guess at a strange face? Was I mistaken in this little brunette, then?

Or had I been mistaken in my judgment of Miss Jenrys?

No, never! I had set her down at once for a lady, in the sweet old-fashioned meaning of the word—womanly, refined, good and true; and had not her letters confirmed this? But this dark-haired, quick-speaking little person by her side—was she, after all, a friend? And had I committed a *faux pas* in refusing to deliver up the little bag? And if so, had I the courage to approach these two and commit myself? Could I tell Miss Jenrys how, failing to think of a better way of finding her, I had read her letters? I had meant, of course, to do this; but could I, with those pert, mocking eyes upon me? No; in my heart I knew that it was not that which vexed me. Could I bear the scrutiny of those clear, straightforward brown eyes in that other presence, which would put me at so sore a disadvantage?

Then I shook myself and my senses together. After all she came alone. Might they not separate soon? How could I tell that there was not a friend, several friends perhaps, waiting for that troublesome brunette back in the Nebraska Building?

They were walking straight down the street toward the lake, with a row of State buildings upon one side and the great spreading Art Gallery on the other. It was a perfect June morning, and the sight of the blue lake at the end of that splendid promenade, and the fresh breeze blowing off it, were inspiriting. There was to be some State function that day, and the crowd was thickening. Made bold by numbers, I came close behind them. Miss Jenrys had unfurled a big blue umbrella, and the two walked in the shade of it; and in order to screen myself, in part at least, should the brunette, whom I was beginning to detest heartily, turn and look suddenly back, I shook out the closely-rolled folds of my own umbrella and poised it carefully between my face and the sun.

And now, made bold by my canopy, and frankly bent upon hearing what I could, I drew daringly near, and when they stopped and stood to gaze at the ornate New York State Building, I halted also.

"By no means," I heard the soft voice of the lovely blonde say, as she moved back a pace to look up at the facade. "That would be quite too enterprising. I am chaperoned by my aunt, who is not so good a sight-seer as myself, and for two days I have ventured——" Here the sharp call of some hurrying chair-boys drowned her words, and I next heard the brunette's voice.

"Things do happen so strangely"—it was impossible to catch all of her words—"mamma is sick so often—and papa—I do dislike being alone, though—in the Art Gallery—acquaintances. That is all—I do wish—"

They moved on, Miss Jenrys increasing her speed perceptibly, and seeking, it seemed to me, to walk a little aloof from her companion, which caused me to wonder if she could be expecting or hoping to meet anyone. I was no longer able to hear their conversation, but they again paused and gazed long at the fine colonial building of the State of Massachusetts.

I had hardly looked to see Miss Jenrys enter the placid New York halls, but when she turned away from Massachusetts without entering or so much as climbing the terrace steps, I wondered; and then, as the pair turned away, and after a moment of seeming hesitation moved on toward the lake, a man, tall and well dressed, passed me so closely and at such a rapid pace as to attract my attention to himself. He walked well, with a quick, swinging stride, and I think I never saw a man's clothes fit better. His hands were gloved, and in one of them he carried a natty umbrella, using it as a cane. I had not seen his face, for he turned it neither to right nor left; and his splendid disregard for the beauties all about him was explained when I saw him halt beside Miss Jenrys and hold out a hand with the assured air of an old friend. I was near enough to see the smile on her face when she turned to greet him, but the few quick words they exchanged were of course unheard. Then I saw her turn toward the brunette on the other side; but that brisk little person had already drawn

New York Building.

back, and now she said a word or two, nodded airily, and, turning, went quickly away.

A moment later Miss Jenrys and her companion turned about and went toward the Massachusetts Building, and I saw his face. It was dark and handsome; and as they mounted the terrace side by side I pressed boldly forward, under the shadow of my umbrella, and thanking my lucky stars that I had it with me, and that—because it was on the cards that at ten o'clock I was to go to the rendezvous where Farmer Camp was to meet, or await, Mr. Smug, for he knew him by no other name—I was lightly but sufficiently disguised in a wig slightly sprinkled with gray, and long about my neck and ears, and a very respectable looking short and light set of moustaches and whiskers, the whole finished with a pair of gold-rimmed glasses.

Wearing these, I ventured so close that I heard, while toiling behind them up the broad old-fashioned stairway, a few fragmentary words from the lips of Miss Jenrys, who seemed replying to some question.

"I cannot, indeed—the best of reasons. My aunt is not here, Mr. Voisin."

"Mr. Voisin!" I fell back and meditated. So this was the handsome Frenchman, the rival of "him"! I did not again attempt to overhear their conversation, but I followed them about the building as they moved slowly from room to room, and now I did not follow with my eyes upon the graceful and stately movements, the lovely profiles and turns of the head, of the fair woman moving on before me, but I noted carefully every gesture, every pose and turn, the gait, carriage, and as correctly as possible the height, weight, and length of limb of Mr. Maurice Voisin of France, and I felt that I was doing well.

When at last they turned from the building, which neither had seemed in haste to leave, I looked at my watch, and knew that I had barely time to reach the southern end of the grounds even aided by the Intramural. As I came out upon the street once more, and was passing hurriedly by the eastern portico of the New York Building, I chanced to lift my eyes toward it. The great curtains between the fluted columns were swaying in the breeze, and from between two, which she seemed to be trying to hold together with unsteady hands, the face of the little brunette, dark and frowning, looked cautiously out.

CHAPTER VIII.

"STRAIGHT FROM THE SHOULDER."

WHEN FARMER Camp had presented himself at the rendezvous after his visit to the bureau, he had found Smug awaiting him, but in company with a muscular stranger, with whom he represented himself to have important business; and after a few "leading questions," which Camp answered quite naively, the two excused themselves, Smug making a second appointment for the following day.

Again the farmer was prompt, and this time Mrs. Camp also. I did not make my presence known to them, and Smug did not appear, so I left them to digest this clear case of perfidy, while they viewed the wonders of the Transportation Building and the great golden doorway; and, believing, like Brainerd, that the Midway was a mine likely to yield us at least a clue, I turned my steps westward, my thoughts a singular medley, in which the Camps, Miss Jenrys, Delbras, Greenback Bob, the little brunette, and Monsieur Voisin were strangely intermingled; and—I am obliged to admit it—the young fellow who had accosted me upon Midway, and avowed a knowledge of Miss Jenrys, was also in my thoughts.

If it was true that he knew the owner of the black bag, why not question him—carelessly, of course? Perhaps—well, perhaps he knew Monsieur Voisin also.

I could hardly have given myself a reason for this sudden anxiety, but it was there, and it sent me straight down Midway Plaisance, as nearly in my former tracks as was possible. It was too late for breakfast, I assured myself, and far too early for luncheon, ergo, if my friend the guard was still upon his beat, I must surely see him, sooner or later.

And so it proved. As I emerged from the shadow of the viaduct, over which the Intramural rattled and rolled, I saw him, not far ahead and coming toward me, his hands clasped behind him, his chin-strap down, his face absorbed, and seemingly oblivious of all about him.

When we were but a few feet apart, he turned upon his heel

and began his backward march, with the same air of indifference to all about him.

As he neared the long low cottage opposite the village of the little Javanese, and having "Java or Home Restaurant" over its door in big letters, and as I was nearing him, I saw him suddenly throw up his head and spring forward. At the same moment I noted a man—hatless, coatless, and wearing upon his waistcoat the badge which indicated his position as "head waiter"—come running from the direction of the Home Restaurant, pointing as he ran, breathlessly, toward a man and woman who were walking rather briskly eastward.

As the guard came opposite this couple I saw him halt just a perceptible instant, his eye upon the hurrying waiter; then he stepped quickly before the coming couple and made a courteous but positive gesture, clearly an order to halt. The man did not halt, but brushed past the polite guard with a scowling face. He was a big fellow, flashily dressed, and with a countenance at once coarse and dissipated; and as he made a second forward movement I could distinctly see his hand drop, with a significant gesture, toward his right hip.

"Stop him!" cried the almost breathless head-waiter. "A beat."

At the word the woman made a little forward spring, and the man made a movement to follow.

"Halt!" commanded the guard, at the same time clapping a hand upon the man's shoulder, and then—

It was only the work of a moment.

There was a quick movement on the man's part, and I saw the butt of a big revolver, and called out in warning: "Take care!" I might have saved my breath. The tall guard stood moveless until the weapon was actually in sight, and then the arm in the blue coat shot out, strong, swift, straight from the shoulder, and the pistol-arm dropped, the weapon fell to the ground, and the man staggered back, to be received in the unwilling arms of the head-waiter, to struggle there for a moment, and then to submit, quite as much to the fire in the young guard's eye as to the strength of his arm. The woman at the first sign of struggle had drawn away from her companion, slipped into the crowd about them, and was making off in haste, when I said, addressing the waiter:

"Must she be stopped?"

The fellow shook his head. "Let her go," he said; "they were dodging their breakfast-bill."

It was the common trick of a common sharper. Having ordered and eaten a late breakfast, they had called for something additional, and in the absence of the waiter had left their places near the door and slipped away.

It was over in a moment. The man, forced into honesty by strength superior to his own, sulkily paid the bill, while denying the claim, and then, like his companion, he slipped through the crowd and was soon out of sight.

Meantime, my friend the guard, with a look of disgust and weariness upon his face, had turned away the moment his duty was done, and I followed him, smiling a little over this reversal of our positions.

"Well," I said, as I reached his side, "I see there is good reason for your ability to judge a 'straight-from-the-shoulder' knock-out blow."

He turned quickly, and with a shade of haughtiness upon his face, which was lost in a smile as he recognised me.

"Ah," he said courteously, "good-morning! So you witnessed that pitiful affair. It does not fall to my lot to serve ladies." He hesitated slightly, and then asked, "Did you deliver up your find?"

I laughed and shook my head. I had fallen into step with him, and we were now moving slowly along his beat.

"If you refer to the lady with the dark eyes, who had the poor taste to ignore your presence," I said, "I did not. I may have committed a blunder, but my judgment condemned the little person."

He turned toward me a quick look of interest.

"Then you thought—" He stopped, and the red blood dyed his face as on that first day.

"I thought," I instantly took up the word, "that she was an adventuress, not a companion or friend to the owner of the little bag."

"And you were right," he exclaimed. "The lady who—who dropped the bag you found was alone when those foreign brutes with their palanquin ran against her. I was not near enough to reach her promptly; but I saw—and the other—the brunette, it is a strange fancy, perhaps, but I have thought that she had been following Miss—the lady, though for what purpose—" He stopped. "It is no affair of mine. I—I am glad that the lady has her property."

"But she has not got her property."

"No? Pardon me, I did not understand."

Against Odds

He had turned his face to the front, but I could see that he was agitated, and was holding himself under with a strong hand. As I walked beside him and noted his fine physique, the well-set head and clear-cut features, I felt genuinely attracted toward the manly fellow, and wondered what was the secret of his interest in that lovely girl, whom he had yet shunned; for, looking back upon the events of the previous day, I could see that he had purposely held aloof from the moment when he saw that a champion and protector was at hand.

"I had thought," he said after a little, "that is, I fancied there might be something—some clue to her whereabouts in the bag."

"It was not complete," I answered. "When I could not overtake her, and the brunette did not recommend herself to my confidence, I opened the bag, after some hesitation."

"Yes?" The syllable was a direct and eager question.

"I found nothing by way of identification save two letters, both unsealed, and these, after some reluctance, I opened."

"Ah!" A trifle stiffly.

"The first was from a lady in Boston to a lady here at the World's Fair."

"Indeed!" A freer tone, almost a sigh of relief.

"This gave me so little information that I was obliged to open the second letter, which was written, I suppose, by the owner of the bag, and not as yet posted; even this did not give me her address."

"How strange!"

We had reached the end of his beat, and now I turned with him, and we sauntered slowly toward the Ferris Wheel. I felt that he was worthy of a grain of comfort, if I were able to give it, and I said:

"It was like this. The letter from Boston was written on the eve of a start for this place. The other letter, if posted, would have passed the lady for whom it was intended upon the road. This last letter, written supposedly by the owner of the bag, states that she, having left her New York home some time since, is now in the World's Fair City in company with an aunt, whom she describes as rustic, but delightful, and that because they are stopping very near the Fair she feels safe in coming alone on such days as her aunt elects to pass in the quiet of her own apartment; the only clue to an address is the statement that she enters the grounds by the Fifty-seventh Street gate."

"Ah!" It is a sigh of genuine relief. At last he has a clue, if a slight one. But what does he want of a clue? Having gotten thus far, I relate briefly my experience of this morning, omitting description and the name of Monsieur Voisin, whom I describe as a tall dark-haired gentleman, evidently a foreigner, and then I play my card.

I am here upon business of an important nature; my time is limited; I do not know the lady; and having committed the folly of holding back first because of the brunette, and last—well, because I had an especial reason for not coming under the notice of this strange man—in short, had I found the lady alone I should have returned her property; in the presence of a third party I did not wish to do so; and then I put my question.

He had said that he knew this young lady, and, being here day after day, he would be likely to see her again. She would be sure to revisit the Midway; and what could be more easy than for him to return her lost property, explaining as he chose? It would relieve me much; it would be to me a genuine favour.

The guard was silent for a time; then he paused in his measured walk and turned to face me.

"If I have not misunderstood," he said slowly, "you set out this morning for the purpose of restoring to the lady her lost property?"

"True."

"And—do you mean to tell me that because of the presence of this brunette first, and then of the man, you gave up the idea?"

"Quite so."

"I confess," he said, "that I cannot understand why those people should be a hindrance; nevertheless, I am ready to believe that your reason is good and sufficient."

"Thank you."

"I trust," he hastened to add, "that you will judge me as generously when I say that I cannot oblige you. I know the name of the lady, it is true; but, much as I may desire to serve you, I cannot do so. My desire to avoid the lady, to remain unrecognised by her, is as strong as is yours to hold aloof from her escort. It's an odd position," he added, with a slow half-smile. "I trust the contents of Miss—of the bag were not of too great value—not indispensable to her?"

"By no means—quite the contrary; and this being the case, we will trouble ourselves no more about it. Of course I can't urge my request under the circumstances." I could not repress a smile at the absurdity of the situation. "And to say that I don't bear malice, as they say in making up a quarrel, let us exchange cards." I produced my card, a simple pasteboard of the size known as the visiting-card, and with only my name engraved across it.

The guard drew back a step, and again that ready flush dyed his face.

"Pardon me. You are addressing me as one gentleman to another, and if I were to give you the name by which I am known here it would not be my true one. I will not give you a fictitious name, and—I can give no other."

I was silent a moment, then—"I will not urge you," I said; "but at least, as man and man, equals, we can shake hands." And I held out my own.

His face cleared instantly, and he promptly placed his palm upon mine.

"I can do that," he said, "as man to man, as an equal, and"—he threw back his handsome head—"I shall never, I trust, have reason to hesitate before giving my hand as an honest man to an honest man; and now—" He paused, and I with him.

"And now," I supplemented, "we are neither of us idlers. This is your beat?"

"For the present."

"Then—I hope we shall meet again. Success to you."

"And to you." He lifted his hat as I turned away, and looking back a moment after, I saw him once more a Columbian guard on duty, piloting an old woman across the street and away from a sprinkling-cart.

"Handsome enough to be a prince," I thought. "An American prince, and poor, doubtless. Honest, I'll wager; and with a mystery. I wonder if the world is pouring all its mysteries into this White City of the world."

CHAPTER IX.

IN DISGUISE.

TWO DAYS had passed since my talk with my friend the guard, and although Brainerd, myself, and others had thoroughly searched Midway Plaisance, hoping to obtain a glimpse of our quarry or a hint of their presence, we had been unsuccessful. We found many things in Midway, but neither Greenback Bob nor his friend Delbras.

"I tell you," Dave had said on the previous night, when we were discussing our failure and its probable reasons—"I tell you, Carl, these men began their business in Midway—I'm sure of it; and I solemnly believe that you're the fellow that scared them away."

"I, indeed—how?"

"Simply by springing upon them in that Camp affair. I believe they spotted you."

I felt chapfallen, for I was more than half inclined to believe that Dave's notion was the correct one, and I wondered that I had not thought of this myself.

"And if they did," went on Dave, "it would be the most natural thing in the world for them to 'fold up their tents like the Arabs,' etc. Don't you think so?"

"Granting your first premises," I conceded grudgingly, "your second, of course, are tenable. Perhaps you have an idea where their 'tents' are now spread?"

"Oh, you always try the sarcastic dodge when you are beaten a bit," grinned Dave good humouredly; "but that's all right. I think we may as well give the Midway a rest, at any rate."

"I suppose you have noted that the Woman's Building has had more than its share of stealing of late?" said I.

"M—no."

"Well, you should read the papers, and look in at the bureau, once a day at least. They've had an attack upon the exhibits—failed, I believe—and a number of pockets picked."

"Do you suggest the Woman's Building?"

"To-morrow I suggest the vicinity of the Court of Honour and the Administration Building. It's the Princess Eulalia's day, you remember; or had you failed to note that?"

"Go on, boy; wound me where I'm weakest," scoffed Dave.

But I chose to ignore Dave's chaff.

"I suggest that we join the crowd early, and stay with it late."

"Done!" cried he.

"It's hard to tell where they will elect to work. There will be a thinning out inside the buildings, but a crowd outside, and such a crowd as this will be—all with necks craned and attention fixed; ladies in gay attire, the cream of the city's visitors as well as the other side; and there will be at least half a dozen false cries of

'There she comes!' and somebody's pocket will suffer at each cry."

"Right you are!" agreed Dave. "It'll be a swell crowd, and it's my opinion that our men will be in the thick of it."

* * * * *

Early the next morning I went to see if anything had been reported concerning the diamond robbery, for as yet little had been accomplished. There was one of the attendants, a young woman, whom I had felt uncertain about. She was pretty, and I thought artful and vain; and I had learned from another employé of the Lausch Pavilion that she had formed the acquaintance of a rather flashily dressed person wearing much jewellery, and that just before the robbery she had been seen to receive two or three slyly-delivered *billets-doux*. The girl was being closely watched, and one of the guards, who was stationed near, and who was said to have been seen loitering near the pavilion oftener and longer than was needful, was likewise under close surveillance.

But this morning there was something to report. It did not come through any of the men at work upon the case, nor was it in the nature of a discovery. It was an anonymous letter, and it came through the United States mail, having been posted in Chicago, at the up-town post-office.

It was addressed "To whom it may concern," at the bureau, and was brief and to the point.

"If you do not want to waste time," the letter began, "turn your attention to the men in charge of the robbed jewellery exhibit; and if you also keep an eye upon a certain up-town man who keeps a place advertised as a 'jewellery-store,' and with rather a shady reputation—a man not above doing a little business in uncut gems, say, in a very quiet way—you may find some of the lost gems between the two."

There was no signature, and I saw at a glance that the writing was carefully disguised.

I was not inclined to treat this document seriously, though I could see that it had created quite a sensation at the office, and when asked my opinion concerning it I said:

"If this letter means anything but to mislead, it can mean but one of two things; either it is written by one of the thieves to draw us away from the right track, or it is written by someone who belongs to a gang, and who means, if possible and safe, to sell out his comrades for all he can get and a promise of safety. I've seen this done."

"And what is your opinion?"

"I'm more than half inclined to think it is a hoax."

"As how?"

"It may be the work of a crank or a practical joker," I replied; and I thought it possible, though hardly probable.

"If we had advertised this thing," said the officer slowly, "I should think little of this letter, but it has not been made public."

"It is known," I reminded him, "to some three hundred men here in the grounds, and it has been told to—how many sellers of jewellery up in the city, not to mention their employés? Half a dozen picked men have been detailed to work upon the case. I don't think it likely, but some officer who covets a bit of special work might have thought it worth while to muddle the job for us; or some revengeful clerk up-town may be trying to get even with some enemy. However, the thing can't be ignored, and my advice would be, trace the letter to its author, if possible."

There were no letters for us that morning, and I left the place soon, certain that the machinery of the bureau was quite equal to the task of looking after the anonymous letter, which, after all, did not occupy a large place in my mind.

Since my talk with my mysterious guard, I had made next day another effort to see Miss Jenrys. I had waited at the gate at Fifty-seventh Street for three long and precious morning hours, and then I had turned away anathematizing myself, and vowing that hereafter I would attend to my own legitimate business, and not prowl about after an evasive beauty, who, no doubt, had already purchased a new bag and forgotten her loss. But in my heart I knew it was not to restore the bag alone that I so earnestly looked for Miss Jenrys. I had not fallen in love, not at all; but yet somehow I had a singular anxiety to see again the face of this sweet blonde, and to hear her mellow, musical voice, if only in the two words, "Thank you."

Even as I turned away after my long and fruitless waiting, I did not promise myself to forget her, nor altogether to quit the chase. I hypocritically said, "Now I will trust a little to chance." How Dave would have laughed could he have known my thoughts!

* * * * *

Against Odds

By nine o'clock that morning there were thousands of people thronging the Court of Honour, drifting out and in under the arches of the Administration Building, and up and down upon the streets on either side of it. Everywhere there was a look of expectancy, and no apparent desire to move on.

As the morning advanced, and the active guards began to stretch ropes at either side of the entrance through which the procession would pass, the throng drew together from various directions and massed themselves, as many of them as could drawing close to the rope outside; some with the narrow comfortless-looking red chairs seating themselves with the great rope actually resting upon their knees, to be hemmed in and pressed upon at once by row after row of crowding, pushing humanity, while others swarmed boldly between the ropes and filled the smooth gravelled space reserved for the honoured guests and the city magnates attendant upon them.

It was a good-humoured crowd, but it held its place until, from the entrance of the building, a line of guards in full uniform came slowly out, while from the east a second company came forward, two by two, and these spreading into a line, single file, and facing about, united with the others in forming an L, and thus slowly, quietly, but none the less surely, they advanced, while just as slowly and almost as composedly the crowd fell back, and outward, until the roped-in space was cleared, only to partially fill, and to be again cleared, once and again.

Brainerd and I had separated upon reaching the place, and I had not seen him since, although I had moved about from point to point almost ceaselessly.

As eleven o'clock approached the crowd began to grow restless, and questions to be bandied about from one to another, while guards, as ignorant for the most part as their questioners, were interviewed endlessly.

"When is she coming?"

"Is she coming soon?"

"Are you sure she will come here?"

"Is it eleven o'clock?" etc.

It was eleven o'clock when I drew out from the throng that had pressed within the ropes, only to be slowly driven out again, and passed through an aisle of fans and parasols, which had been opened and kept open, the width of three men, shoulder to shoulder, by a constant passing of its length; and I was skirting one side of the building slowly and with my eyes searching the crowd of faces, when I heard a familiar voice near me speaking in impatient tones.

"Law, pa, it's no use! I ain't a-goin' to set on that tottlin' thing one minit longer—not for all the infanties in Ameriky! What more's a furrin infanty than a home-born one, anyhow?" There was a stir next the rope and a break in the wall of humanity about it, and then Mrs. Camp emerged, her bonnet very much awry, and her husband bringing up the rear, puffing and worried, with a little red chair hanging from one shoulder and the faded umbrella clutched in one hand.

They saw me at the same moment.

"Wal," began the lady, "I'm glad I ain't the only simpleton in the world! If here you ain't! I can't get over thinkin' what a ridickerlus thing it is fur half of Ameriky, a'most, to turn out jest to see a baby that's brought acrost from where Columbus used to live! Jest as if a Spanish baby was a-goin' to enjoy sech a crowd as this! One thing's certain, I ain't goin' to wait; if the pore leetle creetur is half as tired's I be, it'll want a nap fust thing! Come on, pa!"

A shout of laughter drowned her last words, and after explaining to Mr. Camp that I was "looking for a friend," I got away from the absurd old woman, who, with her husband at her heels, was marching toward the lake—"Where there was enough water, maybe, to make a ripple and where one wouldn't get stepped on ef one happened to tumble down."

As I found myself upon the outskirts of the crowd, someone set up a cry of "There she comes!" and there was a movement toward the west end of the Administration Building.

Two or three carriages had drawn up inside the roped-in space, and several smiling gentlemen with *boutonnieres* upon their immaculate coats stood in waiting near. I turned the corner to the north, where the crowd was less dense, and had begun to deliberate upon the wisdom of moving on, when, straight across my path, half running and evidently in pursuit of some one, I saw the little brunette. I had made a quick step in pursuit, when a gloved hand was thrust out before me. "Stand back!" was the order. There was a rush from the south end, a sudden prancing of hoofs upon the gravel, and a carriage drawn by four fine bay horses came into view around the corner of the Mines Building.

"Here she comes!" is again the cry. I am pressed back against the wall, and close beside me the soft-rolling carriage is drawn up; a gentleman alights, and, waving aside the obsequious

Against Odds

Princess Eulalie

footman, assists a lady to descend. In a moment they are gone, swallowed up by the big arched entrance, and a murmur runs through the crowd. If not the "infanty," they have seen one as fair and as gracious, the first lady of the White City, the able and beloved president of the Woman's Board.

When she has passed within I replace my uplifted hat and seek an egress through the crowd, past the restive four-in-hand and down the street which leads to Wooded Island, in pursuit of the little brunette, who had vanished in that direction. And now there seemed a breaking up of the crowd, strains of music could be heard in the distance, and rumours of an approaching parade are rife. Wooded Island, at the south end, seems quite alive with moving forms; and I saunter over the first bridge, cross the tiny island of the hunters' camp and Australian squatters' hut, cross a second picturesque bridge, and begin to examine the faces moving about the flower-bordered paths, thronging the rhododendron exhibit, and resting upon the scattered benches.

I pass some time in this way, and have turned my face toward the mainland once more, when a burst of music, near at hand, draws my eyes to the opposite bank, where, between the west facade of the great Manufactures Building and the lagoon, the "wild riders" led by Buffalo Bill, prince of showmen, are defiling past, with their fine horses curvetting and restless under their gorgeous trappings and the weight of their fantastic and variously costumed riders; their banners are fluttering and their weapons glisten in the breeze and the sunshine.

There is a grand rush toward the two bridges, and as I hasten on with the rest I catch a glimpse once more, as she comes down a side-path, of the elusive brunette.

She is close in the wake of two women, who are running hand in hand, and I hasten to place myself as near her as possible, but discreetly in the rear.

And now, from the opposite side of the lagoon, we hear another burst of music and a cry, "The princess! the princess!" We cross the first bridge and dash upon the next, which, being high and arched in the centre, is at once filled with spectators, while the more venturesome hurry over and line the banks of the lagoon and the sides of the two opposite roads, by which, from the east and west, the two cavalcades will approach—that of the "Wild West" coming from the east, filing past the north end of the Electricity Building, and turning opposite the bridge to file southward, straight down from our coigne of vantage to the entrance to the Administration Building opposite us.

I had followed the brunette closely, and when she arrived at the end of the bridge, where the head of the "Wild West" column was just turning southward, the crowd upon the sloping south end was dense, and some hardy spirits were scaling the five-foot pedestals of the great deer upon either side.

Upon these pedestals, straight-sided and square, there was "standing-room at the top," as some wag observed, and I pressed forward, meaning to mount with the aid of the iron handrail; as I reached the pedestal on the left, near which the brunette had halted beside the two women before mentioned, and who I began to think were in her company, the wag at the top bent down and put out an inviting hand.

"Help you up, ladies; good view up here, and nobody to make us get down in this crowd. It's quite easy; just step on that rail."

One of the two women stepped forward, put out her hand, paused, measured the distance with her eye, put a foot upon the rail, and uttered a little squeak.

"O-w! I ca-an't, pos-sibly!"

Without a word the little brunette, at least six inches shorter, stepped forward, put out her hand, set one foot upon the rail, and went to the top of the big block with an agility that was amazing in a woman.

As for me, I had been quite near her, and it almost took away my breath.

I kept my eyes upon her like one fascinated, until the beautiful princess, preceded by the white-plumed hussars and escorted by the mayor and city council, came from the west, and passed us so close that her charming face, aglow with smiles and bright looks of interest, was distinctly seen and roundly cheered.

We watched her drive slowly down the avenue formed by open ranks of her escort, and then the crowd was ready to follow her and surround the Administration Building, watching wondering—an American throng attendant upon, and admiring, not royalty alone, but royalty, beauty, and gracious womanhood combined in one charming whole.

When the cheer which announced the infanta's descent from her carriage had died away, I turned to see what my brunette, safely bestowed upon her pedestal, would elect to do next.

I was soon enlightened, for she turned at the first movement of the crowd about her, and, seating herself upon the edge of the pedestal, dropped lightly to the ground and walked briskly away.

I followed, of course, determined not to be easily left behind again; and as I went, my mind was occupied with an entirely new thought. I had made a discovery, and it might be an important one. I had found that the brunette, like myself, was in disguise.

CHAPTER X.

CARL MASTERS.

WHEN BRAINERD and I compared notes that night, we came to the mutual conclusion that the Camps were ordained to mingle their destiny with ours in some measure, we chanced upon them so often; and they seemed, since our encounter at the bureau, to take it for granted that we were to continue the acquaintance, now set, in their opinion, upon an official basis, and that it would be a mutual pleasure.

After leaving me, or, rather, after I had separated myself from them at the Administration Building, they had wandered down the Grand Plaza and made their way to the Peristyle, where, after some time, they had encountered Brainerd; and in the course of their amiable converse they had given him some valuable information, or so he thought it.

"You see," he said, "to begin at the beginning, I had mingled all the morning with crowds here and there, and as it was nearing noon I wandered across the Plaza and came to that handsome bridge spanning the canal at the north-west corner of the Liberal Arts. As I crossed this bridge I saw a launch slip out from the landing at the further end, and in that launch two men, one of whom I was sure was Greenback Bob, and the other, from your description, I'll wager was your friend Smug."

"Are you sure?" I demanded.

"Morally certain, yes. Well, as you may guess, I scurried across the little bridge and jumped into the next launch, for they were not easy to follow by the land route, with always the chance that they might go ashore on the wrong side of the lagoon. Well, I kept them in sight until we had made the round of the basin, and they made no offer to land, although the launch filled and emptied before we were back at the bridge from which we started. As we passed under the bridge my heart was in my mouth, for the boat was out of sight for some moments, but when we shot out into the sunlight there they were, not so far ahead of us, and about to run underneath the bridge at the end of the south canal. I wondered a little at their going away from the crowd just then, but that was their affair, so I just shifted my position in order to keep a better watch upon their boat as we came abreast of the bridge, and then, as the mischief would have it, a launch coming from the other way pushed through and under the bridge and struck us such a blow that the women screamed, and one of them let her parasol fall into the water. Then, of course, there was an exchange of compliments between the two crews, and a scramble and delay in securing the parasol; and when at last we were out on the other side the boat ahead was so far away from the landing, where she had of course made her stop, that I could just make out that the two men had left her and she was almost empty. To add to my agony, two boats had passed us while we floundered after that parasol and exchanged compliments with the other boat, and as we lay there waiting I looked wildly about me, and saw at last, on the bridge almost over my head, my two men, standing close by the railing and talking with a little dark woman, who—"

"Describe her!" I broke in.

"Well, now—"

"Was she something under five feet?"

"Yes."

"Dark eyes and hair?"

"Exact."

"A broad black hat with plumes, a red veil, and four-in-hand tie?"

"Upon my word, she had 'em all."

"I knew it; but go on."

"I can't, not very far at least. I just kept myself from swearing while I sat and saw those three so sociable up there, and I not in it. Before I got to the landing I had seen the woman trip away."

"Toward the Plaza?"

"Precisely. Everybody seemed going that way. It was almost time for the infanta to appear. When I set foot on shore I made for that bridge. I had seen them start slowly on after the woman; but when I got upon the bridge I could just see the hat of your friend Smug in a jam some distance ahead, near the Electricity Building, and Bob, the eel, had vanished once more."

"At what time was this?"

He named the time, and then I told him how I had encountered the little brunette, lost her, and found her again, and of her agile leap at the bridge.

"Lively girl!" Dave commented. I had told him the story of her agility with some *empressement*, but he did not seem to see my drift. "You're sure it's the same who tried to claim the young woman's bag?"

"Quite sure—from your description."

"Umph! Mine? And she's the one who met the lady at the gate, and left her when the man appeared?"

"The same."

"Um-m! She tries to secure the young lady's bag; she meets her as though by appointment; and she meets our quarry, too. She seems to know them all. Query: Does she, by any chance, know—well, say you? Who is she? What is she?"

"Who she is I don't know, what she is I can tell you," said I.

"Well?"

"She, as we have called her, is a man."

I had nothing to add to this, and Dave was not willing to accept my statement, based as it was upon that leap at the bridge. "No woman ever made that jump; I knew it. It showed practice, and that not of the sort that is taken by women." This had been my argument, and after some discussion and difference of opinions Dave got back to the Camps.

He had met them wandering about the Peristyle, and gazing across the grand basin at the splendid MacMonnies Fountain.

"Which ort," Mrs. Camp had declared, "to sail out, leastwise, the boat with that white woman settin' up there on top, and come across to serlute that big gold goddiss. For my part," she added, "I've seen one thing that was as it ort to be. They took an' set a woman up in the midst of their court, and made her bigger and brighter and handsomer than anything else. But if they was bent on calling her Justice, why," she opined, "that there court ought to be called a court of justice."

The two old people had evidently grown lonely and sated with grandeur, and when she had aired her views concerning the golden goddess, Mrs. Camp began to talk about our adventure with the counterfeiters.

"That friend of yours was right," she said. "That Sunday-school chap didn't come to time; and we ain't seen him sence not to speak to." And then she related how, on coming away from

Against Odds

their rooms on Stony Island Avenue that morning, they had seen, just across the street from them, the man Smug in earnest conversation with a tall man whose back was turned toward them, and who after a few words had turned and walked away southward, while Smug had entered a cafe close at hand, doubtless to breakfast.

Dave had questioned them closely, hoping to learn more; but beyond the facts as first stated little was added.

The men had met at a point "a few squares" from the Camps' "boarding-house"—possibly four or five. The man in conversation with Smug was tall, and very straight, "sort of stiff like," and well dressed. They were quite sure, also, that he was dark, and that he wore a beard. Incidentally they gave Dave the number of their Stony Island residence.

"We shan't have much trouble to find the Camps," Dave said in concluding his narration. "The old lady has taken a great fancy for the Liberal Arts Building, and she generally spends her time sitting upon a chair in the centre of Columbia Avenue and admiring at her leisure. She says she'd rather see things in the lump, sort of. And I believe they take a walk every morning around the Plaza, the Court, the Peristyle, and then up the lake shore from Victoria House, which she won't enter—because she 'hates old England and all the Englishers'—to the point where Fifty-seventh Street drops into Lake Michigan. And every afternoon, I verily believe, they walk arm-in-arm up and down the length of Midway, without stopping or entering anywhere."

In our summing up we found we had accomplished very little legitimate business. We had established the fact that Greenback Bob was at the Fair, and the presumption was strong, amounting almost to a certainty, that Delbras was also there. We had connected the man Smug with one, if not both, for Dave was sure that the man's companion on Stony Island Avenue was Delbras, and now this brunette, whom I believed to be a man in woman's attire, seemed to be identifying herself, or himself, with the "gang."

"If you can prove that the brunette's a man or boy," said Dave, "then I'll say don't look farther for the third party who came with Delbras from France; and if that should prove the case, tell me, what designs have this gang upon Miss—what do you call her?"

I started. It was Dave who was growing imaginative now. And yet—

"I had only thought of the brunette as having seen the bag fall, and hoping for a find," I said doubtfully.

"Then how did you account for her being at the entrance gate two days after?" queried Dave scornfully.

"Supposing it to have been an accidental meeting, I fancied she might have thought of telling Miss Jenrys what she knew of her loss, hoping for a reward, perhaps."

"Carl, you are growing stupid! You have thought too much of the blonde and not enough of the brunette! Think! In the first instance both are alone; Miss J. drops her bag; why does this particular—well, say woman for the present—why does this woman see it? She must have been some paces behind, or you would have seen her; or if not you, the guard, or even the young lady herself. That brunette was shadowing Miss J."

I was silent before his arguments. I began to think I had been one-sided in my thoughts of the two; and now how simple it all seemed!

"The girl, you say, was watching the gate through a glass, and from a protected and safe point of view. She rushes to meet the young lady, perhaps introduces herself, perhaps is known, and she leaves her when the good-looking man appears. Carl, what use do you intend to make of that black bag?"

"Hitherto," I replied, "it has been a side issue; now it seems to me that we may serve both its owner and ourselves by restoring the bag, and keeping an eye upon all concerned."

* * * * *

The next day I was early at the Fifty-seventh Street gate, and I waited long, but no Miss Jenrys came through; and after loitering near until almost noon, I took a light luncheon at the nearest point possible, and at noon went back to my post. But if Miss Jenrys entered the grounds that day, it was through some other entrance.

On the next morning she came at an early hour, her fair face radiant as the June weather, and beside her was a small-faced little woman who might have seen forty years or sixty; except for her snowy hair, time seemed to have forgotten her. Her dress was a near approach to the Quaker garb of the followers of Penn. Everything about her was of softest gray; but the face, framed by the prim Quaker bonnet, was as fair as an infant's, and with a child's soft colouring in the cheeks that had not yet lost the

Against Odds

charming curves of young womanhood. She looked like a creature whom Life had loved so well that Time had not been permitted to touch or tarry near her, so gentle, and sweet, and good.

But there was no weakness in the placid, fair face, nor in the smooth, even step, neither swift nor slow, with which she moved on beside the fair young woman at her side.

I had watched for this arrival while I sauntered about, now on one side of the bridge, now on the other, and vibrating between the buildings of Nebraska and South Dakota, on either side the broad promenade beginning at the bridge. The west windows of both these hospitable houses overlooked the little stream, proffering a welcome to the visitor at the very outset; and when the two ladies crossed the arching bridge on the side nearest the Nebraska Building I was not surprised to see them halt, look for a moment upon the shady bit of greensward with the inviting rustic seats beneath the vine draped trees close to the water's edge, and then enter. I was very near them, meaning this time to make a prompt and bold approach, and as I turned to enter I heard the elder say:

"No, June, my child. Thee must let me go my way." She halted and laid her hand upon the girl's arm. "I must take these beauties in slowly, else they will not take lodgment in my memory; besides, this place is too tempting."

They moved on towards the shaded seats, and I took from my pocket a map of the grounds, and, standing on the lowest step of the portico, affected to study it, while the talk went on.

"Thee can go through this house while I look at the place and the people, child, and hear the music. Where is that music?"

"Oh, aunty! That horrid Esquimaux band! They've never happened to be in tune before when we came in, fortunately."

"Fie, June! I'm sure it's very good. Now go. You know I care little for fine furnishings, but if there is anything that you think I shall like to see, you may show it to me when you have seen your fill, and I mine. There, go, child! I am going to knit."

The Quakeress took out her knitting, and her niece, uttering a soft laugh, and giving the shoulder of the other an affectionate pat, turned away, saying over her shoulder:

"You're a wilful auntie, and you shall have your way. I'll not be long, so look and listen your fill."

This was the chance for which I had waited, and I took advantage of it by closing my map and following her into the building and up the stairs.

I did not accost her at once, but waited until she had looked about the larger room facing the south and west, where the case of minerals, the great deer, and other western treasures and trophies were displayed, and had sauntered about the cosy and tasteful parlours, looking at the pictures and bits of decorative work; and when she had re-entered the big sunny south room again, and after a little more loitering among the exhibits went to one of the windows and stood looking down into the street, I, who had been standing near an opposite window, was about to cross the room and accost her, when a sudden shout from the street caused me to look out once more.

My window faced the bridge, and I saw that a chair-boy, coming too hastily over the bridge with his freight, and perhaps unaccustomed to his wheeled steed, had let slip his hold upon the handle at the back of the chair just as he had reached the downward slope of the bridge, and chair and occupant, a burly man looking quite able to walk, went whirling down the slope, charging into a couple of young men dressed in killing style and wearing big yellow *boutonnieres*, and overturning itself and all concerned.

They were gathering themselves up in much disorder, and I could not resist a smile at the ludicrous scene; but the smile soon left my face when I saw, passing the scene of distress with rapid steps and without a glance toward it, and coming straight toward the entrance below, the little brunette.

With rapid steps I crossed to the opposite window, and, taking off my hat, bowed before the surprised and now somewhat haughty-looking blonde.

"Miss Jenrys?" I said interrogatively.

She bowed assent.

"May I speak with you a moment?"

She did not answer promptly, and I put my hand to my pocket and drew out my card—the same that I had proffered to the guard a few days before.

She took it and read the name aloud, and in a tone of polite inquiry:

"Carl Masters?"

Against Odds

CHAPTER XI.

"I DISLIKE A MYSTERY."

I HAD not meant to do it, but while I stood there with her clear brown eyes, not repellent but fearless and full of dignity, fixed upon my face in polite but guarded inquiry, the determination suddenly seized me to be as frank and truthful in dealing with this frank and truthful woman as I had a right to be.

I had meant to return the bag, ask her pardon for tampering with its contents, and say no more; only keeping as much as possible an eye to her welfare and safety if I saw it menaced. Now I meant something more; and so, while she held my card in daintily gloved fingers and looked at me with level, questioning eyes, I said, with the thought of the approaching brunette underlying my words:

"Miss Jenrys, I am the person who was of some small assistance a few days ago when you came near incurring serious injury at the hands of a pair of Turks and a sedan-chair." I saw a look of remembrance, if not of recognition, flash into her face, and I hurried on. "I do not mention this as entitling me to your notice, but I ask you to accept my word as that of one having no personal motive save the desire to serve you, and to listen to me for a few moments."

She was scanning my face nervously, and now she said:

"I do not recall your face, though I remember the circumstance to which you refer. If you are the gentleman who held back that reckless foreigner with a strong arm, and so saved me from something more serious than a little pain in the shoulder, I am certainly your debtor, and I am glad of this opportunity to thank you."

A little back of the place where she stood, in a corner, hemmed in on one side by a long glass case of exhibits of various sorts, was an armchair, placed there, doubtless, for the ease of the person in charge of said case and its contents. There was no such person present, however, at that hour, and I pointed toward the chair, and said:

"If you will kindly take that seat, so that I may not feel that I am compelling you to stand, I will not detain you long."

She turned toward the seat, looked at it, at me, and finally beyond me and across the room, as if debating, and half inclined to pass me and escape; and then I saw a sudden withdrawal of the eyes and a compression of the lips, slight but perceptible. She turned as if in haste, almost, and seated herself in the chair, first turning it toward the windows so that her back would be toward the interior of the room, and then, to my surprise, she beckoned me, with a half-smile, to a place upon the window-seat, which would narrowly serve this purpose.

I had not once looked back or about me, but I did not flatter myself that my words alone had won for me this graciousness; she had seen the little brunette, and desired to avoid her.

"Thank you," I said, when we were both seated. "I will now come to the point at once. You must know, then, that after you had passed on and out of sight in the crowd I discovered at my very feet—so close that no one had ventured to pick it up, if anyone had seen it in that crowd—a black leather bag—a chatelaine, I think you ladies call it."

"Oh! you found my bag!" The look of reserve was lost in a quick and charming smile. "I am very glad!"

"I found it, and I tried to follow you and restore it, but you had disappeared."

"I had indeed; in at the first gate, which happened to be the Javanese Village."

"That explains my failure. I had given up my search, and was about to go on my way, when I was approached by a young lady, a small person with dark eyes and wearing a large plumed sailor-hat, who explained that she was a friend to the lady whose bag I had in my hand, that she had seen me pick it up, and would now restore it to her."

"And you gave it to her?"

"Was it not right?"

"The person was an impostor."

"Is it possible? And yet two days after, as you were entering the grounds, and I was about to approach you, I saw this same person greet you, seemingly, and walk on in your company. It made a coward of me. I dared not approach in the face of a friend of yours whom I had treated as an impostor."

"How do you mean?"

"I mean that I doubted the person, and refused to give her the bag." And I hurriedly made confession, telling her how at last I was forced to read first her friend's letter and then her own, in order to learn her name, and that then her address was still a mystery. "I had but one chance of finding you," I concluded. "You had informed your friend that your apartments were conveniently near the Fifty-seventh Street entrance."

"Oh! Indeed!" I had seen the quick colour flash into her face at my mention of the letters, and of having read them, and the restraint was once more evident in face and voice when she said:

"I thank you, sir; but the contents of the bag—it was hardly worth the trouble you have taken to restore it—that is—"

"I have it with me, Miss Jenrys, and when I am sure that we are not under surveillance I will place it in your hands; and now I owe it to myself to make my own conduct in this affair and my present position clearer. At first it was with me a simple matter of returning a lost article to a lady. Failing to overtake you, I might perhaps have turned it over to some guard but for the interference of the brunette, who at once put me on the defensive and aroused my suspicion. It somehow seemed to me that the young person was more than commonly anxious to possess your bag, and then it occurred to me that the bag might contain something or some information that she especially wished to possess. My interest was aroused, and then I took the liberty of examining your bag, and having done so, I determined at least to attempt to return it to you, and to ask you to pardon the liberty I had taken with your correspondence."

"I suppose anyone would have done the same," she said, rather coldly. "What I do not comprehend is why you did not return the bag to me in the presence of this person, of whom you might have warned me."

"It is that which I am about to explain," I replied gravely. "And I must, for the sake of others whose interests I represent, ask you to regard what I am now about to tell you as a confidence made necessary because of the circumstances. Miss Jenrys, the card in your hand bears my real name, but few know me by it, because I so often bear others, as one of the necessities of my profession. I am known here to those who know me at all as one of those secret service men you have no doubt heard or read of. In other words—"

"A detective?" She bent forward and scanned my face narrowly.

"When I saw you in company with the little brunette, as I have since called her for want of a better title, I was at first amazed and inclined to doubt my own sagacity; but when—I am making a clean breast of it, Miss Jenrys—when I followed you, doubtful what course to pursue, I saw you joined by a gentleman, and I saw the brunette slip away from you as she would hardly have done, as you would hardly have allowed her to do, had she been friend or acquaintance. I am enrolled here as a 'special,' but I came, in company with another, with a definite object in view. Within these grounds are several persons under suspicion, and whom we are hoping to capture and convict, and when I tell you that only yesterday I learned that this same little brunette who claimed your property and friendship was seen in company with two suspected persons, you will hardly wonder that what I had attempted to do from purest courtesy from one stranger to another, and that other a lady, I felt impelled to do from a sense of duty, as well as desire to save one whom I had seen to be alone, and who might, for aught I could tell, be menaced by some unsuspected danger."

There was no fear on her face, only a slightly troubled look, as she asked:

"What do you mean?"

"Simply that it is my duty to warn you, and to ask you if you know of any reason why you should be followed, or watched, or menaced by any manner of danger?"

"No"—she slowly shook her fair head—"no reason whatever."

"And may I ask you about this person, this brunette?" I would not say "this woman."

She started slightly, and leaned toward me.

"Is she here still?" she whispered.

I turned my head and cast a deliberate glance around the room.

"I do not see her," I said; "but she may be below, with an eye on the staircase."

"It's more than likely. It's little I can tell you," she said. "She ran up to me that morning at the gate, her face beaming and her hand held out, and when she was close to me, and I drew away from her, she began the most profuse apologies: she was very nearsighted, and she had mistaken me for an old acquaintance she had not seen for some time; then she kept on by my side, prattling about her 'mamma,' who had not been able to leave the hotel since they came; of her dread of being alone, and her eagerness to see the Fair. She had hoped, when she saw me, that she had found someone who would let her 'just follow along, so that she would not feel so much alone,' etc. I did not like her volubility, yet

Against Odds

I could see no way, short of absolute rudeness, of shaking her off. When I met a New York acquaintance, down near the lake shore, she quite surprised me by quietly slipping away. Do you think—" She paused, and arose with a quick, easy grace which seemed inherent. "Will you come down and be introduced to my aunt?" she asked. "I have great confidence in her judgment of—gentlemen, and she ought to know this; that is, if you can give me the time."

"My time is entirely yours," I declared recklessly, "and nothing would give me more pleasure than to pay my entirely sincere respects to that lovely woman I saw in your company, and who, I am almost certain, saw me playing the spy upon her niece."

She smiled as she moved toward the stairway, at the head of which she turned and paused a moment.

"Do you think she will approach us?" she asked.

"I can't imagine what she will do."

"But she will see you, and—"

I think the smile on my face stopped her.

"You did not recognise me," I said. "She may not."

She looked into my face keenly, and then a quick look of intelligence flashed into her eyes.

"Oh!" It was all she said, but it meant much. She took a step downward, and turned again. "Of course I must not enlighten my aunt?"

"If you are willing to let it lie between us two—at first?"

"Certainly," she said gravely, and went on down the stairs.

At the landing, half-way down, where the staircase turned to right and left, I saw, over her shoulder, a little dark figure standing in the west doorway.

"Turn to the right," I said, over her shoulder. "'The longest way round,' you know."

She nodded, and without a glance in the other direction went down the east side, turned at the foot to wait for me with the air of one quite absorbed in an agreeable companion, and we went out at the door facing the Minnesota Building and the morning sun. As we stepped outside I paused in my turn.

"One word, if you will allow it. I may have to learn more of this person. It may make difficulties for me, and—who knows?—perhaps for you, if she imagines that you know her for—what she is. Or guesses, as she might—"

"What you are?" she interposed. "You may trust me."

We turned at the corner, and came once more to the west side and the little arbour. As we rounded the corner my companion suddenly slipped her little hand beneath my elbow, giving it at the same time a significant little pressure. The brunette, having doubtless watched our progress through the window, was coming down the steps and through straight toward us.

For just a passing moment I knew how Miss Jenrys looked to the friends who knew her, and whom she knew best. She was smiling and preoccupied as we stepped within the inclosure.

"See," she said, hastening her own steps and mine, with a bright look toward the benches, "there is auntie."

The little brunette was almost abreast of us, and my companion's smiling gaze was still fixed upon the figure under the vines; then she turned her head, and, just at the place where we could turn from the walk, let her eyes turn toward the figure just opposite us.

It was charmingly done. Just as she made a step in the direction of the arbour her eyes fell quite naturally upon the face of the brunette. "Good morning," she said smilingly, and with a little nod of her head. But there was no slackening of her steps; with the words on her lips we were off the walk, and crossing the grass to the place, not ten paces away, where the sweet-faced Quakeress sat, knitting and looking her surprise.

"Auntie, I have brought you a new acquaintance," Miss Jenrys said, in a voice slightly raised; and then, looking after the retreating figure of the brunette and seeing that she was quite out of hearing, she added, "and I have found my bag."

I took the bag from my pocket, where it had grown to seem a quite familiar bulk, and laid it in her lap, and she began at once to narrate to the wondering Quakeress the adventures of the little bag. She heard it through, with here and there a soft little exclamation of wonder, and I saw that she was slightly deaf, and quite given to misunderstanding and miscalling words and phrases.

"Thee has been very lucky, my dear," the good soul said when Miss Jenrys had done, "and the young man has been at great pains to restore thy reticule. It was hardly worth so much trouble, do you think?"

"Not in actual value perhaps, auntie, but it contained one or two little keepsakes that I valued"—she breathed a little fluttering sigh—"for the sake of the giver."

"Is that why thee has mourned the loss of the little bag so much, and said so many unkind things about those poor benighted men of Turkey? Then, indeed, I must add my thanks to thine." And she turned and extended to me a soft slim hand, ungloved and delicately veined; and then she began to question me about the Fair and the things I had seen, showing in her questions and comments a singular mixture of innocent unworldliness, and native shrewdness, and mother wit.

In the midst of our talk Miss Jenrys broke in with a low, quick exclamation, which caused us to cease and turn toward her.

"Mr. Masters," she said, in a low tone, "our friend the brunette is looking over from the gallery windows of the Dakota Building—see! the one next the corner, toward the bridge. She does not make herself needlessly conspicuous, and it was only by the peculiar shade her figure threw, as she stood at one side—the eastern side—that I was drawn to observe her. My eyes are very strong—I am sure I am not mistaken."

"It is only what I expected," I replied. "She will wait, no doubt, until she gets an opportunity to speak with you. Evidently she has some object in view, something to learn from you, or something to tell you. I would give something to know what it is."

She looked at me a moment with thoughtful eyes. I had purposely spoken in a guarded tone, and when she answered it was in the same manner.

"Would it help you to learn her object?"

"It might, and it might give us a hint as to their reasons for following you."

"Their reasons? Do you think—" she stopped abruptly.

"I don't know what to think, Miss Jenrys. It looked as if this person were following you on the day you lost your bag, and I am convinced that she is in some way connected with two or more men who are more than suspected of being offenders against the law. Miss Jenrys, do you know of any reason why you should be watched—followed? Have you an enemy? Are you in anyone's way?"

Instead of answering, she turned to the elder lady, who had been listening like one who but half comprehends.

"Auntie, you heard me say that Mr. Masters has strong reasons for thinking that the young woman who just passed us, and who has forced herself upon my notice, and tried to claim my bag, is loitering about now for the purpose of speaking to me?"

"I heard thee: yes, June, surely I did, and I cannot understand the thing at all."

"Nor do we, Aunt Ann," she turned to me again. "I am getting the fever for investigation," she said, slightly smiling. "I am not

South Dakota Building.

Against Odds

alarmed at what you have told me, but I do not doubt it, and if you think it best, if it will help you, I will give that young woman a chance to ease her mind to me. I will leave you here with Aunt Ann, and go, under her eyes, to the building next to this, on to the Washington House, and give her a chance to follow."

I waited for the elder lady to speak, and my own surprise was great at her brave proposition—for it was brave, braver than she knew; and I was asking myself if I had the right to let her go to meet—an adventuress at the least, a criminal possibly. But her aunt gave the decisive word.

"My dear June, thee knows I do not like a mystery. If anything is to be learned concerning this person's strange conduct, we should find it out, and end the following and spying, else it will not be safe for thee to come here alone, even by day."

"Fie! Aunt Ann—with all these guards and half the world looking on? Then I had better go, Mr. Masters."

"If you will."

"Have you any advice or instructions to give me?"

"I think you will know how to proceed. Only it might be well to let her talk, if she will."

"Certainly."

"And, Miss Jenrys, let me beg of you, do not go away from this immediate vicinity, and do not walk upon the streets with this person if it can be avoided. Above all, do not make a further appointment with her."

"I will be discreet. Good-bye for a short time, Aunt Ann." She dropped the newly-returned bag into her aunt's lap and went away, as lithe and careless-seeming as the veriest pleasure-seeker.

She looked up and down at the windows of the South Dakota House and then walked deliberately in.

CHAPTER XII.

"MORE DANGEROUS THAN HATE."

WHEN WE had watched her vanish within the walls of the opposite building, Miss Ross—for "Aunt Ann" was a spinster—

deliberately arose and took the place beside me.

"We can talk better so," she said placidly, "and I want to talk with thee." And she began to roll up her knitting with care.

As we sat there I was almost hidden from view from the streets, because of the thick vine tendrils that fell like a curtain between me and the passers-by, while it did not prevent my looking through the green drapery at my pleasure. But Aunt Ann had placed herself where she was plainly visible to all who passed.

"Now," she began, having put away her knitting, "I ask thee honestly, sir, does thee think my niece in real danger of any sort? I cannot understand this strangeness."

"Truly, Miss Ross," I answered, "I know no more than you have heard; but I could do no less than warn the young lady, knowing what I did."

She bent toward me and scrutinized my face closely, keenly.

"Thy face is a good face," she said then, "and I like thy voice; but, young man, I am only a woman, and I have no right to do rashly. My niece trusts thee, but she is but a girl, with all her self-reliance. Forgive an old woman's caution, and—tell me what is thy reason for the interest thee takes in my niece? Cannot thee give me some credential, some voucher for thy good faith, before I say to thee what I wish to say?"

Again I found myself forced to a sudden decision. In my experience as a detective I had found myself in many strange situations, but never before had I felt that I must speak the truth, or not at all, in a position like this. I answered, with scarce a moment's hesitation:

"You are right and wise, madam, and I am sure that I can confide to you the truth concerning my business at the Fair—only asking, because others are concerned with myself, that you regard my information as confidential."

"Surely," she said quietly. "Thee may trust a Friend. We are not given to overmuch speaking. Of course thee has my promise."

"Then I may tell you that my business here is to watch for and guard against just such people as this person, this brunette, seems to be. I am a member of the Secret Service Bureau."

We were alone in the little arbour, and I showed her first my badge, sewn inside my coat, and then my photographic pass.

"I thank thee; and may I ask now does my niece know this?"

"I should have found extreme difficulty in gaining her ear or her confidence otherwise," I answered.

Against Odds

"Ah! I felt sure—I know the child so well—that somehow she had found a reason for her faith in you. There is no prouder or more womanly girl living than my niece, June Jenrys; and now tell me frankly, what does thee fear or anticipate for her?"

"If I knew your niece, Miss Ross, her friends, her foes, her history, I might venture an opinion. As it is, cannot you help me?"

She pondered a little, then:

"Tell me again," she said, "all about the bag and this woman."

Now, I wanted to learn one or two things from this interview, and I realized that our time was short, so I rehearsed the story again, and quite fully, but as briefly as possible. When I had finished, the clear-headed Quakeress was thoughtful again, then she said:

"I don't like this, not in the least; and I feel that thee has been right. I fear my girl is, in some way, in danger. Will you advise me?" she asked, with sudden energy.

"To the best of my ability, willingly." And then I risked a first repulse. "If I might ask you to tell me something of your niece—her position—your plans—"

"Of course. My niece there is an orphan and an heiress."

"Oh!" She gave me a quick glance and went on.

"Her home has been in New York City, with an aunt, formerly her guardian. June is now of age and her own mistress. Of late she has been with me in my little home, less than one hundred miles from this city. She came of her own accord, and was most welcome, and we came here together a little more than a week ago, June declaring that she meant to stay all summer, and I nothing loth." She stopped and smiled. "This is all very barren," she said. "I think thee will have to question me."

"Then I think we must be brief. First, are you stopping near the grounds?"

"Very near; on Washington Avenue, little more than two blocks away;" and she mentioned the number.

"Is it a boarding-house, a—pardon me, what I wish to know is if you have made any acquaintances there; if anyone has learned, for instance, that you are ladies of independent fortune, meaning to make a long stay, and consequently likely to have with you more or less money."

"Ah! I was sure thee could get on. We are in a private house, found for us by the Public Comfort Bureau, and we have taken their only suite; there are no others."

"And the family?"

"Just the two, man and wife, and a servant. It's a cottage, but very cosy."

"Has your niece an enemy?"

"An enemy? Oh, I trust not! I do trust not! I can't think so. Still, June is a society girl; I know little of that side of her life."

"Then do you know if she has a friend who is, or may be, a fortune-hunter, one whom you distrust?"

I saw the quick colour flush her sweet face and leave it pale again, and again for a moment she seemed to hesitate.

"I don't quite like to say it," she began then; "but since we have been here I have seen a person who, I think, would be a suitor for my niece if she would permit it. I am not versed in the world's ways, but I have seldom found myself deceived in my judgment of man or woman, though I ought not to boast it. But of this man I think three things. He is madly in love with my niece, and his sort of love is not the true sort. It is not lasting, and it is more dangerous than hate. He is a foreigner, with the soft, insincere ways that I cannot like nor trust. He has a strong will and a cruel eye, and—he likes me not at all. Mind thee, I do not accuse him—only he is the one person we have met here and spoken with except thyself; and—" She broke off and shook her head.

"Do you think—" The question did not fall from my lips, but she interpreted it.

"Thee means does she care for him? I do not think it. She is courteous to him, nothing more. Out of his sight I do not think she gives him a thought. But he is here, and she is young. I am poor company for a young girl."

"I wish all young girls could enjoy such society as yours, Miss Ross. Do you think this business has disturbed Miss Jenrys?"

"Disturbed? June Jenrys has not one drop of coward blood in her veins! I have thought, since she has been with me—I am almost certain, indeed—that something has saddened my girl just a little; she seems quieter than she used, and is almost listless at times, which is not like her. Sometimes she seems quite herself, and that is a very bright self, then at times she is quite preoccupied. I think this affair has aroused her interest, perhaps—ah—"

She was facing the street, and the little quietly-uttered syllable caused me to look through the leaves in the same direction. Miss Jenrys was approaching, on the opposite side, in the shadow of the Dakota Building; and with her, walking slowly and talking volubly, was the little brunette. I was watching her narrowly, and as the two crossed to the side nearest us I saw her start, stop suddenly, and turn toward her companion; as she thus stood, her back was toward the bridge, and a glance in that direction showed me a tall, well-dressed man, who carried a bunch of longstemmed La France roses, and whose brisk steps brought him in a moment face to face with Miss Jenrys. There was a brief pantomime of greeting between the newcomer and Miss Jenrys, and then she turned toward the brunette, and there was a short exchange of words. Then the man lifted his hat, the brunette bowed and turned away, going toward the entrance, while Miss Jenrys and her companion, whom I had recognised as Monsieur Voisin, came toward us.

He was not aware of my presence, I know, until he had passed the point where the arbour opened opposite the west door of the Nebraska House, but he acknowledged Miss Jenrys' introduction with a perfect bow and an amiable speech, intended for my companions as well as for myself.

He had taken the liberty of calling at their cottage, he informed us, to ask if he might not serve them as escort, but had been told that they were already at the grounds. He considered himself very fortunate to have met them at the very gate, as it were; and then he presented the roses to Miss Jenrys.

She received them with a smile, and a word of praise for their beauty, and then, in that charming way a clever woman has when she chooses to employ it, she made him aware that his kindly offer of escort service must be declined, since, with a nod in my direction, they "were already provided with an escort."

I took my cue at once, and after a few more words, addressed to each in turn, and a short exchange of courtesies between him and myself, Monsieur Voisin lifted his hat, saying that since he was so much a laggard as to have lost some charming companions he would endeavour to recover his lost time by travelling to the Convent of La Rabida *via* the Intramural Railway; and so, smiling and bowing, he went back over the bridge to the station above the entrance.

When he had gone Miss Jenrys turned to me.

"I must ask your pardon for that little implied fib, Mr. Masters; and, auntie, don't look too much shocked. I could not allow Mr. Masters to lose his time, which is no doubt of value, or to go away perhaps before he had heard my experience." And then, before the elder lady could utter her gentle reproof or I could reply to her speech, she began to tell her story.

"I thought," she began, "that I would take the shortest way to my object, so I went in, as you saw, to view South Dakota. It was so small that I was soon upstairs, walking around the little gallery under the dome. Of course I came upon our friend the brunette almost at once, and greeted her so amiably that she joined my promenade without hesitation. Of course you don't care to know all that we said. I let her take the initiative, only keeping an amiable and fairly interested countenance and following her lead. She began by telling me how she 'happened to meet me again.' She had entered early, and had passed the time looking at some of the State buildings, in order to be near the entrance, where her 'mamma' had partly promised to meet her in an hour or so. She did not want to miss her 'mamma,' and so had loitered, after a little time spent in some of the buildings opposite, in these two houses, where she could overlook the entrance and the bridge. It was not 'nice' to be alone so much, and her 'mamma' did not like her to be alone, but she could not bear to lose the Fair, any of it. Did I like going about alone? They were stopping at a hotel quite near. Did I like a hotel? etc. In short, one of her objects, I am sure, was to learn how long we mean to stay here in Chicago; and another, who were in the house with us, if it were large, and if there were other rooms to let—"

"One moment," I broke in. "Did she ask for your street or number, or both? and how did you reply to her?"

"My answers were politely vague. She did not ask for our address, and I thought it rather strange. She knows that there are 'several people at our house, but no room for more,' and that our stay depends upon circumstances; but she had one important request to make, and she made it very adroitly. Seeing that I, like herself, was alone, at least sometimes, she had wondered, if it were possible, if I would not like to see the grounds by night. Her 'mamma' did not care to come out after six o'clock, she feared the lake breezes; and she did so long to explore the grounds at night. Would it be possible—would I be willing to accompany her, when I had no better companion, of course, for an hour or so, some evening soon, to see the grounds and buildings illuminated? Her 'mamma' had told her she might ask, provided of course she was sure, which of course she was, that I was 'quite nice and proper.' As for herself, she was quite prepared with her cards and references."

She stopped here, and challenged my opinion with a piquant, questioning look.

"My child!" ejaculated Aunt Ann, "thee did not accept?"

Against Odds

"Was that all?" I asked.

"It was quite enough," she replied, quite gravely now. "She gave me a card with a written address upon it, and I told her I would let her know to-morrow morning by mail."

"June, thee must not go!"

She turned to me, without replying to her aunt's exclamation. "What do you think of it?" she asked calmly, but quite earnestly now, in contrast to her light manner of telling her story.

"I think you have done well, both in going to meet this person and in your manner of meeting her modest requests, but I think it has gone far enough."

"You think, then, that there is a plot—something serious?"

"I can see no other explanation; and now, Miss Jenrys, before another word is said, will you promise me not to allow this person to approach or address you again?"

She looked at me in some surprise. "You think her so dangerous?" she questioned.

"Yes; you have used the right word."

Again she watched my face intently, but she did not give the asked-for promise, and her aunt broke in anxiously.

"Mr. Masters, does thee think we would be safer, and wiser, if we went away quickly and quietly?"

"Auntie!" exclaimed the young lady, "how can you! I thought you were braver. Don't speak of going away. I will not hear of it. I am willing to be advised, within reason, but I would rather risk something than go away from this beautiful place before I have seen all of its wonders, or as many as I can. I am not afraid, and I will not run away. You do not advise such extreme precautionary measures, Mr. Masters, surely?"

"Not since I have heard your wishes so strongly expressed. No, Miss Ross, I think there is no need of going away, now that you are warned and will use caution; but, Miss Jenrys, you will be cautious about going out alone, and especially at evening—you should have an escort, a protector."

"One might as well be a prisoner at once as be compelled to remain indoors on these lovely nights," said the girl rebelliously. "Auntie, I will carry my little revolver. Oh," in answer to my glance of too plain inquiry, "I can shoot very well."

"I shall feel much safer without it, my child," said Aunt Ann uneasily. "Mr. Masters, is there not some way—these guards in uniform, or are there not guides who could be employed—in the evening, that is?"

"Auntie dear, I have a better thought still—the chairs. We can secure two reliable men for them, and do our sightseeing by night in comfort and safety in that way." She turned a smiling face toward me. "Don't you think that a simple and sensible arrangement?"

"I do; that is, if you will permit me to choose the men who are to guide the chairs and see that they understand their duty."

"Why, to be sure. Mr. Masters, we are very stupid, auntie and I. If you could—"

She hesitated, and glanced from her aunt's face to mine.

"June, child, I think I know what is in thy mind; I know the nature of this young man's business in this place, and you are right. If he can spare the time, it is right that we should know, if possible, what we have to guard against, to fear or avoid. Is it thy pleasure, sir, to undertake this for us?"

I turned silently toward Miss Jenrys.

"Aunt Ann is right," she said, with decision. "Can you take this matter in hand?"

"I will take it in hand," I replied. "But tell me just what you wish. Do you simply want insured protection against annoyance, or do you want this brunette followed up until we learn why she has singled you out for her peculiar attentions?"

"I have heard it said," Miss Jenrys replied, "that the detective fever is contagious, and I feel now as if I must have this little mystery unravelled. I dare say it will end in something stupid and commonplace. Still, let us unravel it if possible. What say you, Aunt Ann?"

"I have already told thee that I detest mysteries. Yes, we must know what it means."

"And know you shall," I declared, "if it rests within my power."

The sun was fast travelling toward the zenith, and I had promised Dave a rendezvous at noon.

It was not difficult to impress upon these two clever women the need for perfect secrecy, and that no one must guess at the truth concerning myself. I had observed that Monsieur Voisin addressed me as Mr. Masseys, and that Miss Jenrys had spoken my name in performing the introduction very indistinctly, and before I left she spoke of this.

"Perhaps you noticed the mistake of Monsieur Voisin in addressing you," she said. "It occurred to me, just as I was about to speak your name, that I might be making a blunder, so I mumbled your name, and was glad to hear him call you by another."

"Your tact was a kindness. Let me remain Mr. Masseys to him and to anyone I may chance to meet in your company. I may be obliged to call upon you, and should we meet, Monsieur Voisin and I, it will be best that he knows me for a visitor like himself."

When we parted it was with a very thorough understanding, and I went toward my meeting-place wondering what new thing would turn up in this city of surprises, and what Dave would think of all this. I had determined to put a shadow upon the heels of the brunette when she should appear to get the note from Miss Jenrys, which was to be couched in diplomatic language, and take the form of an indefinite postponement rather than a refusal.

When Dave and I met, I gave him, as usual, ample time to say the things of no moment first, in his usual manner; but I did not mention my own affair of the morning, leaving this to be told later and at a time of more leisure, for Dave and I had no secrets from each other when we were together.

And this was the part of wisdom as well as for friendship's sake. I knew always just how his work stood, and should disaster or delay overtake him, I knew just how to report or to go on with his work, as he with mine.

When he joined me, I saw at once that he was more than usually animated, and, contrary to his usual custom, he came straight to the business upon his mind:

"Old man, I have seen Delbras."

CHAPTER XIII.

FACE TO FACE WITH DELBRAS.

"YOU HAVE found Delbras?" I echoed. This was news indeed, and I waited eagerly for further information.

"Yes, sir. I'm sure of it. I don't doubt it; and it was in Midway Plaisance."

"Go on, Dave."

"Well, it's a short story. I had been lounging around the big wheel for some time—that monster has a sort of fascination for me; it makes me feel like a small boy, unable to gape enough. I was looking at the people coming and going, and I almost forgot that it was noon, until I heard someone say close beside me, 'Almost noon, Jack. Let's get out of this.' That startled me. I had not thought it was so late, and I took a look at old Sol and started on. I was walking pretty brisk, and all at once I came up behind a couple that made me start. One of them was Greenback Bob, past doubt, and the other was, or so I first thought, an Arab dressed in American trousers and coat and wearing a fez; but when I came closer and looked him well over I was sure it was Delbras—there were all the points, everything; and I followed them, feeling as pleased as if I had them already in bracelets; and then, just as I was wondering where they were going, they brought up in a crowd before one of those Turkish theatres. The hustler was hustling in his last crowd before dinner, and when the two pushed their way to the ticket booth I kept close behind them.

"Well, sir, they were close by the place, but they bought no tickets, that I'll swear; nevertheless, before I could take in the situation they were walking past the man at the entrance and into the show, and I made all haste to buy a ticket and follow them.

"Of course I felt sure that I was following, for I had seen them pass through the inner door; but when I got inside, and began to look around me, they were not there, neither of them. I looked through the audience, it was a very thin one; made my way down to the stage to look for the door by which they had escaped me, and I did some mental profanity that'll be forgiven me, I know, and then I gave it up and went outside to reconnoitre the old barrack.

"On one side its windows overlooked a lane open straight from the street, and there was a small door in the rear corner, while in the other a door that must have opened behind the scenes inside gave upon a sort of court-like quarters where a lot of fellows where lounging, and a few cooking, at an open fire. I made this discovery through a crack in the high fence in the rear, and I prowled about until I assured myself that my gentlemen were not there.

"I suppose I had hung about that rear inclosure some twenty minutes, or perhaps more, when I suddenly bethought me of the other Turkish booth and the big bazaar, and I came around to take a final look at the front and then move on. When I reached

Against Odds

the front, one of the dancing-girls was posturing before the entrance, and a new voice was calling the crowd to 'come and see and admire the only original,' etc.; and, sir, there upon the upper step, exhorting the public, was—Delbras himself."

"The clever rascal!" I exclaimed.

"You may well say so. Well, sir, it did not take me long to do my thinking. It was almost noon, a quarter to twelve in fact, and I said to myself, 'This fellow is playing Turk, and he has turned showman. He has just relieved the other fellow, and will be likely to be here all the afternoon.' I couldn't have stayed there if I would without being spotted, for the moment I got myself a little nearer to him he spied me, and began a pantomime of roping me in hand over fist with an imaginary cable. He would have known my face if I had tried to keep near enough to be safe in case of a sudden move, so I took the chance of keeping my appointment with you, getting up a different mug, and hurrying back."

"And you expect to find him there?"

"I hope to find him there. It would never have done to have stayed. He would have spotted me at once. The fellow is a long remove from a fool. Carl, what do you think of this deal? What, in your opinion, is their little game?"

"Precisely the same that you and I would play in their places. What could a man ask better if he wants to dodge arrest, or evade surveillance, than such a chance as Midway affords him? All he needs is a 'pull' with some of these Orientals, and they are here for the most part for the 'backsheesh.' Besides, you remember, Delbras is said to have crossed at the time many of these fellows were coming over, and he had plenty of chance to make himself solid on the way, or even before they crossed the water. Who knows how much fine work he has done among these Turks, Syrians, Algerians, Egyptians, Japs, and so on?"

"Jove! you're right enough."

"And then, Delbras has just the face and figure to disguise well; as a Turk, for instance"—Dave made a wry face—"or as an Arab, and even Bob could manage to transform himself into a passable Algerian. Your discovery of this morning, Dave, simply means that, from this moment, in addition to the task of watching all the European faces in search of our men, we shall have the added perplexity of peering under the hoods, turbans, fezes, etc., of all Midway."

Dave's face was very grave, and he was silent for some moments.

"The very fact," he finally resumed, "of finding Delbras in a Turk's fez and playing the 'jay' for one of their theatres shows that you're right, Carl. Well"—getting up suddenly and catching his hat from off the floor—"we didn't exactly come here to play; and as for disguises—why, we've played at that game ourselves."

We took a hasty and somewhat meagre lunch at the nearest "stand," and prepared for an afternoon upon the Plaisance. But I saw clearly that some other way must be devised to entrap our quarry; that, given the open sesame of the temples and pagodas, the booths and pavilions, the villages, with their ins and outs, and our tricky and elusive trio would have an advantage against which it would be difficult to contend.

And in this I was right. We found Delbras, or the man we believed to be Delbras, still occupying the "lecturer's" place at the entrance to the theatre. He was disguised to the extent of a pair of black whiskers and some slightly smoked gold-rimmed noseglasses, just as he had been in the morning; and he did not labour continuously. Instead, he exchanged often with a second person, who took up the strain of flowery superlatives at about every other half-hour, during which relief the disguised Delbras gave some portion of his time to the box-office and making of change, and the remainder to puffing innumerable cigarettes. But in spite of our combined vigilance, before the afternoon was over, and while the crowds were thickest and rapid movement impossible, the man escaped our vigilance. It did not surprise me. Those Midway throngs made veritable sanctuary for a fleeing criminal, but it made me more than ever determined to find some other and quicker way of getting our hands upon this gang.

All that week we haunted Midway to little purpose. Once in the very centre of the big Turkish bazaar—where everything was sold, and which was extended from time to time out of all proportion to its original size—where, too, I had been arrested and ignominiously marched away, to be rescued by Dave Brainerd—I caught a glimpse of Delbras, this time in full Turkish costume, and minus the beard and smoked glasses.

I followed him recklessly, thrusting aside those who obstructed my way with an impatient and ruthless hand, until I came to a spot, almost at the southern exit of the long and narrow L, where a crowd was packed from side to side of the eight-foot aisle, with mouths agape listening to the exhortations of a boyish-looking fellow, wearing a Turkish fez and a sort of smoking–

jacket, and looking, in spite of this, far more like a Jew than a follower of Mahomet. He stood at one side, close to the entrance, and a curtain framed and partially concealed him. Behind him, towering above him by a head and shoulders, was a tall Soudanese, his face black, and shining, and round, and his white robe and turban emphasizing the arm, bare, black, and massive, that waved a continuous accompaniment to the words half spoken, half shouted, by the other:

"Buy your tickets! Buy your tickets now, now, now! Come and see how to get married! Come to see how to get divorced! Come to see how the ladies quarrel with their husbands! Come and see how the ladies quarrel with each other! Buy your tickets now, now, now!"

In this singular combination of the modern fakir plying his trade and the huge black steadily and systematically beckoning toward a stairway partially concealed beyond the curtain, and looking like some giant eunuch of ancient romance, there seemed something which caught and held the public eye and the public wonder; and they crowded about the improvised entrance, and formed an impassable wall between me and the man so short a distance ahead, yet so utterly out of reach.

It was vain to struggle. That Turkish fez had been to Delbras an open sesame through the packed mass of humanity, and for a time I saw it nodding above the lesser heads half-way between the door of exit and that half-concealing curtain. Then, presto! it was gone; and though I went wildly around to the farther entrance, pushing and jostling to right and left, and bringing down upon myself anathemas without number; though I reached the south end of the building in a moment, seemingly, and gazed in every direction, Delbras had vanished.

It was while making this wild rush that I brought upon myself the attention of one of the very guards who had led me ignominiously away from the presence of Smug and the Camps.

He had seen my hasty rush from the building, and, without at first recognising me, had followed me to inquire the cause of my haste.

I knew him at the first moment; and when I had answered his inquiry, he knew me.

"The matter? Oh, I was trying to overtake a—a person whom I particularly wished to see," I replied; and I saw on his countenance the dawning look of recognition. "Seems to me you and I have met before. You don't want to arrest me again, do you?" I added testily; and then I pulled myself together and asked more amiably, "Did you think I was running away with another wallet?"

The young fellow's face brightened. Dave's words had told him and his companions who I was, and he answered, very respectfully:

"No, sir, not this time; though I had not recognised you at first. Can I help you in any way, sir?"

"N—no, I'm afraid there's no help for me this time. By the way, did you happen to see any of those parties again after you marched me off so cruelly?"

He knitted his brows to assist his memory, and finally replied:

"Come to think, sir, I did see one of them; at least one of the persons who had been swindled like yourself."

"Swindled?"

"Yes, sir. You see, we didn't quite catch on at the time; it was all done so quick, and I got the idea that it was a sort of pocket-game; but it happened that I met the other gentleman, the next day, if I remember, and I spoke to him, for I knew his face at once."

"Describe him."

"Why, not very tall, and—well, not very light nor very dark, I should say; not much hair on his face, and dressed in a sort of gray suit."

"Yes, I see." I recognised the description as that of Smug, and determined to hear more. "And what did he say?"

"Why, nothing at first; but when I saw him looking at me sort of sharp, I just stepped up and asked him how the row finished after the other guard and I had hustled you off; and then I told him how we had found out our mistake, and how your friend had let us off easy, although both were on the detective force. And then he explained how, as you and he were trying to keep the old man and his wife from being fleeced, one of the gang had set up the cry of 'Pickpocket!' and had pointed at you; and then, you know, when we fished that wallet out of your pocket it looked a—"

"Yes," I replied gravely; "it certainly did."

"He said," went on the guard, "that he had tried to make us understand that it was all a mistake about you, you know, but we didn't hear him."

"So you told him that my friend and I were upon the S.S.?" I said.

"Why, yes; was that—"

"Never mind. What did he say about the others—the tall man with the fez, for instance? He had a note-book and some bills in his hand, you may remember."

"Yes, sir, I do. Yes, he told me about him. Jumbo! but didn't you all get into a muddle. He had a narrow escape, too—the tall man, you know. Did you know who he was?"

I shook my head.

"Well, sir, he came very near being fleeced too. He wanted to change a bill, it seems, and the old farmer and the other fellow—the one that told me, you know, had both been getting some change from a man that claimed to make a business of changing foreign paper and large bills, to accommodate people."

"Oh!" I ejaculated.

"Yes, sir; and this gentleman—he was a big man, you know; one of them foreign managers, and couldn't speak very good English—was just going to change with them, a hundred, I think he said, when somebody sets up the cry of pickpocket, you know."

"Yes, I know; go on."

"Well, sir, after you was gone, of course in the crowd the real pickpocket got off scot-free. It turned out that the farmer and him that told me had been 'done' by some sharper, and that they was just ready to pass off on this foreigner a lot of counterfeit money."

"Great Caesar!" I ejaculated, and then checked my hasty speech. After all, why should I expend my breath or wrath upon this guileless guard, who, after all, was doing me a service? and how cleverly Smug had twisted the story, and made it serve his turn! But it must not be repeated—if it had not been already.

"Look here," I said in a more amiable tone, "have you told this affair, all or any of it, to anyone?"

"Who—me? No. Haven't had the chance. The fellow that was with me that day was taken off next day, and I've not seen a soul I know since. I did want to tell him."

"It's well you did not. Look here, if you want to keep out of trouble, you must keep perfectly dark about this matter. It's being sifted on the quiet, and they'd take it very ill at headquarters if one of the guards was to 'leak' on them, and maybe spoil their game. And if you should chance to meet this party again, remember, mum's the word."

"I'll keep mum, sir. I don't want to lose my job, not yet, before I've seen half the Fair."

"Very good. Now, how long have you been on duty about this place?"

"Two weeks, sir—ever since I was put on the force."

"And this foreigner—manager as you call him—did you have a good look at him?"

"Oh yes, sir."

"Ever seen him before?"

"Now that you ask, I'm quite sure I have, but not knowing who he was. Yes, I'm sure I've seen him about the village among the Turks more than once."

"Describe him."

"Why, he's good-looking, and tall, and dark; got a sort of proud gait, and square shoulders; always dresses swell."

"Thank you." I had squeezed my orange dry, and was anxious to leave him. I had suspected it before, and was now convinced that unwittingly, in my attempt to play the guardian angel to Adam Camp and his wife, I had come face to face with Delbras.

When I compared notes with Dave that night he was quite of my opinion.

CHAPTER XIV.

MISSING—CARTE BLANCHE.

IT HAD been decided between Miss Jenrys and myself that the little brunette should not be altogether ignored, at least for a time; and I had taken it upon myself to provide the letter which was to put off until a more convenient season the proposed survey of the White City by night.

After some thought I had written the following, and posted it according to directions, in care of a certain café on Fifty-seventh Street:

"DEAR MISS B——,

"I find that I can hardly evade the duties one owes to courteous friends, and must for a few evenings devote myself to these. It is very likely that some of the friends of my chaperon will visit the Fair, perhaps this week, in which case she will perhaps be able to dispense with me for one evening; therefore please inform me if you should, as you suggested, change your address, so that I may drop you a note when the right time comes.

"Yours, etc.,
"J. E. J."

This letter was submitted to Miss Jenrys, and then posted, but not until the superintendent had secured for me the services of a half-grown boy who had won a reputation as a keen and tenacious "shadow." Him I set to await the coming of our brunette; and, lest he should mistake or miss her, I waited in attendance with him until she came, which was at an early hour and in haste.

I had also placed a man upon Stony Island Avenue, armed with minute descriptions of Smug, Greenback Bob, Delbras, and the brunette, and with instructions to watch the cafés and houses upon a line with the Fair-grounds, and especially within a certain radius within which we knew parties of their peculiar sort were received "and no questions asked."

As for Brainerd and myself, we had laid out a new system, and upon it we founded a strong hope for ultimate success; though we recognised more and more the fact that we had to cope with men who were more than ordinarily keen, clever, and skilled in the fine art of dodging and baffling pursuit. In fact, I was now thoroughly convinced that they were living and working upon the supposition that they were constantly watched and pursued, and that they governed their movements and shifted their abode accordingly.

There was one thing which weighed upon my mind—I had almost said conscience—and troubled me uncomfortably, and that was the attitude I was permitting the disguised brunette to maintain toward Miss Jenrys.

Since she had entered so earnestly into the work of ferreting out the motive for the brunette's persistent attentions, she had manifested such a willingness to aid me by allowing that personage to continue the acquaintance already begun, that, while I appreciated it as an earnest of her trust in me, it was, nevertheless, embarrassing.

I was not yet ready to tell her that I believed the brunette to be a man in masquerade—I must be able to prove my charge first; and yet I had determined that they should not meet again if I could stand between them.

It was to speak an additional word of caution, and to tell the two ladies that two stalwart and trusty chair-pushers were engaged for their evening sight-seeing, that I set out one morning to make my first call upon them at their apartment on Washington Avenue. It had been decided that, even in such a throng as that of the White City, it would not be wise to meet within the grounds too often, or too openly. We were sure of more or less surveillance from one source; and I was quite ready to believe that from more than one direction interested eyes were watching the coming and going of Miss Jenrys, if not of myself.

Already I had tested the cooking and service of a variety of the restaurants, cafés, and *tables d'hote* within the gates, and I had also found that outside, and especially within easy reach from the northern or Fifty-seventh Street gate, were to be found a number of most cleanly and inviting little places, more or less pretentious, and under various names, but all ready, willing, and able to serve one a breakfast, dinner, or luncheon such as would tempt even chronic grumblers to smile, feast, and come again.

I had breakfasted that morning at one of these comforting places, and upon leaving it had crossed the street to purchase a cigar from the stand on the corner, and having lighted it had kept on upon the same side.

I had meant to recross at the next corner, for halfway between two streets, stationed beneath some trees upon a vacant lot, was a boot-black's open-air establishment which I had a mind to patronize. As I neared the scene, however, and glanced across, I saw that both of the boot-black's chairs were occupied, and upon a second glance I noted that one of the occupants was my recent acquaintance, Monsieur Voisin, Miss Jenrys' friend.

He was busy with a newspaper, or seemed to be, and glancing down at my feet to make sure they were not too shabby for a morning call, I kept straight on and turned down Washington Avenue upon its farther or western side.

I had bought a paper along with my cigar, and as I ran up the steps of the pretty modern cottage where the two ladies had established themselves I threw away the one and put the other in my pocket, wondering as I did so if Monsieur Voisin was also on his way to this place, and smiling a little, because I had at least the advantage of being first.

It was so early that the ladies had not yet returned from breakfast, which they took at a café "aroond the corner joost," so the servant informed me. But I was expected, and I was asked to wait in their little reception-room, where a sunshade and a pair of dainty gloves upon a chair, and a shawl of soft gray precisely folded and lying upon a small table, not to mention the books, papers, and little feminine knicknacks, gave to the room a look of occupancy and ownership.

I had just unfolded my paper, and was glancing over the headlines upon the first page, when the two ladies entered, and I dropped my paper while rising to salute them.

In anticipation of or to forestall a possible call from Monsieur Voisin, I made haste to get through with the little business in hand, and obtained from Miss Jenrys, without question or demur, her promise not to hold communication with the brunette, at ieast by letter, and to avoid if possible a meeting until I should be able to enlighten her more fully.

"I do not want to lose sight of her," I said, in scant explanation, "and it seems that we can best keep our hold through her pursuit of you; but I would rather lose sight of her altogether and begin it all over again than let one line in your handwriting go into such hands"—I avoided those false pronouns 'her' and 'she' when I could—"and hope and trust you may be spared another interview. Please take this upon trust, Miss Jenrys, and you too, Miss Ross, and believe that I will not keep you in the dark one moment longer than is needful."

They assured me of their willingness to wait, even in the face of what Miss Jenrys laughingly described as a devouring curiosity; and then, while she turned the talk upon the Fair and some of its wonders, Miss Ross, murmuring a word of polite excuse, took up my paper from the place where it had fallen from my hands.

"Thee will allow me—I have not seen our morning paper."

"Oh, Aunt Ann, I had entirely forgotten it !" cried her niece contritely.

"It is not important, child," replied the smiling Quakeress. "There is very little in it now except the Fair, and that we can better read at first hand."

Nevertheless, she began to turn the pages and to scan here and there through her dainty gold-framed spectacles, while Miss Jenrys began to interrogate me concerning the mysteries of Midway Plaisance.

"We hear such very contradictory stories, and I do not want to miss any feature of the foreign show worth seeing," she said, with an arch little nod and smile across to her aunt, "nor does

Aunt Ann; and I don't quite feel like bearding all those Midway lions unguarded, unguided, and—unadvised."

I was not slow to offer my own individual services, in such an earnest manner that, after a little hesitation and the assurance that it would not only not conflict with my "business engagements," but would afford an especial pleasure, inasmuch as I had not yet "done" the Plaisance in any thorough manner, she finally accepted my proffered services for her aunt and herself, adding at last:

"To be perfectly honest, Mr. Masters, I know Aunt Ann will never enter that alarming, fascinating Ferris Wheel without an escort whom she can trust should we lose our heads and want to jump out one hundred feet above terra firma; and I am quite sure I shall want to jump. I always am tempted to jump from any great height. Do you believe in these sensations? I have heard people say that they could hardly restrain themselves from jumping into the water whenever they ride in a boat or cross a bridge."

"I have heard of such cases," I replied. And so we talked on, discussing this singular and seldom met with, but still existing fact, of single insane freaks in the otherwise perfectly sane, when the gentle Quakeress, uttering a little shocked exclamation and suddenly lowering her paper, turned toward us.

"Pardon me! but, June, child, what did you tell me was the name of the young man to whom thy friend Hilda O'Neil is betrothed?"

"Trent, auntie—Gerald Trent."

"Of Boston?"

"Of Boston; yes. Why, Aunt Ann?"

"I—I fear, then, that there is sorrow in store for thy young friend. Gerald Trent is missing."

"Missing?"

The Quakeress held the paper toward me, I being nearest her, and pointing with a finger to some headlines half-way down the page, said:

"Perhaps thee would better read it."

I took the paper and read aloud these lines:

"'ANOTHER WORLD'S FAIR MYSTERY.—GERALD
TRENT AMONG THE MISSING.

"'Another Young Man Swallowed up by the Maelstrom.

Against Odds

"'Yesterday we chronicled the disappearance of Harvey Parker who was traced by his friends to this city, where he had arrived to visit the Exposition for a week or more. He is known to have arrived at the Rock Island Depot and to have set out for the Van Buren Street Viaduct *en route* for the Fair. This was on Monday last, five days ago, since which time, as was stated in our yesterday's issue, he has not been seen or heard from by his friends or by the police, who are searching for him.

"'Nearly two weeks ago, Gerald Trent, only son of Abner Trent, one of Boston's millionaire merchants, came to this city to see the Exposition and to secure accommodations for his family, who were to come later. He stopped at an up-town hotel for some days, visited the Fair, and secured apartments for his friends, which were to have been vacated for their use in a few days.

"'He had written to his family, telling them to await his telegram, which they would receive in three or four days. When this time had expired and no telegram came, they waited another day, and then sent him a message of inquiry. This being unanswered, they made inquiry at his up-town hotel, and then began a search, which ended in the conviction that young Trent had met with misfortune, if not foul play. On Monday last he left the hotel, saying to one of the inmates of the house that he should have possession of a fine suite of rooms, within three blocks of the north entrance, which presumably means Fifty-seventh Street, within three days, and that he meant to send for his friends that day by telegraph. No message was received at his home, as has been said, and nothing has been heard of him since that day.

"'Young Trent wore, rather unwisely, a couple of valuable diamonds, one in a solitaire ring, the other in a scarf-pin; he also carried a fine watch, and was well supplied with money. The police are working hard upon the case. The list of the missing seems to be increasing.'"

I put the paper down and looked across at Miss Jenrys. I had recognised the name Hilda O'Neil as that of her Boston correspondent whose letter I had found in the little black bag, and by association the name of Gerald Trent also. Miss Jenrys was looking pale and startled.

"Oh!" she exclaimed. "That is what Hilda's telegram meant."

"You have had a telegram from Boston?" I ventured.

"Yes. You perhaps remember the letter in my bag?"

I nodded.

"In that letter Hilda—Miss O'Neil—spoke of Mr. Trent's delay, and of her anxiety. I did not reply to her letter at first, expecting to hear from or see her, for she had my address. It was only a freak my telling her to write me through the World's Fair post-office; but when she did not come—on the day before I met you, in fact—I wrote just a few lines of inquiry. In reply to this I received a telegram last evening. I will get it." She crossed the room and opened a little traveller's writing-case, coming back with a yellow envelope in her hand. "There it is," she said, holding it out to me.

I took it and read the words:

"Have you seen Gerald? Hilda."

"Did you reply to this?" I asked, as I gave it back to her.

"At once—just the one word, 'No.'"

"Do you know this young man?" I asked.

"I have never even seen him, but I know that he bears a splendid reputation for manliness, sobriety, and studiousness. He was something of a bookworm at college, I believe, and has developed a taste for literature. You see, I have heard much of him. Oh, I am sure something has happened to him, some misfortune! You see, she had asked him to call upon me, and he would never have left Hilda—not to mention his parents and sister—five days in suspense if able to communicate with them."

"If he is the person you describe him, surely not."

She gazed at me a moment, as if about to reproach me for the doubt my words implied, and dropped her eyes. Then she answered quietly:

"The simple fact that John O'Neil, Hilda's father, has accepted him as his daughter's *fiancé* is sufficient for me. Mr. O'Neil is an astute lawyer and a shrewd judge of character; he has known the Trents for many years, and he already looks upon Gerald Trent as a son."

"And Mr. O'Neil—where is he?"

"Abroad at present; it is to be regretted now."

I took up the paper and reread the account of young Trent's disappearance; and Miss Jenrys dropped her head upon her hand, and seemed to be studying the case. After a moment of silence, Miss Ross, who had been a listener from the beginning, leaned toward her niece and said, in her gentlest tone:

"June, my child, ought we not to try and do something? What does thee think? Should we wait, and perhaps lose valuable time, while the Trents are on their way?"

Miss Jenrys lifted her head suddenly.

"Auntie," she exclaimed, "you are worth a dozen of me! You are right! We must do something. Mr. Masters, what would you do first if you were to begin at once upon the case?"

"Get, from the chief of police if necessary, the name of the uptown hotel where young Trent was last seen."

"And then?" she urged, in a prompt, imperious manner quite new in my acquaintance with her.

"Obtain a description of him from some of the people there, and learn all that can be learned about him."

"And what next?" she urged still.

"Next, I would seek among the houses within two or three blocks from the north entrance for the rooms which he engaged, and which are perhaps still held for him."

"Mr. Masters, can you do this for me?" She was sitting erect before me, the very incarnation of repressed activity, and I knew, as well as if she had said it, that she would never permit my refusal to weaken the determination just taking shape in her mind to do for Hilda O'Neil what she could not have done for herself, and to do it boldly, promptly, openly. She saw my hesitation, and went on hurriedly:

"I know how busy you must be, how much I am asking, but you have undertaken to follow up that brunette and find out the reason for her interest in me, and surely this is far, far more important—a man's life, the happiness of a family, my friend's happiness at stake, perhaps; for I am sure that no common cause, nothing but danger, illness, or death, could keep Gerald Trent from communicating with his parents and his promised wife. Drop the brunette and all connected with her, Mr. Masters, and give such time as you would have given to my affairs, and more if possible, to this search, I beg of you. At least, promise me that you will conduct the search, and employ as many helpers as you need. I'll give you carte-blanche. Deal with me as you would with a man, and if I can aid in any other way than with my purse, let me do it."

As she paused, with her eyes eagerly fixed upon my face, the sweet Quakeress leaned toward me, and put out her white slender hand in earnest appeal.

"'Thy brother's keeper;' remember that a deed of mercy is beyond and above all works of vengeance. What is the capture of a criminal, of many of them, compared to the rescue, the saving, perchance, of an honest man's life? I beg of thee, consent, help us!"

There may be men who could have resisted that appeal. I could not, and did not. I did not throw my other responsibilities to the winds; I simply did not think of them at the moment, when I took the soft hand of the elder woman in my own, and, looking across at the younger, said:

"I will do my best, Miss Jenrys, and, that not one moment may be lost, tell me, can you describe young Trent?"

"Not very well, I fear."

"And his picture? Your friend must have that?"

"Of course," half smiling.

"Telegraph her to forward it to you at once. And has your friend at any time mentioned the hotel where young Trent would stop? Most of our Eastern visitors have a favourite stopping-place."

"I know." She had made a movement toward her desk, but paused and turned toward me. "I think it is safe to say that the two families would share the same house. They did in visiting the summer resorts, always; and I know where Mr. O'Neil and Mr. Trent went when they attended the great convention in this city." She named the place, and I promptly arose.

"I will go there at once; but you may as well give me the Trents' address, and permit me the use of your name. If I am wrong I will telegraph from up-town for the name of his hotel."

As I turned my face cityward that morning I was not only fully committed to the search for missing Gerald Trent, but I was determined to convert my friend and partner to the same undertaking.

And having now found time for sober, second thought, I had also determined not to relinquish my search for the little brunette and her secret, nor for Messrs. Bob Delbras and company. Had I not carte-blanche?

As I left the house, intent upon my new errand, I was not surprised to see approaching it, almost at the door, in fact, Monsieur Voisin. We exchanged greetings at the entrance, and I had walked some distance before it occurred to me to wonder how it came about that Monsieur Voisin, whom I had last seen at the bootblack's stand, two blocks north and east, happened to be approaching Miss Jenrys' residence from the south.

CHAPTER XV.

THE KING OF CONFIDENCE MEN.

I FOUND a number of people at the big up-town hotel who could tell me a little of Gerald Trent, as he appeared to them after a few days' acquaintance; and these were unanimous in saying and believing that young Trent was not absent by his own will.

"It's a case of foul play, I'm sure of it," declared the clerk, to whom I had represented myself as 'acting for one of Mr. Trent's friends.' "Cowles saw him at the viaduct, he told me, just before he left; that was five days ago now, and Trent was then going down to secure those rooms and see that they were put in order. He went by the Suburban, because he wanted to go over to the avenues, and Cowles went down by the Whaleback."

There was no more to be learned up-town. Gerald Trent had been last seen at the viaduct at the foot of Van Buren Street, where the "cattle cars," the "Suburban," and numerous boats left the Lake Front and the wharf beyond *en route* for the Fair City. This was at ten o'clock a.m., or near it.

I went back to the Fair City, as Trent had last gone, upon the Suburban train; and before noon had begun an exploration, in the vicinity of the north entrance, for the rooms engaged by him.

Bounding the Fair City on the west was the street known as Stony Island Avenue, and after a short survey of such near portions of this street as I had not seen, I satisfied myself that young Trent would not have selected it as a place of abode for his lady mother, his sister, and his sweetheart. One block westward, running south from Fifty-seventh, was a short street called Rosalie Court, and after exploring this I pushed on to Washington Avenue, and then to Madison, running respectively one and two blocks parallel with Rosalie Court.

Something impelled me to pass by Washington Avenue, upon which Miss Jenrys and her aunt were lodged, and to explore the farther avenue first.

"If the rooms are within two or three blocks of the north entrance," I said to myself, "and if they are upon this street, I shall find them within one block north or south from this corner," meaning Fifty-seventh Street, and I turned southward and began my search in earnest.

Not long since this part of the city had been a beautiful suburb, and the pretty cottages and more stately villas were, for the most part, isolated in the midst of their own grounds. Every other house it seemed, and some of the most pretentious, bore upon paling, piazza, or door-post the legend "Rooms to Let," and I applied and entered at a number of handsome and homelike portals, first upon the east side and then upon the west, crossing at Fifty-eighth Street to turn my face northward.

At Fifty-seventh I paused. "It is something more than two blocks from the Fair entrance to this point," I mused, "and therefore I ought to go but one block in this direction." But when I had traversed the block to Fifty-sixth Street, with no success, I crossed the street and went on, saying, "It's easy for a stranger to be mistaken in a matter of distance." At the north end of this square stood a large old-fashioned mansion, of a decidedly Southern type. It stood upon terraced grounds, and was a dignified reminder of better days, with its stained and time-roughened stuccos, and the worn paint about tile ornate cornices. "Rooms to Let" was the sign upon a tree-trunk, and after some doubt and hesitation, I went up the terraced steps, crossed the lawn, and rang a bell much newer than its surroundings.

Once admitted to the wide, inviting hall, with its glimpse of cheerful dining-room beyond, and a large cool parlour opening at the side, I felt that Trent might well have sought quarters in this roomy, airy house; and when the "lady of the house," a woman small, elderly, delicate, and refined, appeared before me, I put my question hopefully.

"Madam, have you among the inmates of your house a Mr. Gerald Trent?" I saw by her sudden change of countenance that the name was not strange to her, and was not surprised when she informed me that a Mr. Trent had engaged her best suite of rooms for himself and four others; that he had called upon her on the Monday previous, paid her an advance upon the rooms, and informed her that his friends would arrive in three days, if not sooner.

"They should have been here," she concluded, "the day before yesterday, but they have not appeared, and we have had no word from them. It is very inconvenient for me. Of course, the rooms are secured until Monday, but I have no means of knowing if they will come then; or when I may consider them at my disposal."

It was evident she had not seen the papers, and I at once put the notice in her hand, and told her the nature of my business.

There seemed but one opinion of Gerald Trent. When she had read the paper and heard my statement, she said, at once, what the inmates of the hotel had said before her:

"Something has happened him. He never went away like this of his own accord. I never saw a more simple and sincere young man." And then, as if by an afterthought, "He had too much money about him; he was too well dressed, and—I don't think he was of a suspicious nature."

I learned from her very little to help my further search. Trent had met none of the guests of the house upon either of his visits there. In reply to a question, she had said:

"He seemed in the best of spirits when he paid the advance money and went away; and he said that he meant to spend the day in the Plaisance. I remember that he laughed when he said this, and added something to the effect that he wanted to decide, before the ladies came, where it would pay to go on the Plaisance, and what were the things they would not care for. He had a rather frank and boyish way of expressing himself."

"And you think he went from here to the Fair?"

"I believe he went from here to Midway Plaisance. There is an entrance on this street, three blocks south, and I walked to the door with him and pointed the way to it."

And this was all. Of course I took from her lips, as from the people up-town, a minute description of Trent's dress and appearance on the day of his disappearance, and then I went back to the Fair by the Midway gate, and wished impatiently for the time to come when I should meet Brainerd and consult with him. This I knew would not be until a late hour, and as I lounged down the Plaisance I began to look about for the handsome guard, in whom I had taken a decided interest.

I found him easily—as erect, soldierly, attentive to duty as usual—and we spent the greater part of two hours chatting, while we paced up and down Midway. He was a bright talker, and he entertained me with a number of amusing incidents, graphically related, and illustrative of the life of the Plaisance.

During the two hours, however, I broke the monotony of a continuous tramp by an excursion, now on one side and then on the other; now to see the glass-blowers; now the submarine exhibit; and, lastly, to the Irish village that clustered about Blarney Castle.

It was on my return from this that, as I approached him, I saw, with some surprise, that he was in earnest conversation with a woman, and as I came nearer and he shifted his position slightly, I saw that the woman was none other than that *ignis fatuus* the brunette. Her back was toward me, and she was squarely facing him, so that, as I came nearer and directly toward them, I caught his eye, and, nodding with a gesture which I think he understood, I turned away and watched the manoeuvres of "the little mystery," as Brainerd so often called the brunette, wondering if this unknown guard was also to be enmeshed in the plot she seemed to be weaving. And then there flashed into my mind that first meeting with the guard, and his avowed acquaintance with Miss Jenrys. Was this interview in any way connected with or concerning her?

The brunette had not seen me; of that I was quite assured, and even so I had small fear of recognition, for while I had not, on the occasion of our two meetings face to face, worn any disguise, I was confident that the widely different garments worn on the two occasions, together with my ability to elongate, twist, and change my features, and to alter the pitch of my voice, was masquerade sufficient. But I did not desire to become known to this anomalous personage, and I lingered here and there, within sight and at a safe distance, until I saw her nod airily and trip away, flinging a smile over her shoulder.

In the time spent in waiting the end of this little dialogue I had decided that I must know this young man—so reticent, yet so frank—better, and that I must win his confidence, and to do this perfect frankness, I knew, would be my best aid.

When the "mystery" was safely out of sight, and on this occasion I had no desire to follow her, I rejoined the guard, and I was sure that I surprised upon his face a look of perplexity and annoyance, which vanished when I put my hand upon his arm, and, falling into step with him, began:

"I hope you understood my meaning when I went into ambush so suddenly? I really did not care to encounter your friend."

"That is hardly the right name, seeing that the lady is a stranger to me," he replied, slightly smiling.

"Indeed!" I retorted. "Then may I wager that I know what she had to say to you?" I saw him flush, and his lips compress themselves as if to hold back some hasty speech, but I went lightly on: "That is the young person who claimed the bag belonging to your acquaintance—you remember the circumstance—and if she is still as angry at me as she was on that day she was doubtless imploring you to 'run me in,' and put me in more irons than Christopher Columbus ever wore. Honestly now, am I not right?"

He was silent and seemed perplexed again, and I promptly changed my tone. "If I am mistaken, and if the young woman is someone you know, I beg your pardon; but, remembering how she turned her look upon you on the occasion of that first meeting—"

"One moment," he broke in. "It is possible that we have been unjust in this case, and I think I may tell you, without a breach of confidence, what this young lady"—I thought he emphasized the "lady" somewhat—"who by-the-by is a stranger to me, had to say just now."

I bowed my assent, lest speech might cause a discussion, and he went on:

"The young lady, after excusing herself for doing what she termed an unconventional thing in addressing me, asked at once after you."

"After me? But—go on."

"She spoke of you as 'the person' I was talking with on the day when her friend lost her bag and she tried to reclaim it, and when I disclaimed all knowledge of you, she told me how 'cavalierly'— that is also her word—you refused to yield up the bag, and how anxiously her friend was hoping to secure that bag—even yet."

"Ah! Indeed!"

"You will pardon me," he went on, not heeding my interjection, and speaking with marked courtesy, "but I almost fear you have mistaken this young lady."

"Why?"

"Because she not only gave me the name of the owner of the bag, but she assured me that the lady recognised me in passing. a thing which I regret, and she called me by my name."

Here was a coil indeed. My head was a nest of queer thoughts and suspicions, but I kept to the subject by asking:

"And may I ask how you replied to all this?"

"In the only way I could. You were a stranger, who was anxious, I felt sure, to restore the bag to its owner. You had assured me of this much. As to your address, I could not give it, and your name I did not know; but I added the promise that should I chance to meet you, as I might, I would ask you to send the bag to the lady's address."

"Pardon—was this the lady's proposition?"

"No. She asked me to get it from you—the bag."

"And to restore it through her?"

"Yes."

"And the address? Did she give you the young lady's address, the owner's, or her own?"

"She gave the owner's address."

"Then if you will give it to me I can promise that tomorrow will see the little bag in its owner's possession."

He took from his pocket a visiting card, upon which was engraved the name June E. Jenrys, and underneath in pencil the address.

I had seen just such a card, minus the pencilled address, on Miss Jenrys' card-tray on Washington Avenue; and that pencilled address! It was that of the cafe to which Miss Jenrys was to send her note concerning the evening excursion.

I had not spoken of the adventure of the bag during the afternoon, and I had not meant to do so. Since our last meeting my position in relation to Miss Jenrys had been changed. I was now in some degree the guardian of her interests, and while I believed in, and admired this handsome and secretive stranger guard, and might have entrusted him with a secret all my own, perhaps, my mouth was closed concerning the young lady whom he professed to know yet was unwilling to meet.

As I looked at the tall, lithe figure, the erect head and handsome face, I wondered what this mystery could be which caused him to withhold his name from those who might be his friends; to shun a lovely girl whom he knew and in whom he was evidently interested; and, above all, which linked him, as was now fairly proven, through the wily brunette, with the strange pursuit of Miss Jenrys. Was it possible, I asked myself, that this medley of mysterious happenings could reach back through the brunette to Greenback Bob, the counterfeiter, and Delbras, the king of confidence men?

CHAPTER XVI.

THAT LITTLE DECOY.

I STOWED the false address in my waistcoat pocket, and after promising to see the guard again on the next day, a promise which I fully intended to keep, and exchanging a few friendly but important sentences with him, we shook hands and separated. We had grown almost friendly in our manner each toward each, in spite of the fact that neither knew the name of the other. He had told me where he lodged, among the number who were housed within the grounds; and we had agreed to dine together at an early date at a place which he had recommended in reply to my inquiry after a satisfactory place to dine within the walls of the Fair. He had dined there regularly, he assured me, and I was glad to know this, for I foresaw that I might need his help in the defence of Miss Jenrys and her interests, and I could not know too much of his whereabouts.

"Till we meet and wine and dine," I said flippantly, upon leaving him, little dreaming how soon and in what manner we were to meet again.

As I left the Plaisance the handsome guard was still the subject of my thoughts. That he had told me the truth concerning his interview with the brunette I did not doubt, but was it the whole truth?

All that he had rehearsed to me could have been said in much less than half the time she had spent in brisk conversation with the guard, whose part seemed to have been that of listener.

Not that I had any right to demand or expect his full confidence; still, why had he withheld it; and what was it that the brunette had slipped into his hand at parting?

Another thing, we had planned to dine together soon, and he knew that I was, or seemed to be, quite at leisure, while he would be relieved from duty very soon, and yet—well, he had certainly not grasped at the opportunity.

I did not expect to meet Brainerd until a late hour, and I had decided to do nothing further in the matter of the Trent disappearance until we could talk it over. In fact, there was little to be done until I had seen Miss Jenrys and her aunt, and reported to them, as I had engaged to do at seven o'clock. At this hour I called and made my meagre report, which, however, was better than nothing, as the ladies were good enough to declare.

They had remained at home all day, and late in the afternoon received a message from Miss O'Neil. The picture, it assured her, would be sent at once.

A little to my surprise, I found that the ladies were prepared to go to town in company with Monsieur Voisin, to hear a famous monologue artist. He had persuaded them, Miss Jenrys said, rather against their wishes, but they had at last decided that this would be better than to pass the evening as they had already passed the day, in useless speculation, discussion, and anxiety.

Of course I agreed with them; but I came away early, not caring to encounter the handsome Frenchman again, and I re-entered the gates of the Fair City a little out of tune, and wandered about the brightly-illuminated and beautiful Court of Honour, finding, for the first time in this place, that time was dragging, and wishing it were time to meet Dave, and begin what I knew would be a lively and two-sided discussion.

At eight o'clock there was music upon the Grand Plaza, and the band-stand was surrounded by a merry, happy crowd. At nine the band was playing popular airs, and a picked chorus that had been singing in Choral Hall in the afternoon was filling the great space with vocal melody, in which from time to time the crowd joined with enthusiasm.

Coming nearer this centre of attraction, I saw, seated near the water's edge, and quite close to the great Fountain, the little brunette and a companion. It was impossible to mistake the brunette, for she wore the costume of the afternoon—a somewhat conspicuous costume, as I afterward remembered; but her companion puzzled me. She was tall and slight, and quietly well dressed, and her face could not well be seen under the drooping hat which she wore. There seemed, at the very first, something familiar about this hat. It was broad-brimmed, slightly curved upward at the sides, and bent to shade the face and fall over the hair at the back; but long dark plumes fell at one side, and a third stood serenely erect in front; and suddenly I remembered that I had seen Miss Jenrys wear such a hat upon the day of our first meeting. But Miss Jenrys, in a dainty white theatre bonnet, had gone up town; and there was no monopoly of drooping hats and feathers—so I told myself.

But I wondered what mischief, new or old, the brunette was bent upon, and I decided to give her the benefit of my unoccupied attention.

Against Odds

From time to time the two changed their positions, but I noted that they kept upon the outskirts of the throng, and seemed to avoid the well-lighted spaces, sitting or standing in the shadow of the great statues, the columns, and angles.

For nearly an hour the music continued, vocal for the most part, and the crowd kept in place, singing and applauding by turns. I had been standing near the east facade of the Administration Building for some time, having followed the brunette and her companion to that side of the Plaza, when I saw a group of Columbian Guards, evidently off duty, place themselves against the wall quite near me. They were strolling gaily, and after a little, as the singers began a national anthem, some of them joined in the chorus or refrain. It was amateurish singing enough, until suddenly a new voice lifted itself among them—a tenor voice—sweet, strong, high, and thoroughly cultured. I turned to look closer, and saw that the singer was my friend, the handsome guard. He was standing slightly aloof from the others, and when he saw that his music was causing many heads to turn, he suddenly ceased singing, and in spite of the remonstrances of his companions, moved away from them, slowly at first, and then with more decision of movement, until he was out of their sight in the crowd.

"He wants to avoid them," I said to myself, "and he seems to be looking for someone." And then I turned my attention to the brunette once more.

At ten o'clock the music had ceased, and the people were scattered upon the Plaza. The electric fountains had ceased to send up multi-coloured spray, and some of the lights in the glittering chains about the Grand Basin were fading out. On the streets and avenues leading away from the Plaza there was still sufficient light, but the Wooded Island, which as yet had not participated in the great illuminations, was not brilliantly lighted. In fact, under the trees, and among the winding shrub-bordered paths, there were many shadowed nooks and gloomy recesses.

And yet it was towards the Wooded Island that the brunette and her companion led me, wondering much, and keeping at a distance to avoid the glances often sent back by the little adventuress.

I had just stepped off the path to avoid the gleam of light that fell across it from the light just at the curve, when a quick step sounded close by, and a tall figure passed me in haste, going the way the two had taken—the form of the handsome guard.

I had followed them past the east front of the Electricity Building, and between it and the canal, and then across the bridge opposite, and midway between the north front of the Electricity and Mines Buildings, across the little island of the Hunters' Camp, and across the second bridge, and it was near this last spot that the guard had passed me.

A few paces beyond me he seemed at a loss, and paused to look about him; and as he did so, the two women, who had made a short-cut across the forbidden grass, came out into the path directly between us, and retraced their steps toward the bridge.

It was past ten o'clock now, and very quiet just here, and the lamps at the ends of the bridge, the only lights just here, seemed to me less brilliant than usual. As the two women came toward me, somewhat slowly, I drew back into the shelter of the bushes, and they passed me, speaking low. I remember that, at the moment, the thought of our singular isolation in this spot crossed my mind, and I wondered why we did not see somewhere a second Columbian Guard on duty.

And now my guard passed me hurriedly, looking neither to right nor left, and I crept forward across the grass and under the trees. I could now see that the women had stopped upon the bridge nearest the island, and on the side facing eastward, and looking over the face of the lagoon at its widest, and across to the silent and now almost utterly darkened Manufactures Building, and that the guard had joined them. Rather, that he was speaking with the brunette, while the other, with bent head, stood a little aloof.

And then, as I looked and wondered, two figures arose suddenly, or so it seemed, from the base of the statue at the end of the bridge, just behind the guard, and as he bent his head toward the little decoy there was a silent, forward spring, a sudden heaving movement, and a splash. With a shout for help I bounded forward, tearing off my coat as I ran. I was conscious of four flying figures that passed me, hastening islandward, but my thoughts were all for that figure that had gone over into the lagoon silently and without a struggle.

As I tore down the bank at the side of the pier, I heard low voices, and could see a boat in the shadow of the bridge; and as I was about to plunge into the water, a voice said sharply:

"Keep out, mate, we've got him!" And in a moment the boat came out, and I saw two men were supporting the guard, half in, and half out of the water, and the other pushing the skiff to shore.

As I stepped into the water to their assistance, I saw at one glance that my friend had fallen into the able hands of two of the emergency crew, whose duty it was to patrol the lagoons by night, and that he was insensible.

"He struck our boat in falling," one of them said to me, "and I'm afraid he's got a hurt head. Too bad; if he hadn't fainted we'd 'a' winged one of that crowd, sure."

CHAPTER XVII.

"THOSE TWO WOMEN."

MY FRIEND the guard had received a blow upon the head, painful but not fatal. He would be about in a few days, the hospital surgeon said. But in spite of the fact that I visited the hospital every day, five days passed before I was allowed to speak to him or he was allowed to talk.

I was very anxious for this opportunity, for I had now a new reason for my growing interest in the young fellow who so stubbornly refused to give me a name by which to call him. He was enrolled among the guards as L. Carr, and I at once adopted this name in speaking to or of him.

I had determined at the first moment possible to have a confidential talk with him, confidential upon my part, at least, and I meant to win his confidence if possible.

In the meantime I had laid all the story of this day's adventures before Dave Brainerd, beginning with the discovery in the newspaper, and my search up-town and down for trace of missing Gerald Trent, and I ended by adding to all the rest a few ideas and opinions of my own, which caused Dave, in spite of his lately expressed lofty opinion of my imaginative qualities, first to open his eyes, and then to roar with laughter.

But he was my hearty second at the last, even to the point of agreeing with me that, if we could accomplish but the one end, it were better to find and rescue Gerald Trent, if he were living and in duress, which we both doubted, or to solve the mystery of his fate if dead, than to arrest a pair, or a trio, of counterfeiters, or possible diamond robbers. As to Miss Jenrys and the mysterious guard, he would no more have given up the thought of solving the problem of the brunette's pursuit of these two than would I at that moment. But we needed all the light possible, and we agreed at once that to obtain this it would be wise, at this point, to make certain confidences to the two persons most interested.

* * * * *

As to the elusive brunette, her "shadow" had followed her for days more faithfully and at closer quarters than we could have done, because of his small stature and his easily managed "lightning changes," managed by the aid of a reversible jacket, three or four vari-coloured silk handkerchiefs, and two or three hats or caps, all stuffed into convenient pockets. But his report was, after all, far from complete or conclusive.

"I've follered her," he declared, "till my laigs ached, an' I never seen a woman 'at c'ud git over the ground like her. Ever sence that first trip my laigs 'a' bin stiff!"

The boy had followed her on the first day by devious ways, and until after mid-day, without losing sight of her; and had lost her at last, as Dave and myself had lost our quarry, in the intricacies of the Plaisance.

"Ye see," Billy had said, "'twas this way. She'd stopped afore one of them Arab places"—he meant Turkish—"where there wuz a pay show, an' she must 'a' got her ticket ahead, fer she jest sort o' held out a card or somethin' afore his eyes and went right in, an' I had ter wait till two or three fellers got tickets 'fore 'twas my turn, an' when I got in she wa'n't nowhere." A look of boyish disgust emphasized the emphasis here. "But wherever she was, she stayed a good while," Bill went on, "an' then, all at once, out she come ag'in, an' went into another big Place clos' by, an' I went in too that time. She went round behind a big table, where they had piles o' jimcracks, an' popped behind a curtain, an' jest as I was gittin' scared for fear she wuz gone agi'n, out she come an' took the place of a tired-lookin' woman that set on a high stool sellin' the jimcracks. She had took off her hat an' things, an' she had on a little red jacket all spangled up, an' a red cap, like the Turks all wear, with a big gold tassel on it, an' she'd made herself blacker round the eyes, an' redder in the cheeks, an' she looked jest sassy."

At least it was something to have our theories in regard to the lurking places of this trio verified. It was something to feel sure, as we now did, that these people were quartered in the Plaisance; but I felt very sure that they had more than one hiding-place, probably each of them a separate one, as well as a general rendezvous.

I questioned the lad closely regarding the "tired-lookin' woman," whom he described as "tallish, an' slim, an' not much on looks," but dressed in Turkish fez, and Zouave jacket, and "painted thick." He had watched her till evening came, and then the tallish woman had returned and the brunette had stepped behind the curtain once more.

"I watched that doggoned curtain," Bill declared, "till 'twas time to shut up shop, but she didn't come out, an' I couldn't git in."

"Did anyone come out from behind that curtain while you waited, Bill?" I asked him carelessly.

"Yes, there was; pretty soon after she went in a young Turk came out, smallish, with a little dudey moustache. He had a pitcher in his hand, an' he smacked the tired woman on the back, an' stuck the pitcher under her nose an' went out."

"Did he come back?"

"Come to think, I guess he didn't; I know he didn't."

"Well, Bill," I said, "I can't blame you; I only blame myself; but if you should see that woman go behind a curtain or door again, and presently see a man come out, if he is the same in size and looks anything like the one you saw tonight, you just follow him, and you'll be on the right track."

"Jim-mi-netti!"

"And, Bill, I want you to be on the Plaisance in the morning early, and if the brunette starts out, don't lose her. If she has not appeared by noon you may go down to the Plaza and look about there, but get back to Midway by three o'clock; she'll show herself there sooner or later."

The next day Bill had nothing to report. The day following he had followed her, late in the afternoon, when she had emerged from the Turkish bazaar down Midway, and had seen her stop and speak to one of the guards, then she had left the grounds by a Midway gate "opposite Hagenbeck's lion circus, ye know."

"And I followed her," he continued, "till she come to that rest'runt where you an' me see her git the letter; she turned off right by the Midway gate, and went acrost to Wash'n'ton Avenue, an' down that till she turned to come to the rest'runt. 'Twas most supper-time, and she didn't come out no more, I'm sure, for

I watched till most midnight, an' there wa'n't no back way, I know, for I looked."

I could well believe that she had taken a room as near the grounds as possible, where she might rest when rest was required, and she was off duty, and I did not doubt but that Delbras and Greenback Rob had each a similar lair outside the White City, but conveniently near it.

This last report had been made to us on the morning of my visit to Miss Jenrys, Bill having appeared at our quarters at an early hour, and I had been studying the expediency of letting Miss Jenrys into the history of her brunette acquaintance, as far as I myself knew it, before visiting the two ladies, at last deciding that I would wait a little and be guided by circumstances, the episode of Gerald Trent's disappearance finally putting it altogether out of my mind.

On the morning after the attempt to drown the guard, Dave and I waited for a time in our room, expecting a report from Bill, which might, we hoped, throw some light upon the events of the night before. But he did not appear; and after breakfasting together, Dave went back to our room to await him, while I made haste toward the Emergency Hospital, where our wounded guard lay, carefully watched, skilfully attended, and not permitted to talk or receive visitors.

Assured that his recovery would be only a matter of days, I went back to find Dave still alone, and this time we both set out, after leaving a message with the janitor, Dave to look after the men who had been detailed upon our business in different directions and to hear their reports, and I to see that more men were at work upon the Trent case before I ventured, as I was most anxious to do, upon a visit to Miss Jenrys and her aunt.

Having done what I could in the Trent case, I found it nearing noon when I approached their place of residence, but I had little fear of finding them absent, and was hastening on, only a few paces from their door, when I saw Monsieur Voisin come hastily out, and after seeming to hesitate a moment upon the threshold, run down the steps and move rapidly away southward. I could see that his face wore a sombre look, and I wondered if he had seen me in the hasty glance he had cast about him. There were others upon the pavement between him and myself, and I trusted that he had not; still, I felt a strange reluctance to being seen by this man so often in the same place, and I slackened my pace and finally stood still, reading the "to lets" upon the opposite houses, until he turned the corner and went, as I was very sure, to the Midway entrance a little way beyond.

I found the ladies at home, and eager to hear the little I had to tell them regarding the Trent case. I had put a good man in the hotel where Trent had stopped, to find out, if possible, whether the young Bostonian had been spotted and followed from that place by any swell adventurer; and I arranged with the mistress of the place where Trent had secured rooms to hold them until I heard from Boston, whether any or all would come on and occupy the rooms and assist in the search. Miss Jenrys felt sure they would come, all of them.

"Hilda O'Neil will not rest until she is here, as near the place where he was last seen as possible. You were very thoughtful to secure the rooms," she sighed heavily. "I suppose now we must simply wait until we receive the picture?" she added.

"There is little else to do," I replied. "Of course I have had other advertisements inserted in various papers, and have offered a reward, as you directed."

"Ah," she sighed again, "we may hear from that."

"I doubt it," I replied. "If he has been abducted, it is too soon for that," and then I turned the conversation by saying:

"I have some news from your friend, the brunette."

"My friend! Mr. Masters!"

"Pardon me; your satellite, then. She was revolving near you the day before yesterday." At this point the door opened and a voice said:

"Miss Ross, the laundress is here about your washing."

Miss Ross rose with alacrity, a benevolent smile upon her sweet face.

"Mr. Masters," she said, "thee must save thy story or tell it twice over, for I must beg thee to excuse me now. I can't send this poor woman away, and I ought not to make her wait."

"It's one of Aunt Ann's protégées," explained Miss Jenrys, "and she has come by appointment."

Mentally thankful for this interruption, I assured Miss Ross that my story should wait, and when she had left us alone I turned at once to Miss Jenrys.

"I am glad of this opportunity," I began at once, "for I have something to tell you which I prefer to make known to you first, although I should have told my story, even in your aunt's presence, if necessary, before leaving to-day."

And as directly as possible I told of my acquaintance with the handsome guard.

Beginning with her encounter with the Turkish palanquin-bearers, I described my interview with the guard, repeated his words, his questions concerning her welfare, his statement that she was not a stranger to him, and then, with her interest and her curiosity well aroused, I described him.

"I wonder who it can be?" she had murmured before I began my description, and I kept a secret watch upon her features, while I said:

"He is a tall young fellow, and very straight and square-shouldered, though somewhat slender. He is blond, with close-cropped hair that is quite light, almost golden, and inclined to curl where it has attained an inch of growth. He wears a moustache that is but little darker than his hair, and is kept close-trimmed. He has a broad, full forehead; honest, open blue eyes, not pale blue, but a fine deep colour, and they meet one frankly and fearlessly. His mouth is really too handsome for a man, but his chin is firm enough to counterbalance that. His manners are fine, and he has evidently been reared a gentleman. I chanced to hear him sing last night, and he has a wonderfully high tenor voice—an unusual voice; clear and sweet, and soft in the highest notes."

Before I had finished my description, I saw clearly that she recognised the picture. Her colour had changed and changed again, from red to pale. But I made no pause, telling how I had seen him in conversation with the little brunette, and what he had told me of that conversation, and then I described the adventure of the previous night.

When I had reached the point where I had offered my card and he had refused to give me a false name, I saw her eyes glow and her head lift itself unconsciously; when I described him in converse with the wily brunette, a slight frown crossed her face, and her little foot tapped an impatient tattoo quite unconsciously; when I pictured him as following the two women toward the Wooded Island, her head was lifted again and her lip curled scornfully. But when I had reached the point where the two figures, springing suddenly from the darkness behind him, had hurled him over the parapet into the deepest part of the lagoon, a low moan burst from her lips, and she put out her hands entreatingly.

"Was he—quick! tell me!"

"He was rescued, unconscious but living, by two of the emergency crew who guard the lagoons by night, who, luckily, were lying in their skiff under the shadow of the bridge engaged in watching the mysterious movements of the very men who were lurking behind the big pedestal on the other side of the pier, awaiting the signal from the women, their confederates. In going over, his head was quite seriously hurt. At first it was thought that he had struck the edge of the boat in falling, but the doctor says it was a blow from some blunt instrument with a rounded end—some manner of club, no doubt."

"And now—how—is he?" she faltered.

"In very good hands, and doing as well as can be expected. I was not allowed to see him, and he does not seem fully conscious, although the doctor says he may recover if all goes well."

"Where is he?" Her face was very pale, but there was a change in her voice, a sudden firmness, and a total lack of hesitancy.

"At the Emergency Hospital in the Fair grounds." I had purposely made his case as serious as I consistently could, and I now made the important plunge. "Miss Jenrys, I have taken a great interest in this young man from the first. He is a fine fellow, and now, added to this personal liking, is the duty I owe this helpless young man, who evidently has an enemy, and that enemy seemingly the very person who has been dogging you so persistently and so mysteriously. You see the strangeness of the complication. Are you willing to help me?"

"I?" she hesitated. "How?"

"This young man knows you. Do you not know him?"

"I—almost believe so."

"And—are you under any vow or promise of secrecy? He lies there, unknown, friendless; and he has an enemy near at hand. I want to serve him, but to do this intelligently I must know him."

She hesitated a moment, and then, to my surprise, arose quite calmly, went to her desk, and came back with a photograph in her hand.

"Look at that," she said, as she held it out to me.

It was a group of tennis-players upon a sunlit lawn, one of those instantaneous pictures in which amateurs delight; but it was clear and the faces were very distinct. One of them I recognised at once as the subject of our conversation. He wore in the picture a light tennis suit, and his handsome head was bare; but I knew the face at once, and told her so.

"That," she said, "is a picture of a Mr. Lossing, whom I knew quite well for a season in New York. Shortly before Lent he left the city, it was said, and I have heard and known nothing of him since."

"And—pardon me—it's very unusual for a young man of society to take up the work he has chosen. Do you know any reason for this?"

"None whatever. He seemed to be well supplied with money. So far as I can judge, I confess I never thought before of his fortune or lack of it." A sudden flush mantled her face, and her eyes dropped. I wondered if she was thinking of that letter to Hilda O'Neil.

"It's a delicate point," I said musingly. "If we could learn something of his situation. He is very proud. Do you think that your friend, Monsieur Voisin, might possibly know something—"

She put up her hand quickly, imperiously.

"If Mr. Lossing has chosen to conceal himself from his friends, we have no right to make his presence here known to Monsieur Voisin." She checked herself and coloured beautifully again.

"You are right," I said promptly. I had no real thought of asking Monsieur Voisin into our councils, and I had now verified the suspicions I had held from the first—fitting the guard's statement and his personality into the story her letter told—that he was the Mr. Lossing from whom she had parted so stormily in the conservatory on the night of her aunt's reception.

And now, as I consulted my watch, she leaned toward me, and suddenly threw aside her reserve.

"Can you guess," she asked eagerly, "how he came to meet those women in that way? It was a meeting, was it not?"

"No doubt of that; and it was also a scheme to entrap him."

"But—how did they do it? How did they lure him to that bridge—those two women?"

I could not suppress a smile.

"Can you not guess? It must be only a guess on my part, you know, but I fancy that in her talk with him that afternoon the brunette led him to think that you would not be unwilling to see him. I particularly noted that the woman with her was of about your height, and that she wore a hat much like the one worn by you on the day I first saw you. Now that I recall their manoeuvres of last night, I remember that the hat almost concealed her face, and that they kept in the shadow."

She did not follow up the subject, but after a moment said:

"Do—do you think I might be allowed to see him if I went with auntie to the hospital? I mean now—to-day! Could you not say that I—that we were—that we knew him?"

"It is quite important that you should do so," I declared unblushingly. "You are the only one who can identify him; and now if I am to tell Miss Ross all these things—"

"Pardon me," she broke in, "if it will not matter, I—I would rather tell Aunt Ann; at least, about Mr. Lossing."

I arose hastily. "In that case I will leave it to you willingly, and if you will come with your aunt, say at two o'clock, I will meet you at any place you may choose, and take you to the hospital; or would you rather go alone?"

"Oh, no, no!" she exclaimed. "We shall be glad of your escort. Indeed, I should fear to venture else."

CHAPTER XVIII.

"IF YOU'LL FIND ONE, I'LL FIND THE OTHER."

IT WAS through the boy Bill that we learned finally how the brunette and her companions made their escape from Wooded Island after the attack upon the guard.

I found the lad waiting upon my return from Washington Avenue, and full of the excitement of his story.

He had struck upon her trail not long after she had parted from the guard, it would seem. He had been watching upon Midway Plaisance until thoroughly weary, when he caught sight of her going east, and followed her to the Turkish bazaar as before. This time she did not retire behind the curtains, much to his relief, but she spoke a few words to the "tired-looking woman" behind the bedecked sales-table, and then left as she came, going straight to the entrance upon Midway which opened upon Madison Avenue, as on a former occasion, and from thence, as before, past Miss Jenrys' rooms, and so to her own at the café.

Here, again, Bill was obliged to loiter three long hours, and then a woman passed him so close that her face was distinctly visible, and entered the place. He recognised her at once as the woman of the "tired" face, though she was now dressed quite smartly and with no remnant of the Oriental in her costume. This

I gathered from his description of her attire, which, while it failed to give things their proper names as set down in the books of fashion, was sufficiently vivid, and enabled me to easily recognise the person who had aided the little brunette by impersonating Miss Jenrys the night before. She had entered the cafe and disappeared again through a side-door, to return, before long, in company with the brunette. They had then partaken of a hearty meal at one of the cafe tables, and had entered the Fair grounds at dusk.

"I didn't have no trouble a trackin' 'em, though I had been dreadin' a reg'lar bo-peep dance, seein' how late 'twas gettin'. But they jest sa-auntered along, quite slow, only I noticed they was always careful not to git into no strong lights; they kept on the shady side of things, 'specially the tallest one with the big cow-boy hat. So I jest monkeyed round till I see 'em start to go round the 'Lectricity B'ildin'. Then I jest slipped over between the 'L'ectric an' Mines, ye know, and come ahead of 'em jest as they turned to'rds the bridges. I tell ye," he declared with enthusiasm in a bad cause, "they couldn't 'a' struck a better place 'an that there second bridge! First, there's the t'other bridge, and that little island on one side, and most everybody goin' round the Mines on t'other side, 'cause 'twas best lighted; then there was them little bushy islands, an' all that lagoon on the west of 'em; an' on the east not a speck of light, 'cept a few clean acrost to the Lib'ral Arts shop, and most all them little lamps on the island gone out. I tell ye, Mr. Masters, I felt sort o' glad when I seen ye come acrost an' hide in the bushes."

"Oh, you saw me, did you?" I said, to hasten him on.

"I should say! I was a-layin' flat 'longside of them little shrubs on the other side the path, right where you turned off."

"Well, go on, Bill."

"Wal, sir, I was so busy watchin' them women that I didn't notice nothin' else 'cept you an' the guard—of course I thought he was tendin' to his biz. When they stopped to talk on the bridge, I begun to crawl along closte to the bridge, an' then—you know how it was all comin' so suddin? When I see the feller go over, an' seen you start to'rds the water, I jest took after the others. Well, sir, 'twas too slick the way they managed. Right alongside them willers there was one o' them little skiffs that's stuck round the island for show, or one jest like 'em. It lay jest where that little woody strip 'ud come right 'tween the island and the other side, an' 'twas all dark there. Wal, they all run that way crost the grass, an' me after 'em, close as 'twas safe to git. Two of 'em, the tall woman an' one of the men, got into the skiff, an' the other two struck off north, keepin' on the grass an' under the shade. I follered after 'em; they went pretty fast, too, till they come most to them Hoodoo tea-shops, you know; we hadn't met a soul so far, but it was lighter there, and I see there was a guard comin' to'rds 'em, an' what d' ye s'pose they did?"

"Oh, go on, Billy!"

"Wal, I had got pretty closte, and I seen them whisperin' together, an' then it seemed to me that they wasn't so far away as they had been a minit before. Then flash came a fizz match, an' sure enough there they was, facin' to'rds me, an' the very way they'd come, an holdin' the match to the ground. Jest then the guard come up, an' they told him they or she had dropped their purse, an' she was lookin' for it; an' when he asked when, she said, 'Oh, an hour ago, when they walked across the island to see the Hor—horty—"

"Horticultural?"

"—'Tyculchural place lighted; an' the guard said he feared they wouldn't find it, an' went on tellin' them they'd better hurry out; an' then he went back the way they'd come, crost the bridge an' all, an' every little way they'd light a match, an' course I got so close I heard her say, 'It must 'a' been when I fell down.' I thought somebody got a fall when they run from the bridge down into the bushes."

"Well, did you find where they went?"

"Drat the luck! No! I'd follered them out Midway, and was jest a little ways behind, when a couple o' guards stopped me, and afore I'd got out of their grip the two of 'em was out of sight."

I was not surprised to hear this. I was quite convinced that the gang had in some manner secured a safe and secret lurking-place in the Plaisance. Still, somehow, I had hoped for something more from Billy's report, and felt somewhat disappointed. But I had yet to learn its true value.

During my absence there had come a message from the bureau asking our presence there. It was the Lausch robbery that "required our presence," so the message read, and Dave had returned an answer promising our presence at the earliest moment of leisure.

We did not feel so deeply interested in the Lausch robbery then as in some other matters, but when we had dismissed our boy shadower we went at once to the bureau.

There was considerable excitement at the office, and with good reason. Some of Monsieur Lausch's jewels had been returned, and in a most novel manner.

Early in the morning a guard had appeared with the treasure in his hand, and a singular story upon his lips.

Last night, he had said, while crossing the north-east end of the Wooded Island, at quite a late hour, he had encountered a man and woman searching for a lost purse. They were quite certain it had been lost on the island, and he being then on duty and "unable to delay," told them that he would search for it next day, and passed on. Early in the morning he had entered upon the search at the place where he had met the two, and, finding no trace of the lost purse, had turned his search into a stroll about the island. He was quite familiar with the place, having done guard duty there, and going close to the water's edge, at a point where a favourite view was to be had, he observed that one of the skiffs that were moored here and there about the island was gone. Going closer, he saw that it had been roughly torn from its moorings, and the soft soil showed that several people had left traces of their presence. It was in stooping closer, to look at these footprints, that he had noticed a bit of string trailing across the grass just beyond; and taking hold of this, he found a weight upon it, which proved to be a little chamois-skin bag containing some uncut gems. He had at once reported this find to his superior officer, being an honest guard, and was ordered to come with it to the bureau.

There was no room for doubt or mistake. The chamois bag contained a portion of the jewels stolen from the pavilion of Monsieur Lausch. There were some half-dozen of the dewdrop sparklers taken with the silver-leaf tray, one large topaz and two of the smaller ones, and there were also two solitaire rings which were not of the Lausch collection.

The bag containing these had been securely tied to a stout cord, nearly a yard in length, and fastened, doubtless, about the body of some person so securely that the double sailor-knot remained—a very hard knot indeed; but, alas for human calculations! something, it was evident, having a fine keen edge, had come in contact with this cord, and had cut it smoothly in two.

As Dave Brainerd and I saw these things, the same thought entered both our minds, and we exchanged one swift glance of mutual meaning, after which we stood and heard Monsieur Lausch ejaculate, and wonder, and question the officers, discuss, and theorize, and prophesy, ourselves saying little, and eager to be away from this place, that we might take counsel together concerning this new thing.

Singularly enough, no one seemed to think of connecting this find with the attack upon the guard at the bridge, and, finally, they decided to advertise the gems, as if they were still in the hands of the finder, who only awaited a reward to yield them up; and, as little more could be done, Dave and myself withdrew from the council, where we had been little more than lookers-on.

As we were taking our leave, the mail was brought in by a messenger, and we were called back from the outer office to hear a letter read. It was from an up-town jewellery house—at least, it bore the card of the house—and it reported that an emerald, "large, fine, and of great value," had been purchased by the head of the firm, under somewhat suspicious circumstances, and from a woman. Further information and a description of the woman, the letter stated, might be had by addressing, or appointing a meeting with, the writer.

And now my interest suddenly awoke, and to such good purpose that I managed to be chosen as the person to go to the city and interview the writer, perhaps also the purchaser of the jewel. And this accomplished, Brainerd and I withdrew in haste.

There was no doubt in our minds, the story told by the guard fitted too well in Billy's tale to admit of doubt. The bag of stolen jewels had been lost by the little brunette, and Dave was fully of my mind.

"I can't see how it was done," he said, as we discussed the matter later. "But it's plain enough that she had missed the bag, and that they were searching for it when the guard came up. Of course she wouldn't say that she had lost a bag of jewels."

"Hardly," I replied. "As for the how, I can very well see how that string might have been severed. You know my opinions about this brunette. A concealed knife may have done the mischief, or one of those steels that help to give ladies a slender waist, broken perhaps by the vigorous running, may have cut the string; it would only require a little rubbing to do the thing. I tell you, Dave, it looks as if we would have a full account to settle with this individual, and I begin to feel the ground under my feet. I'd like to know who the men were who threw the guard over the bridge, though."

"Don't you think Greenback Bob capable of it?"

"Quite."

"And—Delbras?"

"Capable enough, but—he was not in it."

"Are you sure, Carl?"

"I mean to be, shortly," I replied. "Dave, old man, don't ask me any questions yet as to how it's to be done, but I believe that before this World's Fair closes you and I will have gotten Delbras and Bob out of mischief's way, settled the brunette problem, and thrown light on the diamond robbery."

"And how about that lost young Englishman, Sir Carroll Rae, and missing Gerald Trent?"

I turned and faced him. "Old man," I said, "if you'll find one, I'll find the other."

CHAPTER XIX.

"STRANGE! MISTAKEN! HEARTLESS!"

I WAS not disappointed in my interview with the up-town jeweller, who, being as real as the World's Fair itself, must not be named.

In order to identify the jewel offered by the strange woman, I took Monsieur Lausch with me, and he at once declared the description of the emerald to correspond precisely with the one stolen from him, and when I had listened to the description of the woman who had offered the gem, I was quite as confident that this person was the brunette and no other.

True, she had assumed a foreign accent and had laid aside her rather jaunty dress for a more sober and foreign-looking attire; she had made herself up, it fact, as a German woman, well dressed after the fashion of the German bourgeois; but she had added nothing to her face save a pair of gold-framed spectacles; and while I kept my knowledge to myself, I felt none the less sure that I had another link ready for the chain I was trying to forge for this troublesome brunette, who was so busy casting her shadows across my path and disarranging my plans.

The writer of the anonymous letter, for such it was, turned out to be a practical jeweller in the employ of a certain jewel merchant, and I never knew whether he had made his employer's purchase known to us for the sake of the reward, or to gratify some personal spite or sense of injury. Whichever it may have been, it concerned us little. We gave him our word not to use his name in approaching his employer, and our promise of a suitable reward should we find his story of use upon further investigation, and then we sought the purchaser of the jewel.

With him we dealt very cavalierly. We knew, no matter how, that he had purchased an emerald of value, we told him; and I further added that he had bought it from an accomplice, knowing that such an accusation would soonest bring about the desired result, as indeed it did.

A sight of the jewel sent Monsieur Lausch into raptures and rages. It was the lost emerald, the finest of them all!

That he could not at once carry away the gem somewhat modified the rapture, but we came away quite satisfied on the whole, he that the emerald would soon be restored to him, and I that I at last knew how to deal with the brunette—always provided I should find her again after the events of the day and night previous.

* * * * *

On the second day after his plunge into the lagoon I took Miss Jenrys and her aunt to see the injured guard, who was booked at the hospital as "Carr."

The blow upon the head had resulted first in unconsciousness, and later in a mild form of delirium. I had made a preparatory visit to the hospital, and was able to tell Miss Jenrys that the patient would not recognise her or any of us.

I thought that she seemed almost relieved at this intelligence, especially after I had assured her that the surgeon in charge had assured me that the delirium was much to be preferred as a less dangerous symptom than the lethargy of the first twenty-four hours.

"Mr. Masters," she had said to me on our way to the hospital, "there is one thing which I overlooked in telling you what I could about—Mr. Lossing. I—I trust you have not told them at the hospital, or anywhere, that he is not what he has represented himself."

I hastened to assure her that this secret rested still between us two, and she drew a quick breath of relief.

"If he should die," I added, watching furtively the sudden

paling of her fair cheek, "it would become my duty and yours to tell the truth, all of it. As he seems likely to recover, we may safely let the disclosure rest with him."

"I am glad!" she said. "So long as he chooses to be—Mr. Carr, I cannot of course claim his acquaintance. You—you are sure he will not know me?"

"Quite sure," I replied; and she said no more until we had reached the hospital.

We were asked to wait for a few moments in the outer office or reception room. The doctor was occupied for the moment, the attendant said, but an instant later the same attendant beckoned me outside.

"Come this way a moment," he whispered. "The doctor wishes to speak with you."

I murmured an excuse to the ladies, and went to the doctor in his little private room near by.

"When you were here," he began, putting out his hand to me, "I was preoccupied and you were in haste. There is something concerning our patient that you, as his friend, must know. By the way, has he any nearer friends than yourself at hand?"

"I believe not," I replied briefly. "I hope he is not worse, doctor?"

"No, not that, though he's bad enough. But you remember the sailors who came with you said that he had struck against the boat in falling, and we decided, rather hastily, that this was the cause of the wound and swelling. In fact, it was the swelling which misled us. We could not examine closely until it was somewhat reduced; but this morning, after the wound was washed and cleansed for the new dressing, I found that the hurt upon the head was caused, not by contact with a blunt piece of wood, but by something hard, sharp, and somewhat uneven of surface; a stone, I should say, or a piece of old iron—a blow, in fact."

"Ah!" the sudden thought that came to me caused me to start; but after a moment I said:

"I do not doubt it. The fellows that made the attack are equal to worse things than that. I think, from what I know and guess at, the weapon may have been a sling of stones or bits of iron, tied in an old bandana."

I did not tell him that this was said to be one of Greenback Bob's favourite modes of attack, and of defence, too, when otherwise unarmed. In fact, I said nothing to further indicate my knowledge of the assailants of our patient. But I got back to the ladies at once, after thanking the doctor, telling myself that his information would make the charge against the miscreants, when captured, stronger and more serious, if that were needful.

When Miss Jenrys stood by the cot where the injured man lay, pallid and weak, with great dark lines beneath his eyes and his head swathed in bandages, I saw her start and shiver, and the slight colour in an already unusually pale face fade out, leaving her cheek as white as that upon the pillow. The small hand clenched itself until the dainty glove was drawn to the point of bursting; the lips trembled, and the tears stood in the sweet eyes. She turned to the physician, and drew back a little as the head upon the pillow moved restlessly.

"I—I have not seen him for some time. Do—do you think it could possibly startle him—if—if he should recognise me?"

"If it were possible, which, I fear, it is not—now—there is nothing that would benefit him so much."

She went close to the cot then, and, bending down, looked into the restless blue eyes.

"How do you do?" she said clearly.

The restless eyes were still for a moment; then the head upon the pillow moved as if essaying a bow, and the right hand was feebly lifted.

She took his hand as if in greeting, and said again, speaking softly and clearly:

"Won't you go and speak with my Aunt Charlotte?"

A startled look came into the eyes; a look of distress crossed the face. He made a feeble gesture with the right hand; a great sigh escaped his lips, and then they parted.

"Strange," they muttered feebly, "cruel—mistaken—heartless!" His hand dropped heavily, and, quick as thought, Miss Jenrys lifted her head and drew back, her face one rosy glow from temples to chin; and now the sweet Quakeress interposed with womanly tact:

"He does not know thee, dear; and perhaps our presence may disturb him, in this weakened state." She bent over the sick man for a moment, scanned the pale, handsome features closely, gently put back a stray lock of hair that had escaped from beneath the bandage and lay across the white full temple. Then she turned to the doctor:

"In the absence of nearer friends, doctor, we will stand in their stead. Will you give him your best care and let nothing be lacking? When we can serve him in any manner, thee will inform us through Mr. Masters, I trust; and, with your permission, I will call to ask after him each day until he is better."

Sweet soul! How plain to me was the whole tender little episode! I could imagine June Jenrys telling the story of her rupture with young Lossing as frankly as she had written it to her friend Hilda O'Neil, and more explicitly, with fuller detail. I could fancy the sweet sympathy and tender admonitions of the elder woman; and here, before me, was the visible proof of how she had interpreted the heart of the girl, at once so proud, so honest, and so fearless in an emergency like this.

Had the sweet little Quakeress come to the bedside of this suffering young stranger because he was a fellow being, friendless, alone, and in need of help and kindly care, or had she come because she believed that June Jenrys possessed a heart whose monitions might be trusted, and that the man she had singled out from among many as the one man in the world must be a man indeed?

Be this as it would, and whatever the frame of mind in which she approached that white cot at her niece's side, I knew, by the lingering touch upon the pale forehead, the deft, gentle, and quite unconscious smoothing of the white counterpane across his breast, that the pale, unknowing face had won its way, and that what she took away from that hospital ward was not the tenderly carried burden of another's interest and another's anxiety, but a personal interest and a personal liking that could be trusted to sustain itself and grow apace in that tender woman's heart.

We were a very silent party as we came away from the hospital. June Jenrys looked as if the word "heartless" were yet sounding in her ears. I was assuring myself that it was best not to speak of what the surgeon had told me, and the little Quakeress was evidently quite lost to herself in her thoughts of, and for, others. As I took my leave of them, Miss Ross put out her hand, and, after thanking me for my escort, said:

"I will not trouble thee to accompany me to-morrow; I know the way perfectly, and can go very well by myself. Indeed I prefer to do so. I shall not even let June here accompany me—at first."

CHAPTER XX.

"WE MUST UNDERSTAND EACH OTHER."

THE NEXT MORNING brought a telegram from Boston, in reply to my wire asking instructions about rooms on Madison Avenue. It read:

"Hold rooms until we come. Short delay. Unavoidable.

"Trent."

The second day after our visit to the hospital the photograph of Gerald Trent was received by Miss Jenrys, and at once turned over to me, I, in my turn, putting it into the hands of an expert "artist," with orders to turn out several dozen copies as rapidly as possible.

These I meant to distribute freely among specials, policemen, the Columbian Guards at the Fair City; and others were to be furnished the chief of police for use about the city proper, for I meant to have a thorough search made in the hotels, boarding places, furnished rooms, and in all the saloons and other haunts of vice and crime, wherever an officer, armed with one of these pictures and offering a princely reward, could penetrate.

On the morning of the third day another telegram came. This read:

"Still delayed because of illness. Hold rooms.

"Trent."

Accompanying the photograph had come a distracted letter from poor Hilda O'Neil, in which she had described Mrs. Trent, the mother of the missing young man, as almost broken down by the shock and suspense; and we readily guessed that her illness was the cause of the delay.

Twenty-four hours after receipt of this last message came another:

"Mrs. T. too ill to travel. Doctor forbids my leaving. Give up rooms. For God's sake work. Don't spare money. Letter follows.

"Trent."

In addition to these, every day brought across the wires, from Hilda O'Neil to her friend, the pitiful little question, "Any news?" and took back the only possible reply, "Not yet."

And then came this letter from the father of Gerald Trent:

"DEAR SIR," it began,

"I thank you heartily for your kind straightforward letter, and while I see and realize the many obstacles in the way of your search, I yet hope—I must hope—for your ultimate success; first, because Miss Jenrys' letter, so full of confidence in you, has inspired me with the same confidence; and, second, because to abandon hope would be worse than death. The prompt way in which you have taken up this search, at Miss Jenrys' request, has earned my sincerest gratitude. Although I had ordered the search begun through our chief of police here, yours was the first word of hope or encouragement I have received, although I have since heard from your city police.

"My wife lies in a condition bordering upon insanity, and much as I long to be where I can, at least, be cognizant of every step in the search for my son, as it is taken, my duty to that son's mother holds me at her bedside. For this reason we must all remain here, and I implore you to work! Leave no stone unturned! Employ more men; draw upon me for any sum you may require; offer any reward you may see fit; do what you will; only find my son, and save his mother from insanity and his father from a broken heart! Above all keep me informed, I beg of you. Remember all our moments here are moments of suspense."

The name at the end was written in an uneven, diminishing scrawl, as if the letter had taxed the strength of the writer almost beyond endurance, and I heaved a sigh of earnest sympathy for the father, now doubly afflicted.

It was impossible now to do more than was being done from day to day, but every morning I gave an ungrudged fifteen minutes to the writing of a letter, in which I tried to say each day some new word of hope and to describe some new feature of our search, that he might feel that we were indeed leaving no stone unturned.

Meantime, from the moment when our brunette vanished from Master Billy in the Plaisance, no trace of her could be found by the lad or by ourselves.

For a number of days Dave and I gave ourselves to an untiring search, by day and night. We haunted the café where she had found lodgings, but we did not enter, for we did not wish to give the alarm to a young person already sufficiently shy, and we spent much time in Midway and upon Stony Island Avenue, near the places where the Camps had seen Smug, and the saloon wherein he had disappeared one day.

That the brunette had not entered the café since the night of the assault upon the guard, we soon assured ourselves. But we did not relax our vigilance, and for many days the beautiful White City was, to us, little more than a perplexing labyrinth in which we searched ceaselessly and knew little rest, stopping only to let another take up our seemingly fruitless search.

It was not often now that we sought our rest together or at the same time, but one night, after a week's fruitless seeking, I came to our door at a late hour to find Dave there before me, and not yet asleep. He began to talk while watching me lay aside the rather uninteresting disguise I had worn all day.

"Carl, wake up that imagination factory of yours and tell me, or make a guess at least, why we don't run upon Greenback Bob, Delbras, or even Smug, to say nothing of that invisible pedestal-climber of yours, any more?"

"Easy enough," I replied wearily. "They're sticking close to business, and they don't show, at least by day, in the grounds any more. If they're here at all, they are lying perdu in Cairo Street or in some of the Turkish quarters, smoking hasheesh, perhaps, or flirting with the Nautch dancers, and all disguised in turban, fez, or perhaps a Chinese pigtail."

"Do you believe it?"

"I certainly do."

"Jove! I wonder how they managed to get into those foreign holy of holies."

"Backsheesh," I answered tartly.

"Look here, Carl!" Dave jerked himself erect in the middle of his bed. "Suppose you wanted to get in with those people, how would you do it?"

"Dave," I replied, "why weren't you born with just a little

bump of what you mistakenly call imagination? I'll show you tomorrow how to do the thing."

"How?" Dave stubbornly insisted.

"Well, if I must talk all night, suppose in the morning we go to Cairo, and find our way to some one in some small degree an authority—some one who can talk a little English, and most of them can. I might offer my man a cigar, and praise his show a bit, and then tell him how I want to tell the world all about him; how I want to see how they live, not so briefly, you understand. The circumlocution office is as much in vogue in the Orient as, according to our mutual friend Dickens, it is in old England. Well, when he fully understands that I admire their life and manners, and want to live it as well as write it, I begin to bid. They're here for money, and they won't let any pass them—see?"

"Old man!" cried Dave, smiting his knee with vigour, "I'm going to try it on!"

* * * * *

It was seven days before our invalid—as we now by mutual consent called the still nameless guard—recovered his senses fully. There had been two or three days of the stupor, and then a brief season of active delirium; and at this stage the surgeon shook his head and looked very serious; and the little Quakeress, who, true to her first intention, came alone, carried away with her a face more serious still.

"She looks," said the surgeon to me, "as much shocked as if he were one of her own people."

"She has a tender heart," I replied, "and—he is quite well known, I believe, to others of her family."

"To one, assuredly," he said, with a dry smile and a quick glance; and I knew that June Jenrys' interest in the insensible guard had been as plain to this worldly-wise surgeon as to me.

Remembering this brief dialogue, I was not surprised, when I made my brief call in Washington Avenue, to note an added shade of seriousness on the fair face that, since the disappearance of Gerald Trent—unknown, but the friend of her friend—had been growing graver day by day, so that the charms of the great Fair had palled upon her, and she had made her daily visits in a subdued and preoccupied mood, and shortened them willingly, to return at an early hour with the more easily fatigued little Quakeress.

On the morning of the eighth day I called early, sent by the surgeon with a message to Miss Ross.

"She asked me to send her word the first moment when I found our patient sane enough and strong enough to receive a short call, and to listen for a few moments, not to talk, 'that was not needed,' she said," he added with one of his quiet smiles, "and when I told her that when he came to himself the sight of some friend for whom he cared would help him more than medicine, and asked her if he had any such, she said that she could at least tell him a bit of pleasant news, and asked me to send her word at once."

I was very willing to take the message, and when it was delivered the little Quakeress thanked me in her own quaint sweet manner, and a few moments later, while I was talking with Miss Jenrys and giving her some details of our search for a clue to young Trent's disappearance, she excused herself quietly and left us without once glancing toward her niece.

When I visited the hospital in the afternoon, the doctor said:

"Your little Quakeress is certainly a sorceress as well. She came very soon after you left us yesterday, and she did not stay long. I had forbidden my patient to talk, and I heard every word she said. It was a mere nothing, but she has almost cured him."

"If it was so simple," I said, half ashamed of my curiosity; yet having a very good motive for it, "may I not hear the words that so charmed and healed him?"

"As nearly as I can repeat them, you may. I had introduced her, as she bade me, and told him that she had called to see him every day, and I knew, from the look in those open blue eyes of his, that she was an utter stranger, and that even her name was unknown to him. He was pleased though, and small wonder, at sight of the dainty, white-haired, sweet-voiced little lady; and when she took his hand in hers and, holding it between both her own, said, in her pretty Quaker fashion: 'I am very glad and thankful to see thee so much better, and my niece June will be also—I mean Miss Jenrys, who, hearing of thy adventure and injuries, came at once to see if it were really the friend she thought she recognised in the description. My niece's friends are mine, and so I have assumed an old woman's privilege and paid thee a visit daily, and now that thee seems much better I will, with thy permission, bring her with me when I come again.'" The doctor stopped short and smiled.

"Was that all?" I asked, smiling also. "What did he say?"

"Well, sir, for a moment I thought the fellow was going to faint, but it was a pleasurable shock, and he made a feeble clutch at her hand, and his face was one beam of gratitude as he looked in hers and whispered, while he clung to her hand, 'To-morrow.' Then of course she turned to me, and I, pretending to have been quite unobservant, ordered her away, and made their next visit contingent upon his good behaviour during the next twenty-four hours."

I saw that the time had now come when the patient and I must understand each other better, and I began by taking the doctor a little into my confidence, telling him a little of what I knew and a part of what I guessed at or suspected.

"I want now to enlighten him a little concerning this attack upon him, doctor," I concluded, "and if I don't make him talk–"

"Oh, see him by all means. There's nothing worse for the sick than suspense. I begin to understand matters. Since his return to consciousness he has seemed singularly apathetic, but let me tell you one thing: there were two nights—he was always wildest at night—when he talked incessantly about that meeting at the bridge, and he fully believes now that she, whoever that may be, was there. His first question asked, after being told of his mishap, was this: 'Was anyone else attacked or injured besides myself that night at the bridge?' and when I answered no, he seemed relieved of a great anxiety."

I had not seen him since the full return of his senses, and he seemed very glad to see me. When the doctor had warned him against much conversation, and had left us, I drew my chair close beside his cot, so that I could look into his face and he in mine.

"My friend," I began, "I am doctor enough to know that a mind at ease is a great help toward recovery, and I am going to set your mind at ease upon some points at least. Mind," I added, smiling in spite of myself, "I do not say your heart. Now, to do this I may need to put a few questions; and to obey the doctor and at the same time come to an understanding with you, I will make my questions direct, and you can answer them by a nod."

At this he nodded and smiled.

"I dare say," I went on, "you wonder how and why you were treated to that sudden ducking"

Again he nodded; this time quite soberly.

"I am going to enlighten you, in a measure, and I am obliged, in order to do so, to take you into my confidence, to some extent, and I must begin with the adventure of the bag—Miss Jenrys' bag, you know."

Now I was approaching a delicate topic, and I knew it very well. I had not, in so many words, asked permission of Miss Jenrys to use her name in relating my story, but I had said to her during one of the several calls I had made in Washington Avenue, during the week that had just passed:

"When our friend is able to listen, Miss Jenrys, I must tell him, I think, how he came to be assaulted upon the bridge, as I understand it, if only to prepare and warn him against future attacks; and, to make my story clear to him or even reasonable, I shall need to enter somewhat, in fact considerably, into detail. I can hardly make him realize that he has a dangerous enemy else."

I saw by the flush upon her face and a sudden nervous movement, that she understood fully what this would involve, and for a moment I feared that she was about to forbid me. But the start and blush were quickly controlled, and she pressed her lips together and drew herself erect, and there was only the slightest tremor in her voice when she said, slowly:

"You are right; he ought to know," and turned at once to another subject.

Something in the look the young fellow turned upon me when I spoke of the episode of the bag reminded me of her face as she gave that tacit consent; there was the same mingling of pride and eagerness, reticence and suspense, and I plunged at once into my story, recalling briefly the encounter between Miss Jenrys and the Turks, the finding of the bag, my meeting with him, and the appearance of the little brunette, and here I put a question.

"I want to ask you," I said, "and I have a good reason for asking, as you will see later, why, when that tricky brunette turned her back upon you so pertly after making her demand for the bag— why you at once left us both and without another word? Wait," as he seemed making an effort to reply. "Let me put the question direct. Did you not leave us because you thought that person was really a friend of Miss Jenrys, and had, perhaps, been warned not to speak too freely in your hearing?"

The blood flew to his pale cheeks, and there was a momentary flash of haughtiness in his fine eyes, but as they met my own, this look faded from them and he murmured "Yes."

"Thank you," I said. "And now, before going further, let me tell you that I am violating no confidence; it is not for me to explain more fully here than this: The young lady of whom I am about to speak knows that I am telling you these things. I am not speaking against her will."

And now his eyes dropped as he said faintly, "Thank you."

I next told him in as matter-of-fact a manner as possible how I examined the bag, and how, when all other hope of a clue to the owner failed, I read Miss Jenrys' letters; how, when the first letter failed to give me the owner's address, I read the second in full.

"And now," I said to him, "before I go further, let me remind you once more that I speak by permission, and add, on my own behalf, that, even thus authorized, I would not utter what I am about to say if I did not believe that by so doing I can set right a wrong, a worse wrong done to you than that of attempting your life—a blow at your honour, in fact."

He started, and then, as if remembering his condition, said with wonderful self restraint, "Go on, please."

And I did go on. Before I paused again I had told him almost word for word, as it was implanted upon my memory, the story June Jenrys had written to her friend, the story of that ante-Lenten party—just the fact, omitting her expressions of preference. I told the story as I would have told it of a dear sister whose maidenly pride was precious to me; told how she had gone, at his request, to speak with him in the conservatory, and how, there, she had heard, herself unseen, those flippant, unmanly words, so unlike him, yet from the lips of someone addressed by his name.

For a long moment after I had ceased speaking he lay there so moveless, with his hands tightly clenched and his eyes fixed upon empty space, that I almost feared he had fainted; then he turned his face toward me and spoke in stronger tones than I had supposed him capable of using.

"That letter—did it name that man?"

"What man?" I had purposely omitted the name of the man who had come so opportunely to lead Miss Jenrys away after she had heard the heartless speech from behind the ferns in the conservatory, and while I asked the question I knew to whom he referred.

"The man who came so opportunely after the—after I had gone."

I hesitated. Here was a complication, perhaps, for I had hoped he would not put this question yet, but I could not draw back now, or what I had meant should result in good to two persons, at least, might cause further misunderstanding and render the last state worse than the first. So, after a moment, I answered:

"Yes. It named the man."

"Who? tell me!" This was not a request, it was a command; and he was off his pillow, resting upon his elbow, and eyeing me keenly.

I got up and bent over him.

"I'll tell you fast enough," I said grimly. "And it's evident you are not a dead man yet; but get back on your pillow—he's here in this very White City, and if you want to take care of your own you'd better not undo the doctor's good work. Lie down!"

He dropped back weakly, and the fire died out of his face; he was deathly pale, but his white lips framed the word, "Who?"

"Monsieur Maurice Voisin," I said.

"The dastard!"

"Quite so," I agreed. "Did you know he was here?"

"Yes." He lay silent a moment, then: "I see! He saw it was—he—"

I held up my hand. "If you talk any more I shall go; and I have more to say to you. I want you to get well, and there's someone else who is even more anxious than I am. But you have made one mistake, I think. You think that Voisin attacked you because you were about to meet Miss Jenrys, do you not?"

He stared, but did not answer.

"When the brunette met you in the afternoon of that day, she gave you some reason for believing that Miss J. desired to see you, and that if you joined them that night it would please her."

I paused, but again he was mute.

"My friend," I went on, "I believe that Love, besides being himself blind, is capable of blinding and befooling the wits of the wisest. That brunette is an impostor. As for knowing Miss Jenrys, she does, if following her up and down, and trying to force an acquaintance, is knowing her. Here is the truth: That brunette, as we all call her, for want of any other appellation, is one of a trio, or perhaps a quartet, of adventurers, confidence men, counterfeiters, what you will, so that it is evil. They are here for mischief, and they began at once, through this brunette decoy, to entrap Miss Jenrys, for what purpose I am just beginning to learn. It seems, too, that they have designs upon you, for they decoyed you out the other night, this brunette and one of their woman companions dressed to resemble Miss J., and when they had you upon the bridge and you thought you were about to meet Miss J., two men who had been lying in wait for you behind a buttress sprang upon you, and while one thrust you over, the other dealt you a blow which, an inch lower, would have killed you—so the doctor has said."

All the life had gone out of his face as I ceased speaking. His lips trembled. "Then—it was not she?" he said brokenly.

"My dear fellow," I put my hand upon his, "listen: Until the next morning she did not know you were here, but after reading that letter I could not help believing that you were the man of whom she wrote, and I went to her, told her of my meeting with you, described you, and saw at once that she recognised you. Then I told her how you had been attacked, and the next morning I brought her and her aunt to see you. I don't want to flatter you, and I can't betray a lady; but while it was not she that night upon the bridge—and in your own sober senses and free of Cupid's blindness you would be among the first to know that it could not be she—she is now very near, and she is only waiting to be told that she may come to see, with her own eyes, that you are better, and that you will be glad to see her."

"Glad!" How much the one word said, but in a moment he looked up. "But—these men—how do you know—"

"About the attack? I saw it. I had been following, watching you and them."

He put his hand to his head as if bewildered.

"But, my God! those men! If they are following her—and myself—and if it is not—not Voisin—" He lifted his hand suddenly. "I tell you, man, it is Voisin!"

As his hand dropped, the doctor came up and looked keenly from one to the other. I got up quickly.

"Doctor," I said, "I fear he has talked too much; but if you will let me talk to him a little longer—tell him something that will lift a weight from his mind, once he understands it, I am sure he will promise not to talk; and I will be brief."

The doctor looked at his watch. "Go on," he said; "I give you fifteen minutes."

The guard heaved a long sigh of relief, and I seated myself again beside his cot.

"Now," I said, "I, on my part at least, am going to be perfectly frank with you. We must understand and aid each other."

Against Odds

CHAPTER XXI.

"LET ME LAUGH!"

THERE WERE moments, yes, even hours, during the week while our guard lay upon his hospital cot unconscious or delirious, when I blamed myself severely for my lack of confidence or frankness that afternoon of his encounter with the brunette; times when I felt that he should have been told at least what I believed was the truth concerning her.

Yet, how was I to have guessed her intent concerning him?

Knowing her pursuit of Miss Jenrys, I felt so sure that she was only using him as a means for obtaining information about that young lady, and that this interview was only the beginning of what was meant to become an acquaintance more or less confidential.

As a result of my reticence, the young fellow had barely escaped with his life; even now, so the doctor said, fever or inflammation might put it in jeopardy.

Well, it was not my only blunder, I thought, looking back, with a grim smile, to my first absurd exploit. But I would try very hard to make it my last; at least, where "the gang," as Dave was wont to call Delbras and Company, was concerned. And when thinking of "the gang," I could not but note how both Dave and myself had reversed our first order in naming them, and now spoke, invariably, not of "Greenback Bob and the rest," but of "Delbras and Company." Somehow, Delbras seemed to have taken the foremost place in our thoughts, as I fully believed he was foremost in all the plots, plans and undertakings of the mysterious and elusive three. And yet he was the one out of the gang against whom we had no actual case.

We could see the hand of Greenback Bob in the counterfeit two dollar greenbacks which had started into circulation so briskly, and then so suddenly dropped out of sight. And his work was also visible in that attack upon the guard; for who, according to the police records, could handle a "slung-shot" as could Bob? And that the guard's wound was the work of a sling, we—the surgeon and myself—quite believed.

As for the brunette, we might begin with her little confidence game, in which she did not secure Miss Jenrys' bag; charge her with the sale of the stolen emerald, and bring home to her the loss of the "dew-drops" and other contents of the chamois-bag lost in her flight across Wooded Island—when we found her again.

But Delbras! We might believe him to be the originator of, and prime mover in, the Lausch diamond robbery, but the only shadow of corroboration was our belief—based upon the fact of Dave's having seen the three together—that they were "partners," and that Delbras was credited with being an expert diamond thief. Not a promising outlook, I sometimes said to Dave, in my moments of discouragement, which my practical friend declared were somehow always synonymous with my moments of hunger.

But to return to our guard and his interests. During the fifteen minutes kindly granted by the doctor, and which somehow ran into half an hour before he came and ordered me away, I contrived to establish between myself and the invalid a very sufficient understanding, and I left him feeling that, so far as lay in my power, he was warned against his enemies, and knew them, at least as well as I did.

Upon one question, however, we differed. As I was about to take leave, I said: "There is one thing that I foresee, and that is a renewal of your social relations with Miss Jenrys and a beginning of the same with her aunt. I can see reasons why it might be better—might simplify matters—if you kept up at least an outside appearance of coolness. You understand?"

"Yes." He was silent for a little time, then: "Will this be of actual use or help to you?"

"Only as your meetings may complicate matters by making new trouble for yourself, or—possibly—her."

"Then," said he, looking me straight in the eye, "Miss Jenrys must decide the question."

As I came out from the hospital that day I came face to face with Monsieur Voisin. He paused a moment, as if in doubt, and then came quickly toward me, one hand extended, a smile upon his face. His greeting was the perfection of courtesy, and I, of course, responded in kind.

After a few remarks of the usual sort, a word regarding the weather, which was perfect, and praises of the Fair, Monsieur Voisin, who had seen me emerge from the hospital, said:

"So it is here that this great Fair cares for its sick and unfortunate? Have you been inspecting its methods, may I ask?"

There are times when the truth is best; and I thought I knew my man, so I replied smilingly:

"A hospital is not in itself charming. I have been to call upon a friend."

"That, indeed! A patient, I suppose?"

"A patient, yes." I felt sure that he was not inclined to tarry, nor in truth was I; but I let him take the initiative, and after a few more airy, courteous words he murmured something about an appointment, and went his way.

When he was quite out of sight I went back to the guard near the door of the hospital, who had grown to know me quite well.

"Did you notice the man who just spoke with me?" I asked him.

"Yes, sir."

"Ever see him before?"

"I have that. A few days ago he stopped and asked after one of the patients—feller that fell into the lagoon the other night. Said he'd heard that a young man fell off a bridge."

"And—may I ask how you answered him?"

The guard looked at me quizzically. "Well, you see, we've been ordered not to answer questions about this case, for some reason that you may know better than I do; and so I couldn't tell him much about it, but I offered to ask for him. He wouldn't have that; said it was only a passing inquiry," and he laughed knowingly.

He had seen me when I came with the men who bore the guard upon a stretcher, and felt that he might overstep the rules with safety.

"How is the fellow, anyhow?" he asked. "They say he was one of us."

"He is one of you," I replied, "and we hope to see him about at the end of a week."

* * * * *

Precisely how Carr or Lossing—I called him "our guard" in those days, by preference—precisely how he and June Jenrys met, I learned in detail, but not until the glorious White City had faded in truth to a dream city—a lovely vivid memory; but I had imagined the scene, even before it took place, and I was glad to know that my "imagination machine," to quote Dave, had not gone far wrong.

Miss Jenrys had accepted my proffered escort that morning, and, a little to my surprise, I found that her aunt was not prepared to accompany her. For the first time that little woman gave me a glimpse of a strong foundation of that good sense that is not held in strictly orthodox leash, the sturdy independence that accepts convention as a servant but not as a mistress, that was hidden beneath that gentle, yielding manner of hers.

"My niece is not a child," she said to me, when the young lady had left us to make ready for the walk to the hospital, "and it is best that she should go alone to-day for his sake. Thee must understand?" I nodded, and she went on: "June has told me the story, all of it, I think, and there is something that should be explained; there is error, at least, somewhere. It seems strange to be talking like this to thee, but thee seems to have come so intimately into our lives of late—besides, of course, I know that—having read that letter, which June has let me read also—thee sees the position—"

"One moment," I interrupted her; "I have wanted to speak upon this subject and have hesitated. Nine young women out of ten would have deeply resented my reading of that letter."

"But the circumstances—"

"I know. Still, I might have resisted the temptation to read on after I had discovered your address, and although she grants the mitigating circumstances, still she must resent, just a little, my knowledge of its contents."

She put up her hand, with a soft little laugh.

"I shall be sure to trip myself if I attempt a polite fib, so I will admit that. At first, for a little time, June did feel quite haughty when she thought of that letter and thy knowledge of it in the same moment. But great troubles often swallow up small annoyances, thee knows; and I can assure thee that my niece now looks upon thee as a real friend, to be trusted, not quarrelled with; besides—for thee must know we have talked over this very thing—she realizes that if thee had not read that letter something unpleasant might have befallen her, something terrible; who knows? Besides, there are all these later happenings, all your help to be put in the balance in your favour. No, Mr. Masters, thee has in June Jenrys a friend, who is grateful to thee, and who believes in thee, and she is no lukewarm partisan."

She put out her slim, white hand, ringless and soft, but firm in its touch, and I grasped it and was silent for a moment; then, thanking her for her kindness and confidence, I said hastily, and in momentary expectation of seeing Miss Jenrys enter the room:

"Miss Ross, I believe you have saved me from a blunder. As you have said, your niece is a woman, and a very clever one, and

I have been near treating her like a child."

"A child, and how?"

"There is a word concerning that same letter we have been speaking of, which I have been longing to speak. It should have been said before this visit of to-day, I think; and I have near been telling it to you, when it most concerns Miss Jenrys."

She came closer, with a swift step.

"Does it—does it also concern—him?"

"Yes."

"And—ah—I must ask thee if it is to his hurt?"

"It is not."

"Then tell it to her at once, if it will make their meeting less embarrassing to either; tell it—hush!"

Almost as she spoke the door opened and June Jenrys entered the room, and never had she looked so charming. It was evident in every detail of her simple toilet that she had dressed with the purpose and the power to please and charm.

The gown was simply made, of some soft, creamy-tinted wool, that fell in long straight folds from her silken belt, and was drawn, soft and full, like the surplice of our grandmothers' day, about the shapely shoulders and across the breast; and the hat was black and broad, with curving brim and drooping plume, the same, in fact, worn by her on the now memorable day when we—the guard and I—saw her, all unconscious of the menacing Turks on Midway Plaisance. A soft, black glove with long, wrinkled wrists, and a long, slim umbrella, tightly furled, completed a charming picture of a New York girl par excellence.

As we left the house and I turned at the foot of the steps to lift my hat to Miss Ross, looking after us from the doorway, she waved her hand and sent me a significant glance, which I well understood. It meant, "Speak, and speak boldly."

When we had entered at the Fifty-seventh Street gate, and were crossing the bridge, I did speak, and boldly too, it seemed to me.

"Before we enter the hospital, Miss Jenrys," I began, "there is something which I think you ought to know. I have not spoken of it in your aunt's presence, because it is first and most your affair, to make known or to withhold for a time. Will you sit in that arbour where I first talked to yourself and Miss Ross? I see that it is unoccupied, fortunately."

She assented promptly, and when we had entered the Nebraska House arbour, and were seated side by side upon the shadiest seat, she turned toward me an expectant look, and silently waited my pleasure. Her face was grave and somewhat paler than usual, but there rested in her lovely eyes a look of fixed purpose, a clear, fine light as of some decision, made after doubt and hesitation, in which she now rested and felt strong.

She did not seem eager, as she sat beside me, only waiting, and her mind evidently was "far away ahead."

I came promptly to the point.

"What I have to say, Miss Jenrys, concerns our friend whom we are about to visit, as well as yourself." She let her lashes droop, and slightly bent her head. "And it has been in my mind," I went on, "for some time—in fact ever since I came to the conclusion that our friend was, in truth, the Mr. Lossing whom you named in the letter I was so bold as to read;" here she flushed hotly. "And here permit me to say, Miss Jenrys, that no man ever read his own mother's letter more respectfully than I perused that letter of yours, searching through it for the address of its writer. I hope you will believe me when I say that I hesitated long, and put down the letter more than once, before I ventured to give it a second glance, and that no eye save mine read or saw one word of its contents while it remained in my possession. When I met you first, and talked with you in this same spot, I wanted to say this to you, but I saw that you preferred to ignore this part of the affair—"

"I did," she interrupted, with gentle dignity, reminding me of her aunt. "I confess that at first I felt sore and sensitive about my poor letter, but that is over, Mr. Masters; you have made me again and again your debtor, even by that act, as I now see clearly. Let us not refer to that letter again."

"But I must once more at least, and I beg you to bear with me if I seem unduly meddling with your affairs; they are our friend's affairs too, and I believe he has been grievously wronged."

"Wronged?" She started, and her face flushed and paled in the same moment. "How—how?"

"I will tell you. You may not be aware how much a few written lines can sometimes convey to one in my profession, especially when written by one who speaks frankly, as friend to friend; and when I had read that portion of your letter which describes the scene in the conservatory, I seemed to see it all." I was speaking with my eyes upon the ripples of the little stream at our feet, into which, from time to time, I tossed a leaf or twig from the branches just overhead.

"When I had read that portion of the letter, Miss Jenrys," I went on, "before I had seen you or Lossing, I said to myself, 'She has been deceived—tricked!'"

"Tricked?" she whispered through pale lips, and then she drew herself erect, and awaited my next words.

"Miss Jenrys, I believe you know now whom I am about to accuse. Yesterday I had a talk with Lossing, as long as the doctor would permit, and I, on my part, took him quite into my confidence. He knows me for what I am; he knows what I am doing. I told him, after consulting you, the story of the letter—of the brunette—everything. Was I wrong?"

"No," very slowly.

"And last I told him that I believed someone had played him a dastardly trick. Shall I tell you what he said to me?"

"Yes."

"He swore that the words you heard behind the palms were never uttered by him; that he saw only you and one other in the conservatory."

She clasped her two hands in her lap, and I saw that they trembled slightly; but her voice was low and calm when she turned to me and said:

"If he tells me this, I shall believe him." And then, after a moment of silence, "How was it done?" she asked.

"Can you not imagine a rival overhearing, perhaps, the appointment in the conservatory? If he is a good mimic or a ventriloquist, say, it would be easy to utter a few words behind the palms, impersonating two people; then, as his victim approaches, he glides behind some other leafy screen, to appear before you, perhaps, a little later, smiling and secretly triumphant."

"I see!" she said, with sudden energy. "Tell me what must—what ought I to do?"

"Will you take my advice, with a strong reason behind it?"

"Yes," promptly.

"Then, say nothing, do nothing, for the present. Believe me, it will be best in the end, and an especial favour to me. I will explain more fully at another time." I got up and stood before her, watch in hand. "We are due at the hospital. Do you agree?"

"To wait?" She arose quickly. "Will it really be a favour to you?"

"It will be a great favour. It will disarrange my most cherished plans for unmasking a villain if you make a sign too soon."

"Then I will hold my peace; I will help you, even—can I?"

"Will you?"

"I will." She put out her hand.

"Thank you. I will not cause you to regret your promise. Shall we go?"

* * * * *

Lossing lay eager-eyed and impatient, watching alternately his watch and the door, when June entered, stately and charming, and came alone straight to his cot.

There were no heroics. These were not the lovers of the popular novel, who meet invariably, after long absence or a deadly quarrel, in an empty parlour at early twilight; they were young and ardent, but they were also familiar with *les convenances*, and possessed of the nineteenth-century horror of a scene.

When she paused beside him his hand was outstretched to meet hers; and if the clasp was close and long, what of that? And if, when she sank gracefully into the seat placed for her by an attendant, there was a suspicious moisture in her eyes, which she seemed to wipe away, since her back was turned to the others; and if his lip quivered slightly, for he was very weak you know, what then?

At first no word was spoken, but their eyes had met and exchanged greetings, without the aid of words.

By-and-by, with his eyes devouring her face, he said feebly:

"You—have seen—Masters?"

"Yes, he brought me here."

"And—he told—you—?"

"Everything."

He drew a long sigh of relief, and slid his hand along the counterpane toward hers.

"June," appealingly.

She put her hand in his for a moment, met his eyes for an instant, turned her own away quickly, and glanced over her shoulder; then suddenly she began to laugh softly.

"June!" reproachfully.

"Let me laugh! Oh, you poor boy! If I don't laugh, I'm afraid—I shall cry!"

CHAPTER XXII.

"THERE IS DANGER—NEAR!"

WOMEN ARE strange. This has been said before, I know, but it is doubtful if it is ever said twice with just the same meaning; and it is always true.

When Miss Jenrys learned that our guard was quite beyond the danger line, and that he might leave the hospital in a week, she promptly declared her second visit, in company with her aunt, her last, assuring him that, while one might disregard Mrs. Grundy when a friend was so ill as to be upon debatable ground, it would never do to risk her favour for a rapidly recovering convalescent. "Besides," she said with a smile that was kinder than her words, "in a few days you will begin to pay some of the visits you now owe to Aunt Ann and to me." And this he did.

When he left the hospital his physician forbade him to attempt anything more severe than a very short promenade once a day, and a little sight-seeing, if he choose to do it in a wheeled chair; for the rest, quiet and much sleep. As to his duties as guard, even the lightest of these were forbidden him for at least a fortnight.

It is hardly likely that the originators of the Fair City planned to do just that, or realized at first what they had done, but intentional or not, the White City was a paradise for lovers.

Those cosy nooks all about Wooded Island, those quiet corners about the lagoons, with seats invitingly placed; and what snug recesses, "too small for numbers, roomy for two," in the great buildings, among the pagodas, temples, pavilions and lofty inclosures, hospitably furnished by generous exhibitors; then there were half a hundred and more buildings, model dwellings, cottages, castles, villas, mansions, palaces, edifices, State and national, each with open doors, and many with cosy parlours, reception-rooms, assembly-rooms, where one or two could find quiet and seclusion in the midst of multitude; and last and best, there were the beautiful lake, the lake shore, the lagoons, the skiffs, launches, and the gondolas.

On the first day of his freedom from the hospital our guard tried his strength moderately, and took counsel with Miss Ross.

On the second day June came "half-way," as she expressed it, joining him upon the Plaza and leaving Miss Ross to my tender mercies, for he had unblushingly begged an hour of my time—which he stretched to two hours—that I might "help him entertain the ladies."

Even now I am not certain that Miss Ross was not a party to the plot by which we first found ourselves alone upon the Plaza; and a moment later saw our guard and Miss Jenrys afloat upon the Grand Basin, luxuriously established, because of the invalid, of course, in a canopied gondola, and looking as innocent as if they did not perfectly well know that their picturesque gondolier could not understand the least word of English.

We watched them until they passed under the bridge of the bears at the south end of the north canal, and when they came out into the lagoon and turned westward as if to skirt the island, I turned to my companion.

"Does she speak Italian?"

"June? No; she is a good German scholar, and loves the language. She speaks French also, and reads Spanish well; but Italian, no, I am sure not."

"Then he does!" I declared, "and he has set those fellows to paddling around the island. Miss Ross, let us go and see the cliff-dwellers," and we went.

When our two lovers were gliding slowly along the shores of the island, in the shadows of its western side, our guard turned toward June, and after a long look into the eyes which she dropped, at last said, softly and slowly:

"June—you did not rebuke me when I called you so at the hospital when I was ill; may I call you June now?"

"Yes, because now you are an invalid." There was a little smile lurking at the corners of her mouth, but he went on gravely:

"Thank you, June; and now may I begin where I should have begun that evening when you sent me from you—"

"Stop, please! I could not speak of that miserable time until you—I mean since you have approached the matter, let me ask your pardon for the insult I then offered you. I have felt all the time since those first hours that there was somehow a hideous blunder, and now my reason has been enlightened. I should not have doubted. Forgive me!"

"June, don't! How could I blame you, knowing as I now do how you were deceived? It is noble of you, but don't ask my pardon when—"

"But I want your pardon! Do you think it humiliates me to ask pardon for a wrong I have done? I am too proud not to do it, Mr. Lossing."

And so gliding along that fair waterway, isolated, yet with all the world around them, those two settled the question of questions; and then, with minds and hearts at ease, and beauty all about them, their thoughts became less serious, and she began to criticise the uniform of a guard standing at a boat-landing, with shoulders erect and a military air.

"And you, Mr. Lossing, are really one of those superb personages! and to think that I have never seen you in your panoply of war."

"Shall I resume it to-morrow?" he asked earnestly.

"For duty? You are not able."

"But when I am able? When I donned that uniform I was in search of a new experience; something to take the staleness out of life. I thought it would give me a view of this great enterprise not to be had by the cash-paying outsider. But, June, I am willing to dispense with my panoply of war, and to be a common citizen once more; shall I?"

"Do you wish to?"

"Your will in this matter is my law."

She laughed musically. "'In this matter?' I am so glad you qualified that speech. But now, seriously, let me say to you that if you choose to retain the place you have taken I shall honour you for it. What can you or any man, in time of peace, do more or better than the work of these young men? Their work can only be well done by gentlemen. Courtesy, watchfulness, care for others; help to the old, the weak, the children; guiding, informing, protecting; making this great beautiful labyrinth of wonders, that might be so puzzling, so wearisome, so dangerous, a place of comfort, of safety, of delight. My friend, when I think what a Babel this place would be without the Columbian Guard, I am proud of—your uniform."

"Then you do believe that 'a man's a man for a' that?' Thank you, June."

"I do, assuredly."

"And if I tell you that I am a poor man, with only a little money and just a newly-fledged literary knack to stand between me and the sunny side of life—what then, Princess June?"

"Don't expect to extract one grain of sympathy from me because of any tale of poverty you may tell, sir. You don't impress me as a young man who has been ill-used by the world. But that literary knack—do let me hear more about that;" and her smile changed to a look of eager interest.

"It's a short tale. About a year ago I made my first attempt as a journalist—newspaper hack would sound more modest—and I am succeeding fairly."

"Then I congratulate you. Anyone can be a millionaire, but a journalist who succeeds—he wields a power beyond price."

* * * * *

There was one thing that bade fair to grow troublesome, as I found myself giving some small portion of almost every day to the two ladies; for Miss Ross as well as her niece had made me feel that my duty as well as my pleasure lay in those daily reports or interviews, held sometimes in the dainty rooms upon the avenue, and now and then in some convenient spot within the Fair City.

At our first meeting, at the north end of the grounds, I did not consider the encounter with the Turks in her behalf a meeting, for I scarcely had a full look at her face, while she did not so much as glance at mine; but at the other I had appeared before her in *propria persona*, and my subsequent calls at the house upon the avenue had been the same. On the other hand, whenever I went about the Exposition grounds or beyond them in my capacity of "sleuth," I went in some manner of disguise.

During the first week of my acquaintance with Miss Jenrys I had encountered Monsieur Voisin twice; first upon the occasion of our introduction, and afterward at Miss Jenrys' door; and during the first week of our guard's confinement in the hospital I had narrowly escaped him twice, going to or coming from the same place. As the days went on I found that Monsieur Voisin's attentions were growing more marked, and his visits on the avenue almost constant.

I did not wish to become too well known to Monsieur Voisin, who was a keen observer, for I was posing for him as a "New York newspaper man," and so at last I was forced to tell the two ladies that some, if not all, of my calls, for a time at least, must be made at unconventional hours, and often in disguise.

And now the days, while quite uneventful, were growing more and more busy for Brainerd and myself.

The matter of the diamond robbery, after considerable discussion and some reluctance, had been turned over to a clever

Chicago expert, and to help him on, and at the same time free our hands for other matters, we gave him all the information in our possession; told him our theories and suspicions, and gave him a description of the brunette, together, of course, with an account of her transactions with the emerald, which, by the way, had been restored to Monsieur Lausch, not freely and not willingly, but because the dealer in precious stones was not daring enough to risk a threatened exposure in the newspapers.

To make the expert's way quite clear with reference to the brunette, we told him also of her pursuit of Miss Jenrys and her connection with the attack upon our guard, adding that we were fully convinced she was one of a clique, working always, whether together or separately, in unison. But we entered into no details where Delbras and his other confederates were concerned. In fact, we did not name them.

"We cannot let the Lausch business go out of our hands without letting the other party into the matter as deep as we ourselves have gone," said Dave, "and the brunette has put her finger into the pie. But there's no proof of any sort pointing toward the rest of the gang; and so, old man, before we put another fellow on the track of Delbras, Bob, Smug and Company, we will satisfy ourselves that we are not smart enough to run them down alone."

These sentiments I echoed in full; and although they were proving themselves adepts in the art of vanishing and leaving no trace behind, I felt—for reasons which I had not as yet confided even to Brainerd—more and more certain every day that we should sooner or later entrap Delbras, and through him the others.

But while we could describe the brunette to the satisfaction of the keen young fellow in whom we felt a brotherly interest and any amount of faith, we could do little more. I sent him my "shadow," Billy, and the boy went with him to the café where she had been seen to come and go, and to the places in the Plaisance where she had more than once disappeared; and having done this we could do no more, save to wish him success and to wash our hands, for a time, of the Lausch diamond robbery and the little brunette—or so we thought.

But now I had upon my mind a new case. Our guard, or Lossing, as, in imitation of Miss Jenrys and her aunt, I was learning to call him, was now becoming convalescent, and while he had not yet returned to his duties as Columbian Guard, which he had assured me he meant soon to do, he was beginning to go about by night and by day, as his strength increased, quite regardless, seemingly, of the fact that he had been attacked once, and had every reason to think the act might be repeated in some new fashion.

I had warned him of the risk he might run by going about alone at night, for I saw that when he was not in the presence of June Jenrys—as he was now sure to be, for a little time at least, every day—he was unnaturally restless.

I had learned to know him too well to suggest a companion for his evening strolls, but I kept an eye upon him, and, so long as he did not venture from the grounds, felt tolerably secure of his safety.

Much of the great inclosure was as light and as safe by night as by day, but Lossing, while recovering in the hospital, had fallen in love with the lake, so near at hand, and his first stroll by day was in this direction, as well as his first evening venture.

Out across the Government Plaza, along the shore to the brick gunboat, and on northward where the lights were faint and the risk greatest, or so it seemed to me, he went that night, and the next, and the next.

But not alone, when he took his second promenade lakeward. The boy Billy was at his heels unseen but watchful, and well knowing how to act should danger threaten.

* * * * *

In the meantime, since the night of the attack upon Lossing, the brunette, Bob, Delbras, Smug—all had vanished utterly. Neither in Midway nor elsewhere, as Turks or gentlemen of leisure, were they seen by Dave, myself, or the boy Billy.

"But they're here all right!" Dave declared, "and if we don't find a new gap in the fence somewhere soon, I don't know the gentry!"

During Lossing's confinement in the hospital, after he had begun to mend, I had brought Dave to see him, and after that he had several times looked in upon the invalid; sometimes at my request, and later for his own pleasure as well.

Dave's bluff ways had made for him a friend in our guard, and so one day, the day following that of Lossing's third lakeside promenade, I asked Dave, who had declared himself off duty for the night, to go and see him.

I had just received a letter from Boston which made me anxious to see Miss Jenrys; and as I had not called upon nor met her during the day, I decided to go to Washington Avenue that evening.

"Go early, Dave," I said, when he had assured me of his readiness to go, "and ask him to put in the evening with you. I don't like these lakeshore prowls. The fellow's a good one with his fists, but he don't seem to realize that it's treachery, a blow in the back, that he must guard against."

Dave went his way, and it being rather early for my call, I sat down to re-read Mr. Trent's letter.

It was brief and evidently penned under excitement. He had received an anonymous letter from Chicago, proposing to open negotiations for the ransom of his son, who, it declared, was at that moment a prisoner in the hands of desperate men.

"In short," Trent's letter ended, "it's an alarming letter. I write this in haste that it may reach you at once, and can only say that my daughter and Miss O'Neil, in my absence, opened and read the letter, and have written to Miss Jenrys in full. I am very anxious to know what they have written. See Miss J—— at once; it is important. I have no time for more.

"Yours hastily,

"TRENT."

As I was turning the key in the lock and about to set out at once for Washington Avenue, Brainerd came puffing up the stairs.

"He's gone!" he panted, "and I was afraid you'd be!"

"Do you mean Lossing?"

"Of course! He laid off his regimentals, one of the guards told me, and put on a swell evening suit, and away he went. Want me to follow him?"

"Yes," I answered promptly. "I can't come home with him, I fear; I must somehow see the ladies alone. You know the place, Dave, do you not? He won't stay late, you know."

I was not greatly surprised to hear of Lossing in Washington Avenue, for we knew well enough that his first evening's visit would be to Miss Jenrys. He had been three or four times taken to the gate in a rolling chair, and had walked from there to the house for a morning call; but this was his first evening outside the grounds since his recovery.

As I approached the house I saw that someone was before me, already at the threshold, and ringing the bell. I could not identify the figure, because of the two trees which stood one on each side of the stone steps before the door, the one half concealing his figure, the other the light at the corner below.

The door opened so promptly that he was admitted before I had left the pavement, and the visitor, Lossing as I supposed, passed in.

"Poor fellow," I said to myself, "I won't come upon his very heels. I'll give him a few moments, at least, alone with the lady of his choice," and I turned away and walked at a moderate pace around the block. But I could spare him no further grace, and so upon again reaching the house I ran up the steps and rang hastily.

The rooms occupied by the ladies as parlour and reception rooms were small and cosy, and thrown together by an arch, beneath which a *portiere* was draped, and Miss Ross came forward to greet me at the doorway of the first of these.

I could hear a murmur of conversation from the farther room, but it was not until I was standing beneath the curtained archway that I saw, to my amazement, Lossing and Monsieur Voisin at the farther side of the room, talking amiable nothings, as men of the world will when they meet. Both were in evening dress, and the Frenchman held in his hand a splendid bunch of American Beauty roses.

Voisin greeted me with *empressement*, and Lossing carelessly acknowledged "having met me before."

Miss Jenrys, her aunt informed me, as she had before informed the others, was engaged upon a letter of some importance, which must be sent in the early mail. She would join us soon; and then I learned from our desultory talk that it was Voisin for whose accommodation I had been pacing the block, and that Lossing had been the first arrival.

These two were still seated at the rear of the inner room, with Miss Ross at a little table near its centre and myself opposite her, and with my back to the archway, when there came a sudden sound at the outer door. It opened and closed quickly, and Miss Jenrys' voice exclaimed:

"Oh, Mr. Masters! I have had such a letter! One of those wretches has written that he will ransom poor lost Gerald Trent for—"

"June, my dear, come and receive thy visitors before thee tells thy news."

There was just a second of embarrassed silence, and then Miss Jenrys came forward and greeted her guests, with precisely the same courteous welcome extended to us each and all.

But she only referred to her exclamatory first words in reply to Monsieur Voisin's question:

"You greeted us with some rather startling words, Miss Jenrys. Pardon me, but is it true that you have a friend lost in this wonderful city?"

But Miss Jenrys was not to be made to commit herself a second time.

"Not at all; it is simply some news just given me by a correspondent, who has told me in a former letter about the disappearance of a young man whom I do not know."

"A disappearance! Is it possible? I am interested." He turned quickly toward me. "May I ask from you the details?"

"You can learn from the daily papers as much as I can tell you," I replied, with my most candid smile. "I read some time since of such a disappearance, and speaking of it casually to Miss Jenrys, learned from her that she had the news direct from a young lady correspondent who chanced to know the young man and his family. Is that reported correctly, Miss Jenrys?"

She nodded.

"And he has been ransomed, you say? That is well indeed," persisted Voisin.

There was a brief moment of silence, during which I knew that her eyes were fixed upon my face; but other eyes were also keenly watching, and I did not return her gaze.

"Not ransomed," Miss Jenrys said, "not yet; there has been an offer of some sort, a proposition, I understand;" and she turned to Lossing and began to question him about his health, and then, before the Frenchman could renew his queries, began telling them both of a recent letter from her New York aunt, full, it would seem, of bits of society news, and mention of persons known to herself, Lossing, and Voisin; and she was so well aided by her aunt and Lossing, not to mention myself, that there was no renewal of the former subject, and after a very short call Monsieur Voisin made his adieus, expressed "the keenest pleasure" at having encountered Mr. Lossing in Chicago, and his determination to see more of him.

When the door had closed behind him I arose, and without a

word of explanation crossed the two rooms, and, peering out through the little bay-window overlooking the street, saw Monsieur Voisin standing upon the pavement outside, and casting slow glances, first up and then down the street; after which he walked briskly southward.

There was no need of an explanation where those three were concerned, and I made none. No one referred to Monsieur Voisin, his visit, or his interest in the Trent disappearance, and nothing was said for a time concerning the letter which was foremost in Miss Jenrys' mind and in mine.

For half an hour I conversed with Miss Ross, and left the lovers to an uninterrupted chat; at the end of that time Lossing took his leave. As yet he had heard but the briefest outlines of the Trent affair; but in spite of my own request that he would remain and make one at our councils, he withdrew, declaring himself under orders to keep early hours.

I let him go without uneasiness, for was not Dave Brainerd lurking somewhere very near, and very much to be relied upon?

He had said good-bye to the little Quakeress in the back parlour, and then Miss Jenrys and myself had walked with him the length of the two small rooms, bidding him goodnight at the door.

As the street-door was heard to close behind him, Miss Jenrys turned to me, caught my arm, and said quickly, beseechingly:

"Mr. Masters, won't you follow him home? I—I have a strange feeling that he is not safe. It is not far, and it is early. Can you not come back—please?"

There was no hesitation, no blushes; she spoke like a woman forgetful of self in her anxiety for another; and when I told her that my friend was doubtless awaiting him, she only wrung her hands.

"He may not be now. It is so early, and I shall not feel at ease until I know. Mr. Masters, I am sure there is danger very near us; I feel it. Won't you go—and come back when all is safe?"

CHAPTER XXIII.

"YOU ARE SUFFERING IN MY STEAD."

IT WAS useless to argue, and how could I refuse? For the first time, and greatly to my amazement, I saw that self-contained and sweetly reasonable young woman deaf to reason, and in that strange condition which, for lack of power to understand, we men call "hysterical."

I went, and in spite of myself I left her presence feeling somehow aroused and watchful—quite prepared, for a little time, to see an assassin at every corner and beneath every tree.

"Do not overtake him," had been her last command. "It might offend him. Only see him safe at his own door."

I was not five minutes behind Lossing, and he could not, or would not, I knew, walk rapidly. I expected to come close upon his heels before I had reached the first corner.

That he would take the most direct and nearest route, I felt, was a matter of course. In fact, he knew no other, or so I thought.

The direct route was straight north to Fifty-seventh Street, and east to the entrance gate; but though I walked fast, and then almost ran, I could see nothing of Lossing and nothing of Dave Brainerd.

What did it mean? When I had reached the end of the first block, without a sight of Lossing, I hastened across the intersecting street and hurried on another block, and still no Lossing. I paused, looked around me, and seeing and hearing nothing, increased my steps almost to a run.

At Fifty-seventh Street I paused, before turning, to look about me and to listen. After the first block, going east, this street became quite densely shaded by the trees on either side.

I had now reached the second block on the south side of the street, that which contained the vacant lots and the overshadowing trees, beneath which the bootblack's stand was placed by day; and here again I paused and listened, in the hope that in the quiet about me I might hear and recognise Lossing's slow, even step. But no step was heard, and I moved on.

"It is early yet," I assured myself; "so early that thugs and night-birds are hardly likely to be abroad."

I was now opposite the bootblack's stand on the skeleton uprights which supported his rainy-day awning, and the platform upon which his patrons sat enthroned in state—and here memory fails me.

I had turned my gaze upon the gibbet-like uprights, and simultaneously, as it now seems to me, a voice shouted my name; but the sound and something else came together—something bringing with it a sting and the sounds of a rampant engine. I saw a myriad of flashing lights, heard a tremendous crash, and—that was all.

I came to myself a little later, outstretched upon a wire cot, and with a cretonne cushion beneath what felt like a very large and much-battered prize pumpkin, but what was in reality my head. There was a glow of electric light all about and above me, and bottles of all sizes and colours on every side.

Slowly it dawned upon my dazed senses that I was in the corner drug-store where I had more than once called, on my return from Washington Avenue, to buy a cigar.

I stirred slightly, and then the faces of Dave Brainerd, Lossing, the druggist, and a big policeman came suddenly into view surrounding my cot.

"Hello, old man, glad to see you back," was Dave's characteristic greeting, and the druggist, who proved to be a physician as well, promptly placed a finger on my pulse.

"Better," he said laconically, and turning, took from the desk at his back a glass which he held before me. "Can you lift your head and drink this?" he asked.

I made a feeble effort, and with Dave's assistance got my head high enough to swallow the medicine.

"Now," said the surgeon, "lie still, and I think before long you will be all right, except for a sore head, which you will probably keep for a day or two."

For some time longer I lay quiet, and with no desire to think or speak; then slowly the noise and dizziness wore away, and the strength came back to my limbs; but when I attempted to rise, I found that my head was paining me severely, and I contented myself with resting upon my elbow and asking, with my eyes on Dave:

"What has happened?"

"Sandbag," replied Dave tersely. "Didn't you feel it?"

"I feel it now," I said, trying to smile feebly, for I knew that Dave, now assured that my hurt was not serious, was giving vent to his relief in a characteristic bit of chaff.

"You see, it was this way," he went on. "Lossing here and I

were walking along on the north side of the street, just down here, and we saw you cross the street on the opposite side; the lamp at the corner showed you plainly. We saw you stop and look, and seem to listen, and then go on, and repeat the same manoeuvre after you had crossed the street. We had stopped under a tree, and close against the wall nearly opposite that bootblack's stand; and we meant to cross and surprise you, when all at once out from behind that platform sprang someone. I gave a yell, and we heard you go down. I ran to you, and Lossing ran and fired after the fellow, who cut across the open ground. I called him back when I saw that you were insensible, and the next minute this officer came up. He ran to this place (lucky it is so near), and brought the cot, and here you are. Can you remember? Did you hear me call?"

"Y—yes," I said slowly, "I—I think I tried to turn."

"And that saved you, no doubt," declared the druggist. "The fellow meant to do you deadly hurt—the weapon shows that. He meant to strike you lower, across the back of the neck; but, at the call, you turned, just as he had taken aim, and as a result you received the blow on the back of the skull, the thickest part; and it struck with less than half its force, glancing away as your head moved sidewise. It was most fortunate for you."

And now, as I began to think and remember, I knew that Miss Jenrys would be waiting anxiously, and that delay would mean for her, in the mood in which I had left her, a time of terrible suspense.

I brought myself to a sitting posture, and then got upon my feet, rather weakly. The druggist touched my wrist again.

"If you'll take my advice," he said, "you will stay right here for the night. I have a comfortable room at the back here, and I think, by keeping up an application during the night, a cooling and healing lotion that will keep out inflammation, you will come out in the morning with nothing worse than a sore and tender skull to show for your encounter. I am a regular physician—you'll be quite safe with me."

I accepted his courtesy as frankly as he had proffered it, and then, while he busied himself preparing the cooling lotion, I told Dave how I had promised to return, and that Miss Jenrys must not be kept longer in expectation. I did not tell him why I had left the house, to return again so soon, and Dave was not the man to question.

"Tell her," I said, "that all is right. She will understand; and later I will explain to you. And tell her I find that I must delay the reading of that letter until to-morrow morning; that it is a purely personal matter that detains me, and that I will explain when we meet." He got up to go, and I turned to Lossing, who, with the tact so natural to him, had gone to the front of the long room, and was idly turning the leaves of a directory. "Dave is about to do the thing I failed to do, because of this sore head," I said to him. "I wish you would stay with me until he comes back. He won't be long."

He seated himself without a question, and while Dave was gone, and my host busy in preparing for my comfort, he talked lightly of this and that, and finally of my unknown assailant.

"I believe I hit him somewhere," he said, "for I heard him drop an oath as he ran, and, by the way, he dropped something else, too."

"What was that?"

He got up and went to the place where the policeman had been sitting until, assured that he could do nothing then, he had gone out with Dave, declaring his intention to "go and look over the ground," a speech which caused Dave to smile behind his hat. From the floor, close against the wall, Lossing took up something, which he brought forward and laid beside me upon the cot.

It was a bar of iron at least four inches in circumference, and incased in a length of rubber tubing, which was tied tightly over each end. "That," said he, "is the weapon, and if it had struck you fairly, it would have been your death."

I held it in my hand. A death-dealing weapon indeed, and I shuddered as I put it down, asking myself meanwhile, "Was it meant for me?"

"But for you," I said aloud, "you and Brainerd—"

"Don't!" He put up his hand quickly. "When I think of what you have done for me, and—I—I fear you are suffering now in my stead."

It was the echo of my own thought, and I was glad to see my host reappear, thus cutting short the subject, which I was glad to drop just then.

The next morning found me somewhat the worse for my adventure, yet thankful to find that I could go about my day's business, a little stiffened from my fall, a trifle weaker than usual, and with an aching and somewhat misshapen head. But a detective learns to bear occasional hard knocks with fortitude, and I was thankful to be out of the affair so easily.

As an evidence of my dazed condition of the night before was the fact that I had not once thought to ask how Dave and Lossing chanced to be so near me at my time of need. It was one of my first thoughts and questions in the morning, however.

"You see," explained Dave, "I had not looked for any one quite so early, but I had stationed myself very near, on the side of the street opposite the house, and was pacing up and down, keeping the place in sight. I had a half-dozen cigars and a pocket full of matches, and when I wanted to turn, if anyone was in sight, I stopped and wasted a couple of minutes trying to light my cigar—see?"

"Distinctly."

"Well, of course, I looked to see our friend come out and go north; and so, while I was just on the turn, I was a little upset to see someone come out of Miss J.'s door and turn square south. Of course I went south, too, and to carry out your plan, I, being nearer the south crossing than he, turned and crossed in order to meet him, and all ready to be properly surprised at the encounter, you know, according to orders. Well, sir, we met right at the opposite corner, and instead of our man, there was a tall, dark, well-dressed person, who hastened his steps a bit in passing me."

He stopped, as if for an explanation.

"It was Voisin," I said. "The Frenchman I told you of."

"Um! I thought as much! Well, I stopped to light my cigar, and the Frenchman turned on the east side of the street and went back the way he came; I, on my side, did likewise. At the north end of the block he turned again, this time without crossing, and I did likewise. I didn't try to keep shady, for I thought it began to look like a game of freezeout, and I kept the west side of the street. As might have been expected, after two or three turns he left the field at the south end of the block, going east; and very soon after your man came out and turned south, which surprised me a little. He walked very fast, but I caught up and tackled him, calling him by your name and then apologizing, and explaining that, knowing you were to call upon Miss J., I had been on the lay for you, having a matter of business to impart as promptly as possible."

"Do you think he suspected us?"

"Not then. He told me very delicately that he had left early, feeling sure that you had some matter of importance to discuss with the ladies, and added his fear that you would not appear for some time yet. Of course I gave up all idea of waiting, and went on with him; and to pass the time and make myself agreeable I told him about the other fellow—what d'ye call him?"

"Voisin."

"Yes, Voisin. We had reached the south corner where Voisin had turned east, and Lossing was walking briskly. At the corner he turned to me and proposed taking the longest route home by going over to Madison Avenue. In fact, he felt like walking, he said. It was this queer route that set me to telling him about Voisin's promenade, and I wound up by wondering if you would take a new route, too. At that he took my arm and let me know in that polite way of his that he suspected our little game; that he knew how anxious you were for his safety, and that he appreciated your interest. 'But,' says he, 'don't you see that if there is danger abroad to-night, it is Masters who runs the risk?' I saw that he was really uneasy, and so when he proposed that we should hasten on to Fifty-seventh street and go down past Miss Jenrys' once more, I agreed, thinking, I will admit, that it was a sort of fool's errand.

"Well, sir, we had been walking at a brisk pace and were halfway down the block between the avenues, when we saw a figure start out from the corner beyond, and run across the street. We were almost at the corner, and to avoid the light just there we crossed the street and went along in the shadow of the trees and buildings, past the light and on to the opposite corner. We had just reached it and had stopped to look and listen for the skulkers, when we saw you come into the light, stop, look about, and seem to listen.

"'He's after that fellow,' I whispered to Lossing; 'let's keep quiet and be ready to lend a hand.' We could just see the fellow jump out at you. It's lucky the night was so clear, the shade was so thick just there."

CHAPTER XXIV.

"IT IS OUR FIRST CLUE."

MISS JENRYS met me that morning almost at the threshold. She had passed a restless night, for my message had not wholly allayed her fear, and she did not conceal the fact.

"I have been very anxious," were her first words. "Perhaps I have been foolish, but somehow I seem to have got into a new world, and I might very well pose for a Braddon heroine. I believe I am growing hysterical. What with my own little mystery, which seems to have stepped into the background, happily for me, and all the bigger mysteries—but there," breaking into a nervous laugh, "I can hold my tongue. Now tell me what happened last night. Oh!" catching my look of surprise, "something happened, I know. I felt it."

She was indeed woefully nervous, but to withhold anything would only increase the strain; so I told her as briefly as possible the story of my encounter, and the part played in it by Lossing and Dave. But I did not speak of Dave's meeting with Monsieur Voisin, and I hardly needed to tell her how it happened that my friend and Lossing were so fortunately at hand.

"I am not surprised," she said, when I had told my story, "but I am, oh, so thankful that you escaped with nothing worse. I felt so sure there was danger, and I urged you into it. But if you had not gone, I feel certain it would have been worse."

She talked on in this strain for some moments, and it was plain to me, though she did not put the thought into words, that she believed the attack was meant for Lossing, and not for myself.

Suddenly she sprang up. "I am forgetting poor Gerald Trent!" she exclaimed, and crossing the room, unlocked her desk, took out the letter, and placed it in my hands. It was a long letter, full of lamentations and repetitions; telling the story in a rambling, exclamatory, hysterical fashion; the letter of a young girl, a stranger to sorrow and its discipline, who finds herself suddenly plunged into a labyrinth of fear, terror, suspense; loving much and tortured through that love; and her story was briefly this:

Mr. Trent had seized the opportunity afforded by the change in his wife's condition, which, while neither really better nor worse, was much quieter. "In fact," wrote Miss O'Neil, "while she does not recognise any of us, she constantly fancies us all about her, and she talks to him in such a low, pathetic, pitiful tone, half an hour at a time, and then drops into a doze, only to wake up and begin over again. She does not know us, and while in this state, Dr. Lane says, she is better alone with the nurse. This being the case, Mr. Trent had left home for a day to look after some long-neglected business matter, and in his absence the letter had arrived. It was addressed to Mr. Trent in a strange hand, a woman's hand it would seem, and it was from Chicago. They had waited in anxious suspense until, chancing to think that it might be an important message and a prompt answer required, Miss Trent had, after some hesitation, opened the letter, a copy of which was at this point inserted. It ran thus, beginning with Mr. Trent's full name and correct address:

"SIR,

"In writing this I am perhaps risking my own life, as your son's is risked every day that he passes a prisoner in a place where he is as safely hidden as if he were already out of the world.

"Not only is your boy a prisoner, but he is a sick man. Your advertised rewards have been read and laughed at. The men who have him in charge are no common criminals. They mean to secure a fortune in return for young Trent. They know that his father is a millionaire, and his sweetheart an heiress in her own right.

"It is in my power, as one of the party in possession, to release your son. I waste no time in platitudes, but state frankly here my object in thus addressing you. I wish to leave the clique for reasons of my own, and to do this I must have money. This is why I propose to help you for a consideration. The 'clique' will take no less than a modest fortune, hundreds of thousands of dollars. I will accept ten thousand. For this I will find a way to set your son at liberty.

"This is my plan: You no doubt have in Chicago some friend who can and will oblige you. Request this friend to insert in three of the city papers here an advertisement as follows: If you accept you will say, 'Number three, we decline,' which I will read by contraries. You will then send by express, to be called for, a package containing ten thousand dollars in bank-notes—none larger than one hundred nor smaller than ten—and a letter in which you shall bind yourself not to take advantage in any way of my application for this packet at the express office; not to set a watch upon me, or in any way attempt to entrap me. This done, I will agree on my part to send you, twenty-four hours after receipt of your package, a letter telling you in detail where your son is and how to reach him. I will not agree to betray his captors; I would not be safe anywhere if I did; and it is liberty without a master, and an easier and a safer life, that I seek. I will also let your son know that he may expect a rescue.

"In proposing this I am running a risk, and in accepting it, while you will risk your money, I, if you betray me, risk my life. If you accept this proposal you will see your son alive, and soon. If you refuse—he is in the hands of desperate men, who will never give him up except on their own terms; they will wait until, driven to despair, you will offer them, through the press, a fortune, and—even then you may receive, after long waiting, only a corpse. As to the search you are making, we know your men and their methods, and they are capable of taking a bribe if it is large enough. It may interest you to know that they have already held one amicable meeting with our leaders, and in the end you are likely to pay them double. As to finding your son, the men who have him safe and secure will not hesitate to take his life the moment they know that they are likely to lose the game. I do not threaten, but I do assure you that your best chance of seeing your son alive and in his right mind lies in your sending me the two words, 'We decline,' with express to E. Roe.

"Yours,
"ON THE SQUARE."

A horrible letter, indeed! and the awful pictures which poor Hilda O'Neil's excited imagination drew of the possible situations, in some one of which her lover might be suffering, lent the last touch of gloom to the wretched whole. She saw him in some dingy cellar, ill unto death, neglected, helpless, and heartbroken; she saw him drugged into insanity, a possibility hinted at by the artful writer of the anonymous letter, and which I had more than once, considered as both possible and probable, and she implored Miss Jenrys to help her and save her lover.

"June, my life, my very life is in your hands! I cannot wait for Mr. Trent; eight long hours almost! I must act. Papa left me *carte blanche* at the bank; I was to draw as I needed, and I will go at once, as soon as this letter is despatched, and see that the money is secured and sent to you; and the letter—the promise—Mr. Trent must make it, and he will. But the answer, June, put that in the paper at once, so that Gerry may soon know that he is to be released. You won't refuse, I know; and, June, telegraph me the moment it is done," etc.

When I had put the letter down, after reading the copied portion twice, Miss Jenrys asked breathlessly:

"What must be done?"

I put into her hand Mr. Trent's letter, received the previous night, and when she had read it, she looked troubled.

"He seems to doubt this letter?"

"And so do I."

"But why? how? It sounds plausible."

"Too plausible. I must think this matter over. Mind, I do not say the letter was not written by some dissatisfied member of the band, but don't you see its weak point? He may wish to leave them, and doubtless would like to depart with a full pocket; but he would never dare to release Trent, even if he could. It's simply a trick. They are playing artfully upon the anxiety, the suspense, the wretched state of fear and hope and dread in which young Trent's friends are held, to extort from them a little money, which will keep them in comfort while they wear out either the father or the son."

"How? Tell me how."

"I wish I could! I will tell you how it looks to me. Young Trent has been missing now more than a fortnight—"

"Three weeks, almost."

"You are right. Now, here are three theories: First, he may be dead. He would hardly submit to capture and imprisonment without resistance, and may have died while a prisoner. Next, he may have been so drugged as to have driven him out of his senses. Or, he may be a prisoner in some secure retreat, while his captors are trying to break his spirit and force him to write to his friends for a great sum of money by way of ransom. But we must act now and speculate later upon all these possibilities. Do you think Miss O'Neil can have secured the money?"

"I do; yes. Her father's liberality is well known. She could borrow the amount if need be; she comes into her mother's fortune in a few months."

"Then we must keep a man constantly at the express office on the look-out for E. Roe." I got up and caught at my hat.

"Are you going now?"

"Miss Jenrys, there is not a moment to lose. That money, if sent, must be stopped, if it is possible! And I must see my partner. Thank goodness, we have an actual clue at last!"

"At last! A clue! What do you mean?"

I turned at the door. "Don't you see that this is really the first hint we have had to indicate that young Trent is still alive and a prisoner. Up to this moment all has been theory and surmise. If this letter is not a wretched fraud, a bold scheme to obtain money, hatched in the brain of some villain who has seen the advertised

Against Odds 185

rewards and knows nothing about Trent, it is our first clue, and through it we may find him." And promising to call upon her again that evening, or sooner if possible, I hastened to the nearest telegraph-office.

CHAPTER XXV.

"IT'S A SNARE."

MY FIRST act upon reaching the telegraph-office was to send a message, at Miss Jenrys' request and in her name, to Hilda O'Neil.

"Word it as you think best," Miss Jenrys had said, and accordingly I had sent this message:

"MISS HILDA O'NEIL,

"Yours received. Will do my best for you. Have courage.

"J. J."

This, while indefinite, was at least not discouraging. To Mr. Trent I wired at some length, as follows:

"Has money package been sent? Answer. If sent, order it held until further notice. Send at once original letter. It may prove a clue. Letter follows.

"MASTERS."

This done, I wrote at once to Mr. Trent, setting forth my belief that the letter was only a scheme to extort money, repeating my message with explanatory detail, and outlining a plan of action which would await his approval by telegraph, and then be put into immediate execution. This I posted with a special delivery stamp, and finding my head growing large and exceedingly painful, I went to my own quarters, compelled for a time to give up to the combined pain and fatigue which seemed suddenly to overcome me. But in spite of the pain in my head I could not withdraw my thoughts from this singular letter; and after tossing restlessly for an hour I got up, and having treated my aching skull to a gentle rubbing with my friend the druggist's soothing lotion, I sallied forth and wandered about the exposition grounds until the time for luncheon and my meeting with Dave came together.

* * * * *

Dave was anxious to hear the outcome of my visit to Miss Jenrys, and we made haste with our luncheon and were soon back in our room, when I told him the little I had to tell and put into his hand Miss O'Neil's letter, bidding him read the page containing what she declared to be an "exact copy" of the anonymous letter.

Dave read the singular document, as I had done before him, once and again; and then, placing it upon his knee, he sat looking at the floor and biting his under lip, a way he had when puzzled or in doubt. Finally he looked up. "What do you think of this?" he asked.

"It's a snare. Don't you think so?"

"Yes; but do you swallow this story of the gang?"

"Old man, supposing young Trent to be alive and in duress somewhere, do you imagine that one man, or even two, could keep him day and night?"

"U-m-m—no."

"Well, I said to Miss Jenrys an absurd thing. I said the letter might have been suggested by seeing those reward notices; but those notices did not give Mr. Trent's full name, and street, and number. No, sir, that letter was written by someone who has seen the contents of Gerald Trent's pockets, and who knows where he is, dead or alive."

"But you don't think he means business?"

"No. And neither do you. If Trent is in the hands of the gang, no one out of the lot will be permitted to open the doors to him. Besides, do you think that a party of men who have the daring and the ability to keep a prisoner three weeks safely hidden will release him for a paltry ten thousand, knowing his father to be a multi-millionaire?"

"U-m-m—just so. And how do they keep him?"

"Well, to me that letter is very suggestive. It hints at a possible situation. It's hard to imagine how a young man, in possession of his strength and senses, could be held a prisoner here in Chicago. But let us say he is ill. Suppose, for instance, he was attacked, those diamonds he is said to have worn being the bait; he is injured; they search him and find him a valuable person to have and to hold. If he is ill they can keep him without much trouble. Or, the letter hints at insanity; suppose he was lured somewhere and drugged—kept drugged. An easy way to bring about insanity, eh?"

"Carl!" exclaimed Dave, with one of his sudden, decisive gestures, "Carl, old man, I believe you've struck the trail! What's your next move?"

"My first move," I corrected, "will depend upon Mr. Trent. I can do nothing until I hear from him."

"And then?" urged Dave.

"I can see no better way to begin than to try and break up the gang."

"Before you find it?" he laughed.

"Before I look for it."

"Good Injuns! How?"

"By making that anonymous letter public—putting it in print."

"Jim-me-net-ti!"

* * * * *

In spite of the diligence of the watchers they could not regain the lost trail of the little brunette, nor, indeed, of the others; and after discussing and discarding many traps and plans, Dave ventured a suggestion.

"If that brunette has not given up her pursuit of Miss Jenrys," he said, "why not try to reach her that way? Ask her to make an appointment. Miss Jenrys will consent."

I could think of nothing better, but I did not act upon the suggestion until evening, when I went, this time in company with Lossing, to call upon the two ladies and give an account of my day's doings.

With the perfection of tact Lossing joined Miss Ross in the rear room, and left Miss Jenrys and myself to discuss our plans. I told her the little I had done in the Trent affair, and of my plans, contingent upon Mr. Trent's approval.

"He will approve, I am sure of it," she said with decision. "He has taken every precaution, and has made himself familiar with your record through the Boston chief of police. He has every reason, so he writes me, to have faith in you and in your judgment. I think you know that."

I thanked her for the assurance that my plans would be favourably received, and then told her of my wish to use her name in trying to draw out the brunette.

"I see no other way," I concluded; "and having once written her over your initials she may respond. Of course the reply must come to you at the office in the Government Building."

"But you will receive it. I can give you my card, can I not?"

"Then you do not object?"

"How can I? Did I not promise you my help? Oh, I am quite enlisted now although after such a *faux pas* as I made last night I cannot boast of my finesse. I quite excited Monsieur Voisin by my exclamatory entrance."

"And how?" I asked quietly, but inwardly eager.

"You remember how he questioned me about the 'missing person?' Well, he called this afternoon. Aunt Ann and I had just returned from the Liberal Arts Building, where we had spent three long hours, and though his call was brief he did not forget to ask again about that 'missing person.' He was almost inquisitive."

"And you?" I asked, inwardly anxious.

"He learned nothing more from me, rest assured. His curiosity seems quite unlike him."

"Possibly," I hazarded, "he has some inkling of my true inwardness, and thinks I have made you my confidant. Do you think it possible?"

"Possible, perhaps, but not the fact," she replied, with a little laugh. "My dear aunt has, in some way, given him the impression that you are a friend or protégé of hers. I am quite certain that he believes this, for he had the audacity to ask me to-day how long my aunt's acquaintance with you had been; and when I assured him that you and she were 'quite old friends,' he asked, with rather a queer intonation, if auntie knew what your occupation was, and when I murmured something about journalism, he smiled rather knowingly."

"A clear case," I said, smiling. "He guesses, at least, at my business, and perhaps fancies me deceiving your dear aunt. We will let him continue in that error, if possible."

I went home that evening pondering the question. Did Monsieur Voisin know me for what I was, and, if so, how? Of one thing I was certain. Since our first meeting he had always affected a most friendly interest in me; and that he was secretly studying me, I felt quite assured.

Another thing furnished me with some food for thought: Not long before we took our leave, and while Miss Jenrys and Lossing were deep in the discussion of the latest Spanish novel, Miss Ross said to me, quite abruptly, and apropos of nothing:

"Did June tell you that Monsieur Voisin was here today?"

I nodded, and she went on:

"You know my feeling where he is concerned; at least, I think you do. He is growing really aggressive, and June is blind to it; she is preoccupied. But I see all where she is concerned, and he will make her trouble. He is infatuated and bitterly jealous, and he is a man who knows no law but his own will. Do I not read him aright?"

* * * * *

The next morning I sent a note, written in the same dainty hand as the first, and signed with the initials J. J., to the little brunette, sending it as before to the café where she had lodged, and twenty-four hours later the telegram from Boston came.

In addition to my own letter, I had sent in the same envelope a copy of Miss O'Neil's, or as much of it as would help Mr. Trent to understand all that had been done by the young ladies in his absence.

His telegram read:

"Thanks for all. Carry out plan. Have ordered return of money. Letter follows.
"TRENT."

Two days later came Mr. Trent's letter, and with it the original composition of Mr. E. Roe, "On the Square."

As Miss O'Neil had said, it was written in a small, clear, angular hand, which had the look of a genuine autograph, without attempt at disguise.

In this I quite agreed with her, and I stowed the letter carefully away for future use. Mr. Trent in his letter assured me that he could not make E. Roe's letter ring true, and that he had finally convinced his daughter and Miss O'Neil that they had made a mistake. "Go on in your own way," he concluded; "and I hope before long to be with you. My wife has recovered from her delirium—very weak, but quite sane except upon one point—she believes our son to be ill in a hospital in Chicago, and the doctor has bidden us humour her in this hallucination, as it may save her life. He looks now for a gradual recovery, and when she is a little stronger I shall come to you; already she has planned for the journey, and assured me that our boy needs me most. It is sad, inexpressibly so, but it is better, at least for her. When I can join you in your work, and your waiting, I shall, I am sure, feel more hopeful, and I trust less impatient of delay."

CHAPTER XXVI.

A COLUMBIAN GUARD.

IT WAS still our theory—Dave's and mine—that, granted our original quarry was still in the White City, we must sooner or later encounter it, if we continued to traverse the thickly populated enclosure long enough, and with an eye single to our search.

We believed as firmly, yes, more firmly than at first, that Delbras and his band were still, much of the time, in Midway; and after long watching we had grown to believe that they had somewhere upon Stony Island Avenue a retreat where all could find shelter and safety in time of need.

"But one thing's certain," quoth Dave, when we were discussing the matter, "wherever the place is, they can approach it from more directions and more entrances than one. They, some of them, have been seen to enter saloons, to go upstairs, around corners, and into basements, and are never seen to come out. I can only account for it in one way."

"And what is that?" I questioned.

"They enter always at the side or rear, and never at the front, and they only do this when they know, by signal, that the way is clear."

"If that is true," I said, "we shall find them sooner or later."

One of the characters assumed by me when going about the grounds in my capacity of a detective was that of a Columbian

Against Odds

Guard. I had a natty blue uniform, in which, when donned with the addition of a brown curly wig, and a luxuriant moustache just light enough to be called blond, I became a really distinguished guard. And more than once, when thus attired, I have watched the conscious faces and overburdened shoulders and heads of the multitudes of uniformed martyrs who, on these oft-recurring dedication days, State and national, not to mention receptions to the great—native and foreign—tramped in sun, mud, or rain, arrayed in all the rainbow hues, beplumed, gilded, and uncomfortable, and have thanked the good sense and good taste that evolved for the manly good looking "C. G." a uniform at once tasteful, soldierly, and subdued, in which one might walk abroad and not feel shamefacedly aware that he was too brilliantly picturesque for comfort.

In this array I had more than once passed my acquaintances of the bureau and the hospital, Miss Jenrys and her aunt, and even Lossing, until one day it occurred to me that I might keep him near me, enjoy his society, and still be on duty, by making myself known; and so, until he chose to go on duty for a part of the day, we went up and down Midway, and in and out of the foreign villages together, as Dave described us, "keeping step, with our chin straps up."

We had made our first appearance in the Plaisance as a brace of guards off duty, on the day upon which I posted the decoy letter to the little brunette.

I had made this letter as brief as possible, merely asking her to name a day or evening when she would be at liberty to do the Liberal Arts, etc., in company with the writer, and upon second thought, I saw that it would be a great mistake for me to call for the reply, in case the brunette caught at the bait. She had shown herself a wary opponent, and she might think it worth while to know who received her answer.

It was late in the day when we left Midway, and with this new thought in my mind I dropped Lossing's arm as we approached the Java village, and skirting the west side of the inclosure, left the grounds by the Midway exit at Madison Avenue, and hastened on to Washington Avenue.

As I turned a corner I saw a smart carriage at Miss Jenrys' door, but before I had reached the house I saw the driver turn his head and gather up his reins, and the next moment Monsieur Voisin, attired as if for a visit of ceremony, came down the steps slowly, almost reluctantly, it seemed to me, entered the carriage, and dashed past me without a glance to right or left.

A card brought Miss Jenrys to the little reception-room where I waited, and when she had inspected my disguise, which she declared quite perfect, I made known my errand, and, as I fully expected, she declared my second thought best.

"I will go to-morrow; there will hardly be an answer before that time; and—suppose we should meet?"

Before I could reply, the door opened and Miss Ross came in.

"A disguised detective is a thing to see!" she declared; and then, when she had looked me over and marvelled at the fit of my wig, she turned to her niece:

"June, child, did thee speak of our dilemma?"

"Auntie, you must give me time!" her face flushing rosily.

"Time indeed! did not this young man's card say, 'A moment. In haste'? And can we entertain this strange young man by the hour? Fie upon thee, June! Do thy duty, else—"

June's hand went out in a pretty gesture, and between the two they made the "dilemma" clear to me.

Some time since, when Miss Jenrys had expressed a wish to see the Plaisance thoroughly, I had offered my services, promising to take them safely through the strange places, behind the mysterious gates and doors, where they had not ventured to penetrate alone. Now they had an especial reason for wishing to make this excursion on the next day, and—would I be at liberty?

I assured them that, in any case, I should doubtless pass a part of the day, at least, in Midway; and if they would allow me to include Lossing in our party there need be no change save that, instead of wearing our guards' uniform, we would go as citizen sight-seers; and instead of a party of two, there would be a quartet, and so it was arranged.

Before leaving the house I had been told what I had surmised before entering.

Monsieur Voisin had asked Miss Jenrys to drive with him, and when she had declined, upon a plea of indisposition, he had renewed the invitation for the following day, whereupon Miss Jenrys, in sheer desperation, recalled that proposed visit to Midway, and, falling back upon that, once more declined with thanks.

Certainly Monsieur Voisin was a persistent wooer!

He was much in my thoughts, after I had left the ladies, and quite naturally followed me into dreamland. My head was heavy with pain, and I went to my room at an early hour. It was long before the lotion did its work and I fell asleep, and then I dreamed that Monsieur Voisin had carried off June Jenrys, and had shut her into an old building in care of the brunette, who locked her in a room at the top of the house and then set it on fire below.

I saw the flames shoot forth; I saw June's face, pallid and desperate, at the window, beyond the reach of the highest ladder; I saw Lossing dash through the flames; and with a yell I awoke.

CHAPTER XXVII.

"I'D SWEAR TO THEM HANDS ANYWHERE."

AT ONE o'clock Lossing and I met the ladies at the rendezvous, as we had grown to call the Nebraska House Parlour, and the little arbour beside the stream. Lossing, quite himself again, was handsome in his well-fitting light summer suit, and happy in the prospect of an afternoon with beautiful June Jenrys, as who would not be? and I was humbly thankful that I was not, for that afternoon at least, obliged to wear a skintight wig upon my sore and tender cranium.

That they might reserve their strength for the ins and outs of Midway, we brought to the gate, for the use of the ladies, the two stalwart chair-pushers, whose work, so far as they had been concerned, had been a sinecure indeed since the attack upon Lossing, and we went at once, and without stops by the way, to the post-office. But there was no letter for Miss Jenrys; and, although I looked about me with a practised eye, followed Miss Jenrys at a safe distance when she entered the office, and kept the others waiting while I took a last long look, I could see no signs of the brunette.

Midway Plaisance was almost unknown ground to Miss Ross, and her wonder, amusement, and quaint comments made her an interesting companion.

"We must see it all, auntie," June Jenrys declared, her fair face glowing with the sweet content with her companion and the moment, that not even the sorrows of her distant friends, which had weighed so heavily upon her own kind heart, could for the

Irish Industrial Village, Midway Plaisance.

time overshadow or abate.

"I shall be guided by my escort," was the reply of my companion, "and I do feel that we may forget our anxieties for a time, and take in all this strangeness and charm with our whole hearts."

We did not linger long in the Hall of Beauty, the costumes of many nations being passed by with scarce a glance. But my companions lingered longest before the queer little person described in the catalogue as the "Display of China," who was a genuine child of the Flowery Kingdom, and generally fast asleep.

We turned away from the very wet man in the submarine diving exhibit with a mutual shiver, and rejoiced anew in the sunlight and free air.

The glassworks, interesting as they assuredly were, we passed by as being not sufficiently foreign; and the Irish Industrial Village and Blarney Castle were voted among the things to be taken seriously, and not in the spirit of Midway. Miss Ross was full of interest in the little Javanese, and we entered their enclosure, feeling sure that here, at least, was something novel.

We had peered into the primitive little houses upon their stilt-like posts, and the ladies had spent some time in watching a quaint little native mother making efforts to at once ply the queer sticks which helped her in a strange sort of mat weaving, and keep an eye upon a preternaturally solemn-faced infant, who, despite his gravity, seemed capable of quite as much mischief as the average *enfant terrible* of civilization. And then—"

"Les go an' see the orang-outang," exclaimed someone behind us, and as they went, a sun-browned rustic and his sweetheart, we silently followed.

The orang was of a retiring disposition, and very little of him was visible from our point of vantage. As I shifted my position in order to give the ladies a better place, a familiar voice close beside me cried with evident pleasure:

"Wal! Lord-a-massy, if it ain't you! Come to see the big monkey, like all the rest of us? Ain't much of a sight yit."

It was Mrs. Camp, and she seemed quite alone. She put out her hand with perfect faith in my pleasure at the meeting; and when I took it and spoke her name, I felt a soft touch at my elbow. I had told the ladies of my acquaintance with Mrs. Camp, and they had fully enjoyed the woman's sharp sallies at my expense. I quite understood the meaning of Miss Jenrys' hint, but while I hesitated, Mrs. Camp began again:

"I've left Camp to home this time. I've tramped and traipsed with him up and down this here Midway, but I've never once got him inside none of these places sense he took me to that blue place over there that they call the Pershun Palis; no more a palis than our new smoke-house. But Adam seen so much foreign dancin'—" As she talked she ran her eyes from one of our group to another, and as she uttered the words "foreign dancin'," her eyes fell full upon Miss Ross, who at once said, turning to me:

"Perhaps thee would better introduce thy friend."

It was done, and in a moment Mrs. Camp was standing close beside Miss Jenrys, making note of her beauty, and taking in the points of her toilet with appreciative eyes, while her tongue wagged on vigorously. She had taken up her story of her husband's "quittin' of Midway."

"He hadn't never no notion of dancin'," she declared, "and never took a step in his life—not to music, that is. But he wanted to learn all he could about furrin ways, he said, so in we went. Well, you ort to 'a' seen them girls. Mebbe ye have, though?"

"No," murmured June.

"Well, then, you don't want to. Dancin'! I've got an old hen, a'most ten years old—I've been a keepin' her to see how long a hen would live—an' if that hen can't take more honest dancin' steps than the hull posse of them hourys, as they call 'em. All the dancin' they know they'd 'a' learnt from snakes and eels, an' sich like wrigglin' things. Pshaw! I don't b'lieve that ole monkey's goin' to show hisself to-day, humbly thing!"

When we turned away from the Java Village Mrs. Camp was one of our party, and when we entered Hagenbeck's animal show she was still telling Miss Ross and I how she and "Adam" had not agreed upon a route that day, and how she had revolted utterly when he proposed to spend the afternoon "down to the odds and ends corner of the Fair, among the skeletins and old bones, and rooins, and mummies," and how "fer once" they had each "took their own way."

It was Miss Ross who had kindly asked the "lone woman," as she described herself, to join our party; and she bore with sweet patience and an indulgent half-smile her many remarks, absurd or *outre*, shrewd or unsophisticated.

"I'm sick of that feller!" she exclaimed, as the "Hot-hot-hot!" of the Turkish vendor of warm cakes was heard. "The very idea of a yallow faced feller like that takin' to cookin' hot waffles for livin'! Right in the street, too! I sh'd think he could get enough cloth out o' them baggy trousers to make him a little tent. 'F I was the boss here I'd make him do his cookin' quieter; he jest spiles the street."

In the German Village our party rested, and the ladies enjoyed its quaint and picturesque cottages and castle, and listened with pleasure to the German band—all but Mrs. Camp.

"I don't see nothin' very strikin' here," she candidly observed, "and I don't see the need of puttin' up so many queer-lookin' barns. The house is well enough, but I'll bet them winders come out o' Noah's ark; an' I can't make so much beer-drinkin' look jest right—for wimmin."

As we passed out she was so rash as to pause a moment to look down into a huge vessel, full to the brim of the queer-looking compound which the vendor described in a loud voice as "bum-bum candy."

"Lad-ee! Lad-ee!" He cried, as she turned away. "Fine bum-bum, splendid!" But the look she cast over her shoulder silenced his eloquence.

"That feller," she declared, "has been settin' around here in one place or another ever sence I've been here with his bum-bum candy. I've never got closte enough to git a look at the stuff till to-day; an' I've never saw a soul buyin' it nor eatin' it."

It had been agreed that we should take a trip in the Ferris Wheel. With the ladies it would be a novel experience, but when we were about to enter the car Mrs. Camp drew back.

"Tain't no use," she said. "I ain't goin' to risk my neck that way. It's jest a-flyin' in the face of Providence! I couldn't git Adam to 'smuch as look at the thing when 'twas goin' round. No, sir, I ain't a-going'!" this to the man at the still open door. But when we had taken our places and the door was about to close, she sprang forward. "Hold on!" she said. "I guess I've as good a right to tempt Providence as anybody! Don't shet that door! I want to git in." As she sat down beside me she said, with the air of one who has done a good deed, "I hadn't orter 'a' let you git a ticket for me, but I didn't feel so squeamy till I got right here. Seems safe enough though, don't it?"

Miss Ross assured her of its safety, and I told her how thoroughly it had been tested, but suddenly she broke in upon my speech:

"S-h! Why, we're a-goin'! My, how easy!" She seemed for a moment to hold her breath, and then I saw her hands clutch at the revolving seat. "Land sakes, it's tippin'! Mercy on me, I can't stand this! Say!" to the man in charge, who was just about to

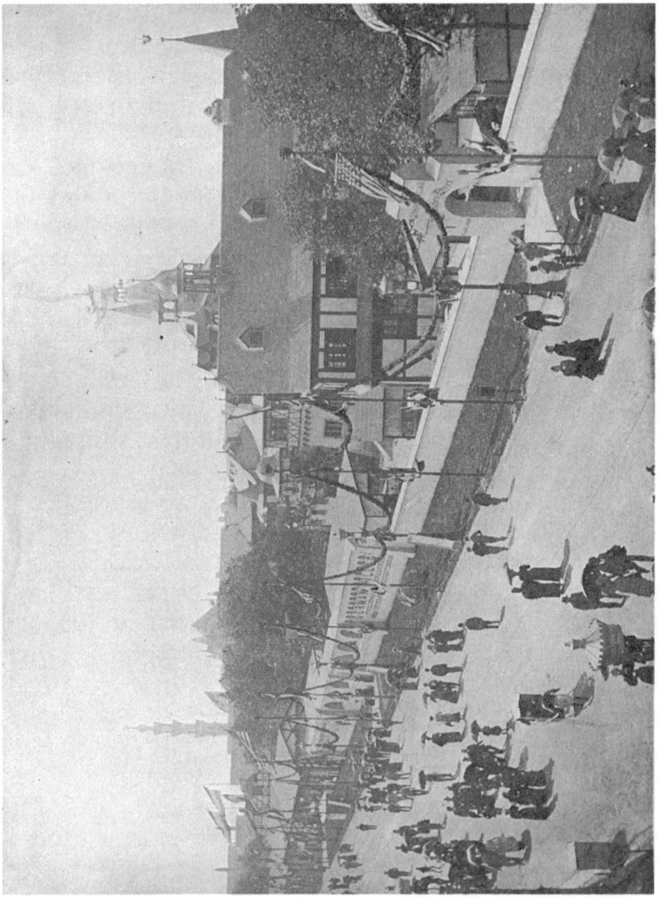

Copyrighted by the World's Columbian Exposition.

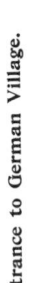

Entrance to German Village.

begin his 'story of the wheel,' "I want to get out! I can't never go no higher. Jest turn back; please dew."

To my surprise, he arose and moved toward the door; then with his hand upon it, he turned.

"It might make you a little dizzy when we reverse the engine, ma'am. Just close your eyes tight until we stop, and you'll feel all right, and not so likely to faint when you begin to walk."

With a sigh of relief and a shudder of terror, she put her cotton-gloved hands over her eyes, and sat crouched over in a very wilted attitude; and I was on the point of speaking rather sharply to the man, when a look in his eye and a rapid gesture somehow restored my confidence in his ability to manage the car, and we went on smoothly and silently up.

We had reached the topmost curve before Mrs. Camp moved a finger, and then Miss Jenrys, gazing out over the wonderful landscape outspread so far below, uttered a quick exclamation of delight. Then the hands fell, she started up and looked quickly around, and for a moment stood with mouth agape and hands thrown out as if for support or balance. Suddenly she drew a long, relieved breath and dropped back into her seat. Mrs. Camp was herself again.

"My!" she aspirated; and after another long look all about her, "Young man, I declare if I ain't obleged to ye jest as much as if you'd 'a' minded me." She ventured near the window, and even put her head out. "My! they look jest like flies a-walkin'! My! we can't look much to the angels lookin' down. They go awful jerky." She said no more until we were almost at the bottom then she turned to Miss Ross: "I've a good mind to go round ag'in," she declared, and when she was told that we were all "going round ag'in," she drew close to the window and made her second circuit in breathless silence.

As we left the wheel and came out from the gate, where a crowd was pushing and pressing for entrance, Miss Jenrys, feeling herself suddenly jostled by some impatient one, uttered a quick exclamation, and at the sound someone just before me, and whom I had not chanced to observe in the crowd, turned quickly, shot a hasty glance at Miss Jenrys, and as suddenly turned back again.

The face was that of a youth, dark-skinned, and with keen black eyes; the hair, cropped close to the head, was as black as the thick, long lashes; the form was slender, and the head scarcely came up to my shoulders; a slight figure, a youthful face, it caught and riveted my attention. After the first glance in our direction, the young man seemed only anxious to extricate himself from the crowd, which he soon did.

We were on our way to Cairo Street, and when we entered at the nearest gateway I saw this same youth just ahead. Lossing and Miss Jenrys went before, and as they turned into the street proper, and moved slowly toward the east court where the donkey-boys were gathered, the youth, who had paused as if in indecision, glanced up and down the street and then hurried away toward the Temple of Luxor at the western end of the inclosure.

There was much of interest in the street, but the ladies soon tired of watching the donkey-boys and smiling at the awkward feats of the camel riders, and turned their attention toward the shops and the architecture; turning finally from mosque and theatre to the more private apartments—they were hardly houses—with their small, high balconies, their latticed windows, their dark doorways, their sills almost level with the street.

It was Miss Ross who expressed a desire to have a nearer view of one of these dark and cool-looking interiors, and as we turned our faces westward I saw across the way, on the inner side of the street, an open doorway, giving just a glimpse of some dark hangings, a brass lantern swinging from the roof, and a couple of men in flowing robes and turbans, lounging upon a divan within.

Beckoning to the others, I crossed the street, spoke to the men, and, finding that one could understand a little English, asked permission to enter with the ladies.

It was granted, after a moment's hesitation and a quick glance at his companion, who did not rise from the divan, and who answered the look with a grunt which, doubtless, meant consent.

There were no seats in the place, save the rug-covered divan, which filled one side from corner to corner. The floor was covered with rugs, and the walls were hung with the same, except where, a little at one side in the rear wall, was a narrow door, painted almost black, and having a ponderous and strange-looking latch.

The wall draperies, to me, looked simply a well-blended pattern in dull blue and other soft tints; just such as one might see in the shops anywhere. But the ladies were of a different opinion, and they at once began a close and exclamatory inspection of each, extolling their colour, their texture, their quaint designs,

Street in Cairo.

their rarity and costliness.

They had viewed the rugs upon the rear walls, Lossing seeming not far behind them in the matter of admiration, and had passed to the side wall opposite the divan, and quite out of sight from the street, there being no windows on that side, in fact on no side of the rug-hung room, which was lighted solely by the door, that, standing wide open, served as a further screen for those behind it.

Mrs. Camp, having faithfully tried to admire the rugs for courtesy's sake, had failed utterly; and to the evident surprise of the silent Egyptian, who still sat in his place, had coolly seated herself upon the end of the divan nearest the street, our host, meantime, standing near the middle of the room, alert, and evidently somewhat curious.

After a brief glance at the second row of rugs, I had crossed the small room and seated myself near Mrs. Camp, and a moment later a big determined-looking woman—American or English, if one might judge from her face and dress, the latter being full mourning and in the height of fashion—entered.

She neither spoke nor looked about her, but went, with the tread of a tragedy queen, toward that narrow dark door in the rear wall. In an instant, before the startled Cairene could prevent her, she had her hand upon the door, and had jerked it half open; but before she could enter, the tall Oriental had reached her side, and somehow instantly the door was closed, and the woman staring at it and him as he stood before it.

He bent toward her, and uttered some word, respectful it seemed, but decisive, and she, with a baked and angry look, turned slowly and went out.

But she took my benediction with her. As I sat near Mrs. Camp, I was in a direct angle with that little door which opened against the inner wall, and in the moment while that door stood open I saw, not, as I thought might be the case, the outer world with the usual *debris* of a "back-door," but an inner room, and in that room, his face toward me as he reclined, his head lifted, startled perhaps from an afternoon nap, I saw a man—a man whom I knew.

I could hardly sit there and wait for my friends to sufficiently admire remaining rugs; I wanted to get out, and if possible to see Cairo Street from the rear. For I now remembered that on each side of Midway, between the houses and villages and the inclosing palings, was a driveway twenty feet in width, for the convenience of the inhabitants, who received their marketing at night, and from this rear avenue.

But my star was in the ascendant. At the moment when I could hardly repress my anxiety and impatience, a man entered; slowly at first, then starting slightly, he threw one hasty glance around him, and strode quickly toward the narrow door, which the Cairene opened for and closed after him.

"My land!" It was Mrs. Camp who had uttered the ejaculation, under her breath, with her eye upon the man by the door. "Say," she went on, meeting my eye, "do you know who that was?"

"Do you?" I counter-questioned.

"Well mebbe I'm mistook, but he looks the very moral of the furrin feller 'at changed that money for Camp and gave him counterfeits!" She half rose. "I'm goin' to ask," she explained.

"Stop!" I caught her hand. "You must not! Leave it to me; I'll find out."

I was too full of my own thoughts to enjoy Cairo after that, and was glad when we set out to visit the Temple of Luxor. I wanted to get away and to see Dave Brainerd.

It was half an hour after our experience in the place of rugs, and we were nearing the Temple, when we were forced to a stand by the approach of the wedding procession, with its camels and brazen gongs, its dancers, fighters, musicians, etc. As we stood, pressed close against a wall, someone came swiftly across the narrow way, dodging between two camels, and greeted us with effusion.

It was Monsieur Voisin, and when the parade had passed and we moved on, he placed himself beside Miss Ross, who at once presented him to Mrs. Camp.

In accordance with her notion of strict etiquette, that good woman put out her hand to him in greeting; and when the formality was over, the way being narrow and the crowd dense, I fell behind with her at my side, Miss Ross having been taken possession of by the cool Frenchman.

For some paces Mrs. Camp, contrary to her custom, was quite silent. Then as we approached the Temple, the others having already entered, she stopped and caught me by the arm.

"Say," said she, in a tone of mystery, "I must 'a' been mistaken before about that feller in that house bein' the counterfeit-money man."

"Why?" I demanded.

"Because, d'ye remember my tellin' you 'bout that feller havin' sech long slim hands?" I nodded. "Well, this feller ahead there with Miss Ross—he's the one. I'd swear to them hands anywhere." I stopped just long enough to speak a few words of caution, and we followed the others.

Late that night I said to Dave Brainerd: "Dave, I have seen the brunette, Greenback Bob, and Delbras."

CHAPTER XXVIII.

"NOW DOWN!"

MISS JENRYS went faithfully to the post-office in the Government Building the day after our visit to Midway, and the next, and the next. On the fourth day she was rewarded, and when I appeared at her door, as I did every day now, by appointment, and at a fixed hour, she put a square envelope into my hand. It was addressed to "J. J., World's Fair P.O.," and the seal was unbroken.

I looked at the initials in surprise. "Is it possible," I asked, "that you two have not exchanged names? Has it always been J. J. and H. A.?"

"Quite so," she laughed. "It was her proposal. It would keep up the romance of the acquaintance, she said," and as I held out the envelope toward her, "No, that is your letter; I have no interest in it, and little curiosity concerning it."

"Then," said I, as I broke the seal, "I shall read it to you because of that little."

But when I had unfolded the sheet, I sat so long staring at it that she asked lightly: "Does it contain a scent, after all?" I put the letter in her hand. "Read for yourself," I said, trying to speak carelessly; and she read aloud:

"'MY KIND FRIEND,

"'I much regret that, because of my mamma's illness, I cannot leave her for the present. But at the first moment of leisure I shall let you know that I am at your service. How much I regret the loss of your charming company, and long for a sight of your charming face, is only known to yours,

"'H. A.'"

"Bah!" She tossed the letter back to me with a little disdainful laugh. "It reads like a love-letter, and is anything but filial." As I folded the letter and put it carefully away, she watched me keenly.

"Mr. Masters," she said, "you have been in some unaccountable manner startled, or shocked, by that letter."

I could neither deny nor explain, and I frankly admitted it, assuring her that she would not remain long in the dark.

"Oh, I can wait," she smiled. "Do not fancy me so unreasonable as to expect the full confidence of a detective. Only, don't fear for my 'nerves,' and let me help in any way that I can. I think," laughing, "that I have said this before."

I was anxious to go now, and, rising, I took her at her word. "You can help me in two ways," I said, "but I must ask you not to demand reasons just yet."

"Go on," she said promptly.

"First, should this brunette, this 'H. A.,' write you again, will you inform me at once, and—I don't think it likely to occur, but if she should call here, will you refuse to receive her?"

"Yes to both. But she does not know my address."

"You forget; she has been seen to pass this house. Don't be too sure."

"I will be on my guard. Is that all?"

"There is another point—a delicate one. I could not but see that Monsieur Voisin's company that day in Midway was not entirely welcome to your aunt and yourself; and—bear with me, please, I am speaking in the interest of another. Promise me that you will not close your doors against Monsieur Voisin, or treat him too coldly, for a little while. Believe me, my reason is one that you will be first to endorse when it is known to you."

She hesitated, and I hurried on:

"The man is of a fiery disposition, and he recognises a rival in the field—pardon my intrusion upon delicate ground. He comes from the land of duellists." She started. "A little patience and diplomacy upon your part, and I think I can promise that he will not annoy you much longer."

"Very well," she assented, "I agree. Auntie, strange to say, has urged the same thing—concerning Monsieur Voisin, that is. At the worst we can go home. It is now the last of June, and we go, in any case, in July. Never fear, I shall not forget your admonitions, any of them." And she gave me her hand at the door with a reassuring smile.

Half-way over the threshold I turned back to say: "By the way, Miss Jenrys, if I chance to appear here at the same time as Monsieur Voisin, please be kind to me."

* * * * *

Late that same night Dave Brainerd and I held one of our long, and, in the past, ofttimes useless and mistaken, symposiums. But this time we were in perfect accord. We had spread upon the table before us our old memoranda from the very beginning of our campaign, and also some few letters and other documents. It had been a long "session," according to Dave, but the conclusion was so satisfactory that, at the last, we had each lighted a cigar, and celebrated thus what we considered a fully mapped out campaign at last.

"Well," pronounced Dave, with a sigh of content, as he tipped back his chair, and elevated his feet to the top of the table between us. "This looks like business! Let us see! First," checking off on his fingers, "we're to keep away from Midway—all but Billy—so that they may not make another flitting, eh?"

"Yes," I assented.

"And we're to patrol Stony Island Avenue and the surrounding country by day and by night, with a full force. Ain't that it?"

"Perfectly. Dave, you are as full of repetitions as an old woman!"

"Or a young one," he retorted; "and you think it is proved that the brunette's a man, do you?"

"It was proved, for me, long ago."

"And that letter? I can't see why it should not be launched at once."

I had written to Mr. Trent, telling him of certain facts and theories, and among them was the suggestion that we should cause a copy of the "Roe" letter, with its proposed barter, to be published in the morning papers, giving him my reasons at length, and requesting his opinion before taking what might prove a very decisive if not aggressive step. Dave was delighted with this idea, and, wearied with our "masterly inactivity," he would, as he put it, "launch the thing at once." My reasons, as explained to both Dave and Mr. Trent, were:

The letter signed "Roe," and offering to liberate young Trent, and at the same time to defraud the comrades of the "clique," if genuine, would, when published, expose the writer, who would then be obliged to "leave the clique," as he had expressed it, and with an additional "reason" for so doing; this would at least lessen their numbers, and perhaps force them to take into their confidence some new colleague. Or, possibly, it would result in a quarrel among themselves, which also might result in some way in our favour.

On the other hand, if it were a scheme of the clique, it would seem that at least they were tired of the game and in need of money; and the advertised letter, if followed up by another advertisement—in which a correspondence might be proposed or some proffer made—might draw them out; and in some way this must be done. In the meantime a warrant must be issued, or rather two, one descriptive of the brunette as a woman, the other as a man; and since the Lausch people had not done so, we would, if we could, arrest her or him on the charge of robbery.

I had to go over the ground once more to quiet Dave, or to tire him out; and we ended at last, as usual, in mutual agreement.

Several days must pass, I knew, before Mr. Trent would arrive. I had written him daily, and he had replied by telegraph. He would be with me soon, and would wire me the date of his arrival. In the meanwhile I was to "act upon my best judgment" in the matter of delaying the advertisement. I decided to wait and watch, and so a few more days passed in routine and quiet.

On one of these quiet days Lossing and I, in a moment of leisure, went down to that interesting, and by many neglected, portion of the Exposition grounds where are situated the cliff-dwellers; the Krupp gun, giant of its kind; the Department of Ethnology, and the great Stock Pavilion, where the English military tournaments were held afternoons and evenings. It seemed to be by mutual consent that we turned away from the little point of land where La Rabida sat isolated, as a convent should; and, crossing the bridge that spanned the inlet between the convent and the stately Agricultural Building, we passed through its spacious central promenade and, passing by the Obelisk and under the Colonnade, paused at the military encampment.

There was no performance at that hour, but men and horses

were being led into the monster pavilion, "for exercise," a big trooper explained to us, "and a bit of drill for the 'orses." At which Lossing slipped his hand through my arm. "Come on," he said, and, a little to my surprise, he led me to a side door, and taking a card from his pocket, held it an instant before the eyes of the soldier on guard, saying a word as he passed him, which I did not catch.

As we entered the great inclosure, a group of officers were standing near the centre of the arena, in busy converse, and a head artillery team was being put through its paces, while nearer our place of observation several cavalrymen were leading their horses up and down. The officers evidently were discussing and arranging some matter of importance. But while I noted this, I also noted that one of them who stood facing toward us lifted his hand in salute, and then moved it toward us in a less formal gesture, and, again to my surprise, my companion lifted his hand and returned the salute in kind. Before he could look at me I had turned my eyes away and was watching with evident interest the manoeuvres of the cavalrymen.

They had mounted their animals and were beginning to put them through their paces, and presently they began the drill known as throwing their horses.

Galloping the animals to a certain point, they were brought to a short and sudden stand, and then by a quick tug upon the hilt, the animal, if well trained, allowed itself to fall upon one side, the rider instantly slipping from the saddle to a position half concealed by the body of the horse from an imaginary enemy in front, and gun in hand, ready to take aim across the saddle.

There was one man who did not at first go through this evolution with the others, but set his horse near the rest looking on. When the others had gone through the exercise, this man rode forward, put his horse at a gallop, stopped him splendidly, and attempted the fall; but the animal was obstinate or only half broken, and began to show signs of both fright and fight.

As his rider turned the excited creature about, and sent him at a mad gallop across the arena, one of the troopers came at an easy trot directly toward us, and drawing rein beside us, with a lift of his hat, said respectfully:

"Good-morning, sir. I hope you are well, sir."

"Good-morning, George," replied Lossing easily. "What is the matter with that horse?"

"'E's a new one, sir, and not quite broke; though I do think, sir, as he 'asn't the best and kindest of riders, sir, and that makes 'im worse."

"Yes," said Lossing absently, with his eyes following the horse, which was a really fine animal, one to attract a horse-lover.

"Hit's too bad," went on the trooper. "Diggs will 'ave to ride 'im this hafternoon, and it'll bait the cap'n horful; for one of our 'orses come a fluke last hevenin'. I be sorry for Diggs!"

"I'm sorry for the horse! George, go and ask the captain to send Diggs and his horse to me."

No doubt my face showed my surprise as the trooper rode obediently off to do his bidding; but Lossing only smiled and moved a step or two away from the rail where we had been standing.

"Diggs," he said, as the man rode up and saluted. "Will you let me try your horse?"

The soldier saluted again, and dismounted without a word; and Lossing took the bridle from his hand, and for a few moments stood beside the horse, stroking him, smoothing his mane, and all the time speaking some low, soothing syllables that seemed to quiet the still quivering animal.

After a little of this he examined the saddle, adjusted the stirrups and bridle, and then, after leading the horse away from us a short distance, he stepped easily and quietly into the saddle. Instantly the creature's head was erected, and his ears put back, but Lossing, with a caressing hand upon his neck, continued his low, soothing syllables, and let the animal walk the length of the long inclosure.

Turning then, he sent him back at a gentle trot, which he increased gradually, until he was careering around the arena in circles, which became shorter and shorter, until he came to a halt in the centre of the vast place. Then after a few more gentle words and light pats upon the sleek neck, he bent over and suddenly drew the rein. Once, twice, three times he gave that sharp pull, but the horse stood steadfast. Turning in his saddle, he said something to the troopers who had drawn near him, and then sat erect in his place, while three of the troopers turned their horses and went careering around the motionless horse and rider. Soon, at another word from Lossing, one of the men rode alongside, while the others drew back.

When the trooper had ranged himself at the side of Lossing's horse and only a few feet away, Lossing nodded; and at the first tug at the rein the trooper's well-trained animal went down and lay supine and moveless.

Then Lossing beckoned a second time, and as the fallen horse got up he was caressed by Lossing, who leaned from his saddle to reach him, and then led away, as the second trooper came up leading his horse.

As the animals stood side by side Lossing dismounted, stood a moment beside his refractory steed, and then, with a gentle pat and a low word as if of reproof, he turned and, after patting the other animal a moment, sprang to its back and sent it galloping around the place; then bringing him back to place, and with a pat or two and a quick "Now down!" threw him, sprang to his feet, and before the animal could rise had again mounted the wayward horse.

Once more he trotted slowly away, caressing and talking to the horse; and then, suddenly wheeling him, he gave a cheery command and sent the creature flying back, past his old place, and across the pavilion; then turning and halting the horse before the group of officers, he gave him a brisk pat, and said cheerily, "Now down!" and, almost with the word, the creature threw up its head and, with scarcely an instant's hesitation, went over and lay quivering upon the ground.

A cheer went up from the onlookers. But without loss of time Lossing had the horse up, turned him about, and, seeing him quite fit and not too nervous, remounted; and now the horse was obedient to his every move or word. Twice more he threw him, and then, returning him to Diggs, he said:

"Diggs, a horse can be as jealous as a woman, and more easily shamed than a boy. And if you are skilful, and love your horse, you can master him; but beware of the first angry word. Anger makes brutes; it never made an intelligent animal yet."

He took my arm, and with a bow and a shake of the head to the officers, who were moving toward him, and a nod to the troopers, he hurried me out of the pavilion.

CHAPTER XXIX.

"FIRE! FIRE! FIRE!"

JUNE HAD passed and July had come. Mr. Trent had arrived and was eating his heart out while the days dragged by. Miss Jenrys waited and wondered, and wrote to Miss O'Neil letters which she tried to make cheerful, until one day she received a telegram. Mrs. Trent no longer needed her, and Hilda O'Neil was coming to Chicago. She would set out on July 3.

Of course I was summoned to meet her when she came, and I learned then something about "ordeal by question." She was a pretty, brown-eyed, gipsy-like, and petite maiden, more child than woman in her ways, but with a warm, loving, and faithful heart, and a wit as bright and ready almost as that of June Jenrys, who was, to my mind, the cleverest as well as the queenliest of girls.

Miss O'Neil's presence was a boon to the sad-hearted father, for she would not despair; and nature having blessed her with a strong and hopeful temperament, and an abounding faith in a final good, she kept the father's heart from despairing utterly.

Miss Jenrys, true to her word, had continued to receive Monsieur Voisin, though she used much diplomacy in the matter, and seldom, if ever, received him alone.

Lossing and I often met him there, and as the days wore on I noted that Lossing was growing melancholy, or at least more serious and thoughtful than of old, and I attributed a part of this to Voisin's ever courteous and too frequent presence in Washington Avenue. I was much with him in these days. Every day almost would find us together for a longer or less length of time, according to my occupation or lack of it.

One day, after a long and learned discussion of the watercrafts of all countries, we, Lossing and myself, turned our steps toward the Transportation Building to see a certain African brinba, sent all the way from Banguella, Africa, and, to my eyes, a most unseaworthy craft.

It was shortly after the noon hour, and Lossing and I had been lunching with June Jenrys and her friend, by invitation, in consequence of which I was not disguised, while Lossing, by command of Miss Jenrys, had worn and still wore his guard's uniform.

As we were passing from the main building into the annex I saw Lossing start, and, looking up, beheld Monsieur Voisin standing alone in the aisle, and evidently awaiting our approach.

He was, as usual, smiling and affable, and "overjoyed to meet with congenial spirits." He fell into step with us at once, and so we were proceeding in the direction of the mammoth locomotive display, when suddenly the alarm of fire rang out all about us, and the cry, "Fire! fire! fire!" seemed sounding everywhere in an instant.

Following in the wake of a hundred others, we hastened out.

We were not far from the scene of that awful conflagration, and we rushed forward, as men do at such times, carried out of themselves often and reckless of danger.

Who can paint the story of that awful fire? What need to tell it? It has passed out of history, and its victims to their rest and recompense.

The mourning caused by that hateful death-trap, the Cold Storage Building, is known to all the world; the recklessness, the heroism, the strict obedience to orders in the face of death, the horror, the suffering, the loss of gallant lives, all these are known; and yet there remains much that has never been told and never will be: tales of reckless daring, of risks taken for humanity's sake, of kindly, humane deeds unchronicled, and of cowardice, selfishness, dishonourable acts that were better left unwritten.

Among those who stood ready to aid, and who showed in that dreadful time neither fear nor undue excitement, was Lossing. Where help was needed his hands were ready, and it was not long, so ill-fitted was the tindery edifice to resist the flames, before the worst had happened, the tower had fallen, and the dead and dying, rather than the burning structure, became the chief, almost the sole care of the earnest workers, firemen and others.

With the falling of the tower one end of the building, from top to base, became enveloped in flames and smoke, and flying timbers borne that way by the wind made the place especially dangerous. As the blackened fragments fell, small wonder that, seen through the smoke and fire, they were sometimes mistaken for human beings by those who had seen brave men making that fearful leap.

It was impossible to keep together in such a place, and we did not attempt it; but as I now and then cast an anxious glance toward Lossing, I noted that Voisin seemed to be all the time near him.

It was some moments after the falling of the tower, and while it was still believed that there were yet men upon the burning roof, that I moved toward the end of the building, where the smoke was hanging like a curtain over everything below, while lifting somewhat above, to look, if possible, toward that part of the roof which might be yet intact. Lossing and Voisin seemed to be eagerly watching something perilously near the choking smoke and falling timbers, I thought, and I shouted a warning to them just as a group of firemen crossed my path.

Almost at the instant a voice—it sounded like Voisin's—cried: "Look! there's a man!"

In the hubbub of sounds the cry was not heard beyond me. I could not have heard it a few feet farther away; but as it struck my ears I saw Lossing look up, and, following his gaze with my own, I saw something black and bulky, something that looked like an arm thrust out, as it fell down and outward and into the thick smoke that obscured that end of the building altogether.

Was it a man falling there in the thick of that suffocating smoke? I saw Lossing spring forward and dash into the midst of it, with Voisin close behind, and then with shudder I rushed after them, seeing nothing, but entering where they had entered the smoke-cloud, and then for instant I paused and held my breath.

The thing that had fallen lay in the thickest of the smoke, and over it Lossing was just about to bend when I halted, seeing a sudden movement on Voisin's part which made me clench my hands.

For the moment, save for my unseen self, they were alone, shut in by the shifting but never rising smoke, and in that moment, as Lossing bent over to peer at the thing on the ground at his feet, the man just behind him drew from his pocket something which I guessed at rather than recognised, something which caused me to spring forward with my fist clenched.

It was the work of a moment to strike down the man who, in an instant, with a criminal's basest weapon, would have stunned Lossing and left him there in the choking smoke to be suffocated.

As Voisin went down I had just enough strength and breath to catch hold of Lossing and drag him out; and, in a moment, calling some others to my aid, we went in after Voisin.

As we lifted him the "knuckles" dropped from his relaxed hand, and, unnoticed in the smoke, I picked them up and hastily concealed them. He was quite insensible, and a little stream of blood was trickling from one side of his face, where he had struck upon some hard substance in falling.

As he lay upon the ground a sudden thought caused me to start; and I bent down quickly, put my finger solicitously upon his wrist, and then pushing back the dark hair, which always lay in a curving mass over his brow, a little to one side, I laid bare a rather high forehead, upon which, clearly defined, was an oblong scar quite close to the roots of the concealing lovelock. Calling Lossing's attention to this, I replaced the lock, smoothed it into place and arose.

"Come away," I said to Lossing, and leaving Voisin in the hands of those about him for a moment, we withdrew to a place where we might see and be unseen. I told Lossing of the attempt upon his life, and he was not greatly surprised.

"I ought to have been on my guard," he said, "for I think he caused me that lagoon dip. But I was carried out of myself by this cursed holocaust. What shall we do?"

"Keep out of his sight, and let them take him to the hospital. He's not seriously hurt. Possibly he's shamming, now; though he was stunned, as well as half-suffocated."

It was as I surmised. Voisin opened his eyes after some time, and made an effort to rise, but he seemed weak and dazed, and they withdrew him from the place where he lay and made him comfortable in a sheltered spot, to await the return of an ambulance, going back for a few moments to note the progress of the fire.

They were not long absent, but when they went back to their charge he was not there, and a bystander had seen him rise, look about him, and move away, at first slowly and then quite briskly, in the direction of the Sixty-fourth Street entrance.

I had persuaded Lossing to remain out of sight, and had myself viewed Voisin's departure from afar, and when I reported the fact Lossing exclaimed, "Masters, this must end! That man must not be permitted to visit Miss Jenrys after this!"

"Rest easy," I answered him. "The villain will at once take measures to learn the truth about you, and when he knows that you are not lying somewhere on a cold slab awaiting recognition, he will know that his matrimonial game is up," I took a sidewise glance at Lossing as I spoke the next words, "and that one fortune at least has slipped through his fingers."

His eyes, sombre and proud, at once turned slowly toward me as I spoke.

"Masters," he said, "I wish to heaven June Jenrys were as poor—as poor as I am!"

To this I had no answer ready, and we walked on for a short time in silence. Then suddenly he stopped short.

"Masters," he asked, "what was it that fell when I went into the smoke, like an idiot?"

"A piece of timber with a burning rag fluttering from it. A coat thrown off by one of those poor fellows. Just the bait Voisin wanted," I replied.

CHAPTER XXX.

"IT SHALL NOT BE ALL SUSPENSE."

SINCE THE coming of Mr. Trent, who had secured rooms next door to the house occupied by Miss Ross and her niece, it had become my habit to pass an hour, more or less, in Miss Jenrys' parlours each day in the afternoon or evening, as was most convenient, and often, besides Mr. Trent, and of late Miss O'Neil, Lossing made one of the party; for he had come to know as much, almost, as any one of us concerning Gerald Trent's strange absence.

On leaving the scene of the fire it was important that I should have a few words with Dave Brainerd, and this done I was as ready to set out for Miss Jenrys' cosy apartment as was Lossing; for I felt with him that Monsieur Voisin must no longer be permitted to annoy the ladies, even for the good of the cause in which I was so deeply interested.

Imagine my surprise, then, when I learned privately, and from the lips of Miss Ross, that Monsieur Voisin had been there in advance of us and had gone.

Seated in the little parlour, with the *portières* drawn, the clear-headed little Quakeress told me the story of his visit.

I had observed upon entering that June Jenrys was not quite her usual tranquil, self-possessed self; that her cheeks wore an unwonted flush, and that her eyes were very bright and restless, while there seemed just a shade of nervousness and a certain repressed energy in her manner.

Miss Ross had led me, with little ceremony, into the rear room, and she lost no time, once we were seated.

"I don't know what thee may have on thy mind this evening," she began, "but whatever it is, I will not detain thee long. Monsieur Voisin has been here. He left, indeed, less than an hour ago. I have had a talk with June since, and she has allowed me to tell you of his call. The man came here between four and five o'clock."

In spite of myself I started. He had left the grounds with a bleeding face, little more than an hour earlier.

"He was pale, and at one side of his face was a small wound, neatly dressed, and covered with a small strip of surgeon's plaster. He was labouring, evidently, under some strong mental strain, and I was not much surprised when he asked June for a private interview, and in such a supplicating manner that she could hardly refuse. Of course he proposed to her; and in a fashion that surprised her; his pleading was so desperate, his manner so almost fierce. He begged her to take time; he implored her to reconsider; and he went away at last like a man utterly desperate. At the last he forgot himself and charged her with caring for an adventurer; a penniless fortune-hunter who might forsake her at any moment; and then he recounted word for word the things said in that conservatory episode; the things that were imparted to Mr. Lossing."

"The scoundrel!"

"Even so. This was too much for June's temper. She ordered him out of her presence, and in going he uttered some strange words, the purport of them being that before leaving this place she might find that Mr. Lossing had vanished out of her life and gone back to a more congenial career, and that she might be glad to turn to him to beg such favours as no other man could grant, and he ended by saying that had she put him in the place of friend and confidant rather than you, he might have made straight the crooked places that were troubling the peace of herself and some of her friends."

I was fairly aglow with excitement when she paused, and I told her at once my story of the day's happenings.

"Tell Miss Jenrys," I said, "that I can, at the right time, explain all the riddles he has astonished her with, and ask her to be patient yet a little longer."

And then I went back to the others, to tell Mr. Trent and Hilda O'Neil that I had now traced the kidnappers of young Trent so closely that I had only to sift one block of a certain street to find the gang and, I believed, their victim; and, in spite of wonder and question, I would tell them no more.

One of the next morning's papers contained this interesting item, followed up by a copy of the letter sent by Mr. "E. Roe, On the Square," to Mr. Trent:

"THE TRENT MYSTERY.

"There is hope that the mystery of the disappearance of young Gerald Trent of Boston may soon be cleared up. And there is reason for thinking that the enemy is weakening. Not long since a letter, signed by the familiar name of 'Roe,' was received by Mr. Trent and promptly handed over to the officers. This letter we print herewith. Mr. Trent is now in this city, and there have been singular discoveries of late. It is quite probable that Mr. Trent even now will compromise the matter provided his son is returned to him safe and unharmed. For, strange as it may seem, to expose and punish the miscreants, it would be necessary to bring into prominence two ladies of fortune and high social standing, who innocently and unwittingly have been made to play a part in this strange affair. For their sakes, doubtless, a quiet compromise and transfer will end this most singular affair. The 'Roe' letter, reads as follows."

Here, of course, came the letter which Miss O'Neil had copied at length for her friend, and which, in the original, had been sent by Mr. Trent to me.

When this notice had been read by the ladies and by Mr. Trent, I was besieged for an explanation of what seemed to them "an unwarranted withdrawal from the battle"; but my purpose once explained, they were readily appeased and their faith in me restored.

It was true that I had tracked the "clique" to very close quarters, but it was one thing to know that in one house, out of half a dozen, were lodged all, or a part, of the gang, and it was another thing to move upon them in such a way as to secure them all, and at the same time rescue and save young Trent, if he were really in that unknown house, and really alive. It was this problem that was taxing all my ingenuity, and which, as yet, I had not quite solved.

I had called alone on this afternoon, Lossing being on guard, and when the newspaper sensation had been explained and I was about to go, Miss Ross, with whom I had grown quite confidential, walked with me to the outer door.

"Friend Masters," she said gently, "I wish thee could tell me something about young Mr. Lossing. The words flung out by Monsieur Voisin were malicious words, and meant to do harm. But are they not partly true? June is a proud girl, but I am sure she feels this reserve of his, and he is reserved. I love the lad; he seems the soul of truth. But there is a strangeness, a part that is untold. My friend, you whom we call upon for everything, can you not make straight this crooked place, too?"

She put out her hand and smiled upon me, but her gentle voice was full of appeal; and I took the hand and held it between my own while I answered:

"I believe I can do it, Miss Ross; and I surely will try, and that at once. It shall not be all suspense."

CHAPTER XXXI.

SIR CARROLL RAE.

I WAS tired with thinking and planning and loss of sleep, and that night I led Lossing away, an easy captive, to the gondola station by the Art Gallery. He had been in low spirits all day, and had not presented himself at Washington Avenue since I had told him of Voisin's visit there, which I did, word for word, just as Miss Ross had related it to me, and with a purpose.

He was a reserved fellow, and I quite agreed with Miss Ross it was time for him to throw off his reserve; so, after I had assured myself that our gondoliers had made no choice collection of "pidgin English," I began to talk, first of Voisin and then of June Jenrys. Suddenly I turned toward him.

"Lossing, pardon the question, but have you ever known Voisin previous to your meeting in New York?"

"I?" abstractedly. "W—why, Masters?"

"Well, it might easily have been, you know. A man meets so many when he travels much."

"Oh" with a short laugh; "and I, you fancy, have travelled much?"

"Why, Lossing, the fact in your case is evident—in your manner, speech, everything." And I went back to Voisin, and his audacity in addressing Miss Jenrys, finishing by calling him a "fortune-hunting adventurer."

Lossing pulled off his cap, and perching it upon his knee, turned his fair head to look up and down the water-way and then faced me squarely.

"Masters, that's precisely what the fellow called me."

"Nonsense!" I said sharply.

"And isn't it true?"

"Not in my eyes."

He was silent for a time, then:

"Masters," he began, "I've been on the point of opening my heart to you more than once. I am discouraged. I have wooed, yes, and won, June Jenrys with hardly a thought of how I could care for her or for myself. Gad! How thoughtless and selfish I have been! And yet you will think me an ass when I say that, up to this moment, I have never troubled myself nor been troubled about money matters. So help me heaven, Masters, I never once thought of her fortune, or my lack of it, in all my wooing of June Jenrys!"

"I don't doubt it," I said easily, "not in the least. It's not in nature that you should be, at your age, half man and half financial machine. It's contrary to your education." And, smiling inwardly, I began deliberately to fold a cigarette paper.

"My education!" He turned upon me sharply. "What—I beg your pardon, Masters, but what the deuce do you know about my education?"

"I'm a very observing person," I replied amiably; "haven't you noticed it?"

He was silent so long that, when I had finished making my cigarette and lighted it, I asked, after a puff or two: "Lossing, is there anything I can say or do that will help you? I see that you are troubled. If it's money only, bless me, your talents will stand you in money's stead. Brains have a money value in this country, you know."

It was more than I at first meant to say. I was treading on delicate ground, and I knew it.

"Brains! Well, there it is! There's where my 'education,' as you say, stands in the way. It's no use, Masters, our points of view are not the same. To understand mine you must know what my past has been. That would convince you how little my brain could be relied upon to stand me in lieu of a fortune in this pushing, rushing, electric America of yours. And my story—well, if I am to tell it, I must tell it to her first, and—good heavens!" he groaned, "when I have told it, I shall seem to her more like a fortune-hunter than even now."

He was in the depths, and if I meant to speak first, now was my time. I tossed my cigarette into the water, and sat erect and facing him.

"What would you give," I asked slowly, "if I could show you a way out—a safe and right and happy way?"

"Give! Man alive! I'd give you my gratitude all my life long, first, and after that anything you could ask and I could grant. But—pshaw!—I know you're immensely clever, Masters, and I know you're my friend, but—"

"There, don't say anything that you will have to retract; and now, I won't presume to advise you, sir," very respectfully, "but if I were in your place I would either go to June Jenrys and tell her my whole story, or else let me tell it to her."

"Let you!"

"And in going, to pave the way, if I were you, I would send in my card, and that card should read, 'Sir Carroll Rae.'"

The murder was out now, and before he could recover from his surprise I launched into my story, telling of my chief's letter, and of the one from Sir Hugo Rae which accompanied it, also of the vivid description which set me to staring at all good-looking blonds.

"My meeting with you in Midway, when you inquired after Miss Jenrys so anxiously, was my first clue," I said. "On that occasion I noted that you answered the description very well, also that you were not an American." He looked at me surprised. "Oh, your English is perfect; but it's neither Yankee nor yet Mason and Dixon's English. It's very fine and polished, but it's different. Oh, I never mistook you for an American, Sir Carroll Rae; but I might not have given heed to that first clue, had I not read Miss Jenrys' letter to Hilda O'Neil; then I said, 'Suppose the good-looking guard is this Mr. Lossing, and that Lossing is Rae?' And then I began to cultivate you."

"Ah! I begin to understand."

"Then," I went on, "came other tests. Rae was an athlete; Lossing knocked out a lunch-room beat scientifically, Rae possessed a high and rich tenor voice; so, I found, did Lossing."

"When?" he interposed.

"On the night you—ahem—fell into the lagoon. I heard you near the band-stand singing in the chorus."

"I see!"

"Then Rae was a fine rider. Lossing can ride also, even a British cavalry nag. In fine, I studied you from first to last, supposing you to be Rae, a member of the English aristocracy."

"Oh, I say!"

"There you go! An American never would say that. Every word of yours, every act pointed to the same conclusion. You were all that a young Englishman of good family and fortune should be; and so, Sir Carroll—"

"Stop! It gives me actual pleasure to find one flaw in your wonderful summing-up. I am not Sir Carroll. Sir Hugo, my half-brother, bears the title, and Sir Hugo and I saw little of each other and were never warm friends."

"One moment, Sir Carroll. Since that first letter from England, my chief has received another. Sir Hugo is dead."

* * * * *

When he had recovered somewhat from the surprise and shock—for a shock it was, in truth—he told how, being left to the guardianship of his elder brother—Sir Hugo was fifteen years the elder—he had yet seen little of him, Sir Hugo being seldom at home for long.

"Sir Hugo's mother, the first Lady Rae, died when he was a lad, and there were no other children by that marriage," he said. "My mother inherited consumption, and three sisters, all my elders, died in childhood. My mother died when I was a babe, and I was given to the care of Lady Lossing, my mother's elder and favourite sister. I grew to manhood in her house at Dulnith Hall, or in London. When Sir Hugo took possession at last he developed a tyrannical temper. He did not choose to marry, and so I must do so. He selected a wife for me, an heiress, of course, and not too young nor pretty, though an English gentlewoman, and a fit wife for a king, if he loved her, which I did not."

"Well, we quarrelled bitterly. I threatened to come to America, and he bade me go and never to return while he lived. Now, my father had left me nothing, only commending me to Sir Hugo's generosity, which, so long as I consulted his wishes, was free enough. Of my own I had a few hundred pounds left me by my mother. I took that and came to this country. I was introduced into society by a fellow-countryman, who thought my change of name a mere lark, and who soon went home, and then straightway I fell in love with June Jenrys."

"Well," I said, after signaling one of the gondoliers to row us to shore, "I have showed you the way out; have I earned my reward, Sir Carroll Rae?"

With a swift movement he caught my hand between both his own.

"Best of friends," he exclaimed, "you can never ask of me a favour that I will not grant, if given the ability to do so; and now—"

"And now," I echoed as our boat came to the landing, "there is yet time for you to make that delayed call upon the ladies."

CHAPTER XXXII.

FOUND DEAD.

ON THE morning of the second day after the publication of the letter signed E. Roe, I awoke at an early hour, after a night passed, for the most part, in thinking and planning.

As the small hours began once more to grow long, and I had reached at last some definite conclusions, I had fallen asleep, but not for long. Sunrise found me awake and astir.

Dave had been out all night, and I was eager for his return. I wanted his cooperation and his encouragement. I wanted to tell him my plans and to hear the result of his night's reconnaissance in the vicinity of the suspected houses.

But whatever his success or lack of it, my morning's programme was laid out. I should "let no grass grow beneath my feet" until I had taken out warrants of arrest for the "gang."

Of charges against them there were enough and to spare; but to make my final success more sure, it would be best, I knew, not to alarm them to the extent of letting them see that their deepest and wickedest game was known. For this purpose it would be well, I knew, to take them first upon separate charges.

Greenback Bob, I decided, should be arrested upon the charge of counterfeiting, with no specified dates or names. Delbras we would charge with an attempt to pass counterfeit money, or with the attempt to swindle Farmer Camp. Smug should figure as a confidence man. And the brunette, whether appearing as man or woman, should be accused of masquerading. And to complete the list, I would also procure a warrant which should charge Monsieur Voisin with an assault upon Sir Carroll Rae.

Smiling at the thought of the surprise this last name would occasion, I closed my door and was turning the key in the lock when Brainerd came hastily up the stairs and toward me.

"Masters," he said hurriedly, "you're wanted at once. Come along!" And turning, he ran back down the stairs, and awaited me at the foot.

"What's up?" I asked, when I had reached his side.

"Dead man," was his laconic answer as he caught my arm and hurried me along. "Found this morning. I want you to take a look at him."

"Why must I look at him?" I persisted.

"See if you know him, of course!" and to prevent any further inquisitiveness on my part he began to tell me how the body had been found at early dawn by two "honest and early-rising Columbian Guards," lying in the mouth of an alley upon Stony Island Avenue.

"Shot?" I ventured.

"Not much! Strangled!" He glanced over his shoulder and lowered his voice. "And the queer thing is, Murphy and I were through that same alley, from end to end, after midnight. He was not there then. There were four of us within a block of that place all night. Neither he nor his assailants could have passed by on the street."

"Ergo?" I queried.

"Ergo, being out all night, and so near, Murphy and I were the first persons the guards met after finding the body. So, while one of them ran to the station we went to the alley, where the other stood on guard. The body lay upon ground where ashes had been thrown, and thickly too. We could see his footprints plainly. Small they were, and others—two others—one long and slim, the other shorter and broader. They're covered at this moment with dry-goods boxes, open end down, with a big policeman sitting upon them. They couldn't take a cast in those soft ashes."

"Has the body been identified?"

"There was nothing upon the body by which to identify, but it had not been robbed. There was money and valuables in a pocket, and—a belt."

I saw that, for some reason, Dave did not want to give me further information, even if he possessed it. And knowing him too well to press my questions, I remained silent until we had reached our destination.

When we were in the presence of the dead, and the covering was about to be lifted from the face, a sudden shock and thrill came over me, and I hesitated for just an instant, feeling a sudden dread and reluctance at the thought of what I might see, yet neither knowing nor guessing.

Then slowly the officer drew away the covering, and I moved a step nearer.

"Good heavens!" There was that natty suit of dark blue, the slight and short figure, the olive-skin and close-cropped hair that I had seen often.

"Do you know him?" asked Dave.

"Not by name," I replied, and then I turned away to collect my thoughts.

It was the brunette who lay there before me, clad now as when last we met at the Ferris Wheel, in the garb of a man.

There he lay, slender and youthful of face and form, with the small, clean-cut features that had made it so easy to masquerade as a dashing brunette; the keen black eyes, seen through half-closed lids, were staring and inscrutable, and the black marks where something had been drawn so tightly about his neck as almost to cut into the flesh were horrible to see.

"I do not know his name," I again assured the officer in charge. "I have seen him several times disguised as a woman, and once only in the attire in which he now lies dead. I have taken note of him as a suspected person, and I have believed him to be a man since June 7," and I related briefly my reasons for this belief. But I did not make known my belief in the dead man's connection with a gang of dangerous criminals. There was time enough for that. Nor did I give voice to the belief, swiftly taking shape in my mind, that he had met his death at the hands of his comrades, and because of the letter I had caused to appear in the morning papers two days before—the letter of "E. Roe, On the Square."

The body of course must go to the Morgue and the coroner, and I told the officer where I might be found or heard of, if wanted for the inquest, and then we withdrew.

"I was quite sure it was your brunette," declared Dave, now grown communicative. "Not by recognition; you know, I only saw 'her' once and then at some distance, but thanks to the honest guards and ourselves—Murphy and I, that is—the body was not rifled, and I myself helped to search the pockets, at the sergeant's orders, and to examine the belt he wore. That gave me my clue; in it were half a dozen more of Lausch's dew-drop sparklers, unless I am much mistaken, and two more of the pink lot. He seemed to vary in his way of carrying his topaz treasures."

"I think I can explain that," I said. "When he carried that chamois bag, while disguised as a woman, he meant, no doubt, before laying aside the disguise, to negotiate the sale of them, and so had them in readiness. He carried the emerald, you remember, and the other things he sold and tried to sell, in a little bag, so the tradesman said."

"Well!" said Dave ruefully; "one of the gang has slipped through our fingers in a way we did not look for. Have you a theory that will account for this, Carl?"

I turned upon him almost fiercely.

"I have, and so have you, Dave Brainerd. I don't for one moment doubt that my mistaken policy has brought this murder about, and you can see how it has complicated things. When I found through the brunette's note—I can't seem to find any other name for him—that in all probability we knew the men who had made away with Trent, I thought the game was almost in our hands, and now—" I dropped my head dejectedly.

"And now we're a good deal mixed," supplemented Dave dryly. "We're in a dilemma!"

It was indeed a dilemma, if no worse.

When Miss Jenrys had put that note from the "little brunette" into my hand, I had opened it with scant interest, for I only desired through this medium to keep, if possible, some trace of her—or him. When I opened the letter and saw the small, sharp, and much-slanted handwriting, I almost exclaimed aloud in my surprise.

The writing was the counterpart of that of the letter written to Mr. Trent, and opened by his daughter and Hilda O'Neil—the letter proposing a way to liberate Gerald Trent!

I could hardly wait until I could compare the two, and verify my belief, and then I had at once told my discovery to Brainerd.

If the brunette were indeed one of the "clique" who had kidnapped or murdered Trent, then that clique was composed of the very men we were hunting down, and we were nearer to the truth concerning Gerald Trent than we had dared to hope or dream.

It was a great discovery. It put a new face upon everything. And then the question arose: How could we best make use of this new knowledge? How quickest secure the miscreants, fasten this last, worst crime upon them, and rescue Trent, if he yet lived?

And then the previously discussed project of making public the brunette's letter—for the handwritings were identical, and we never doubted that the brunette and "E. Roe" were one and the same—was again canvassed.

"It's the thing to do!" Dave had declared. "We are close upon the scent, and what we now want is a clue, just that. They are so secure now, they go and come so seldom, and with such system! And if we make a dash and do go wrong, they are warned; and now that we know our men, we know that rather than be taken tamely, or be betrayed by the presence of a prisoner, they would resort to desperate measures. Let's advertise this Mr. Roe and his letter; it will show them that they have an enemy at home, it will disturb their fancied security; they will begin to quarrel among themselves and forget their caution. Some of them will show themselves and show us the way to the rest."

What I had counted on was the clause referring to the young ladies, which I had published after much hesitation. This, more than all else, would tell the man I believed to be at the head of this scoundrel band that he was known. He would understand the meaning of that particular sentence. He might see in it and the rest an actual bid for a compromise, and so become less cautious and vigilant. In fact, as Dave declared, "the publication of the letter and its attendant statements was meant for a bait."

Having decided upon this course, we had agreed to keep our discovery a secret until we had made this first experiment; and while awaiting results we would not discontinue our efforts to locate our party, by which we meant to make sure that our attack, when made, would find them all, or at least the chief personages, under one roof; for my belief that by devious ways this "clique" came together regularly, if not nightly, with their headquarters under one roof, and that roof not far away, was strong.

The fact that we were about to exploit the Roe letter had in itself aroused fresh hopes in the hearts of Hilda O'Neil and the father of Gerald Trent, and we decided to keep the important fact that the letter had revealed to us between ourselves.

For a few days it should be known to none but our two selves; meantime, from those few days we hoped for much.

We had hoped much; and, after two days of waiting, something had happened indeed! The little brunette who had been so mysteriously interested in June Jenrys, who had shown herself, and himself, an active member of the "clique," lay dead at the Morgue, murdered—by whom?

"I can't look at it as an unmitigated misfortune," declared Dave, in reply to some of my self-condemnatory moralizing. "Let us admit that the fellow's letter did cause his death. Wasn't it because he wrote it quite as much or more than because you printed it? And even grant you it was your deed, all of it, haven't you been labouring to get that chap where he could do no more harm? Mark me! if we ever learn who that lad is, he will prove to be one of the outlaws that the gaol and the halter were especially meant for."

This I could not doubt, and I took such comfort in it as I might.

Of course the detective who had been in search of the brunette was at once summoned, through Dave and myself, and the only information brought out by the inquest was that which, between us, we gave. He was a "crook," and would have been arrested by myself, had he lived, upon a charge of masquerading in woman's dress while carrying out illegal schemes. Corey, the only name I shall dare give the clever Chicago detective, declared the body to be that of a person, name unknown, for whom he held a warrant upon a charge of robbery; and, lying dead in the Morgue, the "little brunette" was arraigned and proven guilty of participating in the Lausch diamond robbery, of World's Fair fame, and a portion of the spoil was produced as having been found upon his person. The jewels were duly turned over to Monsieur Lausch, who had now recovered nearly, if not quite, half of the jewels he had lost, these all having been in the possession of the brunette.

Between the event of the morning and the hour of the inquest I had been busy, and when it was over I hastened to my room to arm myself with certain papers and intent upon securing the warrants, all save one, for which I had so lately planned.

At the door of my room a tall figure awaited me, and when I recognised it as that of one of my chief's most trusted "stand-bys," who seldom left New York, I began to wonder.

He had been directed to my quarters, he said, and finding the surroundings to his liking, had awaited me there. He was not slow in making known his business, and he began with the query:

"Have you got Delbras?"

I had, of course, sent regular reports to my chief, and a week previous had informed him that we were on the trail of the Frenchman, and I answered: "Not yet; but I mean to have a warrant out for him within an hour."

"Don't waste your time," advised Jeffrys. "I have a warrant and all the necessary extras in my pocket. I have been in Chicago long enough for that." And he made haste to tell me how our chief had lately received from France papers authorizing the arrest of Delbras, wherever found, upon the charge of murder. The French police had worked out, at last, a solution to the mysterious murder in the Rue de Grammont.

The victim, one Laure Borin, was found in her apartment stabbed in half a dozen places, and a tall, dark man, name unknown, was searched for in vain for many weeks.

At last the crime was traced to Delbras, through the revelations of a second woman, who, finding that the man she had believed in hiding had really crossed the ocean and left her behind, had at once avenged herself by putting into the hands of the police the means by which they had traced the crime home to Delbras.

"You must not arrest the fellow," Jeffrys had said. "Leave that to me. I have everything—extradition and all—and in Paris they'll not fail to execute him."

This last argument had its weight. I could not speak with equal certainty of the formality which we call "trial by jury," but I began to feel that the fate of the "clique," in one way or another, was being rapidly taken out of our hands.

One thing was assured; Jeffrys must wait and move with us; any effort of his to secure Delbras alone would endanger our chances for securing the rest.

Before going further with Jeffrys I felt that I must consult Dave. He had left me at noon to go back to Stony Island Avenue, where half a dozen places, each more or less "shady," were being constantly watched. Leaving Jeffrys to look at the wonders nearest at hand for an hour, and this he was quite ready to do, I set out in search of my friend and fellow-worker, wondering a little what he would think and say of this new turn of affairs.

CHAPTER XXXIII.

"A MERCYFUL DISPENSAYSHUN."

AS I left the Exposition grounds and came out upon Stony Island Avenue I looked at my watch, for I had in mind much that I wished to accomplish before night came on. It was nearing three o'clock, and I hastened my steps.

Glancing about as I put away my watch, in the hope that I might see Billy or Dave, as they from time to time shifted their place of observation, I saw, to my annoyance, on the opposite side, but coming toward me almost directly across the street, Mrs. Camp. Her eyes were fixed upon me, and when she had reached the middle of the highway, she waved her arm in frantic gesture, which, in spite of my haste, brought me to an instant standstill, knowing as I did that she was quite capable of shouting out my name should her signal be ignored.

As she came nearer I saw that her eyes were staring wildly, and her face wore a look so strange and excited that for a moment I feared that the marvels of Chicago and the Fair had unsettled her reason, and her first words did not altogther reassure me.

"If this ain't a mercyful dispensayshun," she panted, stopping squarely before me, "then I don't know what is! I was goin' to hunt ye up jest as fast as feet c'd travel, an' I never spected to be so thankful for knowin' a perlece officer ez I be ter-day. My!" catching her breath and hurrying on; "if I couldn't 'a' seen to gittin' them wretches arristed afore night, I'd 'a' had a nightmare sure, an' never slep' a wink!"

"Mrs. Camp," I broke in, "not so loud, please."

"Ugh!" The woman suddenly dropped her loud tone and looked nervously around. She was trembling with excitement, and the colour came and went in her tanned cheeks.

And now, to my surprise, I noted dangling from her arm beneath the loose wrap, which she wore very much askew, a black something, which, as she lifted her arm to pass her hand across her twitching lips, I perceived was an ear-trumpet attached to a long black tube such as is used by the deaf, and my fears for her sanity were increased.

"Mrs. Camp," I said, in a soothing tone, "you seem exhausted; let me take you to your rooms, if they are not too far, and you can talk after resting."

Something in my tone or look must have enlightened her as to my thoughts, for she suddenly broke into a short, nervous laugh.

"Oh, I ain't crazy! Though I don't blame ye if ye thought so," she said, with an attempt at composure. "I was comin' to see ye, and it's important. I was goin' to that Miss Jenrys, but I forgot the number her aunt give me, and so I struck right out for that office where Adam and me met ye that first time when I wanted ye arristed right off, ye know. But, land! I be actin' like a plum fool. Come right along!" She caught my arm and turned me about. "My place ain't fur, and I s'pose we can't talk in the streets."

I began to fear that I should not easily escape her, and moved on beside her, her hand still gripped upon my arm as if for support.

"I shan't open my head ag'in," she said as we went, "till we git there." And she did not, but when we had reached her door and I was about to make an excuse, and after seeing her safe indoors hasten on in my search for Dave, she said, much more like her usual self:

"Come right in now and find out what kind of a detective I'd make if I had a chance. It's your business, too, I guess;" and then, as I seemed to hesitate, "an' it's about that counterfittin' man."

Suddenly, somehow, the notion of her insanity vanished from my mind, and I followed her into the house.

She opened a door near the entrance, and, after peeping in, threw it wide.

"It's the parlour of the hull fambily," she explained as I entered, "and I'm thankful it ain't ockerpied jest now, for our room ain't more'n half as big."

It was the tiniest of parlours, but not ill-furnished, and the moment she had dragged forward a chair for me, after the manner of the country hostess, and had made sure that the door was close shut, she drew a small "rocker" close to my own seat and began eagerly:

"I've had an adventer to-day, a reg'lar story-book sort of one. It's made me pretty nervous and excited like, and I hope you'll excuse that; but I'm going to tell it to you the quickest way, for, 'nless I'm awful mistook, them folks'll git out quick's they find out who I be, or who I ain't, one or t'other."

"My time—" I began, hoping to hasten her story, but she went on hurriedly:

"Ye see, Camp has got so sot and took up with them machines, and windmills, and dead folks, and dry bones down to'rds that south pond that he ain't no company for nobody no more; so this afternoon—we didn't neither one go out this mornin', for we'd been to see Buffaler Bill las' night, and we was tuckered all out—so this afternoon I went with Camp down street instead of goin' the t'other way, for he thought 'twould be a good idee to go in a new gate; but somehow when we got there I didn't feel much like goin' in, seemed like 'twould be sich a long tramp, and I jest left him at the gate and sa'ntered back, thinkin' I'd rest like an' be fresh for a good long day to-morrer."

"Yes," I said, as she seemed waiting for my comment, "I see."

"Wal, I come along slow, and right down by—wall, I'll show you the place, I'm awful bad 'bout rememberin' names; but when I'd got more'n half-way home, an' was 'most up to a house that stood close to the street, I see the door begin to open, real careful at first, an' then quick; an' then out of the house came a tall man. He didn't look back, but I c'd see there was someone behind him, an' then the door shut. The man come down the steps, an' then he seemed to see me, an' a'most stopped. I tell ye I was glad then that I had on these."

She thrust her hand into her pocket and drew out a pair of those smoked-glass spectacles so much affected by sight-seers at the Fair, and I was forced to smile at the strange metamorphosis of her face when she put them on and turned it toward me. With the small, sharp eyes, her most characteristic feature, concealed, the face became almost a nonentity.

"Would you 'a' knowed me?" she demanded.

"I think not."

"Wal, I guess he didn't'; anyhow, he give me a sort of inquirin' look an' started off ahead of me. An' who d'ye s'pose he was?"

I shook my head, anxious only that she should get on with the story.

"Wal, as sure as my name's Hanner Camp, 'twas that feller 't changed the money fer Camp; the furriner one that I see in that Cayrow house; the one with the hands!"

"But—you said—"

"Yes, I know I did; but I studied it all over, an' I wa'n't mistook, not a mite! That feller jest went through an' out the back door, and changed his clo's somewhar, an' came back playin' gentleman. But, I tell ye, I knowed them hands! 'Twas him I seen come out of that door to-day."

"Are you sure?"

"Sartin sure!"

"Then—wait one moment. Did you see him go far? Where did you see him last?"

"Wal, there—there was an alley next to the house, and acrost that was another house, and then a saloon. He went into the saloon."

"Oh!" This was the answer I had hoped for. "Pray go on, Mrs. Camp."

"I'm goin' to. You know I said there was a man come and shet the door; wal, I got jest a glimpse of him at the door, and it kind o' started me, and I came by real slow, a-lookin' at the house. I noticed that every winder in the front was shet, and the curtains down, all but one, and that was the front one next the alley; that was open half-way and the curtain was up. I couldn't see inside, but jest as I came oppersite the winder a man's face popped right out of it for jest a minit, lookin' the way the other feller went, and then it popped out o' sight ag'in; but I seen it square!"

"Who was it?" I demanded, now thoroughly aroused.

"It was that feller that was so perlite to Camp and me the time you was arristed; the Sunday-school feller."

I started to my feet, and sat down again. She had been doing detective work indeed! I thought I could understand it all. This was the house we had for days suspected and watched, but the only one ever seen to enter it had been Greenback Bob. Doubtless the murder of the brunette made them so uneasy that, contrary to custom, Delbras had ventured out by day, probably to learn what he could of the movements of the officers. I turned to Mrs. Camp.

"Mrs. Camp," I began earnestly, "I am going to confide in you. Those men belong to a gang of robbers and murderers; we have been watching them for weeks. Fortunately, you have come upon them in such a way as to locate their hiding-place; you can help us very much if you will try to recall everything just as you saw it there, and will answer a few questions, when you have told your story. Or—is this all?"

"All! I guess it ain't all; an' I guess you won't need to ask many questions when I get through!" I nodded, and she went on rapidly.

"When I see that feller dodge back and shet the winder, I remembered what you had said about him and the others, and 'bout their tellin' me, to that office, how you was a detective yourself; and I jest sez to myself, says I, 'I'm goin' to try an' git another look at that house;' so I went on past it till I come to a little store, and I went in an' bought ten cents' worth of green tea, and when I comes out I goes back, jest as if I was going home with my shoppin'. By the way, you ain't seemed to notice these new clo's."

I had noted the black gown and cape-like mantle she wore, both plain, but neat and not an ill fit; and I had also wondered how she had happened to discard her old straw hat with the lopping green bows for the simple dark bonnet she wore, but she did not wait for my criticism.

"I'll tell you how't come," she went on. 'I ain't blind, and I'd been a-noticin' the difference 'twixt my clo's and some of the rest of 'em; and I was specially took with them plain gownds them ladies wore that you interduced me to that day; an' I jest studied on it, and sort o' calkalated the expense, and then went up to the stores. I wanted a gray rig, like that Miss Ross had on, but I couldn't get none to fit, an' the young lady told me 't black was dredful fash'nable now, so I got this rig; an' 'twas lucky I did ter-day."

What could she mean by this diversion? I was growing uneasy when she uttered the last words. "Yes?" I said feebly.

"I s'pose you wonder what I'm drivin' at?" she queried. "Well, it's comin'. Ye see I was wearin' these clo's, and the goggles, as I call 'em, when I went sa'nterin' past that house; but I hadn't got to it, nor even to the s'loon yet, when a cab—one of them two-wheeled things, you know, with the man settin' up behind to drive."

I nodded.

'Wal, it drove up, an' the man opened the door, right in front of that house, an' out got a woman; she was bigger than me, and all drest in black, an' she looked sort of familiar, an' jest as I was wonderin' who she made me think of, an' she was a-paying the driver, up comes another cab, tearin', and out hopped two fat, red-faced perlecemen, an' there was a little squabble like, an' the woman flung herself round so't I could see her face, an' then I knew her."

She paused as if for comment, but I was now too much amazed for words.

"I knew her in a minit," she resumed, "an' it was that woman that come stridin' into that rug place in Cayrow Street that day. She hadn't no long swingin' veil on this time, and she didn't look nigh so big 'longside them big perlecemen. She had give up quiet enough when she seen she had to; an' they put her into the cab an' drove away, with t'other one behind 'em. I walked pretty slow, so as not to come right into the rumpus, an' I thought, as I come acrost the alley, that I see somethin' a-layin' by the sidewalk on the outside. I looked round, and seein' that every last winder was as dark as black, I stooped down to look at the things, an' here they air." And she shook out with one hand a long black veil which she had drawn from her pocket, and held out with the other the snake-like speaking-tube.

"I c'n see you're in a hurry," she said, dropping the veil and tube into her lap, "an' I'll git to the p'int now, right off. I wa'n't never no coward, and I jest ached to find out what them fellows was up to. Mebbe if I'd stopped to think I wouldn't have run the risk, but while I stood there with them things in my hand a idee popped into my mind. I looked round; there wasn't a soul near me, an' the winders was all dark, so't nobody could see me from the house, and of course they hadn't seen the woman git arristed an' took away. We didn't look much alike, but I though mebbe they'd let me in, thinkin' 'twas her; and when I got in I'd tell 'em I'd found the trumpet at their door, and p'r'aps, if I felt like it, I'd say I'd seen a gentleman to the winder that I was 'quainted with; that is if he didn't come to the door. Anyhow, I thought I'd try to make sure it 'twas him I see at the winder."

I shuddered at her cool recital of such daring venture; and yet I could see how, with her country training, she would see nothing so very serious or dangerous in thus thrusting herself into a strange house, gossip-like, "to find out what was goin' on." She took up the trumpet.

"I was used to these things," she said, "for my aunt on my mother's side used to live with me; she was a old maid an' she used one. Stone-deef she was, a'most, but I didn't think then o' usin' this. When I got onto the top step I felt 'most like runnin' off all of a sudden, but I set my teeth and give the bell a jerk. 'Twa'n't long before the door opened jest a crack, and I see an eye lookin' out. I meant to git inside before I said anything, so I kind o' give the speakin' trumpet, hangin' over my arm, a shake; it was 'most hid under the veil, you know; and then the door opened wider, and I see a woman. My! the palest, woe-begon'dest woman I'd ever see, 'most. 'Oh!' she says, in a shaky, scairt sort o' voice, 'come in quick.' She looked so peaked and strange I jest stood starin' at her a minit, and all to once she reached out her hand and motioned to me; and as I stepped in she caught hold of the big end of the speakin' trumpet, and then I see that she thought I was deef; and quick as a wink it come to me to play deef 's long as I could—deef folks are allus makin' blunders—and then to 'polergize an' git out. So I stuck the tube to my ear.

"'You're the nurse?' she says through it, but not very loud, for a deef person, that is. 'Louder,' sez I. So she sed it real loud, an' I nodded.

"Then she motioned me to come into the room to the front, that I had seen the man look out of. It was 'most dark there, only there was a winder on the alley that 'peared to be all boarded up, only jest a slit to the top to let a little streak of light in. 'Set down a minit,' she says; an' when she let go of the trumpet her hand shook so't I could see it. She opened the door in the back of the room, an' I see there was a screen on the other side so I couldn't see the room, but I got up an' tiptoed to the door. The carpet was awful thick there an' in the hall, though it was old enough too.

"She hadn't shet the door tight, an' I heard her say, 'Wake up, Bob.' An' then a sort of question; an' she says ag'in, 'The nurse has come after all, and you can go and sleep now.' Then I heard a man say, 'What made the old gal so late, blast her eyes! I'd go an' give her a good old blessin' if she wasn't sech a crank-mouthed jade.' An' then he seemed to be stirrin', an' I 'most thought he was comin' in; but then he says, 'Git her in here, an' then git me somethin' ter eat. I can't sleep when I'm so holler.' 'Won't you come in an' speak to her, Bob?' says the woman, 'an' tell her 'bout the med'cin'; I'm so tired.'

"Then I was scairt ag'in, though I declare I felt sorry fer that poor crittur of a woman.

"But the man snarled at her, and says, 'Naw, I won't; I'm tired's you be. Hustle now, an' bring me the grub mighty quick.'

"I scooted back to my chair then, and in a minit or so she come in an' motioned me to come into the other room. I see they had mistook me for some deef nurse, an' I begun to think I'd grabbed more'n I could hold, an' to wish I was out. But I went in, an' if ever a woman was struck all of a heap, 'twas me."

She paused as if mentally reviewing the scene once more, and I fairly quivered with anticipation and anxiety for what the next words might develop.

"I had noticed that there was three winders on the alley side of the house," she resumed, "an' there bein' only one in the front room, of course I looked to see one sure in this, an' mebbe two, but there wasn't a winder; the wall on that side was smooth, only at the winder place was a kind of cubbard arrangement like, an' the room was lit by a kerosene lamp. It was furnished quite good, too; but in a corner on the bed laid a young man, as good-lookin' about as they make 'em; only he was dretful pale an' thin, an' he 'peared to be sleepin.

"'There's yer patient,' says the woman, through the tube. 'There ain't nothin' to do now only ter give him drink, an' not let him talk if he wakes. He sleeps a good deal, an' when he wakes up he's out of his head, an' 'magines he's somebody else, an' ain't in his own house, an' all sorts of nonsense.' She went to the bed an' stood lookin' at the sick man in a queer sort of way, an' she give a big long breath, as if she felt awful bad, an' then went out by a door that I knew went to the hall, an' I heard noises in a minit more, as if they come from the kitchin stove.

"Now I knowed she took me for a nurse and all that, but all the same I begun to think I'd better git out. I couldn't play nurse an' ask about that Sunday-school feller too, an' I thought I'd jest made a big blunder, an' I'd better git out 'thout waitin' for her to come back; an' jest then I heard a little noise, an' I looked round, an' the sick man had rolled over an' was lookin' at me straight, an' when he ketched my eye, he says, 'Come here, madam, please.' 'Twas a real pleasant voice, though weak, an' I went right up to the bed. He looked at me real sharp, an' sort of wishful, and then he says, 'You look like a good woman.'

"I didn't say nothin', an' he kep' right on, sort of hurried like. 'I was not asleep when you entered,' he says, 'and I heard that poor woman. I am not insane, and this is not my home. You have come here to nurse me, but if you want money you can earn a hundred nurses' fees by going to a telegraph office and telegraphin' to—'

"Jest then there was a noise in the hall, an' he stopped, an' I picked up a fan an' stood as if I was a-fannin' away a couple of little moths that the lamp had drawed.

"Nobody came in, so I went to the door an' listened. Seemed as if I heard a door shet upstairs, an' I guessed the woman was taking up the cross man's dinner. So I went back to the bed. He laid still for a bit, and seemed listenin'; then he says:

"'I am a prisoner, and have been half-killed first, an' then drugged to keep me so. My people are wealthy. They will pay you royally if you'll help me; if you'll go to the nearest police-station an' give 'em a paper I will give yer, with my father's name, an'—' He stopped ag'in, an' shet his eyes quick as lightnin'; an' the next minit the pale woman came in quick, an' lookin' awful anxious. She went to the bed an' looked at the sick young feller, an' then she took hold of the trumpet and motioned me to listen. 'Can you hear?' she says into it, not very loud. I nodded, an' looked to'rds the bed. 'He sleeps real sound,' she says, 'and won't be likely to wake up, anyhow; I can't leave him alone to talk to you in another room. There's somethin' I forgot, an' some of them may come in any time now. Will you do a wretched woman a small kindness?' She looked at me awful wishful when she said that, an' I nodded my head ag'in.

"'They told me not to let you in unless you gave me a card, and I—I am so troubled I forgot to ask you for it at the door. Will you give me the card now, an' please not give me away to the boys? I can't stand no more trouble. I—I think it was you being so late made me forget. Why was it?'

"For a minit I was stumped, an' then an idee come to me. 'Ter tell the truth,' I says, as bold as you please, 'I've been in a little trouble, an' I forgot that card. You see, I had to put off comin' here on account of a couple of perlecemen that was on the look-out fer me. I've only jest give 'em the slip.' You see I thought when she heard that she'd make 'lowance fer the card, an' I wanted to talk more with that sick boy, fer I b'leeved he was tellin' the truth. But, my! she jumps up, lookin' scairt to pieces, an' she says:

"'The perlece! Do you think they will follow you? can they? Merciful goodness! we can't risk it. I'm almost broke down, but I'll call up Bob, an' you must go right away. Don't you see it won't do?' She snatched a key out of her pocket. 'Come,' she says. 'Mercy, what a risk!' I had took off my glasses and laid 'em down on the table by the bed. I picked up the black veil I had dropped on the chair, and jest as she went to take the key out of the hall-door—she had to turn her back to do it—I went to the table and took up my glasses, and tried to ketch that poor boy's eye and make him a sign; but, my! he laid there with his eyes shet, an' sech a look of misery upon his poor face, an' all at once it struck me that I hadn't spoke once, an' that he hadn't noticed the trumpet till the woman come in, and then he thought he'd been a-beggin' help of a deef woman. But I hadn't no chance then, an' as soon as she'd picked out the key, she says, 'I'll have to let yer out front. It won't do to risk your being seen coming out by any other way.'

"The way was clear when I got out; but I most dreaded meeting one of them men som'ers, and I jest started straight to find you."

"One moment," I said hurriedly, as she now ceased. "You spoke of Miss Jenrys—why did you think of going to her?"

"Why, she was nearest of anybody, an' I thought you was as likely as not to be there."

CHAPTER XXXIV.

"EUREKA!"

AT TWELVE o'clock p.m. a party of men had gathered not far from the house where Mrs. Camp had made her singular discoveries; they came singly and by twos, from various directions, and their movements were so quiet as not to have disturbed the lightest of sleepers, however near, for with one exception all were trained to the business in hand.

When two of the party had made a careful reconnaissance of the premises they returned to the waiting group.

"There's the door and two windows at the front," said one, "and three windows on the alley, the middle one, as we know, boarded on the inside. At the back is a door opening upon a sort of shed, and a window in the same; and in the angle formed by the shed and the rear of the house proper is another window; on the inner side, opposite the alley, the wall is blank. There's no bed in the front room," the speaker went on rapidly, "though someone may bunk there. Of course there's a watcher in his room. Two of you must patrol the alley while Brainerd cuts out a pane or two of that closed-up alley window, to see if anything can be heard through the cracks of those inside boards, though it's probable they are padded to deaden sound. As for the upper rooms, they're sleeping there doubtless, and—"

"Don't forget," interposed Brainerd in a low half-whisper, "about those iron hooks outside those back windows. They're for something more than signalling; they're stout enough to support a rope with a man at the end, and the rope and the man are both inside, no doubt."

"Four to the back then," I said, "and you, Jeffrys, take the lead; three to the alley, you and two others, Dave. If the thing's not accessible, divide to back and front. Lossing, can you and Murphy hold me on your shoulders while I try that window? Now, all to our places; and there ought to be a train soon over there; let's do our cutting under cover of its noise."

The Illinois Central Railway was but a little distance from us, and we took our places to await the sound of its first train. But fortune, having baffled and hindered us again and again, seemed now to have relented toward us.

Before trying the window I crept up the steps to examine the lock of the door, and judge, if I could, of its security. Lossing, as he still preferred to be called, and Murphy, the policeman, were standing below me, one on either side of the steps, and as I stood at the door above them I turned and looked about me. All seemed quiet up and down that often unquiet street, and the lights from either direction hardly served their purpose there, a fact which had been considered, doubtless, in making choice of this place.

It was after midnight now, and as I heard, far away yet, the first faint rumble of the train, I put my hand upon the handle of the door.

Was it imagination, or did I feel a responsive touch upon the other side? I let my hand rest lightly upon the knob, and waited; then, suddenly, as the rumble of the train came nearer, I sprang down the steps, and, crouching at the side of Lossing, whispered across to Murphy, "Lay low and be ready; someone's coming out." There was no time for more words, but I never doubted the readiness of my two helpers, nor their quick comprehension of the situation.

As the rumble of the train came nearer, the door opened, almost without noise, and shut again; and softly, slowly, looking up and down the street, but not below him, almost within reach, a man came down the steps, paused an instant, and stood upon the pavement, to feel, before he could turn his head, a hard grip upon either arm, a cold pressure at the back of his neck, and simultaneously a low whisper:

"One sound and you are a dead man."

It was all the work of an instant, and so quickly and quietly done that our friends in the alley were not aware of our capture until we had secured our prisoner and Lossing had gone to summon Dave.

Then, still in utter silence, we led our first capture across the alley, and Murphy flashed a dark-lantern in his face.

It was a pallid and cowardly countenance that the light revealed, and I was not surprised to recognise the man I had dubbed "Smug" upon the day of my arrival at the World's Fair. He was trembling violently, and thoroughly cowed.

We had no difficulty in searching his pockets; he did not so much as remonstrate—perhaps because of the pistol I had now transferred to the hand of Lossing. By the light of the dark-lantern I selected from among a number of keys taken from his pocket a slender one, which, as it only needed the look upon his face to tell me, was the key to the street-door.

"Listen!" I said to him, holding the lantern high. "It will be to your interest to help us, and you will find it so if you help to make what we are about to do as easy and quiet as possible. We know who are in that house, and if we can take them without noise and trouble, so much the better for them. The place is surrounded; they can't escape alive. Is anyone in the front room, lower floor?"

He shook his head sullenly.

"You were put there on guard—is it not so?" He blinked under the lantern's rays, and I saw that I was right. "And you thought it would be quite safe to slip out for an hour or two; and so it would have been last night or the one before. Now, is Delbras on the second-floor front? You had better tell me!" He nodded sullenly. "And Bob? Remember, your answers can't injure their case and will benefit yours. My word is good. Is Greenback Bob there?" Again the sullen fellow bowed his head. "And how many more, exclusive of your prisoner?" The rascal started, and seemed taken with a new panic. "You had better be quite frank," I admonished. "How many?"

He held up three fingers as well as the handcuffs would permit, and a moment later we had left him at the mouth of the alley, guarded by two officers, while we arranged for our attack.

One man was left to guard the rear, with full instructions covering any and all possible emergencies, and one was told off to guard the front entrance, while the remaining six were paired: Lossing with myself, at his own request; Dave and one officer, and Jeffrys with another. Murphy we had left with Smug, and in charge of the party without.

"Masters," Lossing said, "I want to be with the man that attacks Delbras. I owe it to him." When Jeffrys had heard him he declared Delbras his prey. But I also had my word to say. Jeffrys might serve his warrant and bear off the captive from the city, but he could only take him when I had failed; and so it was arranged.

When all was ready we waited, six of us, upon the steps of the gloomy house, until after what seemed an hour, and was in reality ten minutes, had passed, and then a long freight train came rumbling cityward. As it came near I inserted the key in the lock carefully and turned it slowly, and without noise; and while the sound still covered our careful movements, we entered the hall, leaving the officer in charge of the door.

Then, when Dave and his companion had entered the front room and stood ready to move upon the watcher through the door behind the screen, trusting the other door to the watchful eye of the guard at the front, we crept upstairs, with that sidewise movement which insures one who has the patience to try it a silent if slow passage, to the top, in single file.

At the top we separated, and while we—Lossing and myself—took our places at the door near the front, Jeffrys listened at the two rear doors, to make sure of the location of his prey, and at a signal which the guard below passed on to Dave we moved, each armed with a dark-lantern, to the attack.

I could hear Lossing's breath close beside me as I carefully and slowly tried the knob of the door and found that it yielded silently.

The house was an old one, and we saw as we slowly opened the door that the lock was only a fragmentary one; there was on the other side only a handle like that without. Holding our lanterns low we glided in, and were halfway across the room when I raised the lantern and turned its light carefully toward the bed, from whence long guttural breathing told of a sleeper unconscious of our nearness. With lantern in one hand and pistol in the other, I made a forward step as I saw by the ray thrown across the bed the form and face of Delbras; and then, suddenly, beneath my foot, something cracked and burst with a sharp explosion.

Only a parlour match, but it brought the sleeper to a sitting posture, and broad awake in a moment. He did not seem to so much as have seen me, but his eyes and Lossing's appeared to meet and challenge each other, and quicker than I can tell it he had bounded from his bed, snatching something from under the pillow as he sprang—something that glittered in his hand as he hurled himself upon Lossing, and the two grappled and swayed, with the knife gleaming above their heads, held thus by the strong hand of the English athlete.

As I sprang to place my lantern upon the table at the bed's head, that it might help me to see and to aid Lossing, a shriek rang from the room at the rear, and the next moment I saw the knife sent flying from the hand of Delbras, and the two go down, still struggling. A moment I watched them struggling there, and then somehow the villain wrenched one hand free and gripped it with an awful clutch upon Lossing's throat; the next there arose from below a succession of screeches that might have issued from the throat of a bedlamite.

Once and again I had tried to interfere in Lossing's behalf, but the effort seemed useless, until, as the screams from below ceased suddenly, I sprang past the two, and, turning suddenly, struck at Delbras with my clubbed pistol. I had aimed at the arm clutching at my friend's throat, but a sudden movement brought the villain's head in sharp contact with the butt of the pistol, and his hold suddenly relaxed, and he lay stunned and at our mercy.

When Lossing, not much the worse for his tussle but somewhat short of breath, had risen and shaken himself together, I said: "He's only stunned and will soon come to. Shoot him if he stirs before I come back." And I ran to the room in the rear.

What had happened there can be soon told.

When Jeffrys opened the door of the rear room, which did not boast a lock, he saw a lamp burning dimly upon a shelf in a corner; upon the bed opposite a woman and a man, both sleeping, and under the one window a coil of rope ladder, as if ready for use.

The face of the woman was ghastly pale, and her sleep must have been very light, for suddenly she opened her eyes, and seeing the officers, uttered the cry, which at first only caused her lord and master to growl out an oath and turn over; whereupon she clutched at him wildly and cried to the men to leave them; they would give themselves up if only the officers would withdraw and permit them to rise and dress.

The man, meantime, seemed to awaken slowly, and to be dazed and stupid, and he paid little heed to his wife's cries as he dragged himself to a sitting posture.

"You'd better get up," said Jeffrys sternly, "and give up. You're all in for it."

Possibly the shrieks that came from below at that moment convinced him, for he answered with a scowling face: "I guess I know when I'm beat. If you'll shet the door, or turn yer backs so my wife can get up, I'll be quiet enough. Shet up, Sue!"

"All right," said Jeffrys; and the two officers drew back from the door, and Jeffrys, drawing it half-shut, said, with his eye upon the man, "Now, the lady first," and pistol in hand he waited.

The one window was opposite the door and the bed close

beside it, so that the half-closed door concealed from Jeffrys both window and woman. He heard her spring up, and at the instant, almost, a slight scraping sound, then suddenly, at the very moment when I stepped from the farther room, the light went out—there was a bound, an oath, a shrill whistle, and, as I reached the door, the flash of a bull's-eye, and two pistol-shots came close together.

As I sprang into the room the light revealed an open window, with the rope ladder half out, half in, and upon the floor beneath it Greenback Bob, with Jeffrys kneeling upon his breast, and the attendant officer, with pistol aimed and bull's-eye in hand, at his head. Upon the bed, weeping and moaning piteously, lay the woman, her face buried in the pillow. I went to her and put a hand upon her arm; she lifted toward me the most woeful face it has ever been my lot to see, and said, with mournful apathy:

"Don't fear—I don't want to escape! I knew the end must be near." And she dropped back with an air of utter exhaustion upon her pillow.

I turned to assist Jeffrys in securing Greenback Bob, who, now that his pretence of stolid apathy had failed him, was an ugly customer to deal with, and who was resisting with all his strength and filling the air with blasphemy. It was necessary to secure him hand and foot, and we had but just completed the task when Dave came bounding up the stairs.

"Eureka!" he cried. "It's a complete catch; and Trent's alive, and the happiest man in Chicago, or the world. Hello!"

He had glanced at the prostrate counterfeiter, and his last exclamation was in answer to a voice from the room where I had left Lossing guarding the senseless Delbras.

Following Dave's significant gesture, I went with him to the door of the room, where, to my surprise, Delbras, his face quite bloodless with rage and weakness together, was slowly dressing himself under the sternly watchful eye and steadily aimed pistol of Sir Carroll Rae.

The latter had gathered the garments together while Delbras lay unconscious, keeping a watchful eye and ready weapon the while, and had placed them close at his side, first removing from a pocket a small sheathed knife. And now, with his own weapon in hand and those of Delbras collected on the table at his side, he was compelling the Frenchman to make his toilet at the point of the pistol, and his set face left in the mind of the enraged and baffled rascal no room to doubt him when he said:

"Unless you have put on those garments within a reasonable time I will call a pair of policemen to dress you; and if you make one sound or movement other than in obedience I will shoot every bullet in this weapon into your body, and do it with pleasure."

"How was it?" I asked Dave while this toilet was proceeding, and we stood ready for the trick or attempt at resistance we more than half expected from the Frenchman.

"I guess you heard it about all. Trent lay there wide awake, mighty blue, and too weak to lift his head; and a big negress was half-dozing in her chair by the bedside, with a pistol at her elbow. She made a grab for it, and yelled, as you probably heard. Trent was assaulted and half-killed, nursed back to life for what there was in it, and has just come to his senses, awfully weak, but game enough to resist their efforts to make him appeal to his father for a big ransom. That's all I've had time to hear."

CHAPTER XXXV.

AFTER ALL.

TRENT, of course, was not strong enough to be moved, and that and the late, or rather the early, hour, it being now almost two o'clock a.m., decided us to camp down in the house until morning. So the men outside with Smug in charge were called in, and with our prisoners securely guarded, we passed the few hours before daylight in conversation, Dave, Jeffrys, Lossing, and myself, in Trent's room.

I was doctor enough to see that the poor fellow had been sufficiently startled by our appearance and the events of the night, and so, eager as we were to hear and he to tell his story, we imposed silence upon him until he could be seen by a physician—at least comparative silence; and as he declared himself "all right" except for his weakness, and finding that he was, very naturally, unable to sleep, or even to rest quietly, we told him briefly the story of our search for him, and in telling it led him slowly to the knowledge of his father's presence in the city and the nearness of his betrothed.

More than once his fine eyes filled with tears and his lips trembled as we told of his sweetheart's telegrams and his father's anxiety; and when he had heard it all, he lay a long time silent but wakeful, and evidently thinking, and at last, just as the first faint streak of gray became tinged with a beam of red in the east, he fell asleep, with a smile upon his pale lips.

When the negress had been removed from the room, she had begged to be taken to her "dear Missis Susie," who, she declared, was "sick enough to die"; and I led her upstairs to the room where the pale, worn woman still lay, in the room from which her husband had been removed.

As the negress entered the room the woman lifted her head, and with an inarticulate cry threw herself into her servant's arms; there was a moment of wild sobbing, and then, as I was about to set a guard at the door and withdraw, the negress uttered a shrill cry, caught the slender form in her stout arms and laid her upon the bed, and I saw a thin stream of blood trickle from between the white lips. Restoratives were at hand, for this was not the first attack, the negress said; and when the woman had been cared for, and at last lay sleeping from exhaustion and, I fancied, the help of an opiate, I questioned the servant.

Her mistress, she said, was a southern woman, and she had been her servant since "befo' the war," when that mistress was a child of six.

An orphan with a small fortune, "Mistress Susie" had married Greenback Bob, "Master Robert," she called him, and had followed him and clung to him through all his downward career of crime, as the big, heavy-featured coloured woman had clung to "Missis Susie." When prosperous, Bob was kind; when unlucky or drunk, he was cruel and coarse. "Missis Susie" had inherited consumption, and that and trouble and danger had "wo'n her life away," as the woman said, with big tears dropping upon her dark cheeks.

"This las'," she concluded, "hit's been the wo'st of all. An' that sick boy! Missis Susie prayed 'em to let him go away to the hospital, when he was hurt and couldn't give anyone away. But they nuver heard to Missis Susie—nuver! They wouldn't have been trapped like this if they had."

It was by my proposal to bring the physician—whom at an early morning hour I had summoned to see Trent—to pass judgment upon "Missis Susie" also, that I won the negress to tell me something about Trent; how at early evening he was brought in by Bob and Delbras, whom she called Hector, and whom she evidently both feared and hated; how a physician was called, as the young man was insensible, and how, fortunately for them, he continued delirious for three weeks and more while the two wounds on his head, both serious ones, were healing; how the "gang" had deliberately taken the risk of keeping him until he had so far recovered as to be beyond the danger-line, knowing that they could not safely negotiate the return to his family of a prisoner who might die perhaps while the negotiations were pending.

She told how some one of the gang proper was always on guard in the sick-room by day, and often by night, and that it was only since the going away of one of the gang, Harry by name, that they had entrusted the prisoner to her care alone.

It did not take me long to find out that the person she called Harry was the brunette, now lying dead at the Morgue, and I saw, too, that she did not dream of the fate that had overtaken him, although I felt sure that the woman Susie did.

At early dawn the three men, Delbras, Bob, and Smug, or Harris, as his companions called him, were taken away under charge of Dave Brainerd and Jeffrys, to be locked up and safely kept until Jeffrys should take Delbras to New York, and thence to France. The others would await our appearance against them.

When the physician came, I took him from young Trent's bedside to that of "Missis Susie."

Of Trent he had spoken only words of cheer. His wounds were healing, had healed in fact healthily, and with no danger of after-trouble, mental or other; and now he needed only good nursing, good food, tonics, stimulants, and for a little longer quiet and not too much company. He might be moved, he told us, upon a cot, and for a short distance, that afternoon; and he commended us for our wisdom in not following up the excitement of the previous hours with an instant meeting between the invalid and his father and sweetheart. Now, "after a light breakfast and good nerve tonic," he might see his friends, when they had been prepared and warned against unduly taxing the patient's nerves and strength.

Of the sick woman above stairs there was a different tale to tell. She might linger for weeks, but for her there was no recovery.

When the negress—Hat, her mistress called her—heard this she was inconsolable, and when I had promised her that, if possible, she should remain with her mistress to the end, she was ready to be my slave; and knowing that nothing could help or hurt her mistress more, she was willing to tell me what she could about the gang and their methods.

She had no love for her mistress's husband, and she seemed to have remembered against him every unkind deed or word spoken or done to her "Missis Susie." Delbras she had ever feared and hated, and Smug she despised as the coward decoy of the gang. For Harry she expressed a liking. "He was bad, that's true," she declared; "sharp as you please and tricky; but he was good to my mistress when the others forgot her. He was good to her always, and he bought her books and fruit. When he dressed in woman's clothes she would help him, and he never forgot to thank her. But they quarrelled, Harry and Bob and the Frenchman, and he left night before last."

I told her of Harry's fate, and she cursed his slayers with oaths like a man's; and after that her testimony was ready, and it helped us much. As for Susan Kendricks, for this was the name by which the poor soul had wedded Greenback Bob, there came a time when she told me her story, and a sad, sad page it was, with little light anywhere upon it. She had taken little part in their dangerous enterprises, only now and then appearing somewhere with Harry when he was masquerading as a girl, in order to mislead the officers or the neighbours in their estimate of the number and sex of the gang; or to play a part, as on the night when she personated June Jenrys in order to entrap Lossing.

* * * * *

But when the ship's in port who cares to wait for the furling of the sails? The journey ended, we go ashore.

Little need to describe the meeting between Gerald Trent and his friends, which occurred shortly after the going away of the "gang" and the visit of the doctor.

He told them the story of his "disappearance," and the manner of it was briefly thus:

At one of the small tables in the Public Comfort Café he had dined opposite Smug, whose confiding and kindly obliging manner and general air of being a good but rather slow young man made him an invaluable decoy for the gang. Here Trent's rather careless display of a well-filled purse, together with the fine watch he carried and his valuable diamonds, quietly but mistakenly worn, had no doubt attracted Smug, who made himself agreeable, but not obtrusively so, and had contrived to meet him again and yet again. The last meeting was at evening, when, while chatting easily, he had expressed a desire to visit Buffalo Bill, and Smug, claiming to be a near resident, very modestly offered his escort, and was so unobtrusive and so eminently proper while confessing to a weakness for "horse shows," that Trent had been quite disarmed.

At the close of the entertainment, the Elevated trains being overcrowded, Smug had carelessly recommended the Central, alleging that one of its suburban stations was little more than two blocks away, and proffered himself as guide, as an afterthought, and because he could show him a short cut.

"He showed me several," concluded Trent, with a grimace; "for, having lured me away from the crowd and into an almost deserted and ill-lighted street, we were suddenly attacked, and my 'short cuts' were administered upon my crown."

Some hazy remembrance caused him to believe that they had taken him to their lair, half-carrying and half-dragging him, and representing him to an inquiring policeman as being a victim of too much brandy and beer.

Then came his illness, a dream of fever, pain, and delirium, and a slow return to reason, to find himself a prisoner, too weak to lift head or hand, and yet fully determined not to help his rapacious captors to a fortune at his father's cost.

Since his return to reason he had, as much as possible, rejected what he believed to be opiates, and had feigned sleep to avoid their threats and importunities, and to meet cunning with cunning.

While thus sleeping (?) he had heard some of their whispered plotting, and he was able to explain how it was that Mrs. Camp had succeeded in carrying out her wild but successful adventure.

Among Smug's acquaintances was a certain widow, or a woman who passed for such, who called herself a nurse, and whose services "came high." However, she was "one of the right sort," who "asked no questions," and "always obeyed orders." Upon the night of Harry's disappearance there had been an unusual commotion in the house, and a recklessness of speech quite uncommon; and before morning it was decided that Smug should secure the services of this valuable nurse at an early hour, as they must have "another hand."

Before noon Smug had reported the arrival of the nurse at an early hour, and the fact that she was "hard of hearing" was counted in her favor. Smug had further said, to the satisfaction of Delbras—who by-the-bye had never entered Trent's room without first assuming the disguise of an elderly foreigner—that the woman was especially willing to come because of a little difficulty with "the cops," who were "too attentive for comfort."

Thanks to the successful attention of these same "cops," the woman had left in Mrs. Camp's hands the means whereby she might penetrate this stronghold of iniquity, and so be enabled to do what we had schemed and planned to accomplish, and but for her might have made only a partial success.

Mrs. Camp was the heroine of the hour, and we bent to her our diminished heads, and willingly declared her a detective indeed; for, while we had fathomed the disguises of the gang and tracked them home, it was her masterly coup that had made of our raid the assured success which it was.

To say that Mrs. Camp was made much of by Hilda O'Neil, June Jenrys, and Miss Ross is to put it mildly, and the good woman cared far more for the petting and praise of the two pretty girls than for the gratitude and congratulations of all the rest of us; and the friends she has found through her singular raid upon Smug and company will be her friends for all the years to come.

How I first established a connection between the crook Delbras and the fine gentleman who had taken New York society by storm as Monsieur Maurice Voisin was a wonder to many, until I had laid before them the process of reasoning by which it was done.

I had entered the classic Fair-grounds intent upon searching among the many faces for two, one a blond young Englishman, the other a dark and handsome Frenchman, and a letter picked up in the crowd had given me a mental photograph of these two, though I knew it not.

Before I had ever seen Voisin I had said of him, mentally, "I believe he has tricked Miss June Jenrys and young Lossing." Then I saw him in company with Miss Jenrys that day before our meeting, and I could not help seeing how perfectly he answered the description of Delbras. Next we met, and I could not believe in him; and the glimpses of Greenback Bob's disguised companion in Midway, as agent and fakir, all were wonderfully like Monsieur Voisin, man of fashion; and so from day to day I had watched him as he sought to dazzle the eyes of sweet June Jenrys, hoping for the time when I might unmask him before her.

Then came the attack upon Lossing at the bridge, in which we both saw the hand of Voisin. Mrs. Camp, too, added her quota to the solution of this riddle when she recognised in Voisin the swindler of the Turkish Bazaar, and identified the hand of Voisin as the hand which had held out the spurious banknotes to Camp; and, finally, there came his second attempt to destroy Lossing in the Cold Storage fire, ending as it did in his own disaster and in revealing to me the scar upon the temple so minutely described in the chief's letter as belonging to Delbras.

The man had maintained a stolid indifference and a stubborn silence after his arrest, even when he learned how complete was his exposure both as Voisin and Delbras.

Before his departure for New York a complete record of his misdeeds, so far as we knew them, was made and put into the hands of Jeffrys. The man Smug, or Harris, as might have been expected, was willing to betray his companions in crime, now that he knew himself safe from such vengeance as had been meted out to Harry, the brunette, and in the hope of such measure of immunity as is sometimes bestowed upon the rascal who "confesses" the evil deeds of his associates. It was by his testimony that we fixed the theft of Monsieur Lausch's diamonds upon the gang, and the attack upon Lossing, or Sir Carroll Rae, upon Delbras and Bob; and it was through Hat, the negress, first, and then from Smug, when sharply questioned, that we learned of their last and vilest plot, which was to obtain the ransom for Trent, if possible, or to "put him out of the way" if this failed, and then, with their hands free, to purchase a small yacht and to kidnap Miss Jenrys, keeping her out in the lake until she should buy her release by marrying Delbras.

The only time when Delbras was seen to blench or to appear other than the stolid, sullen, and silent criminal was when Miss Jenrys, accompanied by her aunt, was obliged to appear and identify him as the man who had masqueraded as Monsieur Voisin.

Then, indeed, his dark face paled, his eyes fell before hers, and he turned away with bowed head.

Clearly such love as such a man can feel had been laid at the feet of queenly June Jenrys, who had learned the truth concerning him with amazement, horror, loathing.

While the body of "the brunette," Harry, lay at the Morgue, a tramp, strange to the police and to the city, viewed it with the many others who gloat over the horrors of life, and who, having looked long, and with a startled face, pronounced the body to be that of a professional thief long wanted by the authorities "out West."

"He wuz a born bad un," the man declared, "an' a born thief. He couldn't stay anywhere long on that ercount. I'll bet he's picked more pockets than any lag at the Fair. He was a slick one. Liked the women, and most generally had a lot of friends 'mong 'em wherever he was; but he most generally left 'em the poorer when he got ready to quit. 'Little Kid,' that's what they used ter call him, 'cause he was little an' good-lookin'; but there wasn't a decent hair in his head." And the tramp turned away with a malevolent look at the dead man.

And that was all we could learn about "Harry," for Smug, ready to talk on all other subjects, would utter no word as to the manner of Harry's death. "He had left them," that was all he would say; and by this we knew that Smug was doubtless the decoy who had lulled the suspicions of the victim and made it possible for the bolder spirits to do the deed of death.

Delbras was taken to France, and before the closing of the great Fair had met his fate at the hands of the French executioner.

Greenback Bob and Smug might have spent all their days in prison if they had possessed three lives apiece, so many were the counts against them. Their trials were separate, and came about after weeks of delay. There were no friends with long purses to "influence" the jury, and unless that elastic pardoning power is stretched for their benefit, as has sometimes happened in similar cases, Greenback Bob and Smug will employ their future time honestly and for the good of the race.

Sir Carroll Rae had a very fair reason for remaining in America for a time; and so, placing the business of his newly acquired estates in the hands of the London solicitor who had been Sir Hugo's legal adviser, he remained in the World's Fair City, where, with minds unburdened, the entire party, with at first the exception of Gerald Trent, who was rapidly recovering in spite of the overwhelming attentions of his friends, took up the much-interrupted and pleasant employment of seeing the World's Fair, with eyes that saw no flaws, even in the Government Building.

The Trents did not linger when the invalid was well enough to travel, but hastened to the home where Mrs. Trent, an invalid still, but a happy one, awaited her son's return impatiently, after the long weeks of suspense.

There are no weddings in this tale of strange happenings,

which, nevertheless, are not more strange than many of the unwritten annals of the Fair. But when the early autumn came, two pairs of lovers, chaperoned by a discreet little Quakeress, renewed their acquaintance with the Court of Honour, loitered in the shadows of the Peristyle, drifted upon the Lagoon, and, pacing its length, recalled anew the strange adventures and experiences of that wonderful, impossible, kaleidoscopic, yet utterly and charmingly real Midway Plaisance.

THE END.

Something About the Author of *Against Odds*

VERY LITTLE BIOGRAPHICAL information exists on Emma Murdock Van Deventer, an American detective novelist who wrote under the pseudonym "Lawrence L. Lynch." Her series of thrillers were published in Chicago, and were frequently reprinted in England by British publishers. Following is a bibliography of her fictional works:

Against Odds. A Romance of the Midway Plaisance. Chicago: Laird & Lee, 1894. 272p.
Note: *Fairground Fiction* reprinted the British edition of this novel which carried the subtitle: *A Detective Story.*

A Blind Lead; Daring and Thrilling Adventures, Clever Detective Work. Chicago: Laird & Lee, 1912. 324p.

The Danger Line: The Story of a Mysterious Case. Chicago: Laird & Lee, 1903. 444p.

Dangerous Ground; Or, the Rival Detectives. Chicago: A. T. Loyd & Co., 1885. 462p.

A Dead Man's Step. Chicago and New York: Rand, McNally & Company, 1893. 583p.

The Diamond Coterie. Chicago: A. T. Loyd & Co., 1889. 552p.

The Doverfield's Diamonds: The Great Gem Mystery. Chicago: Laird & Lee, 1906. 359p.

The Last Stroke. Chicago: Laird & Lee, 1896. 290p.

The Lost Witness; or, The Mystery of Leah Paget. Chicago: Laird & Lee, 1890. 557p.

Madeline Payne, the Detective's Daughter. Chicago: A. T. Loyd & Co., 1889. 457p.

Moina; or, Against the Mighty. Chicago: Laird & Lee, 1891. 520p.

A Mountain Mystery; or, The Outlaws of the Rockies. Chicago: A. T. Loyd & Co., 1889. 600p.

No Proof. Chicago and New York: Rand, McNally & Company, 1895. 354p.

Out of a Labyrinth. Chicago: A. T. Loyd & Co., 1885. 471p.

Shadowed By Three. Chicago: Donnelley, Gassette & Loyd, 1879. 738p.

A Slender Clue. Chicago: Laird & Lee, 1891. 650p.

Under Fate's Wheel: A Story of Mystery, Love and the Bicycle. Chicago: Laird & Lee, 1900. 373p.

The Unseen Hand. London & New York: Ward, Lock & Co., 1899. 416p.

The Woman Who Dared; A Thrilling Narrative. Chicago: Laird & Lee, 1902. 471p.

A Woman's Tragedy; or, The Detective's Task. London & New York: Ward, Lock & Co., 1904. 323p.

THE WORLD'S FAIR SENSATION!

No. 776. Published Every Wednesday. Beadle & Adams, Publishers, 98 WILLIAM STREET, NEW YORK. Ten Cents a Copy. $5.00 a Year. Vol. LX.

Chicago Charlie, the Columbian Detective.

BY LIEUT. A. K. SIMS.

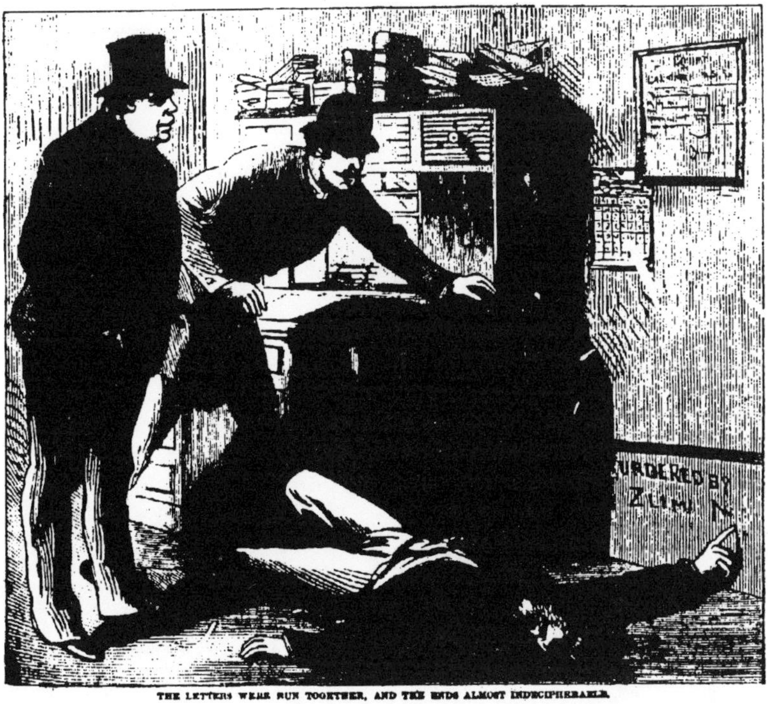

THE LETTERS WERE RUN TOGETHER, AND THE ENDS ALMOST INDECIPHERABLE.

CHICAGO CHARLIE,
THE COLUMBIAN DETECTIVE

CHAPTER I.

A MYSTERIOUS AFFAIR.

A HEAVY-FACED, beefy man, English by birth, but whose features had such strong suggestions of the German that one could not doubt he was an Englishman of German ancestry, approached the door of a room, over which hung a small gilt sign showing it to be the office of John Malcomb, broker.

He advanced hesitatingly, as if he doubted the kindliness of his reception.

His timid knock on the door bringing no response, he rung the bell. Lightly at first; then so loudly that its echoes smote through all the corridors.

No one appeared in response, and he turned away.

He was back again in a quarter-of-an-hour; only to meet with the same experience. John Malcomb was not in; or if in, he had no desire to see visitors.

"The hoddest thing Hi've met with in a fortni't!" the Englishman with the Germanic features soliloquized. "John Malcomb 'asn't the 'abit hof being late. No prompter man hin Chicago, so Hi've told 'im. Hand 'ere 'e isn't down yet! Bejove! Hi b'lieve Hi'll call ha policeman!"

Before doing so, however, he mounted to the top of a stout step-ladder, which he found conveniently near, and, at the imminent risk of breaking his fat neck—for the ladder trembled and groaned under him as if in pain—he climbed to the transom over the office door and looked in.

He climbed down again in great precipitation, and at even greater risk, his red face turning a sickly yellow.

Picking up the high hat, which had been knocked off, he stood for as much as ten seconds rubbing it vigorously with a red handkerchief, not knowing what he was doing;—then he mopped his heated face with the same handkerchief, jammed the hat back into place, and tottered down the stairway as fast as his ponderous legs would carry him.

He did not stay so long as before. He was back within five minutes; and at his heels strode a policeman.

"What cause have you for thinking there's something wrong?" the policeman was asking, and it was noticeable that there was a suspicious, and even an anxious, note in the question.

"Hi don't think ha man would tumble down has 'e seems to 'ave done, sir! Not unless 'e 'ad the 'eart disease hor the hapoplexy, which Hi'm afraid hof hevery minite hof my life. I suppose you 'aven't hany fears hof those 'orrors?"

"Not at all!" and the officer gave the Englishman a distrustful glance—a glance that seemed causeless.

They were at the door, now; and, after trying the knob, the policeman applied a key to the lock.

The key refused to turn; when, without more ado, he thrust his shoulder against the door, and, with a strong surge, forced it inward.

A startled look overspread the officer's face.

On his back, motionless and dead, with right arm outstretched and finger extended, lay John Malcomb, the broker.

It needed but a glance to show that the extended finger had endeavored to trace in blood on the wall some message or word of information—something that should furnish a clue to the murderer, for there could be no doubt that Malcomb had been slain.

He had been stabbed in the back, and had used as ink the blood which had flowed from the wound!

The Englishman seemed as much stupefied and horror stricken as the officer, and stared at the tracings on the wall with a fear-filled and watery eye.

"What do you make hof it?" he questioned, in a shaky voice.

The officer did not immediately answer, but stooped down

and held a magnifying glass over the letters made there by the now stiffened finger. The letters were run together and the words almost indecipherable. But this he managed to spell out, after much study.

"MURDERED BY ————"

There had been an obvious attempt to write the name of the murderer, or a portion of it; but death had touched and palsied the finger before the task was completed, and the only result was a network of meaningless lines and circles.

There was not a keener man on the Chicago force than Charlie Clingstone, better known to his friends and admirers as Chicago Charlie, yet all his keenness and experience failed him here; and when he again looked at the Englishman, there was not only distrust in his glance, but an indication of deepest pain.

"Walesey, when did you see John Malcomb last?"

The inquiry so startled the man that his fat legs shook under him. He was not less surprised that the officer, who was wholly unknown to him, should thus familiarly address him.

"I believe you spoke of an appointment?" still fixing the trembling Englishman with his keen glance.

"Not han happointment, sir! You mishunderstood me! But—"

"When did you see him last? Mind, now, if you don't tell the truth, I'll know it sooner or later!"

"Walesey," as he had been called, lifted his hands and protested vehemently that he had no knowledge of how the man came by his death.

"That is not the question!"

"Well, then, sir, Hi met 'im last night."

"In this office, too!"

"'Ow did you know that?"

"John Malcomb did not always take the trouble to sweep his office, and he employed no office boy to do it for him. You see that dust over there in the corner? There's your footprint in it, and you haven't been in that corner since we came in together!"

"Walesey" shivered as he looked at this mute evidence.

"I'm not accusing you of anything!" and Chicago Charlie turned from the writing to an inspection of the dead man. "I just want you to speak the truth, whenever I ask you a question. John Malcomb has been foully murdered. Anyone can see that; and I'm determined to find who killed him."

"I don't know ha thing habout it, 'pon honor!"

The officer gave no heed to the protest, but quietly went on with his examination.

What had been a pool of blood was now nothing but a suggestive stain, made black by hardened blood clots. The soaked coat was almost dry, showing the crime to have been committed some hours before. In addition, there were indications that a ring had been taken from one of the dead man's fingers. But nothing had been taken from the room.

He saw that if the Englishman *had* been in the room at the time, it was as an accomplice or principal, for some one else had also been there. *And that other person was a woman!* There were prints of *small* shoes, and at one place the tips of small fingers had left their impress in the dust on a table!

He took a tape measure from his pocket, jotted down in a note-book the length of the shoes, the appearance of the finger prints, and made memoranda of the other indications in the room.

Then he threw up a window and called to a brother officer in the street.

"You will take charge here for a few minutes, Mangle!" he said, when that officer came into the room. "See that everything remains just as it is. I shall be back in a few minutes. There has been murder done here, and we must get at the bottom facts."

Having delivered these instructions, he telephoned to the central police station, and turned toward the door.

The Englishman was still standing there, as if not knowing what to do.

"You are at liberty, Walesey. I think I can put my hand on you, should you be needed. There will be a coroner here, though, in a little while, and I'd advise you to attend the inquest and tell all you know, and thus free yourself from any possible suspicion. The fact that you were here with Malcomb the night of his death will surely be looked into."

He passed into the corridor and ran down the broad stairway.

He hesitated on emerging into the street, and then turned resolutely toward John Malcomb's residence, taking a car at the nearest corner.

It has been said that Chicago Charlie seemed much distressed by the discovery that Malcomb had been murdered.

The look of distress deepened on his face.

There was abundant occasion for it, too.

Chicago Charlie

There was not a fairer girl in Chicago (at least Chicago Charlie thought so) than Daisy Malcomb, the daughter of the dead broker.

More than that, the young and popular officer and the broker's daughter were on terms of peculiar intimacy. They were lovers! The fact that John Malcomb had not looked with favor on the officer's suit, did not in anywise change these facts. Chicago Charlie had wooed pretty Daisy Malcomb, and had won her heart, in spite of the objections of her father.

He smiled grimly when the thought crossed his mind that possibly this peculiar state of affairs might bring down suspicion on his own head.

Suddenly a white look rested on his face, and he hastily quitted the car. He strove to put away the thought that had come to him. Nevertheless, he walked back toward the broker's office, and sought the man who had nightly charge of the big building.

"Your room looks out on the corridor leading to Malcomb's office," he began. "Did you chance to be here last evening?"

"All the evening, sir! I was not feeling well. I went down to the street door once, and once I went to the floor above."

"Did you see any woman enter Malcomb's office, or go that way?"

"I did, sir! Malcomb's daughter! She went up there about nine o'clock."

"Any other?"

"None, sir!"

"Did Malcomb leave the office when she did?"

"No, sir. She went away alone."

"One question more: How long did she stay?"

"I cannot tell you that. I do not remember!"

"That will do. I may have some further questions for you after awhile."

He was about to say more, but when he saw the man staring at him in wonderment, he turned away and again descended to the street.

His brain was in a whirl. He knew, in his own mind, that Daisy Malcomb was incapable of such a deed, and yet he saw what the evidence might lead to!

"I must see the inspector at once!" and he groaned aloud, "My God! it will never do for any one else to be detached for this case!"

Then he called a cab and was driven furiously away.

CHAPTER II.

CLOSETED WITH THE INSPECTOR.

BUT FOR his great desire to obtain an immediate interview with the inspector, Chicago Charlie would probably have hastened to the woman he loved, even though he dreaded the effect of the necessary revelation. John Malcomb had not been in all respects a model man; nevertheless, his daughter loved him, and the knowledge of his murder would come to her as a terrible shock.

The officer's heart bled, as he thought of her and of the mental anguish she must be called on to suffer. The vehicle swayed and jolted, but he did not know it; and, even though he looked out on the houses, he did not see them. He set his teeth hard, and muttered:

"I will save her from even the breath of suspicion, if it be possible! Dear girl! She will have enough to bear. *That* would completely crush her!"

He aroused from his meditations, when the cab stopped and he saw that he had reached his destination.

The news of the finding of the body of John Malcomb, who had been murdered in his own office, was already in possession of the inspector, when Chicago Charlie entered the inspector's room.

"Ah! you have come to make a personal report on the Malcomb case!"

Chicago Charlie had counted much on the fact that he was personally known to the inspector and had more than once received recognition at the hands of his superior. His eyes lightened now, for the tone was kindly and even cordial.

"Sit down, and tell me all about it!" and the inspector waved him to a seat.

It took but a few words for the young officer to acquaint the inspector with the extent of his discoveries and conclusions.

"And now I have a request to make!"

The inspector glanced at him keenly.

"The evidence, as I have shown, all goes to prove that the crime was committed by a woman. And a young woman, or one not advanced beyond the period of middle life, for the impress of fingers in the dust of the table showed them to have been firm and smooth. The fingers of an elderly lady would have shown wrinkles or marks indicative of her age."

The inspector nodded. He liked this exhibition of keen insight. Still, the puzzled look remained.

"There is one woman on whom suspicion will likely fall, who I know is as free from this bloody stain as an angel of paradise. That is the dead man's daughter, Miss Daisy Malcomb. She was seen at the office, or going in that direction along the corridor, about nine o'clock last night. I have this from the janitor. He saw no other woman go that way, though that proves nothing. A dozen might have gone without him observing them. He confessed he did not know when Daisy left the office: so you see he was not as alert as he pretended to me to be."

"You had all this in reply to your questions?"

The puzzled look still remained.

There was an answer in the affirmative.

"May I ask you why you prefer to be assigned to the case? We have many good men—men who have shown their capabilities. You have your own particular field. Another would have to be sent to take your place!"

Chicago Charlie had thought the matter all out, during the ride in the cab, and was prepared with his reply. He was resolved to hold back nothing.

"It is very true. My reasons will be plain to you, when I say that Daisy Malcomb, the young lady who is likely to unjustly fall under suspicion, is my promised wife!"

The inspector was amazed, and showed it. He did not immediately reply, but looked hard at the carpet, and chewed at a bit of match which he fished from a vest pocket.

Finally he spoke:

"Only that I know you so well, Mr. Clingstone, I should instantly tell you that your request is a most preposterous one. The worst possible man, ordinarily, to put on a case like this, would be the lover of the woman who is liable to be suspected. Naturally, he would desire to shield her, and would be tempted to suppress anything tending to show her guilt. Is not that a fair inference?"

The young officer could not evade so direct a thrust. He flushed but not in anger.

"It is!"

"You will understand how highly I regard you, then, when I say I will seriously consider your proposition. You are a man of your word. I say this, because I shall ask a promise of you."

"Name it!"

"Before even thinking seriously of this matter, I must have your pledged word of honor that if anything occurs to cause you to doubt the innocence of this young lady you will instantly report it to me."

"You have my promise!"

Chicago Charlie gave his word freely, for he was sure nothing of the kind, more than had already been reported, could occur.

"Now," and the officer seemed to desire to turn from the subject, "What do you know of this Englishman, of whom you have spoken? Do you think he may have been an accomplice?"

"It is possible! I have formed no theory, yet. I know the fellow fairly well. He is a wealthy chap, not the brightest in the world, and is traveling about as fast a gait as any one of so sluggish a disposition can. His name is Selwyn Fisher, though he is usually called 'Walesey,' or 'The Prince,' which he much prefers to his own name.

"He claims to have been a big man in the tight little island beyond seas, and that he was once granted audience by the Prince of Wales. Hence the name was given him by his associates. He is a lover of fast horses, gambling, and all the other things that usually go with them. He spends his money like water, and drinks like a fish.

"He confessed that he was in Malcomb's office last night; though, in spite of the suspicion that might arise because of it, I don't think he has the nerve for such a deed. He trembled this morning at the bare suggestion. He is a man to run away as fast as his chubby legs would carry him;—not at all the man to wield a knife or pistol. Of course, that is only my opinion!"

"And your opinion is what I wanted."

Again the inspector chewed the cud of reflection, while the young officer sat uneasily before him.

When he looked up, it was in a manner to show that the interview was at an end.

"You will be needed at the inquest, which will be held now in a few minutes. After I hear what there develops, I will consider your suggestion. Come again this evening, and you shall have my answer; and my reasons for it, should I decide against you!"

Chicago Charlie thanked him for this mark of favor, and

sought a cab as soon as he was in the street, giving to the driver the number of John Malcomb's office.

Would the inquest develop anything new? The desire now nearest his heart seemed to rest its fulfillment on the result of the coroner's examination.

CHAPTER III.

SOME STARTLING EVIDENCE.

THE FAMOUS and mysterious Borden murder case was then attracting wide-spread attention; a case in which a young woman was charged with having slain her parents in the most cold blooded manner. Column-long accounts of the trial were being paraded daily in the papers, and Chicago Charlie could not but recur to what he had read, as he hastened up the street leading to the Malcomb residence.

He knew how quick is the public to seize on anything suggestive or sensational, and the fear that suspicion might point its dark finger at Daisy Malcomb in that terrible way, filled him with the liveliest fears.

He was troubled, too, lest the inspector should refuse him his request. He knew that if another were detailed to take hold of this already baffling case, that one of the first things done would be the arrest of Daisy.

His pulses were bounding as he walked up the flagged path and rung the door bell. A servant came, to whom Clingstone stated his desire to see the young lady of the house.

It was like receiving a blow in the face, when the servant, who knew him well, refused him entrance, saying that Miss Daisy had given strict orders that she was not to be disturbed.

"Then she knows of the—"

"She knows of the death of her father, yes, sir, if that is what you were going to say! News of it was brought to her some time ago. She is in her room, now, and absolutely refuses to see any one."

"Will you not mention my name to her? Perhaps she will—"

The servant, who was of the supercilious kind, drew back at

this, and closed the door in Clingstone's face.

Charlie choked down his wrath and his great grief, and walked thoughtfully back to the street.

He found the coroner ready for business, when he again sought the office. One or two unimportant witnesses had already been examined, and the janitor was now undergoing the process of telling all he knew, in response to innumerable questions.

The coroner scribbled something on a blank and gave it to an officer, when the janitor told of Daisy Malcomb's visit to the office, and Chicago Charlie groaningly recognized the disagreeable fact that she was to be summoned as a witness.

The body of John Malcomb had been removed, but the suggestive blood stains were still visible.

Clingstone, sitting where he could accomplish it without much observation, pushed a rug across the blood marks with his foot.

Selwyn Fisher, looking shakier and paler than ever, was next asked to make a formal statement of what he knew.

There was only one point in the Englishman's testimony that surprised the pained officer, and that may be given in Fisher's words:

"Yes, sir; I was 'ere hin the office with John Malcomb last night, hand we 'ad a little game hof cards together; not for much money, you hunderstand, but just to pass haway the time, sir! And Malcomb finally got hangry with me, hand hordered me to leave the room!"

The coroner metaphorically pricked up his ears.

"How was that?"

"Well you see, sir, Hi'd been ha bantering 'im habout that girl hof 'is, hand ha tellin' im that she was the prettiest female hin the city, sir; hand finally Hi hoffered to lay 'im a wager.

"Hi hoffered to pay 'im twenty thousand dollars, sir, hagainst the 'and hof the girl! Hand 'e got mad hat that, sir, hand told me to leave the place, sir, hor 'e'd shoot my blawsted 'ead off! Hof course Hi couldn't stand *that* kind of talk from ha friend, don't you know, so I hups and takes my 'at hand leaves!"

Chicago Charlie wished at the moment that he might have his fingers around the throat of the Britisher, and the glare in his eyes would have been observable had any one been looking at him. All attention, however, was centered on the Englishman.

"And you two were alone in the office?"

"We were, sir!"

"About what time last evening was that?"

"Habout nine o'clock, sir; for when Hi got down honto the street, hit was two minutes hafter, has shown by my watch!"

The look of suspicion with which Chicago Charlie had before regarded Fisher deepened again in his eyes.

He was not allowed much time to reflect on the remarkable testimony of Fisher, when all eyes were directed to the door, and he beheld Daisy Malcomb enter, heavily veiled, and walking with an uncertain and quivering step. He saw that her form was convulsed by the agony she was silently enduring, and his great love made him wish that he might hurry to her assistance. But prudence held him in his seat.

If he was to have the management of this special detective work, he realized that he must be cautious how he permitted the public to see what was passing in his mind. He must not let his feelings sway him, for he knew not but that some detective officer was in the room, sent by the inspector for the purpose of watching his conduct during the trial.

Yet it was hard on him to permit another to place for Daisy a chair and assist her to it.

The coroner, probably willing to spare her all he could, called her name immediately, and administered the usual oath.

Then came the customary questions, varied to suit each individual.

"You visited your father in his office last evening, did you not?" queried the coroner.

A number of seconds, during which she was evidently trying to obtain control of her voice, elapsed before she spoke—seconds that seemed interminably long to the breathless, listening crowd.

Many spectators had gathered, for the news of the murder had already been bruited abroad; spectators from every walk of life, almost, but chiefly belonging to the idle and half vicious classes. And these craned their necks and stared at the veil which hid from view the features of the trembling girl.

Chicago Charlie, with heart bleeding for her, wondered if any there thought of the Borden murder case, so strongly impressed at that moment on his mind; and, thus wondering, he prayed that, if such thoughts existed, they might not prejudice the public mind against her.

"I did not, sir!"

The silence became more profound, as these words fell from

the lips of Daisy Malcomb.

Recalling the evidence given by the janitor, the coroner could scarcely credit his hearing.

So he framed the question anew:

"Were you not up there last evening?"

"Yes, sir; but I did not see my father!"

A deep sigh welled from the throng. The sensation was likely to be spoiled, after all!

"Who did you meet, if any one?"

"No one. I was up here, first, in the afternoon, when my father told me to return for him at eight. It was about nine, though, when I came, and he had already gone."

"And you saw no one?"

"No, sir!"

"You did not see that man over there?" indicating the Englishman.

She lifted her veil, showing a dark, handsome face, and glanced at Fisher, but still replied:

"I saw no one!"

Chicago Charlie could see that the exposed face was pained and drawn, as was to be expected.

"Nine o'clock, did you say?"

"Yes, sir. I looked at my watch, to see how much I was behind time, and it was three or four minutes before nine o'clock."

"And no one was in the office?"

"I think not. The office was dark, and I did not enter!"

Every one thought of the testimony given by the Englishman concerning the time, and several curious glances were bestowed on him.

After a few further questions, Daisy was permitted to depart.

Chicago Charlie did not attempt to follow, feeling sure he would be the next witness—as he was.

He told how Fisher had summoned him from the street; of what they had discovered, and going into the minutest details, at the coroner's request.

Again Fisher was called to the stand.

"Why did you wish to see John Malcomb this morning?" was the sharp inquiry.

The Englishman trembled.

"Because hof that quarrel, sir, hif hit may be called ha quarrel. We 'ad halways been the best hof friends, hand Hi couldn't bear that we should be enemies, at this late day!"

The explanation seemed sufficient.

Then a witness was called whose testimony was to startle Chicago Charlie out of what little composure he had left. This witness was the police officer he had summoned to take charge of the room during his absence.

He came forward and produced a bloody knife, which he held up for the coroner's inspection.

"You may state where you obtained that knife, Mr. Mangle!"

"Yes, sir. I found it lying in the corner over there, just before you reached the office; and when you came in you will remember that I showed it to you."

Chicago Charlie looked at the corner indicated, and saw that some papers were lying in it, under which the knife might have lain concealed. But he did not think it had thus escaped his notice, for he felt he had made a close search of the premises. The thought that it had been placed there since, for a purpose, came to him like a flash.

He looked again at the knife, which the coroner was passing around for the inspection of the jurymen; and a cold sweat broke out on his forehead.

He recognized the knife. It was a small knife, but with a long, slender and keen blade. *It was a knife he had given to Daisy Malcomb not a month before!*

He turned aside his face for fear some one would observe the anguish there depicted.

He had seen that the knife-blade and handle were smeared with blood. Had that knife taken the life of John Malcomb? He would not believe it. At least he refused to listen to the suggestion that the owner of the knife had dealt the fatal blow. That was too preposterous, too horrible, for belief. No one but an insane man would harbor it for a minute.

The terror that possessed him during the next few minutes can scarcely be realized. He felt that he ought, as an officer of the law, to tell what he knew concerning the weapon. Yet he shook, clinging almost blindly to his chair, in the great fear that he might be called up and asked some further questions.

He could not reveal *that*! It would be supreme folly, he thought, to give out that information, until he had made an investigation.

His feeling of gratitude was intense, when he observed he was not to be called. The policeman had turned the knife over to the coroner, and the jurymen were deliberating.

How he listened for the result of their discussion!

It came at last: A general verdict of murder, by some person or persons unknown.

Daisy was safe for the present; and the great work of Chicago Charlie's life had commenced; for he was resolved to run down this mystery, even if he had to resign his position to enable him to do it.

Henceforth, he was Chicago Charlie, the detective, and he was destined to prove he was not unworthy of that title.

CHAPTER IV.

"WHO WAS SHE?"

AS SOON as he felt at liberty to leave the room, Chicago Charlie slipped out, and hastened once more to the Malcomb residence.

It was a pleasantly-situated house, with neatly-kept walks and trees, and the sun that morning was flooding it with light. Yet there was about it an air of marked and suggestive stillness. The presence of death brooded there, which not even the flooding sunshine could drive away.

There was crape on the door, and a glance at the curtains of the windows of one of the lower rooms told that the body of John Malcomb was reposing within, robed for the grave. Chicago Charlie would have known this, without any such evidence, for the carriage of an undertaker was drawn up at the curb.

His pull at the bell was answered by the servant who had previously sent him away.

Resolved not to be balked this time, the young detective pushed past the man and into the house.

"You will take this card to Miss Daisy Malcomb!" he commanded, frowning at the man, who had followed. "I am sure she will see me! If not, tell her it is important!"

The man looked doubtfully at the card, hesitating as if he thought of refusing, then disappeared with it, leaving Chicago Charlie to await his return.

He was back, though, in a remarkably short time, and led the way to a little room on the second floor, where the detective

Chicago Charlie

found the girl, sitting disconsolately at a window, a servant having just left her side.

Taking this as a good omen, Chicago Charlie advanced unhesitatingly.

She arose, sobbingly, to greet him.

Without a word he drew her away from the window, and folded her in his arms, as if he would by that act shield her from all harm.

"My dear Daisy! How you must suffer! I came two hours or more ago, but you would not see me; and now I have come again. You will let me assist you? comfort you? do something for you?"

There was entreaty in the tones.

"I did not know you had called!" she asserted, a light flash of pleasure suffusing her pallid cheeks, where were many traces of tears. "I supposed the servant would admit you, even though I had given orders that I was not to be disturbed!"

His arms tightened about her. Then he conducted her to a chair and drew one close up at her side, kissing her as he did so.

She began to sob, showing all the bitterness of her fresh grief.

"It is terrible!" he confessed. "But you must endeavor to remain calm!"

"The manner of his death is what hurts so!" she averred, between the shaking sobs. "That my father should be killed in that cruel manner! It is dreadful! Dreadful! And he was so kind to me, and so good; and he loved me so! Oh! I don't know what I shall do! I feel at times as if I was losing my mind!"

The anguish on the young officer's face was painful to see. Yet, before this outburst of grief, he was silent. Words failed him. He knew not what to do or say;—realizing how weak and impotent are mere words at such a time.

"You must not distress yourself so!" he pleaded. "I know it is dreadful! But tears can do no good, now!"

He took her trembling hands in his, and was startled at their feverishness.

"You are making yourself ill!" he urged. "Perhaps you need a physician more than anything else. Your palms are burning hot!"

"No! No! I am not sick!"

But when she looked up, he observed that while her cheeks were pale, her eyes were feverishly bright.

"What did they learn at the—the trial?" she questioned.

It was the point to which he would have directed speech, had he known how.

"I wanted to talk to you about that!" he averred. "I think I will be assigned to look into this case, for I have resolved to ferret it out and find the—the murderer! I have already applied to the inspector for the assignment."

Her glance showed her gratitude.

"The man must be found and punished!" she declared, with unexpected sternness. "I can never rest until that is accomplished."

"Nor I!" his pulse quickening. "But the murderer was not a man. The crime was by a woman!"

"By a woman?"

Her voice shook with horror.

"Surely you must be mistaken! That seems incredible! No woman could be guilty of such a thing!"

"I have good reasons for thinking otherwise!" and he clasped the hands yet more firmly. "I distinctly saw a woman's tracks in the dust on the floor, and the print of a woman's fingers on the table at which your father must have been sitting when the fatal blow was given. I am sure the murderer was a woman. You say you were not in the office last night; those tracks and marks were made last night; and some woman made them. If I could lay my hands on her, I am sure I should have the guilty one!"

She shuddered, involuntarily.

Chicago Charlie was thinking of the knife, but he thought it best to withhold that information for the time.

"How can you tell when the marks were made?" she queried, her curiosity quickened.

"By their general appearance! If very old—much more than twelve hours old—they would not have been so distinct. Yet they were not sufficiently fresh and clear to have been made this morning. It is not likely any one would venture on a deed of that kind in broad daylight. Therefore, they must have been made last night!"

He looked at her thoughtfully for a moment.

"What I wanted to ask you is this: Has any strange woman called on you lately, or been in the house?"

She started as if stung.

"Why, it could not be! Yes, a woman was here last evening! Her coming was what kept me from visiting the office promptly, as I promised father I would!"

Chicago Charlie's breath came quick and fast, like that of a hound scenting a trail.

"Who was that woman?"

"I cannot tell you who she was! She was dark—very dark—and wore a heavy veil. Her eyes were as black as night, and so was her hair. She wanted me to let her tell my fortune, and—I foolishly consented. You do not think that she—that that could have brought about—that my delay here could have caused father's death?"

Her eyes were filled with remorse and horror.

Even faster came the detective's breath and louder thumped his heart. Here was information worth having! He felt sure that this dark-eyed fortune-teller had not come there simply to tell fortunes. She had come to get a weapon with which to commit that foul crime;—a weapon from Malcomb's own house, so that the crime might be laid at the door of another! At the door of Malcomb's daughter! The mystery of the Borden murder had evidently not only suggested itself to him; it had suggested itself to this murderess, who had acted on it.

In vain he sought to recall the face of some well-known adventuress or desperate woman who might have committed the crime.

"Describe her minutely!" he requested.

"I do not know that I can, any more than I have already."

"Was she young or old?"

"Young! I should say not more than twenty. Surely a girl of that age could not do *that!*"

"Handsome?"

"Rather pretty. Her cheeks and lips were red and plump, and she had a good form."

"How was she dressed?"

"In an ordinary dark dress. I did not notice her clothing closely, for she had on a dark shawl."

"I will find her," he declared, "if she remains in the city! And I don't think she can escape me, even should she leave. She is the woman that killed your father. I feel sure of it!"

Having obtained this information, he was anxious to hurry at once with it to the inspector. The description tallied with the footprints and marks found in the office, and he did not doubt that the inspector would see that this was the murderess, and not Malcomb's daughter. It explained everything. The finding of the bloody knife, and all. Yet he could not refrain from secretly cursing himself for overlooking so important a thing in his search as that knife!

Notwithstanding his desire to hasten away, he lingered for many long minutes, and had the satisfaction, as he left the residence, of knowing that Miss Daisy Malcomb was in much better frame of mind than when he came. And, most important of all, he had gained the clue needed to begin his work.

CHAPTER V.

A REMARKABLE FORTUNE-TELLER

WITH A feeling that was not quite reluctance, yet was akin to it, Daisy Malcomb walked out through the shaded path, leading from her home into the street.

Three days had elapsed;—days that had been filled with grief. And, though the sunshine fell as pleasantly on this day as on that other when Chicago Charlie pushed past the servant into the house, the shadow which then hung over the residence had not departed. Nor would it for many, many days to come.

The last sad services to the dead had been rendered, and the murdered man was now sleeping in Chicago's beautiful city of the dead;—sleeping quite as quietly there as if he had died in the ordinary manner and with the ordinary surroundings.

The papers had teemed with exaggerated accounts of the tragedy, and the many theories they put forth were certainly remarkable for ingenuity. Yet the detective, reading all of them carefully, felt sure none of then hit anywhere near the mark.

Chicago Charlie had been assigned to the difficult task of laying bare the mystery of the murder, the task he had so desired and so earnestly solicited. And it was at his earnest request that Daisy Malcomb was now setting forth on an errand that possessed all the characteristics of novelty.

Seemingly all the world had come up to Chicago to see the great Fair; and if not to see the Fair, then to profit by those who had come for that purpose. And of the latter class there were so many that the great lakeside city fairly swarmed.

Among others, was a band of Gypsies, who had pitched their camp on some vacant lots near the grounds of the Columbian Exposition, and within easy reach of it. They had been compelled to pay pretty dearly for the privilege, a thing to which they were much averse, but they probably reasoned that the golden harvest they would reap in consequence would more than justify this extravagance.

Chicago Charlie, in his search for the dark-eyed fortune-teller, had located these Gypsies, and had gone among them in various disguises; and, though he saw many young Gypsy women, he could not say that any of them fully answered the description of the young fortune-teller who had visited Daisy Malcomb on the night of the murder.

Hence, he desired that Daisy herself should go to the Gypsy camp, and personally inspect the younger women there, in the hope that she might be able to identify the one sought.

The fact that the woman who had called on Daisy that night had been dark, and professedly a fortune-teller, made him think she might be found among this band of roving Romanies.

As shown in the interview between the lovers, Daisy Malcomb was quite as anxious as Chicago Charlie to have the murderess ferreted out and brought to justice. She had never seen the knife that Mangle had exhibited at the inquest; and, though it was now in possession of her lover, the latter never mentioned it to her. What she had seen in the papers concerning it, gave her no suspicion that the knife there spoken of was the one which had once been her own.

Even though thus anxious to bring the guilty one to justice, Daisy had not been able as yet to convince herself that the deed had been committed by a woman, though she thought it possible a woman might have had knowledge of it, and might even have abetted it. But that woman's hand had driven the weapon she would not believe, for the paths which her feet had followed had never brought her in contact with a creature bearing the semblance of a woman who could be so hardened as to strike that murderous blow.

However, at the bidding of her lover, she had put aside her grief for a time; put aside her shrinking weakness; put aside the thought that her act, under the circumstances, might be unbecoming; and taking an Elevated train, was soon whirling in the direction of Jackson Park.

She separated herself from the vast crowds that were pouring toward the gates opening on the great show, on alighting; and, turning into a side street, hurried quickly on toward the Gypsy camp, anxious to escape the public gaze, and fearful lest she should be recognized.

Her heart gave a weakening, tremulous bound, when the dirty white tents of the Gypsies loomed on her vision; but she went on, nevertheless, and was soon near enough to observe the lounging forms of two or three unwholesome looking, Gypsy men, who appeared to have nothing particular to do in this world, save to lie idly on the grass, smoke stinking black pipes, and stare at the sky.

The music of the cowboy band floated to her from Buffalo Bill's mammoth "Wild West" exhibition, the notes drowned occasionally by the rumble and grumble of heavily laden trains.

The Gypsy men scarcely looked at her as she walked past them and toward the nearest tent. There were only three or four women to be seen, but two of these could be called young. Neither of them was the fortune-teller who had called on her.

Entering the tent, or rather hesitating in the entrance, she saw before her a withered crone, with skin like brown leather, who came promptly forward, and, in a wheedling voice, desired her to come in.

Daisy accepted this invitation, though the rough chair offered was not of the cleanest.

"Now, what can I do for you, my dear?" the woman asked. "I see you have come to get your fortune told. It ought to be a good fortune, for you're a purty girl. And you've a handsome lover, too, I don't doubt. I'm Gypsy Nell, and I've told fortunes—true fortunes—since I was that high!" indicating a distance of two feet from the ground.

There was something so keen and bright in this old woman's eyes, that Daisy almost shrunk from her. The crone's glance seemed to pierce her through and through, as if seeking out her innermost secrets.

"Are there no other women here?" Daisy palpitatingly asked.

Gypsy Nell frowned slightly.

"Only those girls out there. They can't tell fortunes, though they pretend that they can. Let me tell your fortune, lady!"

She took Daisy's hand and peered at it, wrinkling her brows as if in thought. The girl did not draw her hand away, for there was in the old woman's manner something commanding and imperious.

"You are a good girl, as I said—a good girl; but, ah! I cannot speak so well of your father. He was a hard man; hard on the poor. Yes, and he was a gambler, a speculator, and what these

Americans call a wrecker!"

Daisy would have drawn the hand away, now, only that the old crone detained it.

"You must not speak that way of my father!" the girl panted, unable to restrain her indignant tears.

"Yes, I know. He is dead! And your grief is yet strong. Let me see! There is a bloody shadow on the hand. Just there! Do you not see it?

"Your father did not die as he should have died. He was murdered. Ay! I see, now. He was stabbed or cut, and so died. It is hard, lady! Very hard! Pardon me, for giving you pain. I will tell no more, if it thus distresses you."

Daisy was not only astonished by what she had heard, but her curiosity was piqued by the woman's accent. She had expected to hear something foreign. Yet this Gypsy woman spoke English almost as well as she herself spoke it. Whereas, the woman who had visited her that fatal night, spoke it very poorly.

Daisy, having heard this much of the so-called "fortune," was extremely anxious that the Gypsy woman should go on, and so expressed herself.

"Very well, lady! But if I say things to make you feel bad, you must not be angry as awhile ago. It is my business to tell what I see, not what people would like to have me tell them. What good is a fortune, if we do not speak true?"

"Do you mean to say that you see all those things in the palm of my hand?" Daisy demanded, incredulously.

"I see shadows and lines in the hand, and when I see them, I cannot tell you how, but their meaning comes up before me. As you see things, lady, when you read a book. You are educated and can read the book, which to me would be only crazy dots and figures. Yet it tells you what is there put down. So, in this fortune telling business. You read the book, and I read the hand!"

"Go on!" said the girl, resigning herself without further question. "What else can you see there?"

"The bloody cloud has got clearer and I see figures of people moving about in it. There is a man who I'm certain is your father.

"How do I know?" as if to ward off another inquiry. "I cannot tell how I know; only I feel it to be so. He is in a small room—a room that has books and papers in it. A light is turned low on the table. It may be he is asleep, for his head is bent down on his arm."

A twinge of pain shot through Daisy's heart. Had her father fallen asleep while waiting for her and been thus murdered?

"Ah!" and the old woman drew in her breath eagerly. "A man has come into the room. He has crept in through the door. He has a knife. He looks at the man by the table. He creeps forward as a cat. He strikes. He stabs the man in the back!"

Her voice had grown to a low and impressive whisper. Daisy snatched away the hand with a little shriek. So vividly had the picture been painted, and in so dramatic a manner, that she could almost fancy she had seen what had been described.

The crone had looked at her compassionately, even tenderly.

"It was terrible, lady! Was it not?"

Daisy's lips were white and mute, and the pupils of her eyes dilated with the excitement.

"Tell the rest of it!" she resolutely ordered, thrusting the palm once more into the skinny grasp. "Tell me all you see! Everything! Are you sure it was a man who struck the blow?"

For the time a thoroughly superstitious feeling had possession of her, and she could not rid herself of the belief that this old, witch-like creature had some magical power by which events of the past were revealed.

"You are sure it was a man?" shakily.

"Quite sure, my dear!" and the Gypsy stared at her in amazement.

"The man is gone now and the room is dark, and the other man—your father—lies on his back on the floor!"

She had turned again to an inspection of the palm, but she continued to cast on Daisy those questioning glances, which, could Daisy have observed them, would have been the source of much conjecture.

"What kind of a man was he?" Daisy urged. "How did he look?"

The detective instinct, that was so strong a trait in the character of her lover, was being aroused in her.

"A heavy-faced man. A man of much size. A beer drinker, with a chuffy, puffy face."

Daisy recognized the description immediately as that of Selwyn Fisher. She remembered him as she sat in the room at the time of the inquest, and Chicago Charlie had described him minutely more than once since.

"His name?" she panted.

"I cannot tell his name. There is nothing about a man to tell you what his name may be. I can only tell how he looks!"

"Go on!"

Chicago Charlie

"I cannot tell more about that! The bloody cloud is past. Now a lighter cloud overspreads your hand, beginning here. That is the region of the heart, my dear; so I know that what I shall see now will be of your lover."

Daisy sat spell-bound under the old woman's influence.

"A tall, handsome young man, my dear. A policeman, I think, by his uniform."

Wonder trod on the heels of wonder. Daisy could scarcely credit her ears. What remarkable power did not this old woman possess?

"He is chasing the fat man; and he is sure to catch him, for the fat man cannot run so fast. He has found out that the fat man killed the man in the room, and for your sake he is trying to catch him. Ah! he has him now. He drags him down, and then pulls him away with him.

"There is a lighter cloud; a cloud with rosy edges. It is what we call the wedding cloud, my dear. The darkness of the past is gone. I see you standing up in a great church with the young man, and the preacher is blessing you. It is a good fortune, for it ends well!"

She dropped the hand, as if to indicate that she was done, and Daisy looked up at her as if coming out of a trance. What she had heard seemed to the girl parts of a dream, though she knew she had not been dreaming.

"And that is all?"

"Is it not enough? Is it not worth the fee? Who could have a better fortune for fifty cents?"

She laughed in a harsh, disagreeable way, that grated on the girl's over-strung nerves.

"It is enough! If I could only believe it all!"

The old woman frowned, as she had once done at the beginning.

"Believing it or not believing it, does not make it true or untrue. It was written in your hand. I have learned never to doubt what I see there."

Daisy took the fee from her purse, and passed it over.

"Thank you," and the crone courtesied. "Not many get so good a fortune for the money. Not many hands show so happy a future. You have a good face, and I hope that all your dreams may come true.

"I had my dreams, once. Ah! well. That was long ago. I have quit dreaming, except for other people, who pay me for it. But dreams are good for a girl."

She courtesied again and turned away; leaving Daisy alone in the shabby tent.

Daisy looked at her watch, and was surprised that so much time had elapsed. She had been there more than an hour, and it had scarcely seemed five minutes. There were voices about her, which she had not before heard. She saw that a number of Gypsies had returned, and that there were several girls among them.

She scanned these closely, noting their features, dress, and manners. None of them suggested the dark faced woman who had called on her on that ever-to-be-remembered night. They were different in many ways. Some of them were as dark, and had eyes and hair as black, but their manners and speech were of a different order.

The faces were all strange, and when she had satisfied herself that the woman she had come seeking was not of the number, she left the tent and walked back toward the crowded streets, her mind filled with the wonderful things that had dropped from the lips of the old woman.

CHAPTER VI.

THE DANCING GIRL FROM CAIRO.

"THERE IS information of importance back of that!" Chicago Charlie exclaimed, when he heard Daisy's account of the result of her visit to the Gypsy camp. "That old woman knows a good deal more than she told; we have struck the main trail!"

He leaned toward the girl, and his earnestness betrayed itself in his quick speech.

It was the evening of the same day, and he had called on Daisy Malcomb to receive her report, and for the further reason that he was always glad of an excuse to court her presence.

Chicago Charlie was rapidly getting his plans in order, and they were, he felt, sufficiently broad and comprehensive to accomplish the desired result: i.e. the capture of the murderer of John Malcomb. A capable shadower had been put on the track of the Englishman, Walesey, and certain interesting facts had already been discovered concerning him.

"What sort of information?" Daisy asked.

"Well, I think it's safe to assume that that old woman knows a great deal more than she told you. Of course, she has no such ability to read the future and pry into secrets as she claims."

"Of course!" Daisy assented, though she could not quite rid herself of the feeling that the crone was really gifted with prophetic power.

She had held back from her lover the account of the policeman, and the future predicted for him; all excepting that portion relating to his chase of the fat murderer.

Even as he spoke, Chicago Charlie was doing some rapid thinking. He was endeavoring to account for the knowledge which the Gypsy appeared to possess.

"These Gypsies have been about town a good deal lately," he said at length, "begging, and probably stealing. This fortuneteller may even have visited this house. All the world knows of the crime against your father, for it has been published broadcast. Does it not seem likely that she may have seen you here, or that you may have been pointed out to her somewhere? Knowing who you were and recognizing you when you came to the camp, with the knowledge which she could have gained from the papers, it is easy to see how she could fabricate the story told you.

"Taking this view of it, makes it seem reasonable and probable. Either that, or she possesses some knowledge of what has really been done—perhaps knows who committed the deed—and thought to astonish you by saying what she did. Even then, she must have seen you before to have so recognized you."

The explanation was clear and sensible, and yet it did not drive from Daisy the queer thrill that had oppressed her as she listened breathlessly to the words of the crone. It dashed aside what had seemed so miraculous, and the miraculousness of the performance was what she was most disposed to cling to. And yet Daisy Malcomb would solemnly have assured her friends and herself that she was not the least bit superstitious. Probably there is a drop of superstitious blood in the best of us, if we did but acknowledge it. Which is not to be wondered at, when we recall how short is the time since the age of witch-burning. The spirit of old Cotton Mather is not yet dead.

Daisy, fearing ridicule, did not essay to put her feelings into

Dancers, Egyptian Theatre.

words, and Chicago Charlie went on:

"I shall have the Gypsy camp shadowed, and something may develop. At the same time, I do not intend to give my personal attention to it. There is other work for me just now, and for you, too."

He anticipated the glance of surprise with which this was greeted.

"Will you explain yourself, Charlie Clingstone!" she demanded, vexed at the silence that ensued.

"I have been looking everywhere for the fortune-teller that called on you that night, as you know. I half-believe, too, that I have located her. She is in one of the buildings about the Cairo street, in Midway Plaisance."

Daisy knew the place. It was one of the special exhibits at the World's Fair, on the mile-long thoroughfare known as Midway Plaisance containing the pay exhibits and concessions.

She drew in her breath quick and hard. She had already visited the Cairo street—having been there earlier, in the season, before the buildings were completed—and she recollected now that there was a marked resemblance in some of the faces seen there to that of the woman who had called on her.

"Can you go with me to-morrow?" he queried, watching the shadows chase each other over her expressive features.

"I will arrange to do so, if you specially wish it."

"Thank you. I especially wish it, or I should not have asked it of you. Now as to this Englishman, Selwyn Fisher, for the Gypsy could have meant no one else, I hardly think he is the man to watch, though I shall have some one constantly on his track. I don't believe that a *man* did the deed. I think it was a woman, in spite of the assertions of the old fortune-teller."

Much more was said, which it is not the present purpose of this story to record.

The next day, Chicago Charlie and Daisy Malcomb pressed with the crowd through one of the turnstiles into the big Fair.

Before and about them lay the wonderful "White City." A poet's dream wrought into towering palaces and artistic forms. A vision of rich magnificence standing with marble feet in the waters of the Michigan Lake.

But they felt that they had no time just then to devote to its wonders and beauties, and so they turned aside and entered Midway Plaisance; where the glancing sunbeams fell on queer buildings of foreign construction, on Javanese, Dahoman and

Irish villages—and where the odd music of a Chinese band brought back to Chicago Charlie memories of the time when he was a ragged urchin and vigorously led a procession of other boys battering away at old tin pans with a stick.

Entering Cairo street—seemingly a section carved out of the heart of old Cairo—where Egyptian hieroglyphics looked down from the walls and solemn sphinxes guarded the mysteries hidden away in the depths of of the buildings, they sought the spot where the Ghawazees, or dancing girls, were accustomed daily to give exhibitions of their dancing in the far-off Orient.

Two girls, fairly comely in features, with rich red lips, were swaying sensuously in the center of the floor, the dance being more a swaying of the body and limbs than anything like the dances Americans are accustomed to.

Chicago Charlie's eyes were on Daisy Malcomb, more than on the voluptuous figures of the dancers, for one of these swaying women he had picked on as resembling the one who had visited Daisy on that fatal night.

He saw Daisy turn pale, felt her clutch tighten on his arm, and knew she had recognized the dancing girl.

Fearing the recognition might be mutual, if Daisy's agitation attracted attention, he drew his sweetheart away, passing out as if in search of other attractions.

"It is she!" Daisy whispered, in much agitation, and with blanching lips. *"That is the girl who called on me to tell me my fortune!"*

"And it is the girl who took the knife, and who committed the murder!" was the detective's inward comment.

Aloud he only said:

"I thought so. I felt I could not be mistaken, for your description was very minute. Now we will go in here to rest awhile, for you seem about to drop. I was afraid your face would betray you, when you saw her."

Daisy was almost too weak to stand, so suffered herself to be led into a neighboring *cafe*, where refreshments and a cup of stimulating coffee were ordered for her by the detective.

CHAPTER VII.

A BIT OF SHADOWING.

IN AN OBSCURE CORNER, where the light did not fall so blindingly and where the tinkling accompaniment to the Ghawazee dance came with melodious softness, sat Chicago Charlie, with his hat well drawn over his eyes, and peering out keenly from half-closed lids.

His gaze was riveted on the dancing girls, and he was especially watching the movements of the one who had been recognized that morning by Daisy Malcomb as the nocturnal fortune-teller.

It was the evening of the same day, and he had returned to the Cairo building to make a study of the girl.

If this dancing girl were the murderess, what had been her motive? Why did *she* do the horrible deed?

This was the question to whose solution Chicago Charlie was devoting his thoughts.

He was well aware that the Ghawazees had been in the country only a few months, and it seemed impossible that this girl could have formed the the acquaintance of John Malcomb in that time, housed as she had been from the gaze of the public. It was not likely, therefore, that the girl could have held against him, personally, any animosity. And robbery had not been the motive for the commission of the crime, for there had apparently been no valuables taken.

Shrewd as was the young detective he found himself at fault and sorely puzzled.

There seemed but one solution of the mystery: This girl—taking it for granted that she had slain John Malcomb—had not done it through enmity, nor through a desire to rob, but because she had been well paid for the deed by some one who was interested in putting Malcomb out of the way.

Who was this person?

The detective's thoughts reverted to the Englishman, against whom his suspicion had first been aroused. Yet, by putting together all the facts known of the Englishman's career, there was little enough to indicate that Selwyn Fisher had had reason for such a murderous desire.

Fisher and Malcomb had been friends or acquaintances, but

not cronies. There was much to show that Malcomb had pushed the acquaintance, for the purpose of handling some of the money which Fisher now and then threw around so recklessly. The Englishman had come to this country fabulously rich, as it was said, the report adding that he had obtained his wealth through inheritance.

About the Englishman, as flies about a keg of sweets, a number of parasites had gathered. They were principally sporting men; men belonging to the "fastest" set of Chicago. John Malcomb did not exactly belong to this set, but he had been on intimate and sympathetic terms with many of the fellows who were reported to be "bleeding" the thick-headed Englishman.

The detective's ruminations were leading him far from the posturing of the dancing girls, when he was brought back to things present by the actions of a man who had recently entered the room.

This man was stylishly clad, and there was something in his general appearance which caused Chicago Charlie to set him down instantly as a confidence-man and a *roue*. His necktie was of the whitest, his hat of the shiniest, and his clothing of the most elegant fit. Now and then he cast an amorous glance at the girls, and clapped his gloved hands vigorously whenever the performance especially pleased him.

"I think I have seen that fellow," Chicago Charlie muttered, eying the man still more closely. "If I am not mistaken, his name is Youngblood. Colonel Solon Youngblood! I think I saw him at the races last summer with Walesey, when they were backing that little black mare against Thunderbolt! They lost, too, if I'm not mistaken. Yes, it's the same fellow. He is one of Walesey's chums, and by that token I suppose he must have been an acquaintance of Malcomb's."

This knowledge that Daisy's father had herded so often with men of questionable character frequently stung him, as it did now.

The dancing came to an end at last; and, when the crowd began to thin out, one of the girls picked up a buttonaire, and, advancing to the swell-looking man, pinned it on the lapel of his coat.

"That is wort' a quarter!" he heard her simper, ogling the man slily. "Don' you t'ink it wort' that much?"

Then, as the man stooped slightly to get at his purse, she bent forward and quickly whispered something in his ear.

The man started, but regaining his composure, took out the quarter and handed it to her, and began to praise the flowers and the beauty of her dancing.

Chicago Charlie saw it all, and was aroused to instant alertness.

What acquaintance had this Ghawazee with Solon Youngblood? Had she whispered a warning of some sort into the ear of the sport and gambler? If so, did it concern him—Chicago Charlie? Had she, then, recognized Daisy Malcomb that morning, and known the detective when he again sought the building?

These wild fancies, flying quickly through his mind, seemed preposterous. Nevertheless, Chicago Charlie was so wrought upon by them that he resolved to shadow the man, when the latter should leave the building, and see what would result therefrom.

Youngblood did not remain in the building a great while after that. Most of those who had been interested in the dances had gone, and Youngblood followed them.

Chicago Charlie also got up from his corner and strolled out.

He caught a glimpse of Youngblood, as the latter turned into Midway Plaisance, and proceeded to dog his steps, as the sport walked slowly down the thoroughfare.

Youngblood took a car of the Illinois Central back to the city, and the detective climbed into the coach just back of the one occupied by the sport.

As the trains were crowded, it was not difficult to do this without attracting Youngblood's attention.

Every now and then the sport glanced keenly into the faces of the passengers about him, as the train rattled swiftly on its way toward the city, but evidently not seeing the one for whom he appeared to be looking, he abandoned these furtive surveys after a time.

He got off on State street, and walked west toward the river.

Probably fearing he was being followed, he halted, after walking a block or two, and took a horse car.

The delay gave the detective time to make some changes in his appearance. He had long before abandoned his policeman's uniform, as being unfitted to the character of the work he expected to do, and wore now an ordinary business suit.

He stepped into a corner, where the shadows from a stone stairway fell protectingly; and, turning his coat wrong-side out and adding to his face a set of chin whiskers and a pair of glasses, he emerged and walked on again, resolved to take the car that Youngblood was manifestly waiting for.

The turned coat—having been made with a lining of black coat cloth, so that it was really a black coat, instead of a light one, when it was turned—made the disguise complete.

Taking the opposite side of the street, he stopped at the crossing; and, when the car came along, he climbed into the seat within touch of Youngblood.

The detective did not know that Youngblood was fearful of being followed, though the indications pointed that way. Neither was there anything to show that the sport fancied the detective might pursue him. In truth, Chicago Charlie felt pretty sure that he had not been seen by Youngblood while they were in the Cairo building.

Notwithstanding all this, he was fully as careful as if certain the sport knew himself to be shadowed.

That these precautions had not been taken without good cause, the events of the night were destined to prove.

On one of the side streets leading off from Adams, in what might appropriately be termed the Bowery of Chicago, stands a rickety, old building, several stories high which has long had an evil reputation.

Youngblood, having dropped off the car at the junction, approached and entered the building by a side entrance—the shadower not far away.

No lights shone from it, which was a suspicious thing in itself. Neither was there any indication that it was occupied. It seemed to have been given over to neglect and decay.

Stationing himself on a corner beneath a stunted tree, Chicago Charlie closely watched this building for a number of minutes. Nothing came of it. The house remained as dark, as forbidding, and apparently as untenanted as before.

He crossed the street, avoiding as much as possible the glare of the electric lights, and, when he felt again safe from observation, drew near and circled the old house. He could not entirely go around it, for on the southern side it was joined to the other buildings, and some of these were occupied.

However, after considerable search and much stumbling, the shadower found a rear door. It was securely locked, but a window near it he succeeded in forcing, and thus gained access to the lower part of the house.

There was a dust-coated stairway leading into the mysterious upper regions; and this stairway Chicago Charlie at once ascended, stepping with the lightness of a cat, lest the timbers and boards should creak or give forth some sound of warning.

He spent almost a half-hour in searching the second and third floors, without finding anything to reward him, and might have continued the useless search for a much longer time, had not the sound of a softly-closing door caught his ear.

It came from below; and feeling sure, now, that the man he had been shadowing was not to be found above, he hastened to descend.

He again heard the sound, when near the foot of the first stairway, and caught a gleam of light as it fell through the entrance from the street.

The detective drew back, for the form of a man was dimly revealed.

This man closed the door after him and stepped away into the gloom.

What little he had seen of the man's general appearance convinced Chicago Charlie that the fellow was not Youngblood, and with his interest now whetted to renewed eagerness he moved stealthily after.

Contrary to his anticipations the man did not ascend toward the upper rooms, but went downward—thus showing that there was a stairway leading to a basement or cellar.

It was a most perilous thing to do, for another might enter the room at any minute, but Chicago Charlie slipped to this descending stairway and, after intently hearkening, noiselessly descended.

A gleam of light came to him, proving that the way led to an illuminated underground apartment. And he heard voices, too, as he proceeded onward.

On reaching the bottom of the stairway, he perceived that it would be impossible to enter this apartment without discovery. A half-dozen men were grouped about a table in the further end of the room, on which a light was burning. All were heavily masked. And though detached words and sentences floated to him now and then with much distinctness, he could recognize no voice but Youngblood's.

From what he heard, it was plain others were expected; and, not wishing to be caught between two fires, he cast about for a hiding-place.

The only one that offered was the dark corner between the wall and the half-open door. It was not the sort of hiding-place Chicago Charlie would have chosen, but it was the best to be had, and he slipped into it—just in time, too, for there were voices in the room above, and the sound of a footstep came from the head of the stairs.

Crouching in breathless suspense behind the door, with every nerve strained to its fullest, resolved and ready to fight or fly as occasion demanded, the young detective waited the descent of the new-comers.

The light coming from the basement aided in screening him, for it illuminated the stairway, thus throwing the corner into still deeper gloom; and the men passed by without dreaming that any one was thus near.

A sense of relief came to the daring shadower when this ordeal was ended; and he was shifting about in his place of concealment, seeking a point where he might see as well as hear, when the door closed from within, leaving him crouching there without any concealment save the intense gloom that instantly prevailed.

He sought the keyhole, however, and kneeling on the damp stones applied an eye to the small aperture, and looked into the basement.

Youngblood, who had arisen, was rapping for order.

He did not speak until attention had been fully accorded him.

Then he said, very quietly and firmly:

"The Lakeside League will now come to order. Sergeant-at-arms, satisfy yourself that the stairway and building are clear, and that all present are entitled to remain!"

CHAPTER VIII.

THE LAKESIDE LEAGUE.

CHICAGO CHARLIE, seeing that this order was to be executed with considerable literalness, scudded up the stairway like a rat in a trap.

The sergeant-at-arms followed swiftly, peering into the gloom

Chicago Charlie

around the head of the stairway, and then walking on toward the entrance. But, he did not see the detective, who was standing within less than ten steps, securely screened by the thick shadows.

No doubt the sergeant-at-arms had thus obeyed the order of his chief many times, and had become careless through a feeling of safety. At any rate he came back in a few seconds; and, returning to the basement, reported that all was as it should be.

Chicago Charlie heard the report, for his eye was again at the keyhole and his gaze sweeping the interior of the underground room.

He was much puzzled by what he saw and heard. The city was filled with secret orders and lodges of all kinds, wherein mysterious rites and ceremonies were nightly performed. Men who were only plain clerks and artisans in the prosaic walks of common life, became in these organizations Grand Key Holders of the Inner Temple and Sir Knights of the Ancient Order of Homo.

Chicago Charlie, in his many-sided studies of human nature, had often remarked how prone are men to rush into societies of this character; and so, when one of the men in the basement arose and respectfully addressed the chief as "Liege and Loyal Lord of the Lakeside Leaguers," he was more than half convinced that the meeting was only the gathering of an ordinary lodge.

Nevertheless, having gone so far, he was resolved to see the thing to the end, not knowing what might result. The fact that the men were masked amounted to nothing, for masking in these secret lodges he knew was not uncommon.

The one fact remained, that Colonel Solon Youngblood and the men who usually associated with him were ordinarily not the kind of men to seek out such a place for a meeting, if the meeting was to be only an ordinary one.

What the men said was of no moment, though it brought from Youngblood an explanatory reply that rooted and fixed the detective to the floor:

"This meeting has been called, brother Leaguers, to seriously consider our position. We are menaced by a new peril. For a number of months, now, we have gone on without danger and without interference from the police, and I need not tell you that we have been making money. Recently, however, a number of our men have been shadowed. I was myself watched to-night, and I think followed!"

He then went on to detail how he had been warned by the Ghawazee to be on the lookout for a man who had been at the time staring at him, in the Cairo building.

"You cannot guess who that man is, for he has but recently taken up special detective work. He is becoming known as Chicago Charlie, the Columbian Detective, and he is likely to prove a dangerous enemy. I can hardly fancy what put him on our scent, but he is after us, hot and heavy, and each man of you must be constantly on his guard."

There was nothing said by Youngblood relating to the murder of John Malcomb, nor of how he had become acquainted with the dancing girl of the Cairo street. Nothing to show that this band had ever heard of John Malcomb!

One of the men rose to a question:

"When is that next cargo of stuff expected in?"

Chicago Charlie could not hear all that was said, but this seemed to be followed by some talk of stolen goods, of diamonds and laces and expensive merchandise.

When he saw that the meeting was about to break up—and it lasted less than an hour—Chicago Charlie hastily regained the streets, and stood there awaiting the coming forth of the men. They emerged one by one, and quietly dropped away in different directions to avoid observation.

When Youngblood appeared, Charlie followed him as before; and was not a little surprised when, at a neighboring corner, the sport crook encountered Selwyn Fisher, as if by appointment!

They took a horse car to the business part of the city; and then an Elevated Railway train for the World's Fair.

The detective was somewhat astonished at this course of procedure, remembering that Solon Youngblood had come from there so short a time before; but that he stuck close to them, with the tenacity of a bloodhound, may be taken for granted.

Once within the Exposition, the two turned into Midway Plaisance and sought out the big German beer garden, where they lounged and talked, and sipped the beer that had been ordered, while they listened to the music furnished by the excellent German band.

The beer garden was crowded, principally by Germans, who were chattering away with all their national vivacity; and Chicago Charlie, relying on the security of his disguise, took a seat at a table near that occupied by Youngblood and Fisher, and also called for a mug of beer.

Chicago Charlie

He was pleased to note that they had no suspicion of his identity, and were therefore not on guard against him.

He slipped along the seat as far as he could without attracting their attention and listened closely to what they were saying.

It was even of more interest than what he had heard in the basement of the old building, for it concerned John Malcomb.

"There can't be any doubt that the officers have you spotted, Walesey, though I am glad to say we have been able so far to keep them traveling on the wrong scent!"

Walesey gave him a look of gratitude, though his fat cheeks shook with the terror which possessed him.

"It was a deuced unfortunate thing that you happened to be playing cards with Malcomb in his room that night! But for that, no one would have thought of *you*. And then, you see, you foolishly volunteered that story about the offer to bet and the quarrel, and told how Malcomb flew into a huffy rage and ordered you out of the room."

"Hi was ha fool!" Fisher groaned, sinking back into his chair and gulping down great quantities of the beer. "Hi guess Hi 'aven't sense henough to keep my 'ead hout of danger!"

"You ought to congratulate yourself, then, that you have friends to look out for you! I was just going to tell you how I disposed of that last fellow. He fancied he had got together enough facts to warrant your arrest, and he came up to my room looking for you.

"'See here!'" I said. "'Walesey don't know any more about who killed John Malcomb than you do, and that is precious little. You think you've got facts, though you haven't; but I suppose you'll go right on and arrest the poor devil, anyway?'"

"Well, he said that was his intention, and nothing I could say would cause him to abandon it.

"Finally I says:

"'Look here, now! What will it be worth to you to drop this thing? Fisher is an innocent man! If money's any object to you, perhaps we can arrange for you to let up on him, and turn your talents in another direction. Come,'" I say, "'what will it be worth to you?'"

"Well, the upshot of it was that I bought him off for a thousand dollars; and, as I couldn't find you at the time, I took it out of my own pocket."

"Hi don't know ow Hi can hever thank you henough for that!" Fisher declared, his tones and manner showing that the huge draughts of beer he had been pouring into his capacious stomach were beginning to affect his head.

He put his hand into a pocket and pulled out a check book.

"Not at all! Not at all!" Youngblood urged, with an impatient gesture. "Don't you suppose I can do that much for a friend? Keep your money! What is a thousand dollars?"

"But, I don't propose to 'ave you go paying hout your good money for me, that way, don't you see!" Fisher protested, laying the check book on the table before him. "Hi can honly thank you for the favor, but Hi can pay you back the money; hand, bejove! Hi will!"

Thereupon he produced a fountain pen, and wrote his check in favor of Youngblood for a thousand dollars, his fat fingers trembling so much that he could with difficulty control the movements of the pen.

Youngblood accepted this check, with many protestations, but the detective observed that his fingers closed on it, nevertheless, with a covetous grasp, and that he shoved it down deep into his vest pocket, as if not in haste to part with it.

These mute evidences were all lost on the befuddled Briton, who likely would not have observed them had he been completely himself.

Chicago Charlie saw through Youngblood's cunning scheme at a glance; and indeed it required no shrewd mind to fathom it. It was merely one of the many tricks practiced by Youngblood to get hold of Fisher's money.

There had been no such detective officer on the Englishman's trail. No one had ever come to Youngblood's room, looking for Fisher to arrest him, as the sport had averred; and, consequently, Youngblood had never paid out any money to induce an abandonment of this object.

Solon Youngblood had simply taken advantage of the Englishman's credulity and lied him out of a thousand dollars. How many thousand more had been filched from Fisher's pockets by similar devices, Chicago Charlie could not guess; but he was pretty sure the figures would represent a large sum.

Solon Youngblood was "protecting" his English friend with a vengeance!

Chicago Charlie, though he had no great regard for the safety or comfort of the Briton, yet disliked exceedingly to see any one so robbed, and so resolved that he would do something to thwart the plans of Youngblood and his fellow harpies, if the opportunity presented.

Javanese Village.

298   Chicago Charlie

Just now, though, he had other and more important work.

The question again rose strongly in his mind, as he sat there straining his ears to catch the talk wafted from the other table, of whether or not Walesey had knowledge, guilty or otherwise, of who killed John Malcomb?

The detective was still of the belief that the Englishman was not himself the murderer, though the talk just caught might lead to the inference that Fisher knew something of it—more than he had confessed at the time of the inquest.

There seemed no way of getting at the facts in the case, at any rate, and so the detective continued his watch, mentally jotting down all he saw and heard of a suspicious character.

It was very late when the two left the table. The Exposition grounds were ready to be closed. Midway Plaisance had emptied itself of its crowding throngs. Only here and there was a man to be seen—some belated sightseer, who had overstayed.

Youngblood and Fisher made their way out of the beer garden of "The German Village," and apparently turned down the street toward the entrance. The detective delayed a little while, to avoid attention on their part, for the security given by numbers of people was now taken away, and he realized he must be circumspect.

What was his astonishment, on reaching the street, to find that Youngblood and the Englishman had disappeared! He could see them nowhere, though the lights ought to have made them visible in the then deserted condition of the thoroughfare.

Somewhat startled by this strange disappearance, and anxious lest they should elude him, he hurried along, looking everywhere for some signs of the missing men.

CHAPTER IX.

A MODERN DANIEL.

THE COLUMBIAN Detective was destined to a rude awakening from the secure belief that all his movements of the night had passed unobserved. He was to discover that the man he had set out to track was as wide-awake as any detective officer that ever followed a criminal.

Passing the Javanese village, there came sounds that momentarily drew his attention. He was standing at the moment where the light was not of the best. Then there fell on his ears the quick patter of nimble feet, and, almost before he was aware of it, a number of dark-visaged men leaped on him from the darkness and bore him to the earth.

He would have uttered a cry, but for the fact that a heavy cloth of some stifling texture had been thrown over his head at the moment of the attack and he was unable to call out.

He fought with desperation, struggling vainly to throw aside the cloth and free himself, when he was struck into insensibility by a heavy blow on the head.

The slight sounds made by the scuffle had drawn the attention of a watchman, but when that officer came hurrying in that direction all was as still as midnight about the scene of the combat!

The Javanese village lifted its queer roofs and turrets in the faint moonlight, and seemed slumbering as peacefully as if naught had occurred to disturb the serenity of its repose.

Who the dark-visaged men were it would have been difficult at the time to say. Only for the apparent fact that the peaceful Javanese could have no motive for the commission of such an act, they might have been thought the perpetrators of it.

Perhaps the place had been selected in the hope that they would be so accused, if the detective escaped and felt disposed to lay charges against any one.

The guardian of the peace of the place returned to his post of observation, a considerable distance away, and then a dark form showed itself in a shadowy corner where it had been lurking. Another came forth at the same moment, and a sifting moonbeam showed between them the white face of Chicago Charlie upturned toward the sky.

The other members of the assailing party had vanished, seemingly with as much mysteriousness and celerity as they had appeared.

When quite sure the attention of the guard was drawn in another direction, these two men lifted the unconscious form of the detective and bore it away from the spot.

There was little enough chance for them to have done this without being observed, only that they selected a time when the guard had turned on them his back and was slowly walking away.

Hagenbeck's Animal Show.

Satisfied that all was right at the eastern end of the Midway, he was setting out to walk to the western end; and after him, as he thus advanced, crept the crouching forms of the two men, with the body of the officer between them.

When they had gained the vicinity of the big building occupied by the Hagenbeck Animal Show, they put the officer down, and one of them crept away as if on a tour of inspection.

He was back in a short time, and again they moved forward with their burden.

The long street was now apparently wrapped in slumber. The lights seemed to wink dimly and sleepily. The last visitor had departed and the gates of the great Exposition had been closed for the night. Should the watchman not turn back, there was little chance that the men would be seen.

They were as stealthy as a pair of panthers in their movements, and, whenever a light shone from any of the buildings, or there was a suspicious sound, they crept with their burden into the shadows lying heavily along the walls, and there waited until feeling that it would be safe to proceed.

They apparently had no fear that the detective would immediately come out of his unconscious state; and, even if he had done so, he would still have been unable to cry out, for the headcloth had not been removed.

But he lay so limply that any one might well have been deceived into thinking him dead.

Approaching now the big building containing the animal show, they pressed close up to it; and, finding a side entrance, which in some manner they managed to open, they crawled through, dragging the unconscious man after them.

After much search, for they seemed not thoroughly familiar with the place, they found a stairway that led them to the rooms above; hurrying on and not halting until they were in the vicinity of some of the big cages.

For a moment a lamp streamed across their faces, which were wet with sweat. Had any one been there to see, the faces would have been revealed as dark and desperate-looking;—not the faces of Americans, certainly.

It would have puzzled the keenest detective in Chicago to have given a plausible reason for this attack, by these men, on the Columbian Detective. Surely these fellows could have had no connection with Solon Youngblood and the Lakeside Leaguers, nor with any of the parties whom it was the desire of Chicago

Charlie to ferret out.

One of the men, who was as fearless as a lion, in his way, approached the great cage containing the lions, whose roarings and scufflings had been so often witnessed from the street; and, removing the bar that held the door securely in place, looked in.

He was greeted by a low growl from one of the aroused lions. He paid no heed to it, however, but picking up the detective in his strong arms, he removed the cloth and hurled him by main force into the lions' den.

When he had done this, he closed the door as quickly, shot the bar into place, and the two men scudded away as fast as they could, leaving the imperiled officer alone with this new danger.

Doubtless they reasoned that he would be torn in pieces by the fierce brutes; probably mangled beyond recognition; and there would be no witness, therefore, to the dark deed that night committed. It would be the talk of the town for a few days, would absorb the attention of the newspapers and the public, be a ten days' sensation, and then be forgotten.

Almost immediately a series of fierce growls, which grew into angry roars, filled the ponderous cage and rumbled ominously through the rooms.

Then a big, black-maned brute got on his feet and shambled lazily forward from his corner; emitted a hoarse sound from his cavernous throat, and showed his yellow teeth in a wrathful way. He lashed his tail from side to side, as he approached the unconscious man with catlike softness.

The moonlight, streaming from without through the bars, gave to the scene a ghastly vividness.

The other lions watched, crouchingly and uneasily. The roars had subsided, and it might readily have been fancied they were awaiting in breathless suspense the result of the investigations of the black-maned monarch from the African jungles.

It was a most fortunate thing for the unconscious detective, lying thus in peril of his life, that the club which had knocked him senseless had not abraded the skin. There was no smell nor taint of blood on his person. He seemed more like a man lying asleep, with his face turned toward the moonlight.

The lion appeared to hesitate. He revealed his teeth again, as if he meant to pounce on the man, but closed the heavy jaws and contented himself with sniffing at the detective's face and clothing. Then, squatting flat on his belly, he gave the man a playful tap with one big paw, much as a cat taps at a mouse in play.

Chicago Charlie

When this failed to arouse the man, he got up, sniffed him over again; and then returned yawningly and lazily to his corner, from whence he watched the prostrate form with his big, staring, yellow eyes.

The other lions likewise kept their gaze fixed on the man in mute anticipation, but remained sluggishly in their places. Having been fed but an hour or two before, they were lethargic and sleepy.

Their eyes were half-closed, their heavy heads resting on their paws, when a groan broke from the pallid lips of the detective, and he moved. Instantly they were alert and growling ominously.

Other groans and other movements of the limbs and body followed, the aroused beasts watching these developments with keen intentness.

Then Charlie came back from the land of clouds and shadow; and with a sigh of pain stared about and endeavored to sit up.

The motion was greeted by a deep-voiced roar, which had the immediate effect of restoring him to full consciousness.

He was bewildered by what he saw, and for a time could not tell where he was or recall the last acts of his conscious existence.

Then the almost deserted street came back to him, as he had last seen it, and with it the memory of those pattering feet. He started up again, when the strong recollection of the struggle near the Javanese village returned and the pain in his head told him how the struggle had terminated.

The rumbling roars of the lions were increasing in volume, and with his faculties once more clear he recognized his position.

The sifting moonlight rendered the interior of the cage distinctly visible and threw the threatening lions in strong relief.

Their angry attitude warned him of the necessity of caution; and a deep sense of terror, such as he had seldom felt, swept over him. To be thrown thus to savage beasts was a most horrible thing; and, in anticipation, he felt those gleaming, yellow teeth rending his flesh.

He drew back in fear, crowding closely against the bars. He would have called out, but a dread of the consequences held him silent. He had often seen those lions, in his walk up and down Midway Plaisance, but had never until then given them close attention.

However, he recalled how he had seen the keeper stalk into their midst, holding them at bay by the mere waving of a stick;

and how they had crouchingly and instantly obeyed this keeper's commands.

The recollection gave him courage. He felt that he might accomplish what another man could, even though not a professional lion-trainer.

He was resolved to escape from the cage, and he was anxious to do it without attracting attention.

If he could reappear on the street, without a single scratch as a witness of what he had undergone, he felt it would be truly a victory. Besides, he was not willing that his name should be paraded in the papers, in the way he knew it would be, if the reporters got hold of the story.

Lifting himself a little, he looked about for the door through which he knew he had been thrust. It was within reach of his hand, and by a little further lifting of his body he might touch the heavy bar holding it in place.

The lions were still growling and shifting uneasily, but he drew himself half-erect and faced them with so stern a mien that they remained in their places, instead of leaping at him as he feared they would.

He then reached up and quietly slipped back the bar, drawing his body slowly toward the door, but keeping his eyes fixed on the threatening brutes.

Their uneasiness increased and their growls now welled in an angry chorus. Only the fierceness of his attitude seemed to keep them from springing on him.

He continued the slow movement of his body until he had brought his back against the door. Then, summoning all his energies, he quickly thrust the door open and sprung backward out of the cage.

The black maned brute leaped up with a roar that shook the building, and dashed quickly forward, his jaws widely distended. But his expected prey had escaped him! The door swung to with a rattling clang; and, the big bolt having been shot into place, the black-maned monarch did nothing but vainly dash his nose against the bars.

Hoarse roar on roar resounded, and the lions, with their angry bounds, shook the big cage from center to circumference.

Charlie heard a wrathful voice exclaiming, from another room:

"Blast them infernal lions! They're always fighting. They'll kill each other some of these nights."

The detective knew the voice was that of the keeper, who had been aroused from his slumber by the uproar, but he knew, too, that the keeper had no true idea of the cause of this outbreak among the big beasts.

So he scudded hurriedly to the stairway, down which he slipped with as much lightness and ease as was possible.

The outer entrance had been left unlocked by the villains who had borne the detective into the building, and Charlie had no trouble in making an exit.

On reaching the street he halted for a moment, listening anxiously. A cold perspiration bathed his body, and he realized that he was trembling as with an ague. He had been cool enough and courageous enough during the period of that trying ordeal. Now he felt faint and giddy, and grasped the wall to keep from falling.

No sounds came to show that the keeper had risen from his bed; and the growls of the lions were subsiding.

Satisfied that he had escaped unobserved, and thankful for his wonderful preservation, the detective slipped away through the deserted street, wondering how he was to get out of the Exposition grounds.

He was not only weak and sick, but he was stiff and sore, and his head ached terribly. He placed a hand to his head. The blow had been a severe one, as shown by the large prominence it had produced. He was so faint that he felt compelled to stop now and then and rest; but he finally reached the grounds of the Exposition proper; and, seeing no one near, scaled the high board wall, and set out in the direction of the city.

CHAPTER X.

WORLD'S FAIR WILLIE.

"ROBINSON CRUSOE had a cat;-
Poor old Robinson Crusoe!
He kept it in the top of his hat;-
Poor old Robinson Crusoe!"

Chicago Charlie, having caught a train at one of the outlying stations and thus reached the city, heard these nonsensical words, as he hurried along the street in the vicinity of the boat landing.

He thought he recognized the voice, and, quickening his footsteps, soon overhauled the singer.

It proved to be a shabbily-dressed boy, but one who had a peculiarly bright face, though the features were very dark. Although not more than fifteen years of age, there was in his manner the assertive alertness of experienced manhood. Such boys as he, cast adrift in the whirlpool of a great city, and who must sink or swim aided only by their own exertions, develop prematurely.

"Whither bound?" Clingstone called out, in cheery tone.

The lad came to a halt, under a blinking electric light, and stared curiously at his accoster.

It was plain he did not recognize the detective, though the latter was well known to him. He had not seen Charlie since the latter had doffed his policeman's garb.

The detective swept aside the disguising beard and again spoke, at the same time coming still nearer.

"What a lark!" the boy cried. "Say, you skeered me! I see you comin' along there and heard you a-hollerin'; and says I to myself: 'Wonder now what the duffer's up to?' Hadn't any idee it was you!"

"What are you doing now?" Clingstone questioned.

"Workin' the World's Fair."

"Like all the rest of 'em, eh?"

"You bet! Say, I've got the jolliest layout, down there! I've got the sellin' of papers in Midway. Made nighabout two dollars today! What's your lay?"

The detective laughed.

"Oh, you needn't grin! I know you're up to something, or you wouldn't be rigged up in *that* style. Hain't a cop any more, I reckon? Git bounced off the force?"

"We'll talk about that as we go along," said Clingstone, lowering his voice, as an example for the boy to do the same. "You haven't told me where you are going."

"Jist now I'm going home to look after the Infant Wonder. Then I'm going 'round to the newspaper offices and get my papers, fer I reckon the first edition is out now; and then you'll see me sliding for the Exposish, about daylight. I'm World's Fair Willie, now, you see, and I've got to hump myself, to keep up with the rush of biz!"

Chicago Charlie

"Not Billy Stubbs any longer?"

"Only to old friends like you. To all my new and swell acquaintances I'm Wide-awake Willie of the World's Fair! *See*?"

The boy was rattling on at this gait, as they turned into a street leading westward from the lake.

The horse cars were already running, early as was the hour;—in fact they seemed to run all night—and Charlie, grasping the boy by the shoulder, led, or rather pushed him toward one.

"We'll get home quicker this way!" was his explanation. "I want to have a long talk with you, and I haven't any time to spare. I've got to get home myself, and get to bed, or I'll be down sick. I've been out all night, and my head aches fit to split. I think you can do some work for me; like you did once before, you remember?"

The boy looked at him inquiringly, winked to show that he understood him; and then the two climbed into the car.

They got off at Jefferson, and in a tenement house they found the home of the boy who had called himself World's Fair Willie.

It was a little room on the fourth floor, not much bigger than a large dry goods box; and to it they painfully toiled up several flights of creaking stairs.

Billy Stubbs pushed the door open, and, searching out a piece of candle from a corner, lighted it and set it on a low table. Then he pointed to a stool.

"Set down and make yourself to home. These here apartments ain't very big, and they're a little hard to git at, but they're cozy. This room an' that there closet there is what I calls my suite."

On a low bed in a corner of the little room a child was sleeping;—a chubby-faced little fellow, with the bed-clothing half kicked off of him, and one plump arm thrown above his head.

"The Wonder is doing all right, I see!" and Billy tip-toed softly to the bed and looked into the sleeping face. "You've no idea how that chap grows! It's a miracle! He was all skin an' bones when I took hold of him and made a hospital out of myself, and now he's as fat as the big woman in the side show. I've give him another name! You know I called him Tommy; but that was too common for a kid like him—an',—bein' it's the World's Fair year—I throwed Tommy aside as no good, 'ceptin' fer ordinary brats, an' christened him Christopher Columbus!"

"Christopher Columbus Stubbs!" and the detective

nodded approvingly.

"I 'lowed mebbe the name 'u'd be a mascot. Mebbe he'll turn out a discoverer, and discover who his daddy and mammy is. Don't want 'im to do it in a hurry, though, for I've jist froze to him; an' the way he's tuck to me is good to see. He calls me 'Billy,' jist like he was growed up; an' when I told him t'other day that I was World's Fair Willie, he shook his yellow head, an' said: 'No! Dess Billy!' Oh! he's a good 'un."

So pleasant were these reminiscences that the boy—who was but a waif himself—gave an awkward step of a dance, then thrust his hands into his pockets and whistled a bar from the latest opera.

"He's doing finely!" Chicago Charlie admiringly commented.

"What was it you wanted of me?" and the boy turned from those interesting disclosures, remembering that Charlie had stated his time was limited.

"You recollect the work you did for me once?"

"Shadowing the tough that hung around Polk street station?"

"Yes. I've got some more work of the kind for you. As you see, by my change of clothing, I'm not on the regular force, just now. I've gone into a bit of special work."

"Private detective biz?"

"Not exactly. I've been assigned to run down a certain case, by the inspector!"

"Cricky!"

The boy drew up his knees, and looked earnestly over them at his visitor.

Then a shade darkened his face.

"'Fraid I can't do it, after all! There's that World's Fair business. I've got a route there that I ought to keep!"

"You can keep it. It's because you have that route that I think you can be of use to me."

"String yer narrative, then!" and the boy bobbed his head "Say yer say; an' I'm with ye, if it's something I kin do."

"You know the Cairo street!"

"Do I know the Infant Wonder? Ask me something easy!"

"There's a girl in that street—one of the dancing girls— that I want you to shadow for me. She's the darkest one, and the best-looking one. She wears a silver girdle, and has a gold crescent set in her hair just above her forehead. She's the only one dressed just that way."

"Oh! I've seen her!" Billy announced, with great eagerness.

Chicago Charlie

"You see I've got the run of everything, with this newspaper lay, and there ain't many things in Midway that I hain't seen!"

"I want you to keep your eyes on her, every minute you can spare from your work. And you must do it in a way that she will suspect nothing. Do you think you can?"

"Yep!" and the boy drew his knees still higher and rested his chin on them. "I kin try as hard as the next feller! Is that all you want me to do?"

"I think you will find it quite enough. Of course you've got to use your wits. For instance, should it seem necessary at any time to watch any one else—some one who has said something or had a talk with her to arouse your suspicion—you are to do so."

The boy's expressive face showed that he comprehended.

"Same instructions as what you give me before!" and he put down his knees and laughed lightly.

Then his countenance grew serious.

"I didn't have the Infant Wonder with me then! That there chap's got to be looked after. Now the question is how am I to look after him and sell newspapers and do the shadder trick?"

He brightened instantly, however, and went on:

"There's the kindergarten. I'd fergot about that. I've been leavin' him there every day, same as the other hard workin' mothers round here has been a-leavin' of their kids. But I don't know how it would be about nights. They told me when I first went there that they wouldn't on no account keep the Infant Wonder after six o'clock in the evenin', and that I'd got to hustle myself back at that time no matter what happened. The old woman's pretty vinegary at times, and I don't know but she'd 'a' pitched Christopher Columbus into the streets. I didn't never give her the chance!"

The child on the bed stirred uneasily, as if this talk awoke in his slumbering mind unpleasant memories.

Charlie looked at his watch. The gray dawn was showing through the dirty east window, the only window in the room.

"It's time for you to be seeing about your papers. Christopher Columbus is doing all right and will probably sleep like a top for three or four hours yet. I'll stay with him, though, for I don't feel like doing anything. I was never more beat out in my life. When you come back we'll go down to the kindergarten and see what arrangements we can make. It must be fixed so that you can have your whole time to give to this work, if necessary."

Billy Stubbs was manifestly delighted.

"All right," he declared. "That suits me to a dot."

Then he picked up his hat, tiptoed quietly to the stairway, and Chicago Charlie heard him bounding and leaping on his way down to the street.

"I couldn't have found a better ally," the detective mused, putting his hand to his paining head. "My! how that lump hurts."

Then he stretched himself on the floor; and in a few minutes was sleeping as soundly as was the Infant Wonder.

CHAPTER XI.

THE NEWSBOY AS A SHADOWER.

WHEN CHRISTOPHER Columbus Stubbs awoke that morning and looked drowsily about him, he was much surprised to find a man sleeping on the floor, instead of his newsboy guardian.

He immediately began to cry; and, this arousing the detective, the two might have been seen the next instant sitting bolt upright, staring at each other and digging at their eyes.

"Hello, Infant Wonder!" the detective laughingly called out. "You've tuned up rather early. Spoiled my nap, too!"

The child continuing to cry, he went over to the bed, and soon had the little fellow snuggling contentedly in his arms.

Billy Stubbs found them thus, a few minutes later, and expressed his approval in his usual boyish, boisterous fashion.

When the newsboy had told all he had to tell of his morning's experiences, the three left the room, obtained a breakfast at the nearest restaurant at the detective's expense, and then took their way leisurely toward the kindergarten, which was only a few blocks distant.

It was a raw, disagreeable morning. The wind blustered around the corners, the clouds hung loweringly, and there was threat of rain. But in the eyes of the Infant Wonder, who toddled unsteadily between the two, the shabby street and the threatening heavens were only vistas opening into wonderland.

Christopher Columbus could talk, so Billy alleged, but it must have been in some foreign language, for Chicago Charlie could scarcely understand a word of his prattle. The kindergarten, which had been established and was run by the Society for the Cultivation of Christian Charity and the Amelioration of the Condition of Working Women—the Alphabet Society, as Billy Stubbs called it, because of its interminable initials—the S.C.C.C.A.C.W.W.—was located in a dingy, brown house, set some distance back from the street, and which was reached by a double flight of stairs.

A thin, nervous woman, with a cast in one eye, and who possessed a buzz-saw voice not at all calculated to soothe a scared infant, responded to their pull at the bell.

She frowned, when she saw that a stranger accompanied Billy and the Infant Wonder.

The latter began to cry to return to the street. Whether this was the effect of her chilling presence and memories of unpleasant days spent there, Chicago Charlie could not tell.

He had doffed his hat, when she appeared, and now began to explain why he had called.

"We couldn't think of such a thing," she asserted, with some asperity. "It's enough to worry with the children through the daytime!"

But after some further conversation, in which the detective offered her ten times what she received for keeping a child throughout the daylight hours, the Infant Wonder was admitted into the kindergarten under the new stipulations:—which were, that Christopher Columbus Stubbs was to be kept there daily from sun to sun, excepting at such times as Billy should wish it otherwise.

When the detective and Billy were again in the street, the boy began a voluminous rehearsal of how he had found the Infant Wonder stumbling about, one dark night, in dangerous proximity to the lake; of how he had taken him home; and of how, when he could not, by advertising and otherwise, gain any clue to the child's parentage, he had resolved to adopt the pretty little fellow and "turn himself into a hospital."

"Why didn't you get the assistance of the police?" Chicago Charlie queried.

"And didn't I? And what good did it do? They was a-goin' fer to send him to some institution er other; and thinks I, 'if they're a-goin' to do that, I'm a better institution than they'll find!' an so I jist kep' him."

The boy and the detective officer separated, almost as soon as this marvelous story was told, each going their different ways. Chicago Charlie to his room, in search of needed rest, and Billy Stubbs back to the World's Fair, to enter on his new mission.

Midway Plaisance was crowded that day, in spite of the threat of a storm. The boy was alert throughout all the long hours, only leaving when it was time for the evening papers.

But nothing rewarded his diligence.

That night, however, he had cause to congratulate himself on the closeness of his watch.

He had wormed himself without observation into the Cairo street, and was lying with nose thrust almost against the paws of one of the big sphinxes, when he beheld the Ghawazee, whom he had been directed to shadow, come out of one of the buildings and walk uneasily about, as if expecting some one.

The expected party was not long in arriving. He was a little fellow, almost as dark as the girl, with a feminine slightness of form, and his tread fell as softly as that of a tiger.

Like a flash came to the boy the thought, that here was the real murderer!

He appeared to start up out of the ground, for Billy did not see him come through the gate.

That the two were lovers was soon made apparent. They withdrew into a dark corner, as if to escape any unfriendly gaze, and remained there for more than an hour, in close conversation.

Then Billy saw the man kiss the Ghawazee, as he arose to go, and saw her steal back through the doorway.

"I reckon I'd better foller that there chap!" the watching newsboy observed. "No use hanging 'round this bit of Egypt all night! I'll not git to see the girl ag'in; that's certain."

When the man slipped out through the gate into Midway, Billy was close at his heels, for the hour was so late that, though the gate had not been closed and locked, the gatekeeper had relaxed his vigilance.

Hurrying to the west end of the thoroughfare, the man sought a concealed point, and scaled the fence, exhibiting remarkable agility.

Not to be outdone, Billy Stubbs imitated his example, scrambling over the high wall in some fashion, and then pursued the little man through the vacant lots that lay thereabout.

It did not take Billy Stubbs long to tell that the fellow was heading for the Gypsy camp, and he knew then that the little man was a Gypsy and a member of the band camped there.

The fact that the Gypsy had thus met the dancing girl struck the boy shadower as somewhat strange, but he gave it little heed at the time, being fully occupied with the task in hand.

When the Gypsy entered one of the tents, he was greeted by a grumbling voice. Billy had never heard it before, but it was the voice of Gypsy Nell, the fortune-teller.

"Ye'r prancin' 'round turrible late to-night, Zelna Magruder!" the voice grumbled. "Why can't you come in like you ought, and let them that wants to sleep, sleep?"

Billy had sneaked close up to the tent, and could readily hear every word.

"Business, Nell! Do you think there's nothin' to do but set around an' tell fortunes?"

His tones were squeaky and thin, and reminded Billy of the squeal of a rat.

"The business you're into will hang you one o' these days. You'll find I'm a true fortune-teller in *that*! What are you up to, anyway? What in the world, Zel, air you scratchin' at?"

"I'm gittin' my heavy coat!" he growled back, irritated by her nagging. "I've got to go out on the lake to-night, and it looks dark enough to blow."

"Better put it off!" she urged, and Billy could tell that she had arisen.

"If I'm bound to be hung, as you say, there's no danger of my drowning!"

"What do you have to go out fer?" she whined.

"Oh! bother! Don't ask me sech questions! You're allus pestering me. You ought to know. There's a cargo of stuff comin' in, an' the off'cers have got scent of it. I've got to warn the boys."

"You'd better pull out of that league business, Zel Magruder! If ye don't, you'll wish, one o' these days, you had. I don' no as I'll care, though!"

"Go to thunder!" was his ungracious exclamation. "When I want yer advice I'll ask it."

He had found his coat and instantly quitted the tent, his form being revealed as he passed through the entrance, in the fan of light from the lamp he had lit.

Billy, still crouching and watching, saw the crone come to the door and shake her fist at the darkness after him.

"You're an evil hound, Zel Magruder, and I'll be even with you yit! Mind my word!"

Then she went back and blew out the lamp, and Billy Stubbs hurried away on the trail of the receding Gypsy.

CHAPTER XII.

FIGHTING FOR LIFE.

BILLY STUBBS permitted the oars to rest in the rowlocks, and bent forward to listen. About him the night winds sung, blowing fresh and strong toward the land. The blackness of darkness was over him. Behind him, lights gleamed from many of the houses, late as was the hour. Before him and beneath him rolled the waters of Lake Michigan, the waves tossing now and then into white crests.

Billy Stubbs had followed Zel Magruder to the lake front, and had there seen him enter a boat and pull out into the lake.

He remembered what he had heard Magruder say to the Gypsy woman!

"There's a cargo of stuff comin' in, an' the officers have got scent of it. I've got to warn the boys!"

Who those "boys" were and what it all meant the newsboy was determined to know. It might be a matter of importance to Detective Charlie, and it might not; but, whatever it was, he felt that it was his business to find out.

There had been another boat lying in the water, close to the one Magruder had taken; and Billy finding little trouble in releasing the painter, had climbed cautiously into it, and now was paddling out into the lake after the Gypsy.

It seemed rather a reckless thing, in view of the darkness and the state of the weather. But Billy Stubbs, when his detective blood was up, was given to doing reckless things.

Bending forward now on his oars, he heard the "thump, thump" of the oars in the Gypsy's boat; and getting his bearings anew from the sound, he also rowed on, endeavoring to keep a direct course by watching the lights in the houses.

Twice the noise of the Gypsy's rowing ceased in that unaccountable manner, each time, forcing Billy to await the renewal of the strokes.

Fancying the sounds of his own oars might have been heard by Magruder and the latter thus warned, he became exceedingly cautious in his movements, lifting and dipping the oars with great care.

Magruder was heading down the lake toward the White City, he having taken to the water more than half a mile above the northern limit of the Exposition grounds. He had swept far out in the lake and was almost in the track daily and nightly pursued by the boat of the World's Fair Steamship Company.

When almost opposite the big brick ship, erected and armed to represent a regular U.S. Line of Battle Ship, Billy Stubbs became again aware that the sounds of Magruder's rowing had ceased.

He lay to on his oars, as he had done before, listening intently for some renewal of the noise to guide him.

A minute; two minutes; five minutes, passed away; and the silence of the night and darkness continued to brood over the waters.

The flashing of lights from the Exposition buildings came now and then, but they served only to render the darkness seemingly more intense.

For some time Billy had known that the wind was increasing in violence and that the waves were running higher. There was not enough of a "blow," however, to give him any uneasiness on that account. He could handle a boat fairly well, and felt at home on the water.

But he became anxious as the minutes slipped by and no sounds came to tell him that the Gypsy's boat was anywhere near.

When nearly ten minutes had passed, and still there came nothing to indicate the Gypsy's near presence, the boy pulled slowly and quietly forward.

He was now thoroughly alarmed, believing that Magruder had given him the slip and that all his work of the night was thus to come to naught.

But he had not pulled fifty yards when he was undeceived.

Magruder's boat loomed out of the darkness, in which it had been hidden, and the Gypsy, pulling at the oars, quickly laid it alongside.

"Curse you, you spy!" came the low words; and at the same instant Billy felt one of the Gypsy's oars strike him.

He gave a low cry, for the pain of the blow stung him, and he was thoroughly startled.

But he did not lose his presence of mind, in the face of this unexpected peril. He grasped the oar, letting his own drop, and clung on so tightly that Magruder could not draw it away.

"Curse you!" the Gypsy cried, striving to draw the oar away.

For reply, Billy clung with the tenacity of a leech, and the two boats, set in motion, bumped together so violently that the occupants came near being thrown into the water.

So nearly did Billy Stubbs come to being hurled overboard, that, in order to save himself, he had to let go the oar.

As a result the boats swung apart, when the Gypsy again lifting the blade, aimed another murderous blow at the newsboy's head.

Billy sought vainly for the oars he had dropped. The shaking of the boat had loosened them from their places, and they had slipped into the lake! Escape by flight seemed, therefore, hopeless.

He had deftly avoided the second blow of the Gypsy's oar by quickly ducking his head; and when another blow was aimed at him—for the Gypsy had again brought his boat within reach, the boy tried to catch it as before.

With a horrible oath the Gypsy jerked it away, almost falling out of his boat. But at that moment Billy was blinded by a lightning-like flash.

There was a loud report, and a pistol ball cut through the air within an inch of his head.

Zel Magruder had grown desperate.

Billy Stubbs saw the pistol-hand lifted again, and raised himself to leap into the lake; but before he could reach the water the report rung out once more, sharp and clear, and Billy Stubbs seemed to sink out of sight like a lump of lead.

"One infernal spy out of the way, anyhow!" Magruder growled, setting his oars in place, at the same time keenly watching to see if the boy arose to the surface.

He observed that Billy's boat was drifting landward. It was but a few yards away, slowly drifting toward the shore, but the gloom already rendered it nearly invisible.

"That last ball caught him between wind and water!" was the heartless comment, peering still over the black, tossing waves. "He'll never come up till he floats up, ready for the morgue. I wonder who he was, anyhow? Spies are getting terrible thick and bold, lately.

"Well, *he'll* not bother *me* any more!"

With this, certain that Billy was done for, he bent on the oars and pulled further out into the lake.

CHAPTER XIII

A REMARKABLE LETTER.

CHICAGO CHARLIE, sitting silently in the seclusion of his room, had much to cogitate on.

He felt nearly done up. The wound on his head still pained him, and he was so stiff and sore from his late exertions that he felt scarcely able to move about.

Nevertheless, his interest quickened, when his mail was brought in and he saw that one of the letters was from Daisy Malcomb.

He tore it hastily open, eager to get at the contents.

As he ran down the page, his eyes dilated, his cheeks whitened, and his breath came in gasps.

This is what he read:

"Chicago, June 7, 1893.

"Dear Charlie:—I must beg your pardon in advance, for writing these lines, that I know will so pain you. But, indeed! indeed, dear Charlie! I have convinced myself that it is the thing I ought to do. I fear you will never forgive me, though I shall pray for your forgiveness to my dying day.

"I am forced to tell you that I can see you no more! No more! My God! how can I write it? But it is true. You must not think of trying to trace me. It would be useless, and I do not desire that you should. I want you to forget that there ever was such a miserable girl on earth. Seek some one else, whom you can marry happily, and forget me.

"Oh! I don't know what I am saying! I feel that I want you to remember me always, yes, I am even selfish enough to want you to remain single; as I shall do. But no! No! That would not be right. There are many girls you might find in this city, or in other cities, much handsomer and in every way better suited to you. Find one; and make her happy by marrying her;—for I am sure that whoever becomes your wife must be a happy woman!

"And do not think of me too harshly, dear Charlie! Do not think me cruel and hard. Do not think, either, that I am driven to do this. It is of my own free choosing. I cannot explain to you why I do it. You will never know. But believe always that I felt it to be best for both of us.

"And, dear Charlie! should you cherish my memory, as I shall cherish yours—do not, for Heaven's sake, do not ever believe that I could be so wicked as to *kill my own father*! I am unworthy of you—and I know you must learn to hate me!—but do not, do not believe *that*!

"Now, good-by!—and do not try to search for me, for it will be useless. Good-by! Good-by!

"Your unfortunate and miserable
"Daisy."

The ashy fingers of the strong, young Columbian Detective shook, as he held the paper and stared at these lines. He could not credit his eyesight. Surely, he felt, this must be some horrible dream. It could not be a reality.

Yet, he knew that those lines had been penned by Daisy Malcomb. This was no counterfeit of her handwriting—no forgery. The letters, the words, were hers. And she had written that way to him! To her promised husband! To the man she had parted from not fifty hours before, with embraces and loving words.

Again and again the detective ran over the lines, feeling that there must be a mistake somewhere; that the letter must have been written in jest, and there was an explanatory key, if he could but find it. But he was driven to acknowledge that this was wholly untenable.

He did not look at the other letters that lay on the table, mutely bidding him to read them; but took up his hat, thrust Daisy's strange communication into his pocket, and strode toward the door.

There he stopped and hesitated.

A glance at the mirror had shown him that his eyes were shining unnaturally and that his face was as white as that of a corpse. He looked more like a dead man galvanized into temporary activity than a man in whom the warm life currents were still coursing.

He felt that he ought not go on the street looking like that.

The letter burned in his pocket.

He could not resist the temptation to look at it again.

He turned to the words, to make sure they were there:

"Do not ever believe that I could be so wicked as to kill my own father!"

Why had Daisy Malcomb written that?

It struck him that here might be the clue to the secret!

Some one might have led her to think that Chicago Charlie, in his detective search, had come on evidence convincing him that she was the murderess!

"Good God! Can anybody have been so base?"

The sweat of despair stood on his forehead.

He could think of no one who could have done it;—who, even if base enough, could have induced Daisy to give heed to it.

The position seemed so foolish that he cast it aside, and sought for some other.

There was no explanation—there could be none! save what appeared in the letter itself!

Daisy had bidden him an everlasting farewell, claimed herself an unfortunate miserable girl, and assured him it would be useless to search for her.

He was struck dumb by the overwhelming catastrophe that had so suddenly come on him. His fertility of resource stood of no avail. He felt bound, helpless, stricken unto death.

"I *will* find her!" he declared, turning desperately toward the street. "If she is alive, I will find her, if it takes all the years of my life! There's some devil's work here! I'll find out what it is! She must have been crazy when she wrote that. Crazy with despair; with grief! Some fiend has driven her to do that?"

Yet, when he came to sift this idea, it seemed to have as little foundation as the exploded ones that had preceded it. Who was there to so frighten or influence Daisy Malcomb? No one! She might, indeed, have lost her mind, and written the letter while under the influence of derangement and delirium! There seemed no other explanation.

He found himself in the street, without knowing just how he got there; and sought the nearest cab.

He had determined to visit Daisy's home, and begin his investigations of the mystery there.

Though the cab rattled furiously through the crowded streets—he having enjoined the driver to haste—the pace seemed provokingly slow.

He was in a fever of impatience, and could brook no delay, chafing under this seeming slowness like a high-spirited horse.

He half-expected, on arriving at Malcomb's, to find the doors closed and the shutters up. But the house showed every appearance of being still occupied.

Hoping that there might still be some mistake, and that Daisy might meet and greet him as before, he dismissed the cab and bounded up the walk.

He observed that a strange man was doing the work about the yard, and the woman who came in answer to his ring had also an unknown face. The house was the same, but the servants were not!

"Is Miss Daisy Malcomb in?" he queried, trembling in spite of his best efforts.

The maid glanced at him wonderingly, struck by his pallid, shaky look.

"I don't know any one by that name," she replied. "I just came here this morning. Shall I inquire of the housekeeper?"

"Send her here," he requested, catching at the door to keep from falling, "You are quite sure Miss Malcomb isn't here?"

The maid darted away, convinced that she had encountered a madman; but soon returned, with the housekeeper at her heels, who was followed by a gawking, curious servant.

It stung Charlie to have these people stare at him as if he were some specimen in the zoo;—stung him the more, for it told him that his agitation had loudly proclaimed itself.

"Who occupies this house, then?" he asked, when the housekeeper assured him that no one by the name of Daisy Malcomb was to be found there.

The answer nearly prostrated the detective:

"Colonel Solon Youngblood!"

Chicago Charlie made the housekeeper speak the name and title again, before he could trust that he had heard aright; then, as quietly as possible, he requested to see Youngblood.

He had been told that Youngblood was at home; and, following the housekeeper, entered the little waiting-room, where Daisy, in the happy days gone by, had so often welcomed him.

The furniture was the same; and, looking at it, he found it difficult to rid himself even yet of the idea that she would meet him there.

But the heavy tread heard in the corridor was not that of Daisy Malcomb; and a moment later, Solon Youngblood stood before him.

If Youngblood knew him, he affected not to recognize him on this occasion; but stood, as if awaiting an explanation of the call.

"Your name is Youngblood, I believe?" the detective said, awkwardly rising, for he had never felt so ill at ease. "You will

Chicago Charlie

pardon me, I hope, when I ask how long you have occupied this house? I came to see a young lady who I thought lived here, and find that a change has been made!"

"Ah! yes." And Youngblood smiled more amiably, and took a seat. "We only moved in here yesterday. The property came to me through purchase. I have owned it for some time, but only took possession yesterday."

"This is the house of John Malcomb?"

"It *was* the house of John Malcomb, before it became mine. Malcomb, as you probably know, is dead!"

"And his daughter?"

"Well, really now, you wouldn't expect me to keep track of people that way? I can't tell you, sir, where she is!"

The tones were rising and testy.

"Was she not here yesterday?"

"Neither can I tell you that, sir! She was not here when we came in!"

"And you do not know where she is to be found?"

"I have already told you I do not!"

He frowned and shifted uneasily, as if annoyed.

"One question more, if you will allow me?"

Youngblood nodded.

"When did you buy this house?"

The new proprietor arose in evident disgust and anger.

"All such questions may be answered by inquiry at the proper place. To save you search, though, I will say, that the property has been mortgaged to me for a long time, and that shortly before his unfortunate taking off, John Malcomb, finding he could not pay out, gave me a clear deed. I hope you are satisfied sir; and now I will wish you, good-day!"

He turned back into the corridor, leaving the detective to pick his way blindly into the street.

Instead of finding a key to the mystery, the mystery had deepened.

Chicago Charlie

CHAPTER XIV

ON THE REVENUE CUTTER, ANDREW JOHNSON.

WHEN ZEL Magruder rowed away into the thick darkness that lay over the lake, he was firmly convinced that the boy spy who had been following him had sunk to his death in the black waters.

Yet Zel Magruder was a sorely mistaken man.

The whizzing bullet had sped by as harmlessly as had the first, and Billy Stubbs went into the water wholly uninjured.

He had not leaped without knowing what he was doing. He had seen that to remain would be to court death, for the Gypsy's shot proved that the Gypsy meant to murder him.

Therefore, when he felt the waves curling over his head, he closed his lips firmly, and, striking out boldly, for he was a reasonably good swimmer—he pulled away from the dangerous vicinity as fast as he could.

When forced to rise, he could see nothing, even after he had freed his eyes from the water. Sure, though, that the Gypsy was watching for him only a few yards away, he remained perfectly quiet; supporting himself, not without difficulty.

Something bumped against him, and, putting out a hand, he discovered it to be one of the oars of his boat.

This was a God-send; and he clung to it, as drowning men are said to cling to straws.

With its aid, he found his position in the water much easier; but he did not essay to swim, convinced that Magruder was still within hearing distance.

Not until he heard the Gypsy's boat moving away, did he turn his face toward the land. Then he put forth all his strength, though his progress was slow, both owing to the high waves and the interference of the oar, to which he thought it best to cling.

Suddenly there came the rattle of more oars; a number of them this time, showing that the approaching boat was not Magruder's.

Then a clear voice rung over the water.

"Ahoy, there! *Ahoy!*"

It was manifestly a friendly call, and Billy answered it, in as loud tones as he could command.

The sounds of the oars told him the course of the boat had

been shifted.

Again the voice called, and again Billy replied.

Then the boat loomed dimly alongside, seeming gigantic because of its illy-defined shape.

Billy shouted once more, to make his position known, and a muscular hand reached down from the bow, and seized him by the collar and drew him into the boat.

The newsboy was as wet as a drowned rat, but the chill produced by his uncomfortable bath was likely to be the only unpleasant effect of his novel adventure.

As soon as he was safe in the boat, he was sharply questioned, and the boat's head was turned about.

Within twenty minutes thereafter he found himself on the U.S. Revenue Steamer, Andrew Johnson, then lying at anchor near the Government exhibits, and learned that the crew of the boat that had rescued him had belonged to the vessel.

The men of the Andy Johnson, as she was familiarly called, had heard the shots from the Gypsy's revolver, and thinking something must be wrong, had sent a boat's crew to investigate the cause of the shots.

Billy had scarcely stepped on the deck of the cutter, his face plainly revealed in the bright light, when a roar of recognition greeted him and a bushy-bearded sailor scrambled forward.

"Well, may I be hanged! if that ain't Billy Stubbs! Come here, you lively rascal! What have you been doin' swimmin' round out there in the lake?"

Billy had partially acquainted the boat's crew with what had befallen him, and he proceeded to give a brief account of his adventures to this sailor friend, Jack Rackstraw.

Before he had concluded, and while he was still dripping wet, Rackstraw seized him by the shoulder and pushed him toward the companion-way leading to the captain's cabin.

"Tell that to Cap'n Stebbins, will ye? Don't go to babblin' too much of it hyer to the crew? mums the word to them!"

Then, pushing him in advance into the captain's presence, Rackstraw bawled out, in a big voice!

"Beg pardon, Cap'n Stebbins! but hyer's a youngster, that I'm well acquainted with, that's got a yarn I think you'll like to hear!

"Spit it out, youngster!"

This last to Billy, who stood somewhat ashamed.

Stebbins was a pleasant-looking man, in a neat uniform—his appearance nothing indicative of the sailor and commander and fighting man that he really was—and he questioned the boy kindly enough, taking no apparent notice of the streams of water that trickled from Billy's clothing to the carpet.

His interest became intense, as Billy plunged into the narrative.

"A cargo coming in, and he went to warn those in charge of it, eh?" commenting on that part of the story which touched on Magruder's words to the old crone. "That seems to be information worth having! I think you and your friend, Charlie Clingstone, are looking after the same rascals that we're hunting. If so, probably we can be of mutual help.

"Here, Rackstraw, take this boy away and give him something to eat and something hot, and warm clothes, too!"

And before Rackstraw could obey the order, he had turned to his desk and commenced to write.

Rackstraw led Billy Stubbs away, gave him some warm drinks, and a suit of clothing that was a world too large for him, talking all the while of what had recently befallen the boy.

The rough sailor seemed to have a friendly spot in his heart for the waif, whom he had met and become acquainted with many months before. It was while Rackstraw had been hanging about the city doing next to nothing but kill time. Billy Stubbs had sold papers to him and blacked his boots, and the acquaintance thus auspiciously begun had grown gradually to its present proportions.

"Shouldn't be s'prised if the cap'n does the has'some thing by you fer givin' him that tip. The feller you had the fight with was most likely one of them smugglers we have been looking for so long. You'd stand high, if we should chance to ketch 'em through you."

The mental picture of the great benefits to be derived by his friend, Billy Stubbs, from this happy consummation, was so rose-tinged that a huge roar of laughter escaped him, indicative of his pleasure.

"When you're a millionyer up a tree, an' I'm still nothing but poor Jack, mebbe you'll drop me down a dollar er two, eh! Master Billy?"

He stood back, cocked his hat sidewise, and critically surveyed the changed apparel.

"If anybody makes any remarks about them clo'es, jist tell them that your tailor went on a strike. Hello! there's the cap'n a-wantin' us a'ready."

When they were again in the captain's room, the captain gave Rackstraw an indorsed letter; remarking, as he glanced at the boy:

"We're going to lie out in the lake, on the lookout for your recent acquaintance and his friends. We can only hope we may run foul of them.

"You shouldn't have taken that boat I suppose, as it wasn't yours; but I'll have it looked up in the morning and restored to its owner. We can arrange about the charges, sometime, should there be any.

"Mr. Rackstraw, here, will accompany you on shore, and together you will hunt up Mr. Clingstone. You will each then be guided by his advice."

"Whoopee!"

Honest Jack Rackstraw gave utterance to this exclamation, as soon as they were out of the captain's apartment.

"There's a leave of absence in that paper, I'll bet a month's wages. And that leave of absence means a lakeful of adventure and fun. Come along!"

They heard a boat drop into the water and knew that they were to be immediately rowed ashore.

Then they were in the boat, with its bow pointed toward the land, and the strong-armed crew sending it along at a gallant speed.

CHAPTER XV.

THE TRIPARTITE ALLIANCE.

THE MYSTERY surrounding the disappearance of Daisy Malcomb proved impenetrable. Do what he would, Chicago Charlie could not clear it away; nor could he form any reasonable theory by which it might be explained. In fact, the more he thought of it and pondered over it, the more inexplicable did it become; until, through grief and anxiety and baffled hopes, he was well nigh insane.

The possession of the house of Solon Youngblood was a piece with the mysterious disappearance of the girl. That Youngblood had a right to the property was, however, soon shown; for, an examination of the proper records revealed that Youngblood's statements concerning the mortgage and deed were in every essential correct.

He wondered whether or not a discovery that the house and ground belonged to Youngblood had had anything to do with Daisy's singular act. Then he accused himself of brutality, in harboring so foolish a suggestion, and put it from him.

He was in this frame of mind when Rackstraw and Billy Stubbs found him—bursting in on him with all the radiance of discovery and hope. But it would have required more than their unusual exuberance of spirits to drive the chill from the heart of Chicago Charlie.

Yet he greeted Rackstraw warmly, when the latter had been introduced by Billy Stubbs; and, when he had read the letter from the captain, had been told that Rackstraw had met John Malcomb, in the latter's lifetime, and had listened to Billy's stirring account of the adventures of the night, he sat down to a discussion of the situation.

He saw that it was essential to continue the pursuit of the Gypsy and his associates, for there was irrefutable proof that the men the Gypsy had started to warn were members of the band led by Solon Youngblood. It was a fair inference, therefore, that among these men were to be found the proofs he was seeking.

Yet this last startling phenomenon—the singular letter and the absence of the girl—had almost turned his thoughts from the slayer of John Malcomb; though duty, and a hope that a solution of one mystery would clear up the other, urged him to continue work along that line.

He had reached the conclusion, however, that the task to which he must give his individual attention was the shadowing of Solon Youngblood and the latter's intimate associates. He felt sure, though without positive proof, that Solon Youngblood could at that moment have laid bare the mystery of the disappearance of Daisy Malcomb, as well as that surrounding the murder of Daisy's father. He felt that the two were linked puzzles, solvable by one and the same means.

These reflections, indefinite and shapeless to be sure, were crowding his mind, even while he talked to the sailor and Billy, and discussed with them plans for the shadowing and ultimate capture of Zel Magruder and his companions.

When he had laid out for them the work he desired them to do—for Captain Stebbins, in his letter, had placed Rackstraw at the detective's disposal, with unlimited leave of absence—he shook them by the hand; and, when he had seen them depart, turned again to the task that was so engrossing him.

Chicago Charlie had seemingly aged in a dozen hours as much as if a dozen years had rolled over his head. Not only had he apparently aged, but there was in his face such a drawn and tense look, that he started back with almost a cry of fright, when he surveyed his features in the glass.

"This will never do!" he thought. "My face betrays me. It tells too much. I must either learn to hold my feelings and emotions in check, or quit the perilous business in which I have engaged!"

He had come to a seeming rash resolve, and now proceeded to get ready for its execution.

With a keen razor, he removed from his face every trace of a beard. The mustaches on which he had so prided himself were ruthlessly sacrificed.

"They will grow again!" he grimly muttered, as he nervously removed them. "At any rate, what does it matter?"

He was thinking that nothing mattered, now that Daisy was lost to him.

When he had cut away the beard and mustache, he got some pigment from his trunk, and by its skillful application tanned his face to a dark hue, and so changed the general appearance of his physiognomy that his best friend meeting him in the street would never have known him.

He surveyed himself again in the mirror, this time with marked satisfaction.

The transformation was really little short of marvelous.

"I think I can run the gantlet, now!" he commented, in a pleased whisper. "And—if my disguise should be penetrated!—"

The black look that overspread his face emphasized an apparent threat.

The resolution he had taken was this:

He would seek employment in Youngblood's house, if possible, even though the employment should be the most menial.

Failing in that, he would obtain such work as would place him where he could constantly watch the house and grounds. He was skilled as a florist, having taken much pride as an amateur in the cultivation of flowers, and he thought it possible that his knowledge in this, would secure him work in some of the gardens near the Malcomb residence, if not in the Malcomb grounds.

With this in his mind, and his plans fully matured, he descended into the street.

So swiftly had the hours sped, that it was now evening, and the streets were thronged by the thousands of working men and women returning from their daily employment, and by other thousands of clerks and business men hastening homeward from their books and ledgers.

All were crowding in Chicago haste, no one heeding his neighbor.

Chicago Charlie stood, after having reached the street, waiting for a coming car, when a carriage dashed furiously around a corner.

He recognized it as the opportune moment of his life, for in the carriage, in imminent peril of their lives, were Colonel Solon Youngblood and the handsome woman who called herself his wife!

CHAPTER XVI.

"I HAVE HEARD THAT GRAVEYARDS YAWN."

COLONEL SOLON Youngblood recognized his peril, but was powerless to aid himself or the woman at his side. The horse, a spirited animal, had taken fright at a fluttering paper that rolled between his feet, and had immediately become unmanageable. Leaping forward, with Youngblood clinging desperately to the reins, the latter had parted, and the animal was now tearing wildly along, not only threatening the lives of the occupants of the bounding carriage, but the lives of the people in the street.

A police officer tried vainly to stay the horse's progress, and men, in that foolish fashion so common on such occasions, "shooed" the animal and waved their hats, unaware of the palpable fact that their antics only served to increase the fright of a beast that was already insane from fear.

Narrowly escaping collision with a huge beer wagon, the carriage bounded toward the side that Chicago Charlie was on, and where he had stationed and nerved himself for an effort at checking the horse's speed.

Youngblood, livid with fear, was trying to get hold of the

Chicago Charlie

broken and dragging lines; while the woman at his side seemed half unconscious through fright.

With a bound that would have done credit to a professional athlete, Charlie left the pavement, hurled himself directly across the path of the scared brute, and, then, grasping the bridle-bit, hung on for dear life.

People scattered in all directions. Men yelled and women screamed.

But the nervy detective never released his hold, though it looked for a moment or two as if he were sure to get his brains dashed out.

His powerful hands at length succeeded in drawing back the head of the straining brute, until the forward movement was checked. Then, with a twist Charlie drew the head still further around, and the horse came down in a heap, piling the buggy almost on top of the detective, who had leaped aside to escape the thrashing heels that beat the air like ponderous flails.

A dozen men sprung to the detective's assistance, some freeing the occupants of the buggy from the wreck, and others helping the rescuer to hold and subdue the horse.

It was seemingly all over in a minute, and the horse, panting and broken in spirit, was standing quietly, but with streaming flanks, Chicago Charlie's hand still securely on the bit.

Youngblood, having convinced himself that he had escaped, and also that the woman was uninjured, came forward to thank the man who had risked his life thus to help him, at the same time effusively drawing out his purse.

There are some men who think that any favor may be offset by the payment of cash, and Solon Youngblood was of the number.

He did not at all recognize Chicago Charlie, but took him for a total stranger.

Flourishing a hundred-dollar bill, he held it out, at the same time saying:

"I can never thank you enough, my good friend, for what you have done, and so offer this!"

Youngblood's tone was offensively patronizing.

"Keep it!" the detective exclaimed, with voice so changed by the disgust he felt that Youngblood never would have known it, even though Chicago Charlie had attempted no disguise.

A policeman was now on the scene, and the crowds, seeing that all had ended well, were again streaming along as if nothing unusual had happened.

Disgusted as he was, Charlie saw that it would not do to offend Youngblood, for the chance of securing a situation might never again be so good.

"Can I not do something for you, if you will not accept money?" the sport asked, staring in some surprise. "You look as if—"

He hesitated to put the thought into words.

"I *am* in pretty hard straits, just now!" confessed the disguised detective. "I do not want pay for what I have done, but—"

"Well, out with it!" thrusting the bill back into the purse.

"If you could secure me a situation, now, where I might do something to earn a living, it wouldn't be bad. I've been out of a job so long that I hardly know what work looks like, but I think I could suit any employer who'd be willing to try me."

This was said with a little pitiful air of pleading.

Youngblood looked at him closely.

The two were standing at the horse's head, while the policeman seemed to be paying marked attention to the flushed and handsome Mrs. Solon Youngblood. No one was giving the speakers any heed.

"I'll tell you what!" and Youngblood lowered his voice. "I'm needing a man, now. A *reliable* man; one who can do his work and keep his tongue in his teeth. If you're that kind of a man, call around at my office in an hour."

He drew out a card and penciled the name and number on it. "You'll find me there!"

Chicago Charlie saw he had been given the address of the Malcomb place!

The gallant policeman was assisting Mrs. Youngblood to re-enter the carriage.

Seeing this, the detective spliced the broken reins with a strong knot; and Youngblood climbing in beside the woman, he gave the reins into the hands of the sport, and saw him drive away.

Fortune seemed once more to smile on him. Scarcely had his plans been perfected for entering Youngblood's service, when the desired opportunity had presented!

And to become Youngblood's private secretary!—for that was what he believed it to mean—he could not have asked for anything better!

Promptly at the expiration of the hour he was at the place

Chicago Charlie

appointed, and was ushered into a little room in the north wing of the building. It was a room which had been much used by John Malcomb, and in which Youngblood had established an office.

Notwithstanding its prosaic character, it was richly and luxuriously furnished. The writing desk, on which stood a typewriter, and where were many bunches of letters and papers, most attracted the detective's attention.

Youngblood came in directly.

"I want some one who is handy at correspondence and can get up a neat and effective letter, for I'm a little awkward at such things. There's a pile of letters there, that's been waiting an answer for a week, just because I haven't had the nerve to attack them."

Chicago Charlie saw that Youngblood was closely watching him.

Feeling secure in his disguise, he announced his readiness to begin work at once; and for an hour thereafter the two were closeted together, Youngblood dictating short notes which he desired to have elaborated as replies to the letters.

Then he went out, leaving the detective to complete the work.

For a long time the typewriter sung under the detective's fingers.

Youngblood had promised to return, but, hearing nothing to indicate that he would soon do so, Chicago Charlie glanced anxiously at the papers arranged in pigeon-holes, wondering if any of them contained the clues he was seeking.

"It surely will be my own fault if I don't succeed now!" was his thought. "No man ever had a better chance given him."

But though he searched diligently, nothing of consequence was revealed.

Finally, as Youngblood still absented himself, he got up to go. There was no more work to be done that night, and no object could be served by remaining longer. He looked at his watch. It had already grown late.

Still wondering why Youngblood had not returned according to promise, he let himself out of the office.

As stated, the room so used was situated in the north wing of the building. A long corridor had to be traversed before the street door could be reached.

Chicago Charlie was moving thoughtfully along this corridor, his mind on Daisy Malcomb, when he became conscious that some one was near. He had heard nothing, but that indefinable feeling which sometimes comes, had swept over him.

Then his blood almost chilled in his veins.

A form that was the exact counterpart of John Malcomb came into view! It was moving from the north part of the building toward the eastern end!

Chicago Charlie stood rooted by a feeling akin to terror. He knew, so far as human knowledge could go, that the original of that shadow was in the land of spirits.

But for the fear that held him fixed he would have advanced to question the mysterious thing.

Less than a minute was the gruesome object in sight, the dim light of a lamp at the further end of the long hall sicklying it over and giving it occasionally a fantastic appearance.

Then it vanished, as mysteriously as it had come.

Charlie Clingstone, with that sense of awe still oppressing him, hurried to the point of disappearance. But nothing was to be seen. Nothing to indicate that any form of man or ghost had passed that way. Neither did a hasty search reveal anything.

A clammy sweat rested on his face and forehead. He was undeniably mystified and scared. He had never believed in such manifestations. Yet, if he had not seen the spirit of John Malcomb, what had he seen?

As nothing was to be gained by a further search, and not wishing to be found prying about the house thus in the night, he turned back along the corridor and descended to the street.

"My God!" was his almost inarticulate exclamation, as he wiped his dewy forehead. "I shall soon begin to think that I'm sure enough losing my mind. That couldn't have been John Malcomb; and yet—and yet—it was wonderfully like him! Who was it? What did it mean?"

CHAPTER XVII.

PLOTS OF THE ENEMY.

ON THE second floor of a big building which was used partly for a machine shop and partly for a warehouse, a dozen men were congregated in a small dark room.

Chicago Charlie

They were anxious faced men and seemed to have sought the place to avoid observation.

It was an interior room, with only a dirty skylight to let in the sunshine and air of the outer world. All about were scraps of old iron and miscellaneous odds and ends of rubbish. The floor was greasy and dirty, and even the chairs and table had the same appearance of grime.

Yet Solon Youngblood was there, clothed in his usual immaculate fashion. The slight form of Zel Magruder was also to be seen, crouched in a big chair.

More than ever on this occasion did Zel seem thin and weakly womanish.

He was recounting some adventures, to which his companions carefully listened.

"They'll be on your track for another murder, Zel Magruder!" Youngblood sharply commented. "You're getting reckless!"

"Well, what was I to do?" Zel demanded, in no pleasant tone. "The young brat was a-follerin' me an' a-tryin' to find out where I was goin'. If he'd 'a' done so, you fellers would likely be in limbo purty quick. I tried to knock him into the water with the oar; and, when he grabbed it and hung on like a bull-dog, I shot him. The police be blowed! How are they ever to know who done it?"

"If it had only been the other one, Zel!"

Youngblood's voice rasped and his eyes took on a heated light.

"If you'd only knocked that Columbian Detective over that way, I'd move that the band give you a gold medal! But, I think *I've* got him, now!"

He smoothed his chin reflectively and stared at the dirty floor.

Two or three of the band eagerly drew closer.

He laughed; then rising, rapped with his knuckles on the table for order.

"I'll tell you all about it later, boys. Business first, then pleasure. The treasurer will make a report concerning that last lot of goods."

It was the same evening, and almost at the same hour, that Chicago Charlie, standing in the corridor of the Malcomb house, fancied he must have seen the spirit of John Malcomb.

The "goods," as was quickly shown, were a part of the cargo whose coming had been spoken of by Magruder. The treasurer's report showed of what they had consisted and of how they had been disposed. One item touched Magruder, and he arose to explain:

"I hain't been able to do so much, sense old Nell got the idee into her head that we'd better pull out o' the biz. Before that, she was the rankest o' the lot, in favor o' handlin' any kind o' stuff that brought in money. I guess she got skeered. Anyway, she's been advisin' the band to let the thing alone, an' she's been givin' it to me hot and heavy, because I don't pay any 'tention to what she says!"

"Your people got away with the silks, didn't they?" Youngblood frowningly questioned.

"Yes, but I couldn't git 'em to push the sale o' the jew'lry! Nell wouldn't touch anything with a hot poker, and them that she had influence over wouldn't either. I'm afraid we can't handle as much o' the truck as we did once."

Youngblood was not pleased with the statement.

"What was done with the other lot of watches and diamonds?" he growled.

"Old Jake Wolfstein is shovin' them out for us as fast as he can."

Wolfstein was a man long suspected of being a "fence" for thieves; but though his place of business—which showed in front of it the three gilt balls of the pawnbroker—had been more than once searched, no stolen goods had ever been found in his possession. He was one of the shrewdest men of his class in the entire city.

"If the Gypsies go back on us we'll have to turn everything over to Wolfstein," Youngblood muttered, "though I'd hate to do it, for he charges such an allfired commission. He's never satisfied with his five hundred "pershent," but wants it all!"

He knew, however, that Wolfstein was indispensable to him, and that he would have to allow any percent the old cormorant demanded.

"Now I'll tell you what I hinted at awhile ago."

Youngblood settled back in his chair, and smiled wolfishly.

The business of the meeting appeared to be ended; and the reports, with the exception of that made by Magruder, had seemed satisfactory.

The band had not been so quiet and secretive on this evening as on that other when Chicago Charlie had watched them. No doubt they felt safer from intrusion and espionage. They had worn no masks.

The fact that they had changed their place of meeting may

Chicago Charlie

have accounted for this stronger feeling of security.

The men drew their chairs about Youngblood, evincing the liveliest interest. It was not often their chief took the trouble to communicate to them his plans or discoveries. As a usual thing, he gave his orders and they obeyed. He was the directing brain; they were the muscles of the organization.

"I have warned you many times, as you will remember, to be on your guard against the disguises of the man who is becoming known as Chicago Charlie, the Columbian Detective; but when I did so I never thought I'd be myself taken in by him. Yet I was, in a most glorious shape; and this very evening. He's my private secretary!"

The men looked incredulous, and Youngblood, noting their startled glances, laughed aloud—a roaring, jolly laugh that caused them to stare more than ever.

Then, still laughing, he proceeded to relate how Chicago Charlie had deceived and "taken him in."

"Do you know, his disguise was so perfect that I never dreamed but that the scamp was a stranger!" he averred. "And I never suspected anything until he called at the house an hour afterward. Likely I then had my wits about me a little better, for I was a good deal rattled by that runaway.

"Something in his voice—something that sounded familiar—caused me to watch him. Disguising the voice is the hardest thing to do in the world. A man may change the color of his face, and put on different clothes, and even wear wigs and mustaches. But, unless he's particularly skillful, whenever he tries to alter his voice it takes on a husky sound that betrays him.

"I began to notice his voice, and then I saw that his complexion wasn't natural;—that he'd used some kind of tan. And when I continued to study him, with my suspicions thus aroused, I soon saw who the man was."

"If he'd been looking at me the time the knowledge came to me, he'd have seen the thing in my face. But he wasn't looking; and I continued to dictate the letter, just as if nothing had happened."

"Why didn't you kill the hound then and there?" one fierce-eyed fellow demanded.

"Which goes to show what a brainy fellow you are, Swipesey!" was the sarcastic retort; under which Swipesey collapsed utterly.

"No! it wouldn't have done to strike, then. No more am I

ready to strike now. But by coming into my own house that way, he has put himself into my power. I shall let him go on fancying that he's playing it cute and deceiving me in the very worst way, until I get ready to dispose of the scoundrel.

"Why! he even went through some of my papers, to-night, and was amusing himself that way when I left to come here. Don't you see that I can put him on more false scents in a week than he can follow up in a month."

He rubbed his hands gleefully, and smiled back at the beaming faces about him.

The Lakeside League ever stood ready to swear by their chief, but never more so than now. They were a brainless lot of scoundrels, the most of them, and worshiped in another intellect and finesse they did not themselves possess.

"Just let him go on!" and Youngblood nodded his head sagely. "I'll give him enough rope and see him hang himself. It will, maybe, save us a more disagreeable job."

"If 'twas me, I'd put a knife inter 'im some dark night!" Swipesey growled, not pleased with the way he had been sat on. "Sich cattle are a good deal safer out o' the way;—that's my notion!"

"Maybe I'll give you the contract for doing that same, yet!" was the smiling reply. "I think I've got him, though!"

With this he got up, indicating he had said all he meant to say, and moved toward the door; but the Leaguers, grouping themselves in twos and threes, continued to talk of what the chief had just told them.

They were afraid of the Columbian Detective, and their words and actions showed it.

CHAPTER XVIII.

UNSUCCESSFUL SEARCHING.

NO MAN could possibly have been more surprised than Chicago Charlie would have been had he known the subject of the conversation in that little upper room.

He believed himself perfectly secure, never once dreaming

Chicago Charlie

that his disguise had been penetrated by the keen-eyed man he had set out to watch.

Neither had he any occasion to change this opinion, as the days glided by; and two days later, having finished his task and seen Solon Youngblood leave the office, he was still resting in the pleasant belief with which he had all along beguiled himself.

His thoughts, as he sat there, comfortably tilted back in the office chair, were on Youngblood, on Daisy Malcomb, and on the shadowy figure so remarkably resembling John Malcomb.

The figure had not again appeared, or at any rate had not again been seen by the detective.

And Charlie was almost ready to think he had been the victim of some optical illusion.

His reason told him that he had not seen Malcomb. Nothing, he fancied, could make him think that. Had he not seen Malcomb lying dead in his own office, bathed in blood? Pshaw! he put the idea from him as being supremely silly.

Still, he could not shake off the feeling that had held him chained that night, when he stood face to face with the spectral thing. Spirit or man, the sight of it had given him such a chill as he would not soon forget.

Sure it could not have been Malcomb, and unwilling to believe he had seen nothing at all, he turned to the only other tenable theories: What he saw must have been a man disguised to look like Malcomb, or one who naturally much resembled the dead man.

This was unsatisfactory enough—and did not answer the question of what Malcomb's double had been doing there that night!—but it was the best he could do.

The seeing of the ghostly thing had had one good effect. It had taken his mind somewhat away from its recent unhealthy brooding. Still, when the eyes of Youngblood were not known to be on him, a look of anguish often swept over his face.

Since the receipt of Daisy's letter, he had scarcely taken time to sleep, all the hours in which he could be away from the office being given up to a vain search for her. He had sought for her everywhere.

Only that morning, learning that the body of a young woman had been taken to the morgue, he had gone thither filled with the most distressing fears.

Each day a similar report had drawn him to that terrible place of the dead.

The almost insane tone of the letter led him to anticipate her suicide.

With his mind thus running from one thing to another, he took the letter from his pocket and gave it another careful study. He had done that probably a hundred times, until he knew every word and sentence, and could even see the curves of the letters without glancing at them. Nevertheless, he read it over with as much avidity as if it had been just received.

It told him no more than he already knew. Of her own accord she had disappeared, leaving neither trace nor clue, and warning him of the uselessness of trying to find where she had gone.

When he had read it over and over he put it up again; and his day's work being ended, left the office and went out into the street.

There was ease for his wounded spirit in the rushing, bustling atmosphere of the great western metropolis. The sight of these hurrying thousands, each on his own interest intent, conveyed a lesson to a thoughtful man.

It revealed the fact—sometimes an unpleasant fact—that among these myriad he was of little more consequence than an ant vainly struggling up an ant hill. He might die and pass away, and few indeed would there be to mourn or remember him.

Rapt in such reflections, Charlie Clingstone walked on and on, along the familiar streets, entering neither cab nor car, until the dusk of coming night was about him.

He had not guided his footsteps, but permitted them to wander whithersoever they would.

Suddenly he was aroused by a voice, that growled hoarsely in his ear.

"Hey, shipmate! Off your cruising ground, ain't ye?"

A rough hand caught him by the arm.

Looking about he beheld the beaming face of Jack Rackstraw.

At Rackstraw's heels trudged the newsboy, a shadow on his smiling face.

"What news?" Clingstone questioned, knowing by their looks they had something to communicate.

"It's the Infant Wonder!" Billy exclaimed. "She's been a-lickin' of him."

"Who?" the detective questioned, finding it difficult to at once adjust himself to their thoughts.

"Why, the Holy Terror!" cried Rackstraw, with ready indignation. "That there termagant that calls herself Mrs. Susan

Tonguegrass. Mrs. Sourtongue would be a heap sight better. We ketched her at it! An' the Infant, he was a-howlin' jist tremenjus.

"We packed him off home; and then I sot out and filed a complaint instanter ag'inst the Holy Terror, an' I think she'll be a-huntin' up another herd of infants by tomorrer.

"From what the leader of the Alphabet Society said I reckon she'll git the bounce, for it wasn't the first complaint that had been put in ag'in her."

Chicago Charlie turned toward a restaurant.

"We'll go in here," he said, "and talk it over."

A happy fate seemed to direct his footsteps, for the girl who came forward to take their orders was an old acquaintance. She had been one of the John Malcomb servants!

Ever since the time of the discovery that Youngblood had taken possession of the house, Chicago Charlie had kept a sharp lookout for some of these servants, but this was the first one he had met.

"You don't know how glad I am to meet you!" he exclaimed, cordially, putting out a hand.

She drew back in alarm.

Chicago Charlie, absorbed in the pleasure of seeing her, had forgotten his disguise, and committed a most egregious blunder.

He saw that she was both puzzled and alarmed, no doubt because of the strangeness of the face and the familiar intonations of the voice.

Rackstraw and Billy Stubbs, who had not been troubled by the detective's disguise, as they had known of it, seemed stupefied, fearing an unpleasant disclosure.

"Bring us something to eat and I'll explain everything," the detective urged, observing that the actions of the girl were attracting attention. "You'll know me well enough when I tell you who I am."

The girl was visibly agitated, but hurried away, nevertheless; returning soon with some hot rolls and butter and some steaming coffee.

"You still don't know me, I see," Clingstone laughingly whispered, as she placed the things on the table. "I'm your old friend, Charlie Clingstone."

She started incredulously at first; but seeing that it must be the truth, for she could not deny that the voice was Clingstone's, she gave him a friendly glance, declaring:

"You almost frightened me to death. Why are you fixed out

that way? Going to a masquerade?"

He did not reply to this; but asked, with quick eagerness:

"Can you tell me what has become of Daisy Malcomb?"

"Indeed I cannot! The Youngbloods came and took possession of the house and told me that my services would be no longer needed. All the others were treated the same way."

"And Daisy?"

"I don't know where she went, nor when. She was not to be found, when the Youngbloods came there."

There were but few people in the restaurant, and, seeing that her services would not be in immediate demand, he urged her to take one of the chairs.

"I have something to say to you! Do you like your place here?"

"Not if I could get better. I've got to do something, though!"

Then he told her the story narrated to him by Rackstraw and Billy Stubbs.

"If you think you'd like that place I believe it can be obtained for you. I'll have the inspector recommend your appointment."

She smiled and showed her white, even teeth.

She was a handsome girl, with an intelligent face and a bright and winning manner; and Jack Rackstraw, the grizzled lake sailor, viewed her with undisguised admiration.

"The pay will be better, I feel sure!" Chicago Charlie averred, taking a notebook and pencil from his pocket. "If you will say the word, I will write to the inspector right now."

It was evident that he desired her to have the situation, and Billy Stubbs was immensely tickled at the prospect. Billy felt that in the hands of this friend of Chicago Charlie, the Infant Wonder would be perfectly safe.

"What do you say?" and the detective poised his pencil as he looked at her.

She nodded.

"I'll try it; for I don't like this place the least bit. Too many rough men come in here!"

"I'll mail this for you as soon as we go out!" he said, when he had written and folded the note.

Then he again fell to discussing the probable whereabouts of Daisy Malcomb.

The next morning Miss Lilly Lilac—for that was the girl's name—was notified that the position rendered vacant by the resignation of Mrs. Susan Tonguegrass was hers if she would accept it, and a liberal salary was named as the recompense for her services.

CHAPTER XIX.

LED INTO A TRAP.

RACKSTRAW AND Billy Stubbs went away together, congratulating themselves on the future prospects of the Infant Wonder, and Chicago Charlie continued his perambulations.

Arriving at his room, two or three hours later, he found a newsboy awaiting him.

The newsboy carried a letter, which he immediately put into the detective's hand.

"It's from Billy Stubbs," he explained. "He said for me to give you this and to tell yer to come quick. He couldn't leave."

Having delivered the letter and the statement, the boy gave a respectful pull at his frowsy foretop, and disappeared.

The letter was a badly spelled scrawl, but it held startling information.

Billy, in his wanderings, had discovered Daisy Malcomb's hiding place.

The note ran thus:

cHicaGO cHarlEy, i Hav fOUn Out wHur DaZy iZ. sHe iS in tHe OLD HOUsE At a HundErd an Ate —— AvEnOO SHE cAnT giT AWAy iM gOin too StAy aN wACH HEr till yeW COme COme RiTe Of

Billy StUBBs

The blank shown in the copy was filled with a name, which it would be impolite to insert here.

Charlie stared at the scrawl in amazement. Then he thrust the note into his pocket, and turned back into the street.

If Daisy was held at the place given he would find her and have speech with her, if nothing else. She had not desired him to follow her, but he would follow her, nevertheless.

Billy's note stated that she was held in the house. Else, what did he mean by saying she could not get away. Manifestly, she had encountered enemies, against whom she had found it impossible to fight.

Whatever might be the trouble, he would go at once, and do what he could—or whatever she would permit him to do—to aid her.

He knew the site of the old house well. It was in a locality similar to that in which he had watched the meeting of the Lakeside Leaguers. She must indeed be in dire straits, to be found in such a place.

With these thoughts whirring in his mind, he stopped short.

The thought had come to him that this might be but a lure of enemies to lead him into a trap. He was not acquainted with the scrawling chirography of the newsboy, Billy Stubbs. He had never even thought to ask Billy if he could write, taking it for granted that he could, for he knew Billy could read well enough to spell out the news in the papers.

His head whirled as he stopped thus bewilderedly, with that fear suddenly pressing in on him.

If this were a trap set for him, and which it was expected he would walk straight into, there could be but one conclusion from it: his disguise had been penetrated.

He recalled, with some feeling of pride, the manner in which Lilly Lilac had stared at him in the restaurant. This was good evidence that his disguise was excellent. He was loth to believe that it had been seen through.

Only for a few moments did he halt in indecision.

His resolve was quickly taken.

Stepping to the nearest telephone station, he put himself in communication with the Inspector of Police.

Happily the inspector was in his office, and Chicago Charlie could pour his story into the ears of the man he most desired to hear it.

He told the inspector of the communication he had received, gave him the name of the avenue and number of the building, and spoke of his fears of a trap.

"Go ahead!" was the reply. "We'll see that the trappers are trapped!"

Thus reassured, Chicago Charlie took the car of the line passing nearest to the old house; and in less than a half hour thereafter stood in the dark street before the forbidding building.

There was nothing about it to indicate that it was inhabited. No friendly lamp or gas-jet poured its light through the windows. No sounds came from behind its closed doors.

"Looks more than ever like a trap!" he mused, running his eyes over the house. "It would be a bad place up there to get into trouble. I'm afraid the inspector's friends couldn't get to me soon enough to be of much assistance."

Nevertheless, the thought that Daisy Malcomb *might* be screened somewhere behind those dingy brick walls, stirred him anew. He felt that he would go through fire, should that ever be necessary, to rescue or aid her.

Circling the building, and watching closely against any sign of treachery, he sought carefully for some place by which he might enter.

He was wondering why he did not see Billy Stubbs, if the boy had really sent the note; and was becoming more and more convinced that an effort was being made to trap him, when a boyish voice whispered down from the gloom.

"Slip this here way. She's above stairs here."

Chicago Charlie turned in that direction, with his hand on his revolver.

He was not yet satisfied that all was as it should be. The voice had sounded remarkably like Billy's, but the words had been so whispered that it was difficult to be certain of this.

"Is that you, Billy Stubbs?" he ventured to call.

No reply came, and he knew the boy had turned back into the house.

Stumbling forward, he found some rickety steps, leading up to a door wherein the boy must have stood.

He mounted these, with his hand still on his weapon.

The feeling that treachery was afoot was strong on him.

The door stood slightly ajar, and he pushed on into the house.

All was dark as Erebus.

There seemed to be a wide hallway, penetrating he knew not whither.

He whispered again to the boy; and, receiving no reply, and with the conviction still growing that evil was meant, he drew out and cocked the pistol, and took another step.

Instantly he felt himself plunging downward through the gloom. The rotten floor, or a portion of it, had been removed.

A wild cry of alarm and fear arose from the gloom.

Then Chicago Charlie struck among a heap of rubbish, and remained silent and senseless.

Again the boy whispered:

"Pards, we've got im!"

CHAPTER XX.

BILLY STUBBS AS A WILD RIDER.

EVEN THOUGH Billy Stubbs had not found Daisy Malcomb as stated by the false letter, he was not idle. The special work given to him by Chicago Charlie was the shadowing of Zel Magruder; and, even while Chicago Charlie was plunging downward to seeming death in the old house, the keen-eyed newsboy was lying in the shadows of the Gypsy tents.

He had seen Magruder enter one of them and was thinking of worming his way to a better position, when the Gypsy came out and walked away into the gloom.

Billy followed with stealthy footsteps, and was somewhat surprised when he saw Zel turn toward Buffalo Bill's Wild West, which was giving daily and nightly exhibitions at Sixty-second and Sixty-third streets.

Instead of going toward the entrance that was nearest, Zel Magruder veered off; and, after making a wide circle, approached the stables.

There was a small door there, used only by employees, and which was commonly to be found locked. Whether Zel found it open or managed to undo the fastenings, Billy did not know; but he nevertheless saw the Gypsy pass through.

This was a disappointment, for the newsboy feared he was now to lose track of him.

But, after creeping up to the door, he saw that Zel had only pushed it to, and had not fastened it.

Hence he crowded in, determined to go wherever Zel went, if he could possibly do it without discovery.

There were horses and men all about and the place where he found himself, though dimly lighted, was not gloomy enough to make him feel at ease.

A couple of Mexicans were standing out far off, hurling their lassoes at various inanimate objects, and a Uhlan guard was striking up a conversation with a Cossack.

Billy was bewildered by all he saw and heard, and for the

Chicago Charlie

moment almost forgot the object of his errand.

Then he looked around for Zel Magruder.

He did not see him at first, but an instant later he caught sight of the Gypsy stealing along in the shadow of the wall.

It was plain Magruder's presence was unknown to the men whom Billy saw about.

"Whatever is the Gypsy up to?" was his mental query.

Magruder was getting further and further away, advancing as if he meant to force his way into the very arena itself.

The exhibition was in full blast. Annie Oakley had given splendid illustration of her dexterity in the use of fire-arms; and now the gathered thousands were wildly cheering the horse races between cowboy, Cossack, Mexican and others, on their native steeds.

Magruder halted, crouching in the gloom until the races were at an end, and Billy Stubbs, with his curiosity worked to fever pitch, kept on until he was perilously near the Gypsy!

The air was still resounding with the plaudits of the multitude, and preparations were going forward for the introduction of the Pony Express, when Magruder, turning in Billy's direction, discovered the boy, who was staring at him from beneath an awning.

With an oath, Magruder flashed out a knife and dashed at him, his intentions being murderous, for Magruder was thoroughly reckless when aroused.

Billy sprung back with a cry of fear, almost falling headlong over some object on the ground.

A broncho, saddled and bridled, stood near.

What induced the scared boy to perform the next act, he could not have told, unless it was his insane desire to get away from that gleaming knife. Almost before he knew it he was on the back of the broncho, clambering into the saddle for safety, as he would have mounted into a tree if pursued by a bear.

The startled broncho gave a bound that bore Billy out of reach of the threatening knife, and at the same time hurled him into what seemed likely to be new perils.

The little beast had been half asleep, when Billy bestrode him in that unceremonious fashion, and, seeing the glaring lights and hearing the applauding shouts, doubtless thought the time had arrived for an exhibition of his running and bucking qualities.

Almost before Billy knew what the broncho meant to do, he found himself the central attraction of the big show!

The sight of those tiers of faces in a measure brought back his wits, and, though terribly scared by what had occurred and much dreading the consequences, he saw that the best thing he could do was to cling to the back of the broncho.

The little brute was tearing along like mad, and the spectators, thinking this a new feature of the exhibition, were, many of them, shouting in their usual boisterous fashion.

The programme said nothing of a wild broncho from the untamed West being ridden by a tatterdemalion boy; but they accepted it as one of the good things which Buffalo Bill sometimes introduced without previous announcement.

The managers and employees of the Wild West were thunderstruck. They knew not what to make of this sudden appearance, and for a minute stood in speechless amazement.

Doubtless they would have interfered shortly, but the broncho, rearing and plunging wildly, began to prance and buck. The way in which Billy clung to the back of the bounding pony assured them that fun was in store for the multitude; and so they stayed their hands, alert, in case the boy should need help.

Fright, and a feeling that he must hold on or be killed, made of Billy Stubbs a most marvelous rough rider. He set his teeth hard, dug one hand into the broncho's mane and with the other clasped the high pommel, screwed his heels into the broncho's sides, and held on for dear life.

There was never a worse scared boy than was Billy Stubbs for a few minutes. The broncho vaulted, pranced, pitched and bucked, in the most approved fashion;—the applause of the audience rose hysterically;—the cowboys stared their wonderment;—and Billy gripped the saddle like grim death.

Then the broncho, discovering that the reins were hanging idly, bolted wildly out of the arena.

It was all over in less than five minutes and Billy Stubbs was back again at the point from whence he had started.

He heard men hurrying toward him.

Zel Magruder was nowhere to be seen.

But Billy Stubbs thought little enough of Zel Magruder just then.

He heard those pattering steps; and, anticipating condign punishment, freed himself as quickly as he could, and darted away.

Like a rat he scudded through the shadows, and finding the door by which he had entered, he slipped out into the night.

CHAPTER XXI.

IN A QUEER PRISON.

ONE OF the witnesses of Billy's miraculous performance, was his friend Jack Rackstraw.

Rackstraw, having been left to his own devices and finding time hanging heavily on his hands, had resolved to "take in" the Wild West exhibition, and was in one of the front tiers of seats, when Billy dashed in so unceremoniously.

Rackstraw was never more astounded in his life, than when he saw his boy chum on the back of the pitching broncho. He could only stare and give vent to his astonishment in whispered exclamations. For the moment he could not believe his eyes, yet a second look told him that it was sure enough Billy Stubbs.

"Blast me!" what'll that boy be up to next? How did he git onto that ferowcious brute, anyway?"

When the broncho had reached the climax of its wild antics, and Rackstraw expected every minute to see Billy hurled to the earth or crushed to a bleeding mass, he rose with the firm intention of hurrying to the boy's rescue.

But a hand on his shoulder checked him.

"Sit down!" growled a voice. "Do ye think nobody else wants to see?"

Rackstraw sunk helplessly back. His better judgment told him he could do nothing, and that if Billy was to be killed he must be killed.

But he muttered:

"Drat the imp! I reckon I'll have to cowhide him fer that."

His mind was still in a bewildered whirl when the broncho vanished with Billy still clinging to his back.

Then, feeling shaky in every limb, Rackstraw climbed down and made his way toward the entrance through which the broncho and boy had passed.

A man barred his way.

"No coming in here, sir!" was the declaration.

"What's become of that boy?" Jack howled.

The man, who was only an employee, and who was as much puzzled as the sailor, growled back:

"Plague take the boy! I don't know where he came from nor where he's gone. He's knocked the programme endwise and set everything wild!"

Rackstraw glared at him wrathfully, then stumped furiously away, and was soon after outside of the big show, with the night wind whistling about and the stars shining down on him.

Making his way now as best he could along the outside toward the point where the stables were located, he stopped at each advance of a dozen steps and watched and listened.

A crouching form hurried toward him.

"Oh, Jack! is that you?"

The voice was Billy's.

"You young hound!" and Rackstraw gripped him by the collar and churned him up and down. "What do you mean by such cantankerin'? How did ye git on the back o' that there hoss?"

"Come on," Billy whispered, "let's git away from here."

Rackstraw was no more anxious to have Billy arrested than was Billy to be arrested, and, though he was as much mystified as ever, he suffered the boy to lead him away.

"Now see here, you young rascal!" he grumbled, when they were in the neighborhood of the high fence inclosing the Exposition buildings. "I ain't a goin a step furder until I know more'n I do at this instant. Where air you goin' and whatever have you been up to?"

Billy Stubbs, with the fear of the Wild West men still strong on him, halted and gave Rackstraw a hurried explanation.

The sailor snorted, but with surprise more than disgust.

"It was jist like you, young feller. Some o' these nights you'll go off smilin' an' come back froze up in an ice box. Well, if you do you needn't blame *me*!"

"I'm sorry I lost Magruder," Billy observed, still shaking from his recent excitement.

"An' I'm sorry I lost that show. Reckon now, you wouldn't care to go back with me an' see it out?"

"No! no!"

Billy clung to his hand almost fiercely.

"All right, then!" looking down with eyes that held a softened light.

He would have said more, but a form slipped stealthily by

them, which they saw to be Magruder's.

Magruder seemed equally anxious to give the Wild West exhibition a wide berth. He was now hastening toward the Fair grounds.

Billy pulled at Rackstraw's hand and drew the sailor along in the Gypsy's wake.

They soon lost the Gypsy, however, for the latter was moving at a good gait.

Satisfied that he had found entrance into the grounds, or would soon do so, they also went in; and for a long time strolled about, looking vainly for him.

The time was growing late, and it seemed unlikely they would get to see Magruder again that night. The people had nearly all departed, though the guides and guards still hung about, and there was a considerable amount of activity in all the buildings.

They sought the Cairo street, with no better success, and turned back into the grounds and approached the lagoon. A few gondoliers were still visible, hoping to yet take in a fare.

"They hain't no use lookin' any furder this night!" Rackstraw averred. "I'm going over to the Andy Johnson an' see if I can't git a good sleep once more. Can't seem to sleep as well as I ought in these hotels and the like. An' you, young 'un, air a-goin' along with me!"

He linked his arm into Billy's, as he half feared the boy would rebel and break away, and together they walked past the Horticultural Building, and on toward the bridge leading to the beautiful wooded island surrounded by its lagoon.

Billy went willingly enough, for, though loth to give up the search, he saw that he could accomplish nothing by a longer stay, and was, besides, thoroughly beat out by his experiences of the night.

They never dreamed of danger, as they turned from the wooded island toward the smaller island, containing the Hunter's Camp. The scene was like a bit out of fairy land, so smiling and peaceful was it under the light of the electric lamps. The shadows of the low trees and bushes were reflected in black masses in the water; and where the shrubbery intercepted the light, there were dark and romantic places, resembling hidden dells.

They had scarcely set foot on the little island when three or four men leaped out of the shadows and beset them.

Rackstraw knocked one of the rascals down at the first blow; but this seemed not to frighten the others, who lunged at him with knives.

It was a most dare-devil attack, considering the time and place.

The assailants were dark-visaged fellows, much resembling those who had attacked Chicago Charlie several nights before near the Javanese village in Midway Plaisance.

Neither Rackstraw nor Billy thought of this, at the time, though they had been told of the attack by Chicago Charlie and been warned to be on the lookout for these scamps.

Rackstraw was armed with a small pistol, but, disliking to use it, he again struck out fiercely, catching one of the fellows under the jaw.

But the one he had previously knocked down, was up and coming at him again.

"Slide out, boy!" he whispered, turning to Billy, whom he had placed protectingly behind him. "They're determined to slice us up! Pull out, I'll foller ye!"

Billy, who was thoroughly alarmed by the fierceness of the attack, obeyed this sound advice, running lightly out on the bridge.

There seemed to be other forms moving in the bushes, as if more black-browed men were hurrying up, and Jack Rackstraw, menacingly waving his pistol, followed the boy.

Not much noise had been made in the short struggle, but it had reached some of the guards, who were now seen to be hurrying thither.

Rackstraw saw these guards coming, and became aware, too, that the attacking force had as suddenly vanished.

A black look came to his face.

He saw clearly what had been attempted. Whoever the assailants were—whether friends of Zel Magruder or not—they had striven to waylay the sailor and his boy chum, and had chosen the island as offering the most favorable point.

Doubtless they had thought to slay the two there and toss the bodies into the lagoon. Found thus, gashed with knives, there would have been a sensation, it is true, but not much chance of discovering the guilty parties.

Seeing that his enemies no longer threatened him, Rackstraw turned to follow Billy Stubbs, but was surprised to observe that the boy had disappeared.

Billy in fleeing across the bridge in advance of Rackstraw, had seen a man on the opposite shore, whom he took to be one of the

Krupp Building.

assailing party.

Therefore, as soon as his feet left the bridge, he turned sharply, and ran rapidly and silently, convinced that Rackstraw was abundantly able to take care of himself and sure the sailor would follow him almost immediately. So he ran on for some distance, scarcely looking back.

When he came to a halt at length, it was in the shadow of the big 120-ton Krupp gun, which had not yet been moved into the building devoted to the Krupp Gun Exhibit.

This monster cannon, the largest ever manufactured, towered above the boy like an immense redwood log from a Californian forest.

Billy, listening and waiting for the coming of Rackstraw, was startled by a sound of light footsteps.

The footsteps were probably those of a peaceful passer-by, but the gamin, being in an extremely nervous state, attributed them to the advance of foes, and cast about for a place of concealment.

Nothing offered but the yawning mouth of the big cannon.

It was like crawling down into the wide-open jaws of death, to enter that black opening; but Billy Stubbs climbed up to it and slid into the big hole feet foremost.

"What if the thing should be loaded, and should go off!" was his scared thought.

Nevertheless, being already in the maw of the monster, he did not deem it wise to crawl out, and reflection soon convinced him that he was in no danger from an explosion of the gun—for it would never have been brought in there loaded to threaten human lives and the safety of the buildings.

The interior of the big gun was not an uncomfortable place, as he found, when his fears had subsided.

He began to wonder, though, how Jack Rackstraw was to find him there, and, when no further alarming sound came to disturb him, he was on the point of creeping out to look for that redoubtable individual.

Then there came again the tread of footsteps, combined with low-spoken words, and Billy knew that a number of men had advanced and were grouped near the cannon's mouth.

Then he heard them mounting, by a stepladder or in some manner; heard their talk grow louder; and then the brightness of the electric lights suddenly disappeared, leaving him in total darkness.

Krupp Gun.

An iron cap had been placed over the cannon's mouth, and Billy Stubbs was a prisoner!

CHAPTER XXII.

BILLY AS A HERO.

A SENSE OF DEEP FEAR smote the newsboy, when he realized that he had been thus imprisoned. His natural thought was that it had been the act of the men who had attacked him and Rackstraw on the island.

Feeling thus, he remained perfectly quiet, until sure the men had departed. Even then he did no more than stir for some time, not knowing but they might come back.

That they were a desperate lot, he had had ample proof.

"This hyer's a go!" he soliloquized, twisting uneasily in his strange prison, "I never thought to get caught, when I climbed up hyer. It's almost as bad as the horse in the Wild West!"

Truly his experiences of the night had been far from pleasant!

The minutes crept by with feet of lead. The men did not return, nor could he hear Rackstraw's voice calling to him, as he had half hoped he might. The air became close, and he wondered if he would be forced to remain in there until he smothered.

The minutes lengthened into an hour. Still Rackstraw did not come.

The Exposition grounds grew strangely quiet. The change struck him strongly, for usually the stillness was not remarkable. He believed that even the guards had sought their rest.

Billy could endure it no longer. He crawled to the cannon's mouth and placed his hands against the cap that excluded the light and air. It seemed as immovable as the Cheops Pyramid. Pushing against it with head and hands did not stir it from its place.

He groaned aloud; then, becoming frightened, shouted for help.

His voice within that confined space, seemed thrown back on him in muffled waves. He was sure it did not penetrate to any distance.

Chicago Charlie 355

Nevertheless, he called again and again, pitching his tones to a shriek, as the thought that he was buried there alive grew firmer and stronger.

It was no use beating his head against the cannon's cap, and it appeared to be quite as useless to waste his breath and strength in this sort of shouting. But he could not forbear, and again and again screamed his fear at the echoing steel.

No one came in answer to his calls; and, thoroughly cowed and almost exhausted, he remained quiet after a time, convinced that help could not come to him.

He blamed himself for abandoning Rackstraw. This would not have occurred, if he had kept close to Rackstraw's side! He almost felt that he was being justly punished for leaving Rackstraw to face their foes alone. He told himself that the act, performed in fear, had been cowardly, even though Rackstraw had urged it.

Altogether, the newsboy never spent more miserable hours than those he passed shut up in the big Krupp cannon.

But day came at last, when it seemed to the weary newsboy that it never would come.

The electric lights burnt themselves out in the rays of the rising sun; though it was not this fact that made Billy Stubbs aware of the arrival of daylight. It was the hum of voices of early risers.

None of them passed near the big gun, and so did not hear the calls that Billy again began to send up.

He longed intensely to be released, and yet feared the result. What would be said and done to him when he should be found in there? Would he be punished or placed under arrest?

His calls ceased, as the dread of this pressed on him.

Then again he heard voices—the same, he was sure, he had heard when the cap had been placed over the mouth of the cannon.

He held his breath in suspense.

He could tell that the men were climbing up, as before.

Then the cap was taken away and the sunlight and air poured in.

Billy Stubbs crouched in his prison like a spaniel expecting castigation.

But the men, who were employees of the Krupp Gun Company, instead of looking in, walked away.

The newsboy crept to the opening and peered out.

There was no one near; no one apparently looking in his direction. With his pulses thrilling, and feeling that this was his golden opportunity, he crept out still further, clutched the rim of the cannon's mouth with his hands and dropped lightly to the ground.

He glanced fearfully about.

No one had observed him; and, feeling that he had made a miraculous escape, he hastened away as rapidly as possible, endeavoring to assume a nonchalant air.

Though the hour was early, men and women were already to be seen moving about the buildings, and Billy realized that it was high time he had his supply of morning papers. Usually he was distributing them at that hour.

A train of the Illinois Central Railway engaged in the business of carrying excursionists to and from the grounds, was ready to pull out for the city.

He deemed it not wise to make any search for Rackstraw at that time.

"I reckon he's safe enough aboard the Andy Johnson" was his inward comment.

He could see the funnels of the steamer, from where he stood—the steamer lying at anchor near the pier.

There was little time for reflection. Rackstraw had always shown himself abundantly able to look out for number one. Therefore, certain that his sailor friend had come all right through the difficulties of the night, Billy Stubbs hurried aboard the train.

It pulled out almost at the same moment, going to the city nearly empty.

In a remarkably short space of time, Billy returned by the same way, laden with his supply of papers.

He glanced over one of them, while making the run to the Exposition grounds.

A lot of startling headlines riveted his attention:

"ROUGH RIDING!

The WildWest Astonished!

A WONDERFUL PERFORMANCE NOT DOWN ON THE BILLS!

How the Auditors of 'Buffalo Bill's Wild West

Chicago Charlie

*and Congress of Rough Riders' Were
Given a Genuine Sensation.*

"The people who went to see the performance given at Buffalo Bill's Wild West last night, were treated to a bit of rough riding for which they had not come prepared. The races had gone off as usual, marked by their customary success; and then came the event of the evening.

"The Pony Express act was in course of preparation, it being the next thing on the programme, when a roughly-dressed boy, but one showing in his every movement that he was a most skillful rider, dashed in, mounted on the most vicious of the bucking bronchos.

"For a moment, those who had been looking for something else stared. But the performance then given was good enough to atone for the absence of the Pony Express act. The broncho pranced and plunged, but his utmost skill was not able to hurl the young centaur from his back. Time and again did the pony take those wild leaps. It is doubtful if any but the best of the cowboys could have held a seat on him. Yet the boy remained as firmly in the saddle as if he were part and parcel of it.

"Buffalo Bill and Nate Salsbury were as much astounded as any. Where the boy had come from and who he was seemed unknown. Then, as an explanation, one of the cowboys whispered aloud the secret.

"The young rough rider, who had taken this singular way of introducing himself, was none other than Gunnison George, celebrated throughout the Rocky Mountain region as the most dare-devil horseman and broncho-buster ever known in the West. Although but a boy in years, it seems that Gunnison George has attained his celebrity through genuine merit. Last season he rode in the famous trick race against Sage–Bush Sweeney, and beat Sweeney at every point; and the year before, when only sixteen years old, he broke and subdued for the Farnham Brothers, of the Texas Panhandle, a herd of as wild and vicious bronchos as ever roamed the cactus stretches of the great Staked Plains."

There was more of the same sort, nearly a column of it. Either the enterprising reporter had given free rein to his exuberant imagination, or some one had "filled him full of fairy stories."

Billy Stubbs stared as if his eyes would pop out of his head.

"Gunnison George!" he gasped, holding the paper limply in

his hands and looking bewilderedly at the title thus strangely bestowed him.

"Rocky Mountains! Ridin' ag'inst Sage-Bush Sweeney! Breakin' ponies in the Panhandle! *What a lot o' rot* that reporter's been gittin' off!"

Yet, he was manifestly pleased at finding himself made a hero in this remarkable way, and did not take his eyes from the account until he had read it through.

A paragraph at the bottom caused him to stare more wildly than ever:

"Gunnison George could not be found at the conclusion of his own performance, though Salsbury, Burke, and even Colonel Cody himself, sought everywhere for him. If he is still in the city, and sees these lines, he will know that Colonel Cody greatly desires to see him, and will favor that gentleman by calling at the Wild West exhibition."

"Phew!" and Billy Stubbs opened his eyes widely and whistled his surprise.

He could hardly believe the paragraph true; but, on turning to the "Personals," he found there one reading thus:

"If Gunnison George will call at the 'Wild West' he will confer on me a favor. W. F. Cody ("Buffalo Bill.")"

Fortunately for Billy Stubbs there were very few passengers on the train at that early hour, else his excited antics must have been noticed.

When he left the train and started out to distribute his papers, his mind was not at all on his task. Indeed, he was so exceedingly absent minded, that more than once he passed a customer, who was forced to call sharply after him to get the morning news.

The boy was in a quandary.

He was extremely desirous of seeing the great scout, of whom he had heard so much, but he feared to make the venture. There was a grand mistake or deception somewhere. He knew that he was the rough rider referred to in the laudatory newspaper account. But he was equally sure he was not Gunnison George of the Rocky Mountains. Whether or not there was any such famous horseman as Gunnison George he had no means of knowing.

When he had sold his papers—he had retained in his pocket the one he had read—he sought a quiet corner and read over again and again that marvelous bit of reporting.

It almost drove his mind from all thoughts of the hours he had

Chicago Charlie

spent in the cannon, and of Jack Rackstraw.

"If I could only find Chicago Charlie!" he mused. "He could tell me what to do. Hanged if I can tell myself. Seems as if I ain't got head enough on me this morning to know who I am. *Gunnison George! Sage-Bush Sweeney!*"

Thus muttering, he turned about and hurried across the intervening ground to the lake front. Thoughts of Chicago Charlie had put him in mind of Jack Rackstraw, and he was resolved to show the newspapers to Rackstraw and to be guided by the sailor's advice.

Rackstraw had not slept much that night—in fact had scarcely lain down. After seeking everywhere for his young chum, he had at last made his way to the Andy Johnson, and gone on board. But, he had not been able to rest, and was now one of the first of those on the vessel whom Billy saw, as the latter came hurrying down the wharf.

"You owdacious young rascal!" were the words that greeted the newsboy; and though they were roughly couched, words had never sounded sweeter, for the kindliness of the tones belied the severity of the form of expression.

"Playin' larks on yer old chum, eh? Is that what you've been doin'? I've a notion to take a boat-hook to ye!"

The Andy Johnson was lying against the wharf, and Rackstraw sprung over the rail at a bound; and the next moment was wringing Billy's hand with as much cordiality and energy as if the boy were some long-lost brother.

"Tell me where you went las' night! Out wi' it, or I'll chuck you into the lake. Here I've been a-turnin' gray thinkin' you was dead, er somethin'!"

Billy drew him away from the vessel's side, and showed him the paper.

Rackstraw, when he saw the staring headlines, and read enough to comprehend what was there printed, was dumbfounded.

"Some of them reporters hain't got good sense, Billy Stubbs! But, hang me! you did stick onto that critter like mud! What else does it say?"

"Buffalo Bill wants to see me!"

Billy pointed a forefinger at the personal.

Rackstraw roared like a steam whistle, so great was his mirth.

"Gunnison George! Hip—hip!"

He seemed about to break forth in a series of cheers.

"But what do you think of it?"

Rackstraw cooled down and rubbed his nose.

"What do I think of it? Why, I do'—I mean, I'd go an' see him!"

"Buffalo Bill?"

"Why not?" said Rackstraw. "He's advertised fer ye. 'Lost, strayed er stolen! A boy rider, as is supposed to be Gunnison George of the Rocky Mountains. A reward of five dollars fer returnin' of him to the Wild West show!'

"Them ain't the words, but, that's about what they means, ain't it? Of course you'll go; an' I'll go along of you! Had any breakfast?"

"Not a bit. Haven't had time!"

"Come aboard, then. We'll talk it over while we're takin' ballast! Where'd you go las' night?"

Billy Stubbs was hungry enough to do justice to the food Rackstraw placed before him; and between bites he placed his friend in possession of the incidents of the night.

They were sufficiently astonishing to make the honest sailor stare.

Rackstraw kept up a running fire of comment, that was sometimes humorous and sometimes serious; and when Billy had stowed away the last mouthful, the sailor announced his readiness to go straight to the grounds of the Wild West.

CHAPTER XXIII.

OUT OF THE SNARE.

PURSUING THE ADVENTURES of Billy Stubbs has led us too far from Chicago Charlie and the dire peril in which he was placed.

But for his forethought in communicating with the inspector, he would have plunged to death, when he fell blindly through the gloom into the basement of the old house.

The crash of his fall had not ceased to be heard, when there came a shrill whistle. It was from the boy who had lured him to the door, and who was now stationed without to act as a sentinel.

The plans against Chicago Charlie had been most complete, and the thoughts and aims of the planners had been most murderous in their character. They had emanated from desperate men:—men who shrunk from nothing that looked to securing their safety.

Two of them were advancing out of the gloom toward the senseless detective, when that shrill and warning whistle reached them. They stopped instantly:

"Cops!"

This expressive exclamation was followed by a muttered curse.

Then, abandoning their intentions concerning the Columbian Detective, their dreaded foe, they sprung away through the darkness and hurried to the floor above, where a window permitted them to look out on the street.

What they saw told them that their worst suspicions were correct.

Two or three men in citizens' clothing were on the street just below the building, and others, similarly dressed, had advanced into the small yard. Still another was to be seen at the foot of the rotten stairway.

"They've got the house surrounded!" one of the men fearfully whispered, drawing back in much alarm. "I reckon we're in for it, Swipesey!"

His companion, who was none other than the fierce-eyed villain of the Lakeside League, in low-toned maledictions, cursed the Columbian Detective.

They saw they were in a trap, from which it would be difficult to escape, and in consequence were much exercised.

"If we'd only done *him* up," growled the amiable Swipesey, shaking his fist in the direction of the basement. "*He's* the cause of this!"

"That feller's comin' up the stairs!" announced the other, who had again placed his face to the window. "We've got the slide!"

They did not take the trouble to discover the fate of the boy, but, plunging again below stairs, they made their way to a coal-hole opening on an alley.

The alley was guarded, but it offered the only way of retreat.

"Two more cops out there!" Swipesey whispered back, drawing in his head like a tortoise. "We've got to make a break for it, or s'render!"

"Not 'slong's I've got good legs under me, an' no bullets in my back!" his companion growled.

Each of them was "wanted" for a dozen crimes, and the

knowledge of what capture meant for them made them desperate.

Swipesey, who was in the lead, and who had peered out of the coal-hole, took a bulldog revolver from his pocket and nervously fingered it, as he again advanced to the opening.

At that moment they were made aware that the officers had gained entrance to the house. They could hear footsteps lightly pacing the floor above them.

"If I go down, there'll be some one go down with me!" Swipesey threateningly snarled, uneasily shifting the revolver. "Hyer I goes. I'm goin' to dive for the alley that's jist back."

The other was crowding close at his heels.

The next moment a revolver cracked at the street entrance.

Swipesey and his "pard" had made a bold rush; and, being detected in the act, had been fired on by the officer stationed there.

Swipesey swung around, recklessly returned the shot, and then sped on.

Other revolvers opened, ominously breaking the quiet of the night. But the shots did no execution; and these daring members of the Lakeside League, having gained the other alley, sped away unharmed.

The prompt intervention of the police had saved the life of Chicago Charlie, but the police had not been able to hold in their net his would-be murderers.

The boy who had given the alarm, had mysteriously disappeared, and, though he was probably in hiding somewhere in the house, the officers were unable to find him.

Those who had descended into the basement—for the broken floor had shown where the detective was to be found—discovered Clingstone, doubled in a heap among some rubbish and broken boards, and still in an unconscious condition.

But no bones had been broken, and his injuries were not severe. They amounted only to some contusions.

"Sound as a dollar, yet!" one of the policemen averred, pressing a brandy flask to the detective's lips. "Send for an ambulance!"

The liquor had a reviving effect; and long before the ambulance arrived, Chicago Charlie was able to sit up, and announce his ability to stand, and even to walk.

"Thanks, boys! You don't know how grateful I am for all you've done for me, and desire to do; but I don't care to be carried to a hospital in a wagon. I'm all right, or will be in a few minutes!"

As a proof of it he got on his legs, which, though they upheld him, were a little unsteady.

However, the feeling of faintness and weakness soon passed away, and, supported by his brother officers, he walked into the street.

There they took a cab for the office of the inspector, where they made their report.

"I was a fool for walking into that trap," Charlie confessed. "Perhaps, though, it will teach me a lesson."

Whether or not it did, will be seen later.

CHAPTER XXIV.

THE SCENT OF A ROSE.

CHARLIE CLINGSTONE was much worried over this singular attack.

Of course, he had no idea who the men were that had made this attempt on his life, but the fact that such an attempt had been made seemed to prove that his latest disguise had been penetrated; and he returned to his room that night, much depressed.

The strain of the last few days was telling on him sorely. Not a trace had he been able to find of Daisy Malcomb.

"No news, no news!" he groaned, sinking his face in his hands.

The hope that she might be found in that old house and be rescued by him had been so rudely removed that it was even yet a shock.

"Where can she be? Where can she have gone?" he repeated over and over, looking at the unanswering walls.

It was scarcely a relief to turn from thoughts of Daisy to thoughts of John Malcomb. The mysterious shape dimly seen that night in the corridor continued to haunt him like a depressing nightmare.

So far, he had not only failed to discover John Malcomb's murderer, but new mysteries, which were insolvable, thickened about him.

There were only three facts to which he could cling:

John Malcomb had been murdered! Could he doubt that?

Carefully he went over the facts known to him: He had seen Malcomb lying with rigid face in a pool of blood, which had oozed from a wound in his back. He had seen the bloody attempt at writing on the wall. He had handled the stained knife—which was even now in his possession. He had seen Malcomb buried!

Yes, John Malcomb was dead. There could not be the shadow of a doubt of it.

What, then, had he seen that night in the Malcomb house?

That was the second mystery!

Had he seen anything?

Groaningly he pressed his hands against his aching head, for the fear smote him that he was losing his mind.

The third mystery was the disappearance of Daisy. And that letter! That letter!

He took it out and read it over again; as he had done so many, many times before.

"My God, why did she do that? Why did she leave in that way? Why did she not give me her reasons?"

The letters swam before his eyes.

"I'm done up!' he at length declared, rising. "I must go to bed and get some rest, or the result will be that I'll be as dead as those rascals want me to be."

Though he went to bed, he slept little, tossing and moaning restlessly throughout the remainder of the night.

He was hardly in condition for the work that might be expected of him that morning; but he went, nevertheless, to Youngblood's office in the Malcomb house, endeavoring to hide his depression under a light and airy demeanor.

He had taken much pains to remove all evidences of the dreadful fall he had received, and had succeeded remarkably well. But there was a heaviness about his eyes that could not fail to attract the attention of a close observer.

It did not fail to attract the attention of Solon Youngblood, who, when he came in, glanced keenly at his secretary.

"Out too late last night, I'm afraid, Dennison! Late hours generally play the devil with a young fellow. I didn't know you were given to such dissipation?"

Dennison was the name which Charlie had given as his own.

He averred that he had not been dissipating, but felt a little under the weather. Then the work of the day was gone through with, in the usual manner.

Chicago Charlie

So far, the Columbian Detective's efforts to secure proof against Solon Youngblood by means of the letters and papers in the office had amounted to nothing. There were letters and papers in abundance, but none of them contained what he sought.

Youngblood seemed to be doing a brokerage business, for his correspondence usually concerned the purchase and sale of various kinds of stocks and securities.

It was in all respects an uneventful day. Youngblood was kind and courteous, the clerk painstaking and quiet; and when the office hours came to a close, Youngblood crowned the kindness of the day by inviting the detective to spend the evening with him at the house.

"I think it will do you good," was the assertion. "You're brooding over something, and I know it. Mrs. Youngblood will be delighted to see you, and we'll try to make it as pleasant as we can. May we look for you?"

Ordinarily this would have been a most pleasing invitation. Just then, however, Chicago Charlie felt in no mood for the frivolities of light and fashionable small talk.

He hesitated a moment before replying.

Then, feeling that no harm would come from it and that something of importance might be developed, he replied, accepting the invitation.

There never was a more gracious and charming woman than Mrs. Solon Youngblood, when she took the trouble to make herself so. She was an intelligent woman, and she was handsome and brilliant—possessing an indescribable chic and fund of vivacity. And on this evening she strove to make herself most agreeable.

There were cards, and afterward a light luncheon, with excellent coffee, served in fragile, egg shell cups.

At any other time, or under other circumstances, Chicago Charlie might have enjoyed the evening. But he felt ill at ease. Nor could the sparkling talk of the beautiful woman who called herself Mrs. Solon Youngblood win him away from morbid thoughts. Besides, he felt that these people were not friends;—felt, somehow, deep down in his heart, that they knew that they were not his friends, but were making this effort for a purpose.

He recalled the experience of the night before. But for that he might not have harbored a suspicious thought. But that told him his disguise had been penetrated by enemies;— and the chief of his enemies, he was quite sure, was this smiling man who sat beside him:—Solon Youngblood.

Nevertheless, in spite of his depressing reflections and conjectures, he strove to appear at ease; and that he did not fully succeed was in nowise his fault. Many another man would have failed even more entirely.

At last, when he felt that it was almost time for him to go, he found himself alone with Mrs. Youngblood. The discovery did not disturb him at once, for he expected Youngblood to return to the apartment at any moment.

But when Solon did not come, he began to fidget, his uneasiness slowly growing.

Mrs. Youngblood's keen eyes were on him.

"I weary you with my prattle," she confessed.

Then she got up quickly; and, placing two small glasses on the table, poured wine into each.

He shook his head.

"Hasn't your husband told you of my temperance proclivities?" he questioned, mildly looking at her. "But for that, I should be glad to join with you!"

She pushed the glass away.

Only a minute before he had refused to taste the bit of apple she had laughingly offered.

He was becoming intensely suspicious and alert, and Mrs. Solon Youngblood could hardly have failed to notice it.

Looking at her, as she stood there, smiling and handsome, he could not but think of the Borgias. Was Lucretia ever so charming, so winning—*so dangerous*?

"You will at least take this as a souvenir of your call?" and she carefully took from her bosom the large rose which he had more than once admired that evening. "I hope you have had a most pleasant time; and am I presumptuous in wishing that we may be able to see you here again, some evening, in the not distant future?"

She extended the rose, which he could scarcely refuse to accept. His distrust of this woman seemed preposterously silly. He was a man and armed. How could she harm him, if he remained on guard against poison? If they had meant poisoning they would have attempted it earlier in the evening.

He took the rose, which was a large and handsome one, and pressed it against his nostrils, clasping it rather tightly with his fingers.

Instantly from the heart of the rose came a blinding explosion. An impalpable, peppery powder filled his eyes and overpowering odors suffocated him and rendered him half-unconscious.

He heard Mrs. Youngblood give a little tittering laugh, and knew that she had advanced close to his chair.

It was a large arm chair, in which he had remained seated most of the evening.

He crouched in it now, blinded and helpless, and hardly knowing what he was doing.

Then he felt himself clasped by strong arms.

The beautiful fiend who had given him the explosive rose, had touched a spring beneath the chair; and iron hooks, which had seemed part of the chair's framework, had clasped him in a steely embrace!

CHAPTER XXV.

A BEAUTIFUL FIEND.

THE GRASP OF THOSE STEELY ARMS, brought him back to a full sense of his peril. The peppery powder still partially blinded him, and his eyes felt on fire. Nevertheless, he strugglingly strove to rise from the chair.

The laugh of Mrs. Solon Youngblood sounded cruelly in his ears.

"Quite a little surprise, is it not?" came the mocking question. "I have another rose here. Do you think you would care for it?"

Through his blurred vision he saw her pluck at her corsage.

But no other indignity immediately followed.

"You were in too great haste to leave me," she sneered. "Do you think I care only for the company of Mr. Youngblood? It is not often I have the pleasure of speech with so gallant a young gentleman as yourself."

There was a bitterness in the words that showed she was not pleased that her efforts to amuse and hold him at her side had seemed so impotent. If there was one thing more than another on which Mrs. Solon Youngblood flattered herself, it was her ability in that line.

"My God, woman! What do you mean to do with me?" the Columbian Detective managed to ejaculate. "What is the meaning of this outrage?"

"You are a very shrewd man and a very capable man, Mr. Dennison, but you're not always as wide-awake as you might be. I do not think the police will appear to-night to release you! You forgot to warn them, did you not?"

Then Chicago Charlie understood the full strength of the plot.

Having failed in their attempt of the night previous, a resort had been had to an even bolder game by those who had then sought his life.

He now knew that, whoever had been the parties luring him to the old house, Solon Youngblood was their leader and directing spirit.

"You're a very smart man, Chicago Charlie! But the smartest men sometimes make mistakes. You will not have the opportunity to make many more."

Any one not understanding the meaning of the words might have thought that this handsome creature was addressing the man before her in the most cordial way, for the sting hidden in their depth was so subtle as to be almost indistinguishable.

Yet Chicago Charlie caught it, and writhed in impotent rage and pain.

She passed a handkerchief delicately across his face, removing much of the substance that had so blinded him.

Then she stood before him, flashing on him a most defiant look. A look, too, that was full of hate and scorn.

"You think we haven't known you," she asserted. "But you were never more mistaken. We have known you from the first day—from the first hour!"

The fierceness of a tigress was now in her tones.

Chicago Charlie groaned and struggled anew. He might as well have saved his strength. The steel arms that had clasped him were tenacious in their grip, and he could do absolutely nothing to release himself. He could only look at the fair fiend who was thus exasperatingly tormenting him.

"Why don't you kill me, and be done with it, if that is your intention?" he questioned, rendered desperate.

But for the thought that he had been so duped, Chicago Charlie would as soon have died there, as anywhere. The despondency of despair was seizing him and life seemed scarcely worth the purchase.

Chicago Charlie

It will be remembered that he had suffered much during the week past; that his fondest hopes had been dashed to the ground, that failure had followed every effort. More than once had he felt that he did not care for life.

Yet he did not wish to die like a rat in a trap.

"Do your worst, woman!" he imperiously commanded. "A man can only die once; and I don't know that it matters much when that one time comes. It's a question whether a long life is better than a short one."

She laughed him in the face.

"You hope to induce me to kill you there, and so end the play. I am not ready, for I'm afraid it might please you, and I do not care to please the kind of man you are known to be!"

She took up from the table another rose, whose perfume—so sweet and fragrant—Charlie had more than once noticed.

Then she took from a pocket a small bottle, and sprinkled its contents lavishly on the petals.

"Another flower!" she whispered, balefully advancing.

He drew back, with almost a cry of terror. The bottle had held chloroform.

"My poor, dear boy! Don't you like the smell of a rose?"

That mocking smile had come back to her lips.

The detective, clutched by those steely arms, could not lift a hand to push her from him.

"There is no trick about this!" she smilingly urged. "It is only a plain every-day rose, with a little perfume sprinkled over it."

She had knelt at his side; and now, laying a hand caressingly on his shoulder, she lifted the flower to his nostrils.

He fought and almost screamed; but he could do nothing, except shake his head, to repel this novel attack.

"Smell it!" she crooningly urged. "You are excited. You are feverish! It will soothe you. It will make you sleep. Sleep is what you want, my poor fellow. Sound, never-ending sleep!"

At every sentence, she crowded the rose against his face, holding it there in spite of his exertions to escape from it.

Notwithstanding his determination to withstand the effects of the chloroform, an indescribable feeling of drowsiness began to take possession of him.

More than once, he roused himself, when he heard the crooning voice of this female wretch taking on a distant and suggestive sound.

Then he would rage again; only to drop back into half-somnolence, under the effects of the Lethean drug.

"Sleep is what you want, my poor fellow! Sound, never-ending sleep!"

These words came to him like the tinkle of a bell, or the lulling voice of falling water.

Once more, he threw off the strange spell, and shook from himself the dragging weight that sat on his shoulders.

"I will not yield to that infernal stuff!" he screamed. "Take it away! Take it away!"

"It is what you need!" came the crooning tones again. "What you need. What you need!"

It seemed to him that those words, "what you need!" were being repeated over and over, until they ran into a lulling song.

His head drooped.

Lower and lower it sunk on his breast. His breathing became labored.

Still Mrs. Solon Youngblood pressed that deadly rose against his mouth.

Lower and lower sunk the head.

Then the muscles of the helpless man wholly relaxed, and he lay as limp as if dead.

CHAPTER XXVI.

IN PERIL DIRE.

CHICAGO CHARLIE WAS AROUSED by a dash of water. A breaking "whitecap," hurling its spray, touching him, and its coolness brought a gasp of returning sensibility. He opened his eyes slowly and strove to rise.

But he sunk back, through sheer weakness, and because of the terror inspired by his discovery.

He was in an open boat, in the midst of a stormy sea, on a starless night! A flash of lightning revealed this; and the roll of the thunder's reverberation drowned the cry that rose to his lips.

Again he strove to lift himself. A sense of peril made alert his mental faculties, but the lethargic influences of the drug still held his muscles in a powerful grasp.

Chicago Charlie

When the Columbian Detective had succumbed to the influence of the chloroform, and Mrs. Solon Youngblood saw that he had become unconscious, she gave him a keen glance, and then moved softly away.

She was back in a very few moments, and at her heels tip-toed two men. Both were masked and armed; though any one with suspicions quickened could have seen that the taller of the two was Solon Youngblood.

"He knows no more than a stone," she whispered, indicating the chair where lay the helpless detective.

She had turned the light low, and only a subdued gloom reigned in the apartment.

Solon Youngblood and his companion advanced as if they feared the victim of her wiles might awaken.

The knowledge of the cruel thing they meant to do, oppressed them with its terror. Besides, they had so frequently been balked in their schemes against the life of the Columbian Detective that they were not certain even yet that their prey would not slip through their fingers.

Solon Youngblood was physically a powerful man, and it was seemingly no difficult thing for him to lift the body of Chicago Charlie, unaided even by the man who had come to assist him.

He drew the limp form erect, while Mrs. Youngblood shot back the steel arms of the chair; and both smiled, when they saw what a harmless-looking chair it became when those hidden claws were once more out of sight.

The two men then bore the detective from the room, descending quietly with him to the street.

A cab was there in waiting, in which their burden was placed; they climbing in after it.

Then the whip was laid on the horse and the cab rolled away toward the northern part of the city, its ultimate destination being the lake front.

For a long time the quick gait was continued.

There were very few people on the streets; for, in addition to the lateness of the hour, the wind was hysterically screaming, and heavy masses of black clouds portended a storm. Occasionally a crooked tongue of flame lighted the sky, which was followed by a peal that caused the houses to shake.

Unmindful of these disagreeable circumstances—being in fact rather gratified by them—the driver of the cab held quietly and serenely on his way. He had no desire to attract attention.

The stacks of tall buildings marking the business portions of the city had been long passed, and they were now nearing the suburbs. The cottages seemed interminable, stretching on mile after mile. It was most exasperating to the two villains in the cab, who were so desirous that the work upon which they had entered should be brought to a speedy end.

Then the cottages began to disappear, clumps of trees became more numerous, and larger plots of ground grew common.

But even yet the driver did not draw rein; nor did he stop until the last house had been left far behind and the sound of waves told him that the lake was near.

When a flash of lightning showed him the tumbling waters just in front, he brought the cab to a halt; and, climbing down, swung open one of the doors.

"A cursed long time you were getting here!" Youngblood growled, scrambling down and stretching his cramped limbs. "Seems to me you have driven far enough to have reached the State line. How many miles are we out, anyhow?"

The fellow was not pleased at the tone and his reply was little more than a surly growl.

Youngblood laughed, bitterly.

"Well, we'll not quarrel. Neither of us can afford to. But I thought we'd never have done with it. My back's broke with stooping over that fellow, applying that chloroform to his nose. I thought the fumes of the stuff would do me up. 'Twould have been a go, if you'd found all three of us lying in there asleep!"

He laughed again, showing a desire to mollify the surly driver.

"Are you ready to take him out?" came the voice of the third member of the party, who was still in the cab.

At this Youngblood and the driver turned to the door; and the limp form of the detective being pushed into view, they seized it, drew it out, and bore it down to the sands of the lake shore.

Then the driver went back to tie the horse and to scout around a bit to make sure they had not been observed.

When he returned, Solon's assistant had produced two boats from some point in the darkness, and he was now standing by these, having drawn them up on the sandy point.

Youngblood was kneeling at Chicago Charlie's side, again applying an odorous handkerchief.

"Curse the fellow, he's got a head like iron! Bear a hand here, and we'll have done with it. I don't like the looks of the lake, but

Chicago Charlie

it's all the better for our little scheme."

The threatenings of the storm were increasing. There had been several dashes of rain; and, as he spoke, there came another. The sand, caught up by the stiff breeze, flew in a shower.

"If we don't hurry we'll not be able to get out on the lake at all."

He had caught the detective by the shoulders and, his companions coming to his aid, Chicago Charlie was lifted into the smaller of the two boats. Both were then pushed into the water.

Seated in the first, or larger, to which the second was attached by a rope, the three men began to strain and tug at their oars, moving by almost imperceptible degrees out into the waste of stormy waters.

For a time they made very little progress, it being about all they could do to keep the head of the boat pointed in the right direction.

Chicago Charlie had not been bound before being placed in the boat; it being the intention of his enemies to cast the boat adrift, when they had made a good offing. It seemed pretty certain that the waves would ultimately ingulf it, and this was the more assured by the gathering strength of the storm. Even should he return to consciousness, a thing they did not deem likely, he would be utterly helpless in that small boat, without oars and uncertain of his position.

They believed that he would be drowned; and that his body and the submerged or overturned boat being found the next day, there would arise a very natural supposition that he had ventured out alone, and been thus lost.

Solon Youngblood was one of the craftiest of his ilk, and never took chances when he could avoid it.

When they had succeeded in placing a considerable distance between themselves and the land, they found the work of rowing much easier. The waves did not run as high as nearer in, and the "white caps" did not break so furiously.

Nevertheless, they were drenched with spray, and but for their exertions would have been chilled and very uncomfortable.

But they did not cease their rowing until as much as a mile yawned between the boats and the shore. Then Youngblood, crouching in the stern of the boat, took hold of the rope and drew the other boat alongside.

Climbing in it, he again applied to the nostrils of the insensible man a handkerchief steeped in chloroform, of which he appeared to have plentiful supply. Then he cast the handkerchief from him, climbed back into the first boat, and removed the rope from the boat in which lay the detective.

He was very careful in all he did, that nothing should be left to indicate the real manner of Chicago Charlie's death.

The wind which was from the north, caught the boat of the helpless detective and soon bore it from sight. But for the frequent play of the lightning it could not have been seen ten feet away.

Something like a malediction arose to the lips of Youngblood, as he saw the little craft float out of sight, and a sigh of relief fell from his lips. They were pallid lips, with almost the hue of death on them; for, in spite of his iron nerve and hardened nature, the deed of this night sat heavy on his conscience.

But he had been so hounded and harassed by the Columbian Detective that he had felt called to resort to extremes; and there was no doubt he would have repeated the act had it been necessary.

The waves rose higher and higher, lashing the breast of the lake with their spray, and the uncertain rain fell in drenching showers, at frequent intervals. It was truly a wild night and growing wilder. But not yet had the storm broken in full force.

The little boat containing the detective already held a great deal of water; and when Chicago Charlie was aroused by that flirt of the waves, and looked so startledly about him, he was made aware of the fact that he was lying in a pool of water that had soaked his clothing through and through.

His mind acted quickly, and it took him but a moment to comprehend to the full his terrible situation. The incidents of the night returned in quick succession. The last he could recall was that scene in the room of the Malcomb house, with Mrs. Solon Youngblood kneeling at his side, pressing the rose to his lips, and whispering those lulling slumberous words.

All that followed was a blank; yet he knew where he was. Not the exact position of the boat, nor how far from land; but he knew that he was out on the lake, and in peril most dire.

Again he tried to lift himself; and finally succeeded so well that he could sit half erect with head resting against the boat's side.

He waited impatiently for a friendly lightning-flash.

It came, showing him his utter helplessness.

The boat was oarless and tossing at the mercy of the waves. The lightning-flash revealed something else. A towering billow that threatened to ingulf him.

He closed his eyes, uttered a prayer, expecting to find himself the next instant struggling in the water. But a yeasty line appeared at the apex of the green roller, which thus broke harmlessly, and the boat rode safely in the milky sea.

But a second lightning-flash revealed another billow, towering still higher, and the detective closed his eyes in terror, feeling that he was indeed lost.

CHAPTER XXVII.

TRACKING ZEL MAGRUDER.

BILLY STUBBS WAS IN HIGH GLEE. No interview he had ever had, had resulted more satisfactorily than the one just held with Buffalo Bill. Not only had the great scout been kind and courteous; but, seeing in the boy evidences of talent in the horseback line, he had offered to give him a position, and train him for the work of a rough rider.

Billy had felt forced to decline this most generous offer. Just now he owed allegiance to Chicago Charlie, and the work Chicago Charlie had given him remained unperformed.

"Well, think over it! There are plenty of riders to be had, but I believe you might make your mark in that line. You have the native ability."

Billy was not so sure of this, remembering the terror inspired by the broncho; but he did not refuse the season pass to the Wild West exhibition, which the famous scout placed in his hand.

Rackstraw was equally favored, and the two went away smiling and happy. Luck had surely been with them.

"I'll be expectin' to kick up gold dollars from the sidewalk, next," Rackstraw averred, his mouth distended in a grin. "I say, now, Billy Stubbs, *that* was the handsome thing! Buffalo Bill ferever! Rah, rah! Hip, hip!"

He swung his cap, and, but for the time and place, would have given vent to his exuberance in a series of roaring cheers.

Two nights later Billy Stubbs was again on the trail of Zel Magruder; and the trail led him, as before, into the camp of the Gypsies.

He crouched for a time in the shadow of the tent usually occupied by Gypsy Nell; and then, finding a favorable opportunity, when Zel and the crone were both talking outside, he crept into the tent himself and sought concealment beneath a pile of straw.

The straw was hardly in place over him when the two came back, continuing the conversation.

The words were of a startling character.

"I don't think you ought to have anything to do with that girl, Zel!" the crone was protesting. "You'll go and git yerself into the worst snarl that ever was. Mind what I tell you!"

"You're always growlin'!" Magruder made answer. "Nothin' I can do any more pleases you. It's Zel don't do this, an' Zel don't do that, tell you run me wild. What in the dickens would you have me do, anyhow?"

"I wouldn't have you lay a finger on Daisy Malcomb—that's what!"

"I hain't laid no finger on her. I hain't teched her. I dunno as I've spoke to her."

"See, then, that you don't!"

"Anything else, old growler?" and Zel threw himself into a rickety chair and squinted up at the crone.

"Where've ye got her?"

He winked and laid a finger against the side of his nose.

"Guess, Nell! You're a fortune-teller an' ought to be good at guessin'. If ye can't, I won't tell ye. It's one of the rules I don't dare to break!"

Billy Stubbs was wild with excitement, and so quick and hard did his breathing become that more than once he was on the verge of self-betrayal.

He could not see their actions; but, when the crone's words again reached him, they showed that she had turned away and was in another part of the tent. But they were as crabbed as before.

"You break them rules ever' five minutes, an' yet you're always talkin' about keepin' them. You'll hang yerself yit, Zel Magruder! Mark my words!"

"Then I won't git drownded, er chopped up in a railroad accident!"

Zel plucked a straw from Billy's hiding-place, and thoughtfully chewed it, as he nursed his chin.

"Say, what makes ye so blamed int'rested in that girl?'

Chicago Charlie

"None o' your business!" grunted the old woman. "You won't tell me nothin', an' oughtn't expect anything better in return."

Zel subsided, but still chewed at the straw.

Billy's suspense was great. Was he to learn anything of importance?

Had he not already done that? He knew that Chicago Charlie would hail with delight any news assuring him that Daisy Malcomb was alive.

There could be no doubt, he thought, that Daisy was alive, and held somewhere by the Lakeside Leaguers. Oh! if Magruder had only told *where*!

But Magruder grew silent and obstinate, after that repulse by the old woman; and, finally spitting away the straw, he got up and sullenly left the tent.

"He'll be hung, yit!" Billy heard the crone mutter. "I do'no', though, as I'll care. He ain't no good. No; he's bad from top to toe; an' he'll bring ruin on all o' us, sooner er later!"

Billy was in a quandary. He intensely desired to follow Zel, and there was no way of getting out of the tent. The crone showed no intention of immediately leaving it, but moved about, engaged in some occupation, all unmindful of the spy, who lay crouching almost at her feet.

Suddenly Gypsy Nell was startled by a sneeze. It was a sneeze, too, of mammoth proportions, and came apparently from the ground just in front of her.

One of the straws had got into Billy's nose, and brought forth that prodigious sound.

In spite of her years, the crone was keen-eyed and shrewd. She knew her senses had not deceived her, and she was equally sure that the sound had not issued from the earth.

Rightly divining that the straw must hold some one concealed, she stepped toward it, and with a stick carefully raked it away, standing back as if she expected a rat to scud out.

She gave a little scream of fright, when her eyes fell on Billy.

The newsboy leaped up, hoping to make his escape.

But the Gypsy woman caught him by the collar of his coat and held him with a grasp that was remarkably firm and strong. In vain did Billy squirm and twist. He could not wrench himself loose.

"No yer don't, you young rascal! Not till you tell me what you mean by this! What you doin' under that straw, in my house?"

Billy saw that he must assume a bold front.

"Call this a house?" he said, facing her bravely. "Thought this hyer was a Gypsy tent. Come in hyer awhile ago, I did, to git me fortune told, and dropped down there an' went to sleep. Wasn't nobody hyer to wait on me."

Nell knew he was lying.

She flung him into a chair, and took a seat where she could prevent his escape.

Something in the boy's face attracted her, and she looked at him keenly and closely, bending forward in her inspection.

Billy stared in surprise.

"Think mebbe I'm Charlie Ross, hay? Well, I hain't, then? If you're a fortune-teller you ort to know who I am."

"I do!" she averred. "I know a good deal more about you than you do yourself. Zel Magruder's lookin' for you!"

Billy half arose in fright.

"Set down there! He's not comin' back right away. Now, what's your name?"

"Lost it awhile ago!" Billy declared.

"What's your name?" she impatiently demanded, tapping the ground with the stick, which she still held.

"Gunnison George, o' the Rocky Mountains!" said Billy.

"Who calls you that?"

"The newspapers! Didn't ye see 'em today? Gunnison George, what beat Sage-bush Sweeney in that big trick race last year!"

"That isn't your name!" shaking her head in a manner to show she was not pleased. "You call yourself Billy Stubbs. That isn't your name, either!"

Billy was quite shaken out of the snarl of falsehoods he was weaving, by this unexpected declaration.

"What is it, then?" he asked, his face showing his sudden interest.

She laughed.

"I thought I'd catch you!"

"Then you don't know what my name is? What made ye say that, I'd like to know?"

"Oh, I don't know! Perhaps it's because I believe you're a Gypsy!"

Billy's mouth flew open.

"A *Gypsy?*"

"That's what I said. A Gypsy! You wouldn't like to join our band, now, would you? I'm sure you're a Gypsy!"

CHAPTER XXVIII.

QUEER TALK OF THE GYPSY CRONE.

BILLY, WHO HAD BEEN MUCH FRIGHTENED at first, had completely lost this fear, and was now intensely interested. Therefore, when the crone imperiously took his hand, he did not offer to withdraw it.

"You said awhile ago you came here to git yer fortune told! You didn't; but I'll tell it for ye, anyway. It must be an interestin' fortune, by the look of yer face. Want to hear it?"

Billy thought of Zel Magruder.

She interpreted his glance, for he had turned in a frightened way toward the door of the tent.

"That rascal ain't comin' back fer a good while. I think he's goin' out on the lake. If he don't, he's got a sweetheart that'll keep him, so you needn't be afraid o' Zel."

Billy wondered why she spoke to him in that manner. Why was she so friendly? Did she entertain evil designs against him?

The questions were unanswerable, and he thought it unwise to put them into words; but they made him uneasy.

The crone was closely examining the palm of his hand.

"It's an interestin' fortune, anyway," she exclaimed. "You've had experience enough to make a book."

Billy became possessed of mingled feelings of fear and awe.

"Sho! You don't see anything *there!*"

"I see the lake. I see a boy struggling in the water. Is the boy Billy Stubbs? Yes, it is Billy Stubbs!"

"Sounds like a lesson out of the second reader," thought Billy. Nevertheless, he wondered much at what he heard.

"He has been knocked into the lake; but he does not drown! He swims ashore!"

"You're off, there," Billy mentally commented; but still he held his peace.

"Now he is tracking a man. It is a little man."

"Of course she knows about me follerin Zel Magruder!" was Billy's scornful thought. "Who couldn't tell them kind o' fortunes?"

"This little man has a sweetheart, who is also a Gypsy—an Egyptian Gypsy!"

This was so manifestly a reference to the dancing girl that Billy's interest quickened.

"She is blood of the Gypsy blood, though she sometimes claims not to be; an' she an' the little man are gitting too thick to thrive.

"Ah! the boy is a Gypsy, too. Three Gypsies!—like the three little Indians all in a row. Blood of one blood; and blood is—is it thicker than water? That's what the Gypsies say!

"It's redder sometimes! and there's a stain of it on the hands of the little man. He has tried to wash it off, but can't. It is the red, red stain of murder."

Billy Stubbs's eyes had taken on a staring look and his lips were parted.

Then the old woman, pretending thus to tell his fortune, recounted the incidents of the murder of John Malcomb; very much as she had recounted them to Daisy Malcomb; only that, in this instance, the murder was manifestly attributed to Zel Magruder instead of the Englishman, Selwyn Fisher.

Billy Stubbs would have been more puzzled than ever if he had known of that other "fortune," told several days before.

He was puzzled enough as it was; though he was keen enough to know that she was striking at Magruder.

What most mystified him was that she should thus seek to cast suspicion on Magruder. She must indeed have hated the little Gypsy intensely!

She was through at last; and Billy Stubbs realized that of himself she had really told nothing—save that he was a Gypsy—blood of the Gypsy blood.

He did not believe this. Was sure it could not be true.

She cast away the hand, showing that she had finished.

"Is that all?" Billy questioned.

"Would you want more?"

Billy looked at her keenly; and would have given much to know what was passing in her mind.

"Why did Zel Magruder go out on the lake to-night?"

It was a bold venture; but the very boldness of the question seemed to please the woman.

"You're a Gypsy!" she declared. "Blood of the Gypsy blood! Otherwise I would not speak to you this way. But Zel Magruder is a bad man. He will be hung. He will ruin us all. If it wasn't for that, I do'no' as I'd care how soon the rope was put around his neck."

"Why did he go out on the lake? There's a cargo comin' in! There's always cargoes comin' in! 'Stuff' *he* calls 'em!"

She bent her head still nearer, seeming to fear her words might be heard.

"Do you know what that 'stuff' is, Billy Stubbs? It's rich goods, smuggled in from Canada; that's what it is. Oh; they're a bad lot, them smugglers; and Zel is about the worst among 'em. As I said, he's bound to be hung!

"He lays around hyer, watches the police an' the officers, an' then slips out in a boat to a certain place, an' tells the smugglers all he can learn."

Her eyes were blazing, her skinny hands worked convulsively, and her voice shook.

Billy would have been as senseless as a block if he had not seen what she intended; she knew he was a spy of the police; and she hoped what she thus communicated would be borne to the authorities.

She sunk her voice still lower, until it was only a shrill whisper.

"They've got a den somewhere on the Michigan shore; I dunno jist where. But it's on the Michigan shore! On the Michigan shore! Zel told me so one night!"

"An' Zel is a-goin' out on the lake to night?"

She nodded:

"He's already gone!"

"Does he go out every night?" Billy asked.

"Not every night. Generally not more than once a week. But he goes out again to-morrow night. It's but a small cargo to-night. To-morrow night the big cargo will come in! To-morrow night the big cargo will come in!"

She bent swayingly forward, and rocked herself as she repeated these words:

"To-morrow night the big cargo will come in!"

Her eyes were blazing unnaturally. Her voice was husky with passion or hate. Her form shook.

Billy, drinking in her words, could but stare at her and marvel.

She checked herself by an effort and arose from her chair.

"I have been a fool!" she declared, with fierce bitterness. "I reckon old Nell is losin' her mind. You'd better go; and I don't think you'd better come back again. Zel Magruder would like to put his fingers on you!"

Her entire manner had changed. There seemed a revulsion of feeling; or perhaps she felt that she had carried her revelations too far. Zel Magruder was a member of the band, and she probably realized that as such she owed some fealty.

"You'd better go!"

The words were snarled, and Billy Stubbs saw that it was not wise to remain longer. Besides, if he hoped to do anything that night—if he hoped to thwart Magruder's plans or learn anything from them, it was high time for him to leave.

He knew not what to say as a farewell; so he said nothing; but picked up his hat from the heap of straw and hastened out into the night and away from the Gypsy encampment.

What a budget of news he would have for Chicago Charlie, to be sure! His heart glowed with the thought. Daisy Malcomb was alive, and held by the smugglers; most likely held in that den on the Michigan shore. He believed the words of the crone meant all that. That was the most important of the many things he would have to tell, though the others were of almost infinite value to his detective friend.

Should he try to follow Magruder, or should he seek Chicago Charlie?

He decided on the latter course; but, when he went in search of the Columbian Detective, the latter was not to be found in his usual haunts.

CHAPTER XXIX.

THE WORK OF THE LIFE CREW.

"HARK!"

Clear and sharp came the explanation; and the bow oar of the life-boat rested, poised in mid-air.

Within the boat sat a crew of hardy men, listening now with straining ears, and watching with straining eyes, as the life-boat rose on the heavy waves.

Thick gloom was about them, except when the bright lightning burned across the sky, splitting the darkness like the flaming sword of an archangel.

Chicago Charlie

The lake storm was on in all its fury, and the reverberations of the thunder rolled like the tones of deep-throated cannon. The spray blew blindingly—seemingly one continuous sheet; and the rain that hissed downward to meet it seemed to cement earth and air in a wall of water.

It was truly a wild night, and the most fearless of the life crew was fully aware of his peril.

The life-boat had bravely pulled out from the lake shore directly in front of the "White City,"—pulled out into the storm and darkness, in answer to a cry that had come ringing over the boiling waves. It had been a despairing cry;—a cry that told of a human life in deadly peril.

On the shore of the lake, and part of the Great World's Fair Exhibition, is the home of the life crew. This home, a model United States Life Savings Station, lies close to the great, brick battle-ship, Illinois; and in the waters in front of the station, the life crews were accustomed to demonstrate to curious crowds of sights-seers the methods by which lives were saved from the sea.

But they were expecting real work, now; not play.

All through the night the men at the life-station had watched the angry sky and the threatening storm; feeling that there would likely be wrecks that night, and human lives in peril.

As the lightning blazed, the men of this boat crew were fully outlined as they sat anxiously in the boat, swinging high on the rollers. Their faces were stern and set. The grasp of the oars had something of nervousness in it. About each strong chest might have been seen a life-preserver.

A backward glance would have revealed, too, in that blaze of light, the towering domes of the great Exposition. It was like a palace of Aladdin, lighted by a torch down-thrust from the sky.

But they did not glance backward toward the White City, but out toward the stormy waters of the open lake.

"Hark!" came the exclamation again.

Again the cry had been heard.

This time the direction was noted; and the boat's head swinging round a point, the men bent to their oars with right good will, and the boat forged toilingly through the sea.

Those despairing cries had come from the lips of the Columbian Detective!

With stiffened limbs, and body chilled and cramped, he was clinging desperately to an overturned boat, hoping and praying that help might come to him, yet almost believing that it could not.

The north wind, breaking into a furious storm, had sent the little boat down the lake, and the tumbling waves had beaten it inch by inch shoreward; until now it rolled less than a mile away and straight out from the Exposition grounds.

A gleam of those white towers came now and then to the despairing detective, bringing a ray of hope.

More than once since the boat had overturned had he thought of abandoning it in an attempt to reach the land by swimming. Had the sea been more calm, such an attempt might have been successful. But in his weakened condition he knew he could not safely trust himself in a fight against those waves.

The fact that the boat was slowly driving toward the shore, though the advance was at times almost imperceptible, gave him renewed courage. But the storm was driving down the lake, not toward the land; and while he moved only by inches toward the longed-for shore, he moved by yards south-ward.

Suddenly a light burned toward him across the gloom. It was an electric search-light, shining from the bow of the life-boat. He also saw—what he had seen before—particolored rockets shooting high in the air from the life-station.

The sight of the electric search-light so cheered him that he again sent out his guiding call, and with more strength and vim than before. Hope returned, full armed and strong. The chill seemed to leave his limbs and a warm glow gathered about his heart. There was life for him yet, he thought.

Time and again his cry rung out, directing the course of the life-boat; and he did not cease his calls until the boat was almost upon him, the glare of the search-light seeming to put out his eyes.

There was no need to call more. He and the boat to which he was clinging had been sighted by the life crew.

A moment later strong arms lifted him from the water, and these skilled men were rubbing his body and extremities, and applying reviving draughts of stimulant.

The little boat was allowed to float away, for the crew had as much as they could do to hold their own craft up against the stiff wind and tumbling seas; and with their work of reviving the half-drowned detective, they had neither time nor strength for anything else.

Almost immediately the life-boat was put about for the shore; and in a remarkably short time Chicago Charlie was in a comfortable room in the life-station; and within less than a half-hour

Chicago Charlie

thereafter he felt almost as well and strong as ever.

But his anxiety would not permit him to remain there throughout the remainder of the night, though he was urged and even commanded to do so. Neither could he give them as full an account of how he came to be out on the lake as he knew they desired.

Finally, just before his departure, fearing some of the incidents of the rescue, coupled with his name, might get into the papers, he took the commander aside; and, telling him enough to show him the need of secrecy in the matter, begged him to say nothing of what had transpired, and to enjoin the same silence on the men.

When he would not consent to remain until morning, the commander directed one of the crew to accompany him to the city; for it could be seen that the detective was still in a weak and shaky condition, notwithstanding his assertions that his strength had entirely returned.

Chicago Charlie was afterward grateful for this favor.

They had but just left the Exposition grounds, and were in the neighborhood of the new hotels that crowd it so thickly on the north, when Chicago Charlie, uttering a low cry, grasped the arm of his companion and reeled back in manifest alarm.

"What is it?" was the instant question.

"There! There! Don't you see that?" Chicago Charlie demanded, in much trepidation.

"That what?"

"Why, that form?"

"'Twas only a man!"

The form that had so startled him had vanished around a corner.

"Was it a man? Are you sure it was a *man*?"

"Why, certainly it was a man! What else could it have been?"

The detective did not reply for a moment.

He had beheld again the shape seen that night in the Malcomb residence—the form so much resembling John Malcomb.

"You saw it yourself?" was his enigmatical inquiry.

His companion was much puzzled.

"I reckon that liquor they gave you down at the station's affecting your head! Of course I saw the man. What about it? Did you think you saw anything else?"

"I thought I saw a man that I believe is dead."

"Mebbe he ain't dead, then! Or mebbe it's only a resemblance.

Shall we go 'round that way and look for him? Perhaps he's standin' there yet."

"Yes! Yes! If you please. Of course I was mistaken; but the resemblance was most marked."

"Nothing so very strange about that. I've run across a good many things like that. There was my old chum, Jim Welch, that died of a fever six years ago. I thought I saw him one night. The light was about like this. To make sure, I hunted the fellow up that I'd seen, and when I had him face to face he looked no more like Welch than you do."

He was walking with the detective toward the corner where the form had disappeared.

When they reached it, no one was to be seen.

"He was too quick for us!" and Chicago Charlie thought he detected a hidden thrill in the man's words. "I reckon he couldn't have heard us talking and skipped out?"

Chicago Charlie had no answer. He was bewildered. The face and form—for he had seen both distinctly, as he believed—were those of John Malcomb—and yet he knew John Malcomb was dead.

"I don't know what to think of it!" he declared. "It couldn't have been a ghost?"

"Ghost, fiddlesticks!" with a scornful laugh.

"Of course, there are no such things. But—"

"It was that liquor you've been taking! I thought they were pouring the truck down you pretty freely. You'll be all right in the morning; and you'll never see any more ghosts, if you shun the tempting bowl."

He laughed again, but his laugh was not merry.

Then they walked on together, without further comment.

Chicago Charlie was not only mystified, he was ill at ease. What did this reappearance mean? Was John Malcomb still in the land of the living in spite of all the evidence to the contrary?

Chicago Charlie

CHAPTER XXX.

THE SHADOW NEAR THE WHARF.

IT WAS DAYLIGHT, when Chicago Charlie found himself again in the city; and one of his first acts was to seek the office of the police inspector.

The inspector had long retired; and when the Columbian Detective discovered he was not to be found at his office, he went to his residence.

The inspector was intensely interested in the story Chicago Charlie had to tell.

"We'll make a move on them!" he declared, at the same time announcing his readiness for the work of the morning. "We'll have the Youngblood place surrounded, and then we'll call on them to surrender, and at the same time bring you forward. Of course, they think you dead!"

The storm had worn itself out; in fact the rain had ceased to fall before Chicago Charlie left the life-saving station. But the clouds still hung heavily, and the wind was not yet entirely still.

The streets were in a disagreeable condition, when the two men walked away from the inspector's home.

Early as was the hour, it was thought the best time for the contemplated raid; and a number of good men were summoned for this service.

But when the Malcomb residence was reached and the cordon was drawn, it was discovered to the intense chagrin of the would-be captors that the net was empty. The Youngbloods had been given warning, in some singular manner, and had fled. The only other tenable supposition was that, fearing suspicion would fall on them should the detective be found dead, they had thought it wise to make a change of location.

It was a most disagreeable surprise, and no man was more pained than the inspector.

He had thought to catch Youngblood, produce the detective, and force from Youngblood a confession by threats. He had known the plan to work well in many cases.

There was nothing more for Chicago Charlie to do but to return to his room and seek his bed.

Some good men were instructed to make a search of the city for the Youngbloods, and to report any discovery promptly; and with this he was forced to be content.

He was worn out. The toils and the excitements of the day and night, with the perils, had told heavily on him.

But even though he so badly needed rest, he could not immediately fall asleep. Thoughts of that vision of John Malcomb intruded.

He remained closely closeted in his room throughout the day and far into the coming night, receiving reports from the police who were making a vain search for the Youngbloods, and wondering why he did not hear from Billy Stubbs.

About midnight Billy came into the room, in a state of great excitement.

"I've been lookin' fer you ever'where!" he asserted. "In all the places you told me to look, when I wanted you in a hurry!"

"And I left word for you to come up here!"

"Well, I didn't git it! Say, there's more stuff comin' in to-night, and Zel Magruder's gone out ag'in. I seen him in a boat—a sailboat—and noticed which way he was headin'. Nell tol' me las' night that the big cargo 'u'd come in to-night!"

"Nell?"

"Yes; the ole Gypsy woman!"

Then, in reply to Chicago Charlie's rapid fire of questions, he told of the occurrences in the Gypsy tent and of what Gypsy Nell had said to him.

As may well be imagined, the relation held for the detective great interest; and when he was told of Zel's words, showing that Daisy Malcomb was alive, his joy was deep, even though it was tinged with fear.

But the revelation deepened, instead of clearing away the mystery of her disappearance. If she were in the power of the Lakeside Leaguers, as Magruder's words would seem to indicate, why had she written her lover that queer letter?

Chicago Charlie felt sure there was a reasonable explanation, but he had to confess it was not discoverable. He could only wait the natural processes of time for the solving of the problem.

There was work, now, to do, and no time for dreaming and speculation. Billy had said that Zel had put out into the lake, and that a cargo of smuggled goods was coming in that night.

Therefore, Chicago Charlie deemed it his present duty to visit Captain Stebbins, on the revenue cutter, and acquaint him with the facts known.

"Where is Rackstraw?" he inquired of the newsboy.

Chicago Charlie

But Billy knew no more of the whereabouts of Rackstraw than did Chicago Charlie.

"I expect he's making good use of that season pass to Buffalo Bill's Wild West," the detective averred. "Well, we'll have to get along without him, for we haven't time to look him up."

Billy had withheld nothing, as will be seen by this reference to the Wild West.

As the nearest station was that of the Illinois Central, they made their way to that, immediately on leaving the detective's room, and were soon being whirled toward the Fairgrounds.

Although the hour was so late, they found no trouble in gaining admission, as the man on duty at the entrance chanced to know Chicago Charlie.

They did not tarry in the grounds, but went straight to the Andrew Johnson, which was lying in its usual place beside the wharf.

They found Captain Stebbins on board, and to him the detective quickly recounted Billy's story.

"This is important!" the captain declared. "What was the direction taken by Magruder?"

This last to Billy.

The newsboy spy gave him the desired information.

A few more words were said, and then the captain walked away to give the necessary orders for immediate sailing.

"We'll lie out in the lake, along the track the smugglers will be most likely to take coming in, and maybe we can sight them," he explained, speaking again to Chicago Charlie. "It may be we'll have some fun yet, before the night is over. I'd like much to get sight of those scoundrels. They've been worrying me for the past two months, and all efforts to bag them have failed."

He hurried away again to hasten the preparations for departure; and Chicago Charlie, having nothing to do but wait, walked slowly and thoughtfully toward the rear of the vessel, leaving the newsboy to his own devices.

That Billy Stubbs was abundantly able to care for himself, and to extract profit and amusement out of seemingly poor materials, he had had abundant proof.

The detective could not get his mind away from the mysteries that were puzzling him; and he wanted to be alone to think of the woman who was dearer to him than life, and who was probably in great distress, if not in great peril.

Leaning on the rail and looking over the strip of water that lay between the vessel and the shore, he reflected on all the strange events of the past few days.

Of the disappearance of Daisy, and the queer letter; and of the even more mysterious reappearance of John Malcomb.

But, thinking it all over, and passing in review the evidences gathered in the office of John Malcomb, he felt sure that John Malcomb could not be among the living.

Caught by this later tangle, Chicago Charlie had partially neglected the search to which at first he had given his whole energies! The search for Malcomb's murderer.

It will be remembered he had believed that the murder had been committed by a woman. He had drifted from that theory, and now held that the murder had been committed by the Gypsy, Zel Magruder.

The proofs were strong:

Magruder was feminine in his general appearance. His hands and feet were as small as those of the average woman. He was in every essential effeminate. His voice was not that of a man; though it did not sound like the voice of a woman! Billy had compared it to the squeak of a rat; and the comparison was good.

Chicago Charlie reasoned that Magruder had induced his sweetheart, the Ghawazee, to visit Daisy Malcomb, under the pretense of wishing to tell her fortune, and to abstract some implement by which the murder might be committed. He had done that, to throw suspicion on Daisy Malcomb; and had left those feminine impressions of hand and feet for the same purpose.

The Ghawazee was a Gypsy. Gypsy Nell had said so, and Chicago Charlie's study of the girl's face made him believe Nell's statement true.

The Ghawazees were a sort of Gypsies, but this particular dancing-girl was not that kind of a Gypsy; but a real Gypsy; a Gypsy from the land of the Pharaohs; just as Nell and Magruder and the others of the Gypsy encampment were Gypsies from England. A Gypsy is a Gypsy the world over, and the widely-separated bands, usually speaking a Gypsy patois, consider themselves blood of one blood, and are constant in their declarations that "blood is thicker than water."

Hence the friendship that had grown up between the Ghawazee and Magruder, which was ripening, or had ripened, into love. This explained how Zel might have been able to induce her to visit Daisy and steal away the knife.

Chicago Charlie

There were other proofs that Zel Magruder was the murderer of John Malcomb. Magruder was a member of the Lakeside League, the band owing allegiance to Solon Youngblood. This band had been systematically bleeding Selwyn Fisher.

John Malcomb had assisted in this bleeding process, as the detective could not doubt. Chicago Charlie was even not sure that John Malcomb had not been a member of the Lakeside League, though he was naturally loth to think it.

At any rate, his shadowings had made him aware of the fact that Malcomb, if killed by Magruder, had been killed by the instigation of the band—or at the instigation of Solon Youngblood. For he had come on proof showing that Malcomb had declared he would assist in bleeding the Englishman no longer, and that, if the thing was not stopped, he would warn Fisher of how he was being daily and nightly robbed.

Chicago Charlie did not know if a twinge of conscience had made John Malcomb take this stand, or whether there had been some other reason. He had only stumbled on the main fact by overhearing a talk between Youngblood and one of the Leaguers.

The inference was natural, he thought, that Youngblood, not wishing to have such a "sucker" as Selwyn Fisher slip through his fingers, and probably enraged at Malcomb, had sought Malcomb's death, and induced Magruder to become the active instrument.

Once or twice already, Chicago Charlie had been on the point of placing Magruder under arrest for the murder; and no doubt would have done so had not the disappearance of Daisy come to turn his thoughts into a new channel.

The evidences that Malcomb had been murdered by Zel Magruder were strong;—but what did they weigh, if the form now twice seen were Malcomb's?

If Malcomb was alive, then he had not been killed, Zel Magruder was not his murderer; the Ghawazee had not stolen the knife with the intention ascribed!

Chicago Charlie's head seemed to spin round, as he strove to follow the conclusions to their logical ending:

There had been no dead man lying in a pool of blood in that office; Daisy was not fatherless; John Malcomb had not been buried; there was no bloody knife; there had been no bloody writing on the wall!

He clutched the rail to steady himself. If he could not believe these things, which he had seen with his own eyes, and which so many others had seen, what could he believe? He could not believe in his own identity!

Not only did he clutch the rail, but he put one hand to his head, and stared at the waves, a low cry at the same time breaking from his lips.

A boat had shot out from the land and was gliding along the wharf.

In that boat was the form seen on two previous occasions—the form of John Malcomb.

His low cry and startling attitude attracted the attention of a sailor.

"What is it, mate?" was the sympathetic question.

"There! There! Do you not see that!" the detective cried, his agitation so intense that his words trembled.

The words had swept beyond the limits of the vessel, and might possibly have been heard by the occupant of the boat.

There was a smaller craft lying between the Andrew Johnson and the main shore, and into the shadow of this craft the boat swung, vanishing before the sailor got a really good view of it.

"Will you have a boat lowered?" Chicago Charlie requested. "I must see who that was. Lower away a boat quick! For God sake, make haste!"

It was known by all that the detective was on board as the confidential guest and friend of the captain; therefore, when this appeal was shrieked at them, the sailor and his companions lowered a boat, leaping into it at once and grasping the oars.

The excited detective was not a moment behind them; and under his commands, they pulled out for the point where the other boat had been seen to disappear.

But when the place had been gained, nothing was to be seen. The little boat and its occupant had vanished.

Satisfied that he must be somewhere in the vicinity, Chicago Charlie urged a thorough search, but, when it was made, the crew had to confess themselves beaten.

Neither boat nor man could be found.

Chicago Charlie

CHAPTER XXXI.

A STIRRING CHASE.

LIKE A BIRD OF PREY hovering on the crest of the waves, lay the Andy Johnson.

She was far out in the lake, on the path which it was hoped would be taken by the smuggler.

All were alert on board the Andy Johnson, though no lights gleamed. The men were at their places; the small brass guns had been run out; and every preparation made for a chase or a fight.

A chase was what was anticipated, should the smuggler be sighted, for it was not believed the latter would make much resistance.

Yet there were very few on board who believed the night would bring anything but disappointment. To many it seemed the wildest of wild-goose chases. Zel Magruder, who was said to be going to warn the smugglers and convey them information, had been seen to sail in that direction; and had been watched by the newsboy until lost to sight nearly a mile from land.

But what did that indicate? The straight sail out into the lake might have been but a ruse. The information that Zel was going to meet the smugglers might even have been false!

Nevertheless, the well-trained crew stood at their places, ready to obey the commands of their officers.

Though the night was dark it was star-lit.

Captain Stebbins, pacing to and fro uneasily, stopped every few seconds and swept the surface of the lake with his glass.

The fires had been banked, but were ready to be stirred into life in an instant. Therefore, no smoke came from the funnel of the revenue vessel to stream out like a warning flag.

There were probably none on board so excited as Chicago Charlie and his boy second. The capture of the smuggler meant much to them. To Chicago Charlie it probably meant the rescue of Daisy Malcomb, and the unraveling of the whole chain of mysteries surrounding her and her father.

A warning command came from Captain Stebbins. He had seen something—some sloop or ship—though just what, he was not yet ready to say.

A tightening of mental tension might have been observable in all the crew. Still, scarcely any one moved.

"It is a sloop," the captain declared, whispering to his second in command.

Then he passed the glass to the man for a verification of the discovery.

The vessel was seen to be bowling along easily. She carried an immense spread of canvas; but, stood well up to the work, showing that she was stanch and dry, as well as a fast sailer.

Information of the characteristics of the sloop went quickly round, whispered from mouth to mouth. All hoped the vessel might prove to be the smuggler.

It was plain the revenue cutter, lying low in the water and having a black and indistinct outline, had not been seen by the stranger.

The fires were unbanked and the steamer moved forward, but at reduced speed.

If the sloop were a smuggler, the fact would now soon be made manifest.

It was made manifest in a very few minutes.

Captain Stebbins, watching her closely and suspiciously, discerned evidence of excitement on board of her, as soon as the black streamer of smoke from the steamer became visible to the sloop's officers and crew.

Still, the sloop held on her way for a time, probably thinking the Andy Johnson might be only a peaceful merchantman.

Then she was observed to alter her course.

This was interpreted as an expression of caution, and even of fear; it being reasoned by the captain and officers that the sloop had changed its tack to make the steamer show her character. If the steamer was a revenue vessel, a chase would ensue, or at any rate she would tack to intercept the sloop.

"We'll make her uncover!" the captain grimly announced.

Then the course of the Andy Johnson was altered a couple of points; and, when the sloop was seen to bear still further away, one of the bright brass guns bellowed out its compliments, commanding her to lie to.

Instead of doing this, the sloop was observed to be crowding on more canvas, and to be bearing further and further away.

There could be no doubt now, of her character, no doubt she was the smuggler Zel Magruder had set out to warn; no doubt that she believed the steamer to be a vessel of the revenue service!

The excitement on board the Andy Johnson leaped at a bound to fever pitch. Every eye was strained across the starlit spaces,

Chicago Charlie

every heart beat in anticipation, every nerve was tense and tingling; yet each man stood obediently in his place, awaiting the time for action.

Chicago Charlie and Billy Stubbs stood near the captain's side, in the forward part of the vessel. Chicago Charlie was painfully calm; Billy Stubbs wildly exuberant.

"Will we git 'er!" Billy whispered, as the steamer was felt to forge swiftly through the water, under the propulsion of her powerful engines. "D'ye reckon we'll git her?"

As he said it, he danced up and down, glancing at the detective and at the lake, unmindful, much of the time, that many of his numerous questions remained unanswered.

The steamer was now moving at great speed—and she was accounted a fast vessel—but rapidly as she moved, it was noticeable that she gained very little on the sloop.

The latter, with its immense spread of canvas, was proving herself a remarkable sailer. She looked not unlike an immense sea gull, or white-winged night bird, as she glided on over the slightly-ruffled bosom of the lake. The breeze was stiff enough to fill her sails, but not sufficiently so to make her heel over, and thus she stood well up under every stitch of canvas that could be set.

The steamer's fires were fed until they roared like small infernos, and the smoke streaming from her funnel was thick and black as soot. The ponderous engines racked her from stem to stern; and at every quivering stroke she seemed to leap through the sea; but her utmost energies did not serve to lessen the distance between the vessels.

The sloop was holding straight up the lake, with the wind astern; and, having several hundred miles of good sailing ground before her, it was evident the chase was not soon to end.

Chicago Charlie looked grave, and Captain Stebbin's usually good-humored face harbored a most fierce-visaged scowl. Affairs were not progressing to suit either.

"Do you think we'll git 'er?" Billy again asked, pulling at the detective's hand.

"That depends!" and Chicago Charlie deigned for the moment to look down on the boy. "If something breaks on board the sloop and nothing on the steamer, or if the wind comes up so the sloop can't carry so much sail; or—we'll git 'er, if we git 'er! That's as much as I can tell you!"

Billy Stubbs needed no plainer answer to tell him that the

chances of overhauling the sloop were of the slenderest.

Still, the fires were fed, the engines kept at full speed, and the men remained at their posts.

Now and then a gun was fired, in the vain hope of striking the spars or cordage of the sloop and crippling her.

"She's the witch of the lake!" Stebbins averred, speaking to the detective. "See how she shows us her heels!"

The words were those of admiration, for Stebbins was an enthusiast on the score of fast sailing.

"See her walk along! Do you know, Clingstone! I'd give a pile of money to be able to own that sloop? She's as fast as they make 'em, and she's a beauty!"

He took up the glass again and scanned the sloop carefully, noting the details of her construction and rigging.

Then he began to fret and fume, consumed by his inability to overtake her.

"Confound it, the Government never gives us anything faster than a tug-boat. It's a shame!"

The chance that Chicago Charlie hoped for did not come. Nothing broke on the sloop, nor did the wind arise sufficiently to make her shorten sail. Within an hour she had left the steamer away behind; and in another hour the captain's glass could nowhere reveal her.

The stirring chase had ended in signal failure.

CHAPTER XXXII.

THE FIGHT IN THE FERRIS WHEEL.

JACK RACKSTRAW, disconsolate, with no friends or acquaintance anywhere discoverable, found himself in front of the ungainly monstrosity known as the Ferris Wheel. He had sought everywhere for Billy Stubbs and Chicago Charlie; he had sought everywhere for some of the sailors from the Andy Johnson. The Andy Johnson was not in position at the wharf, and no one could tell him whither she had gone.

"Beats all!" he avowed, speaking, perhaps, to the wheel, for he

Chicago Charlie

was looking at it. He was not referring to the wheel, however; though a bystander might have thought so.

The Ferris Wheel, from which a bird's-eye view may be had of the entire Exposition, is somewhat to the Columbian World's Fair what the Eiffel Tower was to that of Paris. Visitors are carried two hundred and sixty feet into the air, in cars similar to railway coaches in construction.

Jack Rackstraw had no special desire to go whirling round on this great pin-wheel, but a lack of something else to do caused him to enter one of the cars. It was at the time unoccupied.

Two ladies soon came in, however, and after them a gentleman. Rackstraw scarcely perceived them, for he was looking down Midway Plaisance. Had he but glanced at the man, his interest in his fellow passengers might have quickened.

The great wheel began to revolve. Still, Rackstraw paid no heed to the trio, but looked out on the queer buildings and queerer people of Midway.

Up, up they went, seemingly into the clouds, until the whole region round about unfolded itself like a map.

Rackstraw uttered an exclamation of admiration.

Instantly the man bent on him a glance, which was dull and unquestioning at first, but which speedily kindled into rage.

The man was the Englishman, Selwyn Fisher.

Fisher had evidently been making a fool of himself in more ways than one. Excessive drink had made his eyes stupid and heavy, as well as blood-shot, and his puffy cheeks were puffier than ever; while his rotundity had enormously increased. He seemed even then suffering from a too free indulgence in spirits, or from alcoholism. His hands shook, his gaze was uncertain and wavering, and his suddenly-kindled anger had in it something suggestive of delirium tremens.

Rackstraw was giving him no heed, and only looked up when a cry from one of the women came as a warning.

Fisher had arisen unsteadily, pitched across the car like a boat reeling under the influence of the sea, and now made a dash at Rackstraw with a keen knife.

"Whatever are you up to?" Rackstraw demanded, warding off the blow and getting on his feet.

"Hi knew you, you 'ound!" the Englishman gurgled, again lifting the knife. "You 'ave followed me henough, Hi tell you!"

It was plain he recognized Rackstraw, and believed him to be an enemy; though at first Rackstraw did not know who the

Englishman was, so greatly had the latter changed.

"You mean to 'ave me harrested, do you?" lunging with the knife. "You think me ha murderer, do you? Hi will be, Hi tell you, before Hi'm through!"

"Stand off, you scoundrel!" the sailor roared, again brushing aside the knife and giving the Englishman a stinging blow. "Stand off, or I'll knock you out of the car!"

The women had sprung up in fright and were screaming.

It was an exciting and novel situation; this fight in the car of the Ferris Wheel, more than two hundred feet above the earth.

The screams of the women were heard on the ground below, and drew all eyes upward. The fact that such a fight was in progress seemed to become instantly known, for a surging crowd of excited humanity collected on the moment.

With his ardor in nowise dampened by Rackstraw's stinging blow, which had purpled one of his cheeks, Fisher again lifted the knife, swaying most unsteadily.

At this the sailor's blood came up.

"Take that, will you!" he said, delivering another right-hander.

Then, clutching the knife hand of his assailant, the two came to the floor in a struggling heap.

The Englishman fought like a tiger, striving again and again to free the hand and deliver a blow with the knife; and for a time it was as much as Rackstraw could do to keep him from accomplishing this purpose.

The crowd below was roaring out its excitement; and the women, cowering in one end of the car, were uttering little, terrified screams.

All the while the car was descending, with its even, unjolting motion.

Getting a firm clasp of Fisher's massive throat, Rackstraw crushed it with his powerful grip, until the waving knife-hand ceased its eccentric and threatening movement, and the Englishman's face began to change from purple to bluish black.

"You infernal scoundrel!" Rackstraw hissed, taking a good look at the discolored face and recognizing the man. "I ought to kill you fer that!"

The fight seemed to have developed in him an unexpected ferocity. Usually kindhearted, he appeared to have been changed by this encounter into a man of tigerish inclinations.

He drew Fisher half erect, by an immense exertion of muscu-

Chicago Charlie

lar power, and held him thus for a moment, as if he contemplated hurling him through the nearest window.

Then his grasp relaxed and his face brightened. He let the limp form slip to the floor.

"Bah, I'm a fool! You did make me most thunderin' mad, though. What in the dickens did ye mean by jumpin' onto me that way? I've never been botherin' you!"

A reply was not expected, for Fisher was too nearly senseless to make any.

Then the car reached the earth, the crowd surged forward, and Rackstraw turned toward a police officer, who had elbowed his way in.

One of the women had fainted.

"Have some one take care of her," Rackstraw requested. "Then, I'm ready to go with you. Hain't done nothin' that I'm ashamed of. That feller jumped onto me with a knife. I wouldn't let him stick me. That's all!"

Other policemen advanced, and Rackstraw left the car in charge of one of them.

With some difficulty Fisher was helped out, and placed in an ambulance. Then a Columbian Guide sprung away to clear a path for the ambulance, whose warning gong was already sounding; and almost before Selwyn Fisher knew what had occurred he was lying on one of the clean, white beds in the hospital substation on Midway Plaisance.

On examination he was found to have no injuries of a serious character, though the severe choking had left him temporarily helpless.

When dismissed from the hospital, which dismissal occurred about half an hour later, he found himself under arrest for his attempt on the life of Jack Rackstraw, and was borne away to a police station.

There Rackstraw, who had followed, again met him.

Rackstraw was anxious to get at the reason of his strange conduct; and was not a little mystified when Fisher raved out, almost as soon as his eyes fell on the sailor's face:

"Why 'ave you sent me 'ere? Hi did not kill John Malcomb! Hi'm an innocent man, sir!"

"Who in Jeremiah ever said you did kill him!" Rackstraw demanded.

The sailor knew of John Malcomb's murder, certainly, but he had not been made acquainted with all the developments of

Chicago Charlie's shadowing.

"Why ham Hi 'ere then, sir! Hi tell you Hi'm innocent! Why 'ave you been 'ounding me?"

His excitement grew every moment; until Rackstraw saw that, if the conversation was continued, another fight would be precipitated.

"Crazy as a loon!" was his comment.

Then he turned away, considerably puzzled, and with mingled feelings of pity and disgust.

It was plain to him that Fisher was on the borderland of that terrible form of insanity induced by alcoholic indulgence.

CHAPTER XXXIII.

RACKSTRAW IN THE TOILS OF CUPID.

CHICAGO CHARLIE WALKED with earnest tread along the street toward the kindergarten establishment, kept now by Miss Lilly Lilac. He anxiously desired to see Jack Rackstraw, and he thought that the place where the sailor was most likely to be found.

The Andy Johnson had returned from its short and unsuccessful cruise; and Billy Stubbs had been again assigned the task of shadowing the wily Gypsy, Zel Magruder.

The mystery of the murder of John Malcomb—if he had been murdered!—and the disappearance of Daisy, oppressed Chicago Charlie like an unpleasant dream.

Just now he was thinking of the statement of Gypsy Nell, that somewhere on the Michigan shore the smugglers had established a "den."

If that den could be found, these mysteries might be laid bare. Could it be found? No doubt it was in a secluded and hidden place, not easily discoverable, and seldom visited by man. Rackstraw was familiar with the shores of the great lake. Possibly Rackstraw could assist in determining its location.

This was the thought impelling the detective, as he strode up the street.

Chicago Charlie

But no thought was further, at that moment, from the mind of Jack Rackstraw.

Rackstraw had been caught in the toils of Cupid. He was a lover, "sighing like furnace." Sitting on a small drygoods box, which Miss Lilly had covered with a crazy-patchwork cushion, he awkwardly caressed his chin with the fingers of his right hand, and stared first at the girl and then at the Infant Wonder.

The children had long departed for their respective homes; or, rather, each individual mother or elder sister had come for the child in which she was most interested and had borne it away, made happy by the fact that the day's toil was ended and that *that* particular Infant Wonder was to gladden the little room or cottage through the quickly-speeding hours of the night.

All had been pleased that Mrs. Tonguegrass had gone out and Miss Lilly Lilac had come in, for there was as much difference in the two women as there is between the taste of acid cider and the pleasant sweet of an orange. Miss Lilac was held in great favor by the children and the patrons of this institution.

Perhaps no one thought more of her than did the Infant Wonder, or took more pains to show it than he, except—Jack Rackstraw.

Miss Lilly called him the biggest baby of the lot; and it must be confessed that if Rackstraw could have had his way, and had not been ashamed to do so infantile a thing, he would probably have enrolled himself as one of the Infant Wonders and remained there as many hours out of each twenty-four as the rules of the institution allowed.

Truly, Jack Rackstraw was in the toils of Cupid.

"I say, Miss Lilly, you wouldn't want to adopt twins, now?" and Rackstraw made a grab at the Infant Wonder and drew him to his side. "Hyer's two of us, and we're a hand to draw to. The knave and the king! Hain't it a strong hand? Well, if it ain't, you won't lose anything in a game of hearts. What do you say?"

Rackstraw was getting his references slightly mixed, perhaps; but he was sure Miss Lilly could not misunderstand him.

"I reckon you're the knave, Jack Rackstraw," and the girl jabbed the needle into the sewing in a vicious manner.

Rackstraw laughed.

"Likely I am. I'm willin' to be most anything, Miss Lilly, and will call myself anything in the world if—"

He looked at her shyly.

"If what?"

He seemed to hesitate about replying, and churned the Infant Wonder up and down in a vigorous manner, probably to hide the flush that had come unbidden to his tanned cheeks.

Miss Lilly gave the sewing another savage stab.

"If you'd only call me— Oh, dod rot it! of course you wouldn't!—if you'd only call me—*husband*?"

Miss Lilly laughed outright, for Rackstraw had squeaked the important word in a most awful and suggestive manner. Not only did Miss Lilly laugh, but Miss Lilly blushed redder than the reddest rose.

What she might have answered may not be known; for, at that moment, a step was heard mounting the stair; and Miss Lilly, blushing furiously, quickly caught up her sewing; and Rackstraw, lifting the Infant Wonder high in the air, began to waltz crazily about the room.

Then there came a knock on the door; and when Miss Lilly, striving vainly to hide a very red and suspicious-looking face, opened it, the Columbian Detective stood on the threshold.

If Chicago Charlie suspected anything of the real state of the case—and it is very likely that he did—he managed very well to hide the suspicion. Indeed, his words and manner were so natural that Miss Lilly soon forgot her blushes, and Rackstraw ceased his waltzing and put down the Infant Wonder to hear what the Columbian Detective might have to say.

"You should have been with us last night," Chicago Charlie began, accepting the chair Miss Lilly placed for him, and directing his words to Rackstraw. "We had a lively chase after a vessel of the Leaguers. But she cleared out, leaving us badly. It is thought the smugglers have a den in a cove somewhere on the Michigan shore."

The statements were of a character to make Rackstraw almost forget the disappointment he had felt at the coming of Chicago Charlie. He could say those words to Miss Lilly Lilac again—and he resolved he would at the first opportunity—and keep saying them until he had received an answer—an affirmative answer.

"We were sorry you were not alone, but we couldn't find you!"

Then Chicago Charlie rehearsed the saying of Gypsy Nell concerning Zel Magruder and the den of the smugglers. He also told of the ghostly manifestations, and of how he was puzzled by them.

Rackstraw could throw no light on this latter mystery; neither could Lilly Lilac, who trembled at the merest mention of ghosts.

"As to that there cove or den I 'low I know jist where it is! At least, I know of several sich places, any of which could be used in that way. I've calculated all along that Youngblood's fellers were bringin' them things from north'ards; but they could bring 'em from Michigan jist as well, likely. Likely easier; though they'd have to carry 'em acrost the peninsula—an' that's a thing I shouldn't think they'd want to do. Perhaps they believe it's the safest way. 'Tany rate, I kin take ye to them coves, or I kin pilot the vessel to 'em. Which way was the sloop holdin' when ye seen her last?"

Chicago Charlie gave him the desired information, or as nearly as he could.

"I thought she might 'a' took the back track, but she didn't! The coves don't lay that away."

Miss Lilly jumped again, being still nervous from the start given them by the Columbian Detective. Another footstep was heard coming up the stairs!

CHAPTER XXXIV.

THE FLASHING OF A RING.

BILLY STUBBS WAS AGAIN SPRAWLED in the shadows of the buildings of the Cairo Street.

But a few feet away, and dimly revealed by the light from an electric lamp, sat Zel Magruder and the Ghawazee.

He had seen them come out of one of the buildings, and had succeeded in diving into the shadows in time to escape discovery.

Much of their conversation was carried on in a Gypsy *patois*, difficult of speech for both. Zel was more familiar with English, the language of the country of his nativity and of his adoption, and the dancing-girl spoke better than any other the dialect of the land of the Pyramids and the Sphinx. Hence they occasionally, because it pleased Zel to do so, dropped into English;— which was much to Billy's delight, for the boy felt that if they kept up their "gibberish," as he called it, he would be no wiser when he went away than when he came.

"Unless you can go with me I will have to leave you, Malma!" he heard the Gypsy say, in squeaky tones that were intended to be affectionate. "I have got to leave the city!"

Her reply was a carcass of pleading tenderness.

"I have got to 'git up and git'! as they say in this country."

"Why shall you leaf me?" was the inquiry.

"Well, hang it, Malma! you'd ought to know. That John Malcomb job, for one thing!"

Billy Stubbs, watching with the keen sight of a rat, thought he observed a shudder convulse her.

"They've been after me for that, all the while, as I've told you!" Zel went on. "And have made it confounded unpleasant for me, too, I can tell you. These off'cers air regular bloodhounds, when they git to trackin' a feller. They're purty shore to pull me for *that*, one of these fine days, if I don't cut out. So you see, I've got to go.

"I hate to leave Chicago most mightily, while the World's Fair is on and there's scads o' money to be made, but it ain't my choosin'!"

"Oh! eef you had not that doan!" she murmured. "I warn you, you know. I to you say, you know: Eef you-a that man keel, you will-a have what you call?—trooble. That what I say."

"How many more times you goin' to tell me that, Malma?" Zel growled. "You're 'most as bad as Nell. I 'low I was a fool for doin' a job of that kind; but it's done, now, an' can't be undone.

"That ain't the only thing, though, that's going to make me leave Chicago. I've been spotted in'that other business. That infernal boy—blast 'im—has been after me again! He must 'a' tracked me out into the lake last night; though I thought I'd shorely throwed him off my track, when I took that cat-boat of Westover's, what I'd never used before.

"But he spotted the cat-boat, just as he had done the others, and he put the off'cers onto my little game. Consequence was, they come mighty nigh scoopin' in the sloop. Curse him, anyway! And now the boss says I'd better clear out fer awhile.

"The boss is skeered, you see, and he's afeared to have me hangin' 'round any more. I used to be the mascot of the gang; now it seems I'm the Jony! Hang it all, anyway!"

The Ghawazee was much impressed by this account, and by Zel's manifest danger; and she was not backward in showing the fact. And Zel, pleased by this exhibition of affection, continued

Chicago Charlie

in the same tone:

"Yes, I've got to cut out; an' what I'm worryin' 'bout most, is the leavin' of you. Some o' these here Columbian guides or guards will be waitin' to run off with you, I'm afeared."

"Does my little crocodile loaf hees dancin' girl?" she playfully asked, tapping his whiskerless cheeks. "Does he loaf her eez I loaf the Nile?"

"You may bet that I jist do!" Zel averred.

Never before had he succeeded in gaining the heart of any member of the gentler sex, and it tickled him immensely. All previous attempts in that direction, and they had not been few, had been scornfully regarded, because of his scant stature and womanish appearance.

"You jist bet I do, my red rose of Egypt!" he avowed. "There ain't any girl in this whole Chicago that I'd turn my finger over to get, exceptin' of you!"

Zel was slightly treading on the domains of falsehood, in making this sweeping statement, for there was more than one girl in Chicago on whom he had looked with adoring eyes, and who, by a slight nod, might have brought him to her feet. But Zel had never regarded the truth highly, when a lie served him better.

"I love you well enough, to want you to go with me, when I cut out o' here!" he asserted. "Do you think you—"

The rest of the sentence was spoiled for Billy by Zel's attempt to snatch a kiss.

The question and reply must have been eminently satisfactory, however, for a moment later Billy Stubbs saw him produce an odd-looking ring and slip it on the girl's finger.

Billy's eyes opened wide with renewed interest. He knew he had seen that ring, or its counterpart; but for the moment he could not recall where.

The Ghawazee looked pleasedly at the shining bauble, turning it round and round on her finger to the better admire its beauty.

It was a handsome ring, of queer design. Of engraven gold, it held two clasped hands upbearing a broken heart. In the center of the heart, like a drop of blood, was a ruby. In addition, the ring was massive and suggestive of oriental workmanship.

Where had he seen that ring?

Again and again the question came to torment the boy, as he listened to the further talk of the lovers.

"That means that you will go with me!" said Magruder, bending on her a tender look. "That's what it means, don't it? You may bet I want you to bad enough!"

"Where the Ghawazee's heart is, she will-a there go!" the girl asserted, with burning cheeks and bright eyes. "With her crocodile she will-a go!"

"That'll be our weddin' ring!" said Zel, beamingly. "I do'no' who the bu'sted heart b'longs to, but yourn and mine'll be the clasped hands."

Like a flash came to Billy Stubbs the recollection of where and under what circumstances he had seen that ring—no, no! not that ring—he was sure it could not be the same; but another like it, which was its mate.

Daisy Malcomb had had such a ring, and John Malcomb another.

He had seen Daisy wearing her ring once, when he had been sent to her home with a note by the Columbian Detective; and its queer design had then impressed him. But in the excitement of more recent things he had forgotten all about it.

He had casually spoken of this ring to the detective; and then Chicago Charlie had told that there was another like it, that belonged to Daisy's father, but which was missing when Malcomb was found dead.

Had this ring, now on the Ghawazee's finger, been taken from the hand of John Malcomb or from that of his daughter?

Daisy, according to Gypsy Nell's statement, was now held by the Leaguers. Being one of them, might not Zel Magruder have taken or stolen it from her?

Billy Stubbs had long believed that Zel Magruder was John Malcomb's murderer.

The ring that had been on Malcomb's finger almost constantly for many months previous to his death had not been there on the morning of the discovery of the murder. What had become of it? Who had taken it?

The more Billy Stubbs thought it over, the stronger grew his belief that the ring which the dancing-girl was admiring was the one that had belonged to Malcomb;—and with this came the added certainty that Zel Magruder was Malcomb's slayer.

"I've got to git to Chicago Charlie with this hyer little item!" Billy told himself, anxious now to be up and gone. "If he could ketch 'em with that ring, it'd be a stunner! I wish't Magruder would git a move on him!"

Chicago Charlie

CHAPTER XXXV.

CROWDED INTO A CORNER.

THE FOOTSTEP ON THE STAIRWAY, which so startled Lilly Lilac, was that of Billy Stubbs.

Zel Magruder had failed to "get a move on him;" but Billy Stubbs, unwilling to remain longer in the Cairo Street, had succeeded in extricating himself without alarming the Gypsy lovers. He had not done it without difficulty, nor without much sly crawling and creeping; but he had accomplished it, and now he was searching for Chicago Charlie.

When admitted into the room, his eyes were shining with excitement and it was very evident he had a story to tell.

He told it quickly; and there was an immediate adjournment of the meeting in that upper room of the kindergarten establishment. Lilly Lilac and the Infant Wonder remained; and Chicago Charlie, Jack Rackstraw and Billy Stubbs hastened into the street, and as fast as steam would carry them toward the Columbian Exposition.

On reaching the grounds, a number of police officers were collected, and the Cairo Street was entered for the purpose of placing Zel Magruder and the Ghawazee under arrest—the belief and hope being that a confession would be thus forced from one or both of them.

But when the Cairo Street was entered, the birds were found to have flown.

"To the Gypsy camp!" said Chicago Charlie, turning back into Midway and walking toward the nearest exit gate. "Perhaps we may find them there."

It was plain that Magruder had induced the girl to leave her employers and go with him in his flight from the city. Still, there was a chance that they might be found in the Gypsy tent. Zel would probably wish to visit that place before taking a final departure.

The Gypsy camp was approached with great caution, though

they found it too large and spread over too much territory for the successful accomplishment of their plans. Chicago Charlie had not a sufficient number of men with him to throw a cordon completely around it.

However, at the suggestion of Billy Stubbs, they approached the tents in the vicinity of the one occupied by Gypsy Nell, for in that neighborhood Magruder had always been found by the boy.

The plan worked to perfection; for Zel Magruder and Malma Nareen, the Ghawazee, were found in the tent of the Gypsy crone, engaged with her in earnest conversation.

Now and then Magruder stopped his talk and made search for some articles, which Malma was tying up in a bundle for him.

The Columbian Detective instructed some of the officers to pass to the rear of the tent for the purpose of preventing Zel's escape in that direction; but in executing this movement, Magruder, whose ears were of the keenest, heard them.

Like a flash he leaped to the half-finished bundle, and, seizing it, threw up the tent canvas and bounded out into the night; leaving Malma Nareen and Gypsy Nell bewilderedly staring.

His exclamation had been:

"Scat! I've got to slide!"

Instantly a revolver cracked in the darkness without, startling the women still more.

But Zel Magruder had sped on unharmed; and, in spite of the utmost exertions of the officers, he succeeded in making his escape.

Malma Nareen, much excited and alarmed, was also on the point of flying from the tent, when she was confronted by a number of blue-coated men, who were headed by Chicago Charlie.

She dropped back with a gasp, to the straw seat on which she had been sitting, and her eyes took on a hunted look.

Gypsy Nell turned about with a smile that was hard to fathom.

"Blood of the Gypsy blood!" she cackled, bending a glance on Billy Stubbs. "And blood is—is it thicker than water? That's what the Gypsies say!"

She nodded and smiled and courtesied; and, beckoning to the men, said blandly:

"I do not often have the honor of seeing so many gentlemen come to have their fortunes told. One, two, three, four—" running her eyes over them—"how many dollars will it be to me, anyway? Fifty cents apiece, gentlemen! Fifty cents apiece, for a true, good fortune!"

Her face was wrinkling and puckering, and she continued to courtesy in a most obsequious manner.

"She's a witch!" thought Billy Stubbs.

And, as if she had caught the thought, she declared:

"I'm a witch, gentlemen. The modern Witch of Endor! What is it you would have me show you? Would you see the past, or the dead of the past? Or, do you prefer the future?"

The Ghawazee was twisting and fidgeting uneasily, and edging toward the wall as if she contemplated making a dash for liberty; and Chicago Charlie interrupted the words of Gypsy Nell by pushing hurriedly forward.

"We must place this young lady under arrest," he observed, stepping in front of Malma Nareen and thus interposing to prevent her escape. "We think she will be needed."

At this the dancing-girl sunk down in a cowering heap. At first her attitude had been that of fright, but holding a crouching and subdued fierceness. Now this was changed. The fierceness was swept away by hysterical sobs.

The Columbian Detective stretched out a hand as if he would take her by the arm.

"No! No!" she shrieked, drawing back.

Gypsy Nell cackled aloud.

"Do not harm her, gentlemen. Her heart is like water. It is as soft as that of her beloved crocodile."

There was something so gloating in the words that Chicago Charlie could not but look at the old woman, wondering what she meant.

"We do not intend to harm her," the detective avowed. "We only want to know the truth. If she will tell us what she knows, in answer to our questions, perhaps we will let her go."

The Ghawazee had put up her hands beseechingly, and her attitude and evident distress were extremely touching.

"We don't intend to hurt you," the Columbian Detective reassured. "All you need to do is to answer our questions. What has become of Zel Magruder?"

"I doan' know!" she asserted. "He leaf me!"

"You were going away together?"

She nodded.

"Why?"

"I doan' know."

"But you do know! This boy—" indicating Billy Stubbs—"heard you and him talking to-night, in the Cairo Street. So, you see, there is no use to deny anything; and we'll get along better if you'll just speak the truth.

"Why did Zel Magruder kill John Malcomb?"

This was a random shot, fired at a venture.

Immediately the girl began to cry.

"I doan' know!" she wailed. "I doan' know!"

"Then he killed John Malcomb?"

She did not instantly reply.

Chicago Charlie repeated the inquiry.

"He-a—what you call?—stab-a heem with the knife!"

A look of triumph came to Chicago Charlie's face. This was a confession of moment.

"Where did he get that knife?"

Again she shook with convulsive sobs.

"Oh, I doan' know! I doan' know!"

Chicago Charlie repeated the question, with considerable sternness. He thought he could see why the girl should fear to implicate herself.

"I-a geet it for heem!"

"Ah! you got it for him! Where did you get it? Tell me all about it. It will be the better for you. You needn't fear to tell us."

Still she hesitated.

"Whose knife was it?"

"A woman's knife!"

"Whose?"

"I-a doan' re'lect the-a name."

"Did you not get the knife from a girl whose fortune you told?"

She nodded an assent.

"And you went there, pretending to want to tell her fortune, for that purpose?"

Again the Ghawazee indicated an affirmative.

Gypsy Nell was bending intently forward, one of the most interested of the listeners.

Then, bit by bit, Chicago Charlie forced the confession from the cowering Ghawazee.

It was as he had thought. She had gone to the house of John Malcomb, at the instigation of Zel Magruder, and had there purloined Daisy Malcomb's knife for the bloody deed which Zel purposed to commit.

Chicago Charlie

The dancing-girl was constant in her declarations, however, that she did not know what Magruder wanted to do with the knife, until afterward, or she would not have stolen it for him. She asserted that he had said he wanted it because it was of great value and had been the property of a friend; that he could not purchase it, and that she must thus get it for him.

She had found it lying on the table in Daisy's room, and had abstracted it without difficulty, while Daisy was absorbed in the fortune that was being told her.

Afterward, when it was too late to recall the act, Zel had shown her an account of the murder in the papers, and had confessed to her that he had committed the murder with that knife; to the Ghawazee's great fear and horror, as she averred.

"Where did you get that ring?" the Columbian Detective suddenly questioned, pointing to the ring that glittered on the girl's finger. "It is the ring of the murdered man!"

Instantly Malma Nareen slipped it off and gave it to him.

"Take eet!" she gasped. "I-a vear eet no longer."

She glanced at the ruby and shuddered. Perhaps it was too suggestive of blood—blood murderously spilled.

She was crying again most bitterly; and Chicago Charlie, chancing to look round, saw that Gypsy Nell was rocking herself to and fro in seeming high glee.

The actions of the crone puzzled him, even though he had heard so much from Billy Stubbs concerning her odd character and oddity of manner. He was forced to the conclusion that the occurrences of that hour were extremely pleasing to Nell; and he determined to apply to her the inquisitorial pump, as soon as he found time.

Then he turned back to the Ghawazee, and once more plied her with apparently endless questions.

He found, however, that he had already extracted almost all she knew. She knew very little of the Leaguers, and nothing at all of the location of the den on the Michigan shore. She was in a manner, acquainted with Solon Youngblood, regarding him as Zel's best friend; and had taken the trouble to warn him of peril, whenever she could; and had transmitted messages between him and her lover, for which they had come to the Cairo Street.

But all this did not implicate her in the many crimes committed by the Lakeside League. She had been used as a tool, it was clear; but seemingly as an ignorant tool.

However, Chicago Charlie thought it the part of wisdom to

detain her for a further hearing; and placed her in charge of an officer; while he sought to obtain some information from the croaking old Gypsy woman.

The officer was not as alert as he should have been.

He turned to converse with another for a moment, and walked toward the door of the tent.

It was the opportunity long sought by the Ghawazee.

She lifted the flap of the tent, and was outside and speeding away in the darkness, before a hand could be raised to detain her.

CHAPTER XXXVI.

THE INFANT WONDER HAS AN ADVENTURE.

"I DO'NO' AS I'LL GIT BACK," Jack Rackstraw solemnly averred, looking earnestly at Lilly Lilac. "So, if you'd only answer that question I asked you last night?"

Miss Lilly's face, which had been covered alternately with smiles and blushes, darkened with anxiety.

"What do you mean Jack?" she asked.

"Hain't I told ye? I've been runnin' on so, blamed if I know what I have said. Thought I mentioned it, while I was a-tellin' of what happened down at the Gypsies' camp last night!"

They were in the same upper room of the kindergarten, but the time was a night later than that which saw them together there last.

The Infant Wonder, neglected by his sailor crony, was playing near the door that opened on the stairway, building houses out of blocks and knocking them down again in great glee; thus working to as little purpose as some men. But it brought him pleasure, which cannot always be said of the men.

"What do you mean by saying you don't know that you'll get back? Where are you going?" Miss Lilly anxiously inquired.

"That's jist what I was tryin' to explain. You see, the Andy Johnson has been ordered on a cruise, and sails exactly at midnight. Likely there'll be a fight before the cruise is over. Captain Stebbins don't want to put out till that time, because he's

Chicago Charlie

afeared of the spies of the Leaguers. He thinks he can make a sneak of it about midnight, and git out without bein' seen."

It always took honest Jack Rackstraw a long time to tell what he had to say; and this was so when he was engaged in conversation with Miss Lilly. Perhaps on this occasion he was slow for a purpose; as his eyes twinkled pleasedly beneath his shaggy brows, when he observed that Miss Lilly had drawn closer to him.

"A fight!" she was gasping. "You don't mean a fight on the lake! A fight with a ship?"

"Mebbe not on the lake. More likely on the shore. More likely, yit, in a cove. I hain't no prophit. Wheres'ever we find them Lakeside Leaguers, there we're a-goin' to jump onto 'em, teeth an' toenail; and if somebody don't git hurt, then it won't be the fault o' the crew of the Andy Johnson. They've worried with them there scoundrels tell they've got their mad up, and would as lief fight as eat, and a good deal liefer!"

He was apparently not looking at Miss Lilly Lilac, yet his pleased glances saw her every attitude.

"So, not knowin' what may come out o' that fight, I says to you that I don't know whether er not I'll git to see you ag'in; an'— well, if you'd only answer that question that I asked you last night!—if you'd only—I'd go 'way feelin' a heap sight better."

Miss Lilly's face was changing from red to pale and from pale to red, though she held it so that Jack Rackstraw could not see it, even by the most intent peering through his bushy eyebrows. But Rackstraw saw that she was twisting nervously at her apron, and that her fingers had a suggestive tremble.

If Jack Rackstraw—the rascal!—could have been soundly thrashed at about that time, probably it would have served him right; for he was making a base pretense of his fears. There was not a braver man on the Andy Johnson than this same Jack Rackstraw, nor a man who thought less of what the results of such a cruise might be. It had even been said of him that he rushed to battle as to a feast.

Yet Jack Rackstraw was a kind-hearted man, not given to blood-thirstiness, nor to vainglorious boastings. He was naturally a warrior, trained to battle on the seas. Fighting as the warriors of old, for his king and country;— which king and country were the flag and soil of his native land, America.

To do him justice, however, it may be admitted that his love for Lilly Lilac may have made him more than ordinarily concerned on such points; and he may really have felt something of what he was saying.

But his twinkling eyes belied this.

"I'd go 'way feelin' a heap sight better," he continued, "if you'd only answer me that there question?"

The Infant Wonder tumbled down the Tower of Babel at that moment, and Miss Lilly gave the child a grateful look.

"What was the question?" she next innocently asked.

"Why—why—" and a great lump got in Rackstraw's throat and almost choked him. "I—I asked you, if you—if you wouldn't be—if you wouldn't be my—*husband*?"

Miss Lilly got redder than any beet, stuffed her handkerchief so deeply into her mouth that she could hardly keep from coughing, and shook more violently than ever; while Rackstraw, feeling that he had hopelessly ruined himself and committed a blunder beyond all pardon, was so much mortified that he nearly fell over.

"I'm a dod-rotted idiot!" he at last blurted out, struggling again to the top of the waves that were ingulfing him. "I'm a teetotal, flabbergasted oyster without any brains, er a head to put 'em in if I had a bushel. I'm a—"

"What was it you said?" Miss Lilly interrupted, having got the better of her emotions and pulled the handkerchief from her mouth. "What was it you said awhile ago? I didn't get the last of it?"

Miss Lilly, it will be seen, was showing herself quite as violently in love with honest Jack as he was in love with her.

Rackstraw swallowed the lump in his throat and rose still further out of the wrangling flood. If Miss Lilly had not caught that awful—that inexcusable blunder, there was hope yet.

"I said would you—would you be my—wife?"

He dwelt a long time on the final word, to be sure that it was the right one before letting it slip.

"You don't really mean it, Jack!" Miss Lilly protested; and another Tower of Babel fell thunderingly to the floor.

Rackstraw looked up with uncommon boldness, and saw that she was blushing like a peony.

His courage grew with the sight; and, feeling his feet touch the firm earth once more, he clasped her hand and drew her down against his heart.

"Mean it?" he ejaculated, in a high-keyed whisper. "May I be cut into bits and fed to the fishes, if I don't mean every word of it! I want you to marry me, Miss Lilly; an' if you'll only say you will, I'll be the happiest man between the oceans."

His tongue was regaining its fluency.

Whether Miss Lilly was blushing or not, Rackstraw could not tell. She had hidden her face against his breast.

Thinking this a good indication, he drew her closer, in a firm embrace; and was startled by a sob.

"You're not mad at me, Miss Lilly?" he pleaded, his voice shaken by fears.

"Of course not, Jack!"

"What ye cryin' fer, then?"

"Because, Jack, I *do* love you, and I'll marry you, if you want me to!"

"Hear that, Infant Wonder? Hip! Hip!"

The Infant Wonder heard something else, just then, that concerned him more directly.

The door had opened softly, and a man reached over and clasped him about the shoulders and drew him into the stairway.

His frightened yell smote the air, causing Rackstraw and Miss Lilly to spring asunder.

Rackstraw caught a glimpse of the man, with Christopher Columbus Stubbs in his arms. The man was turning about to descend. Then the sailor echoed the cry of the Infant Wonder, and leaped in instant pursuit. Either the man was John Malcomb, or the kidnapper was John Malcomb's ghost.

Rackstraw believed it a veritable man, for ghosts do not usually play such pranks; and, as he leaped for the stairway, the small revolver he carried in a hip pocket came out with a swing.

The "bang" of the weapon quickly followed.

The would-be kidnapper had reached the foot of the stairway, and was on the point of bounding into the street.

The shot must have taken effect, for the fellow pitched forward, and the child was dropped, howling, to the floor.

Rackstraw was following the bullet down the stairway, two steps at a time.

It may be that no wound had been made; for, before Rackstraw could reach him, the man scrambled up and plunged headlong into the street.

Christopher Columbus Stubbs was making the air vocal with his screams of fright and indignation, and the voice of Miss Lilly was calling anxiously from the head of the flight.

Unheeding them, Rackstraw bounced through the door, still

swinging the revolver.

The street was almost deserted, and the would-be kidnapper was not to be seen.

With a smothered curse, honest Jack retraced his way, picked up the still yelling Infant Wonder, replied as best he could to Miss Lilly's hysterical questions, and toiled up-stairs.

"Ghosts a-ragin' round like that!" he snorted, setting the Wonder down gingerly and looking to see that none of the Stubbs bones were fractured. "Tell that to the marines! John Malcomb's alive this minute, I don't keer a fig what them there Gypsies says.

"But what in the land o' the livin', did he want with Christopher Columbus?"

CHAPTER XXXVII.

IN THE WOODED COVE.

THIS WAS THE SENSATIONAL and utterly bewildering story that Jack Rackstraw carried to Chicago Charlie on board the Andy Johnson, not an hour later.

Rackstraw had not left Miss Lilly defenseless, however. He had secured a policeman to watch at the foot of the stairs opening on the street, and had left with Miss Lilly the revolver that had been instrumental in saving Christopher Columbus Stubbs from the kidnapping ghost; though Miss Lilly had vowed over and over that she would not—could not—touch the weapon, if a dozen ghosts, on kidnapping bent, should mount the stairs and enter the room.

Not the least excited, when the tale was rehearsed, was Billy Stubbs. It alarmed him for the safety of the Infant Wonder, and so unsettled all his preconceived notions, that he hardly knew whether he was on the deck of a vessel or on the land. Surely, he thought, it could not be!—it could not be possible that John Malcomb was alive.

Sure that the idea was foolish, he fell back on the theory that the man must have been, for some inexplicable reason, disguised to look like John Malcomb.

But why did he seize on the Infant Wonder?

To that he could find no reply. It was as unsolvable as the riddles of the ancient Sphinx.

Chicago Charlie's talk with the Gypsy crone had not been barren of results. She had readily told him all she knew, and had given him a roughly-drawn chart of the lake, which she had stolen a few days before from Zel.

It contained some markings that were thought to be routes of the smuggler sloop, and a point was indicated on the Michigan shore that was presumed to represent the "den."

Rackstraw examined the chart with great care, and decided that it was too crude to be of much benefit. It helped in one way, however; by showing that the den was toward the southern end of the lake.

Rackstraw was acquainted with several coves, any of which might have been meant by the dot, and it was determined to steer for the most southern of them, and then to sail northward, making a close search of every suspicious- looking inlet.

At midnight, according to previous arrangements, the Andrew Johnson was got under way, and steamed as quietly from the wharf as possible.

No lights gleamed from her decks, and no signals were shown. One lone fisherman, tacking lakeward, was perhaps the only man that beheld her thus putting to sea, and he stared his amazement, wondering what it meant, and not knowing that she had been privileged to so depart.

The run across the lake was of no great interest, save to Billy Stubbs, who was making his longest, as it was his first, voyage.

But the interest intensified when, the next night, the Michigan shore was approached, and it became known to all that the search had begun.

Still, there came of it nothing to produce any undue excitement. The deserted coves that were entered held nothing to indicate that they were, or had ever been, the den of a band of smugglers.

But the ensuing night there came an event to arouse every man.

A light was seen displayed on a lonely part of the shore line; and it flashed out and disappeared at such regular intervals that there was no doubt it was meant as a signal for some person or vessel.

Chicago Charlie

The Andy Johnson was lying well out in the lake at the time, but the light was distinctly visible to those on board.

After waiting an hour or more for the vessel to run in, should one have been signaled, the Andy Johnson was put about, and a short southernly run was made, which brought the steamer close to land at a point where heavy forest growth came quite down to the water.

Rackstraw knew of no harbor, so the anchor was let go there, and several boats' crews went ashore, in charge of Captain Stebbins and Chicago Charlie. They were heavily armed, in anticipation of a fight should the smugglers be discovered, and Rackstraw and Billy Stubbs were of the number.

The boats were landed on the sandy, wooded point, and left there in charge of a few men; while the others stole through the woods in the direction in which the light had been seen.

When it was thought the place must be near, Chicago Charlie and Jack Rackstraw crept on in advance, leaving the men, under command of Stebbins, to await the results of their investigations.

They were gone a long time—so long that Stebbins almost lost his proverbial patience.

And this is what they saw, and what they heard:

At the extreme end of the cove, almost hidden from view by the heavy timber and dense undergrowth, was found a small camp of log houses.

The smuggler sloop lay in the cove. It had been the vessel for whose benefit the signal lights had been displayed, and it had been not long at anchor.

There were but few lights in the log houses, but most of the members of the Lakeside League were grouped about a small fire near the water's edge.

Chicago Charlie was almost beside himself with excitement. He seemed so near a solution of the mysteries that had so vexed and puzzled him; so near, perhaps, to the woman he loved, and who had treated him so strangely, that he was on the point of losing his head and bringing discovery on himself and companion.

"Jist take it cool, mate!" Rackstraw urged. "I know how you feel, I reckon, sence I've got a girl now t'other side the lake what's a-waitin' an' watchin' for me! But a-rushin' and hustlin' hain't the things that's goin' to win in this here game. Coolness is the little joker what'll rake in the pot."

The advice and caution was altogether so good and sensible

that the Columbian Detective strove to control his excitement and to regain his old-time caution.

Bit by bit, they worked round the border of the fringing trees, until they reached a point to the rear of the log cabins.

Selecting one of these, from which there came both a light and the sound of voices in conversation, they drew near. Something in the tones—though the words were still indistinguishable—sent an unwonted thrill to the detective's throbbing heart.

They saw that, though they might crawl up to the walls of the house, it would be difficult to look in, for the window was high set; and, therefore, they sought better to accomplish their purpose, which was to see as well as to hear, by mounting a small tree.

A large limb of this extended toward the window, giving them a fairly good view, as well as enabling them to hear all that was being said, for the window was open to the night air.

As soon as Chicago Charlie looked through that window and beheld the faces of the occupants, he started so violently that he came near falling from the branch.

"Steady, mate!" came Rackstraw's warning whisper. "I sympathizes with you, fer I've got a girl—"

The sentence was not completed; for at that moment, Rackstraw, hitching forward, saw what Chicago Charlie saw.

There were two persons in the little room.

One was Daisy Malcomb, and the other was John Malcomb.

They were talking in low tones, but the words could be readily understood.

The subject of their conversation was quite as bewildering.

"Why won't you tell me that, father?" Daisy was heard to beg. "I've asked it so many times. It seems to me an explanation is surely due by this time!"

Chicago Charlie drank in the tones with almost pitiful eagerness. How long it seemed to him since he had heard the music of that voice!

"That's what I want to talk about!" they heard Malcomb declare.

The voice was the voice of John Malcomb, even as the form was his. *He had not been murdered!* He was not dead! More than that one fact concerning him, Chicago Charlie could not hold in his mind at that moment.

"There is an estate in New York," Malcomb was heard to continue, "which is tied up in the most singular manner. I shall tell you about that estate, and then see if you are a true daughter to me!"

"Oh! father, can you doubt it, after what I have done?" came the reproachful question.

"That estate belonged to my father, who has been dead for several years. He took a dislike to me—to me, his only son! The only child, I should have said. The property is worth now two hundred thousand dollars; and it would be mine, every cent of it, but for a nonsensical provision in his will.

"As I said, he took a dislike to me. He cast me off. He said I should no more be considered his son, and all because I would not order my life in accordance with his wishes."

There was a growing pain in the eyes of the girl.

Chicago Charlie had already observed how thin and pale she was—how like a shadow of her former self.

John Malcomb did not notice this look, or, if he did, he did not care to heed it.

"His treatment of me I always thought unjust and cruel. The provision of the will cut me off without a penny, and gave to my children the entire estate—*but not until after my death!* You see, he thus showed that he feared if they got possession of it during my lifetime, I might get some benefit from it.

"If that was not an outrageously cruel thing for a father to do, then I don't know what to call cruel! He was determined that not a cent of all that money should ever pass through my hands."

Daisy Malcomb had bowed her head and was picking nervously at the chair. No comment passed her lips.

For a moment the silence was so great it might almost be felt. John Malcomb was apparently studying her, and thinking how best to proceed with his narration.

"That will serve as an explanation; and will tell you why I wanted the world to think me dead!"

She glanced up inquiringly.

"Of course the fortune would go to you, Daisy, at my death! But not before. I might live a long time—ten, twenty years! I proceeded to hasten the matter. Not by slaying myself, nor by having another slay me; but by making the world believe I had done the latter.

"You have so often told me how you loved me. I believed that you would be willing to appear in the courts as my daughter, obtain possession of the money; and then we could go away and enjoy it together!"

Chicago Charlie

She bent her head again and did not reply, and once more he anxiously studied her attitude.

"Did you think I could do a thing like that?"

She glanced up, as she put the question, and her hot, tearless eyes held a horrified light.

"Why not?" he demanded; and there was a snarl in the intonation.

"It would be perjury! Not even for my father would I perjure myself!"

"Bah! Nothing of the kind. You would not have to prove me dead. That has already been done. The coroner's record shows that, and all about my untimely taking-off. Those records would make a case. All you need to prove is that you are my daughter!"

The look of horror fled, to be replaced by one of indignant anger.

"And this is why you induced me to come with you, and to write the letter that has forever wrecked my life?"

Chicago Charlie's pulses leaped.

"Is it asking too much?"

"It is asking what I will never do. Never! *Never*! NEVER!"

Her voice rose to a shriek.

Then she flung herself at Malcomb's feet, crying out, bitterly:

"Oh, papa! take back those words. Tell me you never said it. Tell me that I have been mistaken in you. That you would not—could not do so base and wicked a thing! Let me trust in you again! Let me believe that you are honest and true!"

"And you refuse to do what I ask you?" he demanded, his anger getting the better of him. "Have I schemed for this? Do you refuse to obey me, *your father*?"

"Oh! I cannot believe that my father asks me to do a thing like that! That he could for a moment harbor the idea! Please tell me it is not so!"

"I ask again, if you will do what I want you to?" he furiously questioned. "I have had quite enough sniffling and tears. You must do what I command! You have been in this sort of temper, half the time since leaving Chicago. Am I to be obeyed or not?"

The Columbian Detective found it difficult to restrain the inclination to launch himself through the window at the scoundrel's head. But Jack Rackstraw's hand was on his arm, held there restrainingly.

"I'm afeared to leave you hyer," Rackstraw whispered, "but don't you think I'd better slide out an' bring up the boys? I'll do it, if you think you can hold yer temper that long!"

"Go, for God's sake!" the Columbian Detective pleaded. "Go! Go! I'll not be able to control myself much longer. Bring 'em up on the run!"

Jack Rackstraw "crawfished" back to the body of the tree, then slid quickly to the ground and disappeared in the dense shadows.

All unconscious of this little scene and dialogue, Malcomb asked again:

"Am I to be obeyed or not?"

"I will never do so base a thing!" Daisy declared getting on her feet, and stiffening with inherent pride. "Never! *Never!*"

"Then, you are no daughter of mine!" was the assertion. "Begone from here! *You never were my daughter*, and I refuse to have anything further to do with you."

She seemed petrified.

"Oh, don't stare at me that way!" was the brutal command. "It is the truth. I loved you, or thought I did, as a man should love his own daughter. But that is gone! No; you are not my daughter. So clear out!"

He was beside himself with rage.

"Is it true?" she asked, in tones that were so hollow they made the listening detective shiver. "Tell me again, is it true?"

"Yes, it's true! You are not my daughter. You never were my daughter; and I thank God for it!"

"I thank God, too!" was the solemn and fervent declaration. "*My* father could never have been so base a thing!"

CHAPTER XXXVIII.

THE CRASH OF THE THUNDERBOLT.

JOHN MALCOMB, DRIVEN TO FURY by this declaration, lifted his hand to strike the girl he had taught to call him father.

The sight drove the Columbian Detective to madness.

Grasping an overhanging branch, he swung himself through the window and struck Malcomb to the earth with a furious blow.

Chicago Charlie

At the same instant, almost, there came the crack of a rifle; and the men under Captain Stebbins, who had been hurried up by Rackstraw, gave their charging cheer.

The scene that ensued baffles description. The smugglers about the fire, among whom were Solon Youngblood, seized their weapons, and, retreating toward the shore, attempted a resistance.

But they were scattered at the first volley of the men from the steamer, and broke for the cover of the underbrush.

Rackstraw gave them no heed, but made a wild dash for the cabin occupied by John Malcomb and the girl. There were sounds coming from it that made him anxious. He had heard the shout of the Columbian Detective, when the latter had precipitated himself to the cabin floor; and now screams arose.

Thrusting open the door, he saw Chicago Charlie engaged in tying the hands of the archconspirator, and again heard the cries of the bewildered and scared girl.

He sprung toward her, but Chicago Charlie was the first to gain her side.

And, Rackstraw, remembering his own experiences in meetings and partings from the idol of his bosom, discreetly turned away, giving his undivided attention to the fallen man.

Malcomb glared up at him like a caged beast. The scoundrel had not been hit by the bullet sent speeding after him down the stairway, as Rackstraw was quick to discover. No doubt he had stumbled and dropped the Infant Wonder, through fright.

"Needn't look at me as if you wanted to eat me!" Rackstraw commented. "I hain't no sugar man."

Then, he bent to an investigation of the knots made by Chicago Charlie, to be sure they were strong and secure.

Outside, a lively scene was being enacted.

Solon Youngblood, who was no coward, was leading such of his men as had not bolted from his side, in a desperate countercharge, in the hope of gaining the sloop. There were a few men on board the vessel, and these were climbing wildly around, trying to hoist the anchor and to set sail, for a breeze was springing up from off the land.

Captain Stebbins rallied his followers to repel the charge of Youngblood's force, and for a time a desperate combat raged on the sandy shore of the lonely inlet.

But the rascally crew of the smuggler was no match for the trained men under command of Stebbins. Inch by inch, they were forced back, until they broke again; and Stebbins's men scattered them like chaff.

Two or three had been killed, and one of the men of the steamer was said to be mortally wounded. In addition, there were stabs and minor injuries; and pistol wounds, without number.

Youngblood was among the prisoners taken; and, when he saw that he could not escape, one of his first questions concerned Mrs. Youngblood. She had been in one of the log huts, but had not been seen since the beginning of the attack; nor was she ever afterward seen by any who might have desired her arrest.

John Malcomb had been dragged into another house, away from the sight of Daisy, and there he was raving out his fierce anger and venomous hate.

Rackstraw's was the command that caused the removal of the miserable prisoner, whose wicked scheming and unhallowed plans had so suddenly come to naught.

As for Daisy and the Columbian Detective, the former was hysterically happy and unhappy by turns, while the latter, with pulsing exultation, held her in an embrace that he almost hoped might last forever, and listened to her incoherent attempts to explain why she had written that awful letter and afterward fled with the man whom she believed to be her father.

To follow and record her halting sentences, and Chicago Charlie's rapturous and pitying exclamations, would require pages. But the substance can be compressed into a few paragraphs:

She had thought her father dead, until one night, when he walked into her room; frightening her sorely. Then he explained that he had not been killed, or even injured, but that all that had been done had been only a pretense. He claimed that he had got into trouble, which would force him to leave the city, and to remain in hiding for some time; that it had been brought about by some business transactions, which had been perfectly fair and honorable so far as he was concerned; but to which he had been instigated by partners and agents, of whose criminal deeds he had no previous knowledge. That they had charged him with being an accomplice; and so he must fly.

He said he had sold his city property to Solon Youngblood, who was ready to take immediate possession. And he had begged Daisy to accompany him; and by systematic lying had induced her to do so.

He also made her think the idea was abroad that she had killed her own father; and had caused her to promise that she would leave no trace or letter by which the officers could follow her.

It was a pitiful story, pitifully told; of confidence and daughterly love abused.

She had been taken first to Detroit, and afterward to the cove; where she had since remained, shocked by the companions which Malcomb had seen fit to gather about him. In addition, she had been depressed by his reticence, and had wondered more than once if his representations had been as true, and his business dealings as honorable, as he had maintained.

CHAPTER XXXIX.

A DEFIANT DEVIL.

"I DEFY YOU to do your worst. You can only imprison me! I haven't murdered anybody!—no, nor I haven't been murdered!"

The scene was a cell in a city prison, whither John Malcomb had been borne after the return from the Michigan Cove.

Chicago Charlie was present, and so was Jack Rackstraw; and also another, who was a prison guard.

John Malcomb had grown defiant, obstinate and self-willed. No doubt he realized that the hopes of his life were blasted, and that no worse could come to him than had already come. His carefully-laid plans had failed. He would never have the handling of the fortune he had so cunningly schemed to obtain; and when he should go from prison a free man again, his record and the knowledge of his crimes would turn the hand of every man against him.

Realizing this to its full, he was bitter and insolent; and inclined to glory in a past which held only shame.

"You can't more than jail me!" he snarled again, "and I reckon I can stand a few months or years of that if I have to. As for those who helped me, they're beyond your reach. All except Youngblood. And he would have been if he hadn't made that last fool flight. As for me, I wasn't given any show."

The look he bent on Chicago Charlie was withering in its hate, but the latter only smiled good-humoredly.

"We are prepared to admit your cleverness, Malcomb. You were deucedly clever. Too clever for me, I must confess."

The statements were made with a purpose; that purpose being to flatter John Malcomb into a further confession.

Malcomb laughed harshly, and with a sort of satanic glee.

"You police think you are very smart, but you are only a set of wooden-heads, after all. And the great, blustering Columbian Detective!—he can't tell a dead man when he sees one!"

He laughed again, showing his teeth in a cruel way.

His face had grown thin and hatchety, and his eyes were so bright and hollow that he was not a pleasant sight to contemplate. Deep down in the depths of each eye there lurked a dancing devil, that now and then took on a shape of fire.

"How did you do it, anyway?" Chicago Charlie ventured to question.

"Easy. Why, it was the easiest thing in the world. I wanted that fortune of two hundred thousand, and I had to die to get it. If I'd 'a' died really, you see, it wouldn't have done me any good. So I just pretended to die. Magruder and some more of the boys helped me, for which they were to have had half of the fortune, if the scheme had worked.

"Well, it didn't work, though that was no fault of mine! The scheme was a good one. Magruder knew of a drug, which he'd run across in some of his Gypsyish wanderings, that would give to whoever swallowed it the semblance of death. He secured it, got a cup of blood from a slaughtering establishment, and then we were ready for the trick."

A scowl flitted for a moment across his face.

"Curse that fool Magruder! I'd like to choke him, yet. He had to muddle things straight from the start, instead of obeying orders! He thought he knew more about it than I did, who was the most interested. I think, too, he was a little afraid of the police.

"So he got that dancing-girl from the Cairo Street to steal the knife from Daisy's room. If it hadn't been for that visit of the girl to Daisy's room, and the ring he took from my hand, you'd never have got on the trail of the thing."

The scowl faded to be followed by a smile.

"I thought that fool of an Englishman would never go away that night; and he wouldn't, likely, if I hadn't claimed to be mad over that betting offer and ordered him into the street. Poor old Walesey! How the boys did bleed him! And they kept it up after my supposed death, and got thousands and tens of thousands out of him, I guess, with which they pretended to bribe policemen and detectives who were said to be wanting to arrest him for murdering me. I think, if I was Walesey, I'd kill Youngblood for that, yet!"

The recollection was so exceedingly pleasing that he laughed aloud.

Then the scowl came back, and he continued:

"When we were all ready, I dipped my finger in the blood and scratched that nonsense on the wall, to mislead you smart fellows of the police force; and then Magruder got in his artistic work on my back, painting a place to look like a wound with blood crusted round it. After which we sopped my clothing in the blood; poured the balance of it on the floor; and I laid down in it, with my finger pointed toward the nonsense on the wall; and Magruder gave me the drug.

"I was a little bit afraid to swallow it, not being right sure there mightn't be a dead man found there, sure enough, in the morning; and I shouldn't have taken it, I reckon, if I hadn't known that Magruder was as much interested in having me pull through all right, as I was in pulling through all right.

"You see, if the drug had finished me, that two hundred thousand wouldn't have been among the possibilities, and Magruder would have lost all chance of sharing it.

"So I swallowed the stuff. And it was powerful enough to kill, seems to me; for I hadn't much more than downed it than I began to feel the numbing effects; and in ten minutes I couldn't have moved a hand or batted an eye for the life of me.

"And that's the way you and Walesey found me in the morning!"

"But the coroner and his jury? I confess I didn't look closely at the supposed wound. But how did you manage to deceive them?"

Malcomb winked unpleasantly.

"I didn't deceive them. They deceived you and the public. They—every mother's son of them—were Lakeside Leaguers; and those were the men who were to share with the Gypsy chief the half of the fortune."

"And the undertaker?"

"Another Leaguer!" chuckling in horrible glee. "Oh, it was a daisy lay-out, and a scheme to fool the Old Boy! I don't wonder you were deceived. But you can't get them! They have all skipped."

"Then you weren't buried, nor anything of the kind?"

"I went into the coffin, but I didn't go into the ground. And a deuced unpleasant night I spent in that box, too. It gives me the creeps, yet, to think of it.

"When the coffin went to the cemetery, there was a counterfeit John Malcomb in it; and I was looking out from a window to see that the solemn *cortege* wound all right on its way. The Gypsy had come in the night, stolen me away and brought the bloom back to my erstwhile faded cheek, and Richard was himself again!"

He laughed, as if he felt the clever trick to have been one worthy of honor; and his utter heartlessness was unpleasantly revealed by the fact that he could thus treat the girl who believed in and loved him.

"The only thing that troubled me," he laughingly commented, "was that I dared not tell any of you wise officers how far you were off the track;—but it did me good to know that you were thrashing this way and that, hunting for my supposed murderer."

CHAPTER XL.

A SINGULAR REVELATION.

THE MORNING that witnessed the return of the captured Lakeside Leaguers found Selwyn Fisher dead in his room; he having died, as the doctors said, of alcoholism.

Not much had been seen of Walesey since his attack on Rackstraw in the Ferris Wheel. He had been given a preliminary hearing on the charge of assault with intent to kill, and had been released under bond to await a regular trial.

It was known that he had been drinking heavily;—even more heavily than before, if that were possible.

There were few or none to mourn his demise, except certain

Chicago Charlie

members of the sporting fraternity. He had lived a fast life.

When his effects were searched, a most singular letter or confession was discovered in his trunk. It had been written some time before; and, as it seemed, in anticipation of death.

The confession covered a number of foolscap pages, and was, therefore, too long to quote.

It began by giving a short history of his life, stating that he was born in England and was forty-five years of age. He had come unlawfully in the possession of a large sum of money, three fourths of which was already dissipated. There were only twenty or thirty thousand dollars of it left; and he considered himself on the brink of poverty.

To a man of his habits and style of living it probably appeared to be a very small sum, for he had spent more than half that much in the year preceding his death.

The points of most interest to the readers of this story, concerned the fortune. It had been inherited, according to English custom, by his elder brother, who was also his only brother.

This brother, having become wildly infatuated with a Gypsy woman, had wandered off and had married her. Afterward he had died; though not till two children had been born to this marriage.

It was not known to the public that there were such children, though the fact was well known to Selwyn Fisher; for his brother had written to him at various times.

Selwyn Fisher saw, as he thought, an opportunity to acquire his brother's fortune. In the absence of children he would have been the next of kin; and the temptation came to him to pretend ignorance of these children and to take the property.

When an investigation showed him that the mother was also dead—she having died shortly after the father—the temptation became irresistible. Selwyn claimed the property; and, having converted it into cash sailed for America. What remained of the fortune was now in one of the Chicago banks. He had never invested any of it, nor done anything except to draw freely on his bank account.

He stated that he wrote this confession to do justice to the heirs, though he had not sufficient strength of will or manhood to give up the money while he lived.

Then came the startling statement:

"I have been acquainted with one of these heirs for more than a year. She is the girl known as Daisy Malcomb, and commonly supposed to be John Malcomb's daughter. The other heir I have not known so long. He is the newsboy, Billy Stubbs!

"I once saw my brother's wife, the Gypsy woman. She was exceedingly handsome, and I don't wonder that my brother fell in love with her. I know I should have done so, if in his place. The girl called Daisy Malcomb is her living image. That was the fact which first attracted my attention to her.

"One day, in conversation with Solon Youngblood, he told me she was not Malcomb's daughter; and then I knew that she was my brother's child. Malcomb had found her in an almshouse or orphanage, or some such place. Malcomb was a married man at the time, and had no children. He desired an heir; and so he took the girl, and called her his daughter. But when I first knew him, he had no living wife.

"Billy Stubbs, whose real name is Marlton Fisher—and the name of the girl is Gertrude Fisher!—looks as much like my dead brother, except as to age, as the girl resembles her dead mother. Zel Magruder says the boy is a Gypsy. Of course, I cannot be sure that he is my brother's child, though I am sure of it as I am of anything I can't plainly prove. If he is a Gypsy, I know he is my nephew, for his face is my brother's face.

"John Malcomb never had a child by his wife; though he did, or rather has, a child by another woman. He told me that, himself, one day as we were driving through the streets. We saw the newsboy, Billy Stubbs, leading a small boy by the hand.

"'Do you see that brat?' said Malcomb to me. I told him I did; and then he said the 'brat' was his; but that he didn't care just then to own it. He said he would have taken it home and acknowledged it as his, only he was sure Daisy would kick up a row. These are his words as near as I can remember them."

But a small part of the confession—which was a record of the man's life—has been quoted. Only that part pertaining to the characters of this story. For the rest, there is not space; nor would it be of great interest.

It was evident, though, that the dead man had set down only truths. The statement that Christopher Columbus Stubbs was John Malcomb's son, explains why Malcomb had desired to kidnap the boy from the kindergarten; and when Malcomb was approached on the subject and shown the words of Selwyn Fisher, he acknowledged their correctness.

"I didn't really want the boy," he declared, "only as he would help me. I thought if Daisy went back on me, I could have the boy put forward by some one as the heir, and through him I could get hold of the fortune. Yes, I told Fisher the boy was mine; and of course, in the absence of other heirs, he would have come in for the fortune left by that fool father of mine.

"As for Daisy, I knew she was dark, but I never knew she was a Gypsy. Fisher never breathed that to me. No doubt he was afraid, for I would have been wanting her to have the money he was fingering. I don't suppose there's much of it left, and I don't care. I got a good deal of it while it was going!

"Fisher was not one of the Leaguers. He was too big a fool to have been admitted there. I must give the fellow credit, though. I didn't really believe he was such a rascal as he makes out. You can't always tell a man by the way he looks. I thought he was only a fat whisky and beer guzzler, and a sucker of the greenest sort.

"If he was alive, I'd beg his pardon for thinking so poorly of him!"

CHAPTER XLI.

CONCLUSION.

THE SCENE SHIFTS AGAIN, and for the last time.

This time it reveals Zel Magruder, with body water-swollen, and sightless eyes staring up at the dirty peak of the tent, in whose interior he had been temporarily placed.

He had rowed and sailed for the last time on Lake Michigan.

The tent was that of the crone, Gypsy Nell, and the crone was bending moaningly above him. She had not loved him, even though he had been distantly related to her, but she was realizing now that after all "blood *is* thicker than water."

They had had many quarrels, had bickered constantly, had nurtured the demon of hate, and the woman had even turned against him and sought to injure him by causing his arrest—still he was a Gypsy, blood of the Gypsy blood; and because of that she wrung her hands and poured out her lamentations.

There were others in the tent: Chicago Charlie, Jack Rackstraw, Billy Stubbs, a policeman and a Columbian guide.

Zel's boat had been overturned that morning on the lake, in front of the Exhibition grounds. The accident had been seen, but not in time to effect his rescue. And at the request of Chicago Charlie the body, when taken from the water, had been borne to the Gypsy encampment, instead of to a morgue.

He felt it was the proper place for it, as that was the Gypsy's home; and, besides, he had a purpose to serve in making the request. He desired further light thrown on the parentage of Billy Stubbs; and hoped the crone, who had grown sullen and uncommunicative, might be driven by the fate of Magruder into making further statements.

It will be seen that Zel Magruder had not left the city, as he told the dancing-girl he meant to do.

He had basely deceived the Ghawazee in many things. Thinking to impress her with his prowess, he had made her believe he had killed John Malcomb; and the theft of the knife he had more than once held over her head as a menacing club to bend her to his will.

Yet, in spite of it, she had loved him. So strange a thing is love!

She had been guilty of no evil intentions, doing what she did through a desire to aid the Gypsy and his friends. It was this that had caused her to become the bearer of mysterious and warning messages between Magruder and Youngblood, and had caused her to commit other indiscretions.

She had returned to the Cairo Street, when she knew she was not to be punished, and when it became certain that Zel Magruder had lied to her. This lying deceit of the Gypsy had been made plain, at a surreptitious interview between them on the night of their flight from the officers in the Gypsy tent. Zel still claimed then to love her, but he did not want her to accompany him, and she departed from him in disgust. She was not only a Gypsy, but she was oriental in her changeful fickleness.

Chicago Charlie questioned the crone, who had ceased her moanings and turned to the men who had brought in Zel's body.

"Yes," she admitted, in reply to his questions, "what I said about the newsboy being a Gypsy, is all true. I don't know about the girl that you call Daisy, though I had suspicions about her when she came here to have her fortune told.

"But the boy was once, for a short time, with this band in England. He was a little chap, but I am sure I am not mistaken. His father came to visit us one day, bringing the boy with him.

Chicago Charlie

The father was not Gypsy, but he said the boy was half Gypsy. I thought I recognized the boy's face when I first saw it, though that visit was so long ago. The face hadn't changed much. He looks like the man, now, more than he did then; but it is the same face.

"Yes, I am sure he is of the Gypsy blood!"

The proof—what additional proof was needed—was secured to give to Daisy and the newsboy their inheritance; and it was secured through the exertions of the Columbian Detective.

He is Daisy's husband, now, and Billy Stubbs makes his home with them. Likewise, the Infant Wonder, who is the richest of the lot, for he has come into possession of the magnificent New York estate which his father, John Malcomb, schemed so hard and vainly to obtain.

As Jack Rackstraw said, when he heard it:

"The Infant Wonder forever! 'Rah! 'Rah! Hip!"

Rackstraw expects to marry pretty Lilly Lilac at no distant day, and in consequence there is no happier man above ground.

He and Chicago Charlie, and the newsboy—who is a newsboy no longer, but who is still called Billy Stubbs—are rapidly becoming a famous trio of detectives, and a terror to the evildoers of Chicago and the harpies of the great World's Fair.

Solon Youngblood and John Malcomb—perhaps the least said of them the better!—are in prison garb, learning the sad and old, old lesson, so difficult for mankind to learn—that "the way of the transgressor is hard!"

THE END.

Chicago Charlie

Something About the Author of *Chicago Charlie*

JOHN HARVEY WHITSON, the son of Aaron F. Whitson and his wife Tracy McNamee, was born in Seymour, Indiana on December 28, 1854. In his early years he taught school and practiced law. In 1880 he helped establish and was editor and part owner of the short-lived *Jeffersonville Evening Journal*. In 1885 the Whitson family moved to Garden City, Kansas, where he and his father took up homesteads. His father went into the cattle business, and John helped him, but at the same time he began writing professionally. In 1888 he wrote his first story for Beadle & Adams entitled *Captain Cactus, The Chapparal Cock; Or, Josh Peppermint's Ten Strike*. He wrote the story under the pseudonym "Lieut. A. K. Sims"; all his longer stories for Beadle & Adams were published under the same name, while his informative articles, poems, and sketches were under his own name. Whitson published over forty-five dime novels for Beadle & Adams. He also had several other works published in periodicals, some of the magazines being: *Golden Days, Golden Argosy, Golden Hours, The Youth's Companion, Good News* and the *New York Ledger*.

In 1898 Whitson was ordained into the Baptist ministry and he preached for two years at Buckfield, Massachusetts. He married Flora Josselyn of Cambridge, Massachusetts in 1900. In the early 1920s he taught Bible history and literature at a girls' school in Nashville, Tennessee, and from 1923 to 1931 was head of the department of religious education at Hardin College, Mexico, Missouri. He died on May 2, 1936. [Biographical information on Whitson from Albert Johannsen's *The House Of Beadle And Adams*, Volume 2, pages 299-300].

Some booklength fiction by John H. Whitson:

Barbara, A Woman Of The West. Boston: Little, Brown and Company, 1903. 314p.

Campaigning With Tippecanoe. New York: The Federal Book Company, 1904. 247p.

The Castle Of Doubt. Boston: Little, Brown and Company, 1907. 283p.

Chicago Charlie

A Courier Of Empire; A Story Of Marcus Whitman's Ride To Save Oregon. Boston and Chicago: W. A. Wilde Company, 1904. 315p.

Justin Wingate, Ranchman. Boston: Little, Brown and Company, 1905. 312p.

The Rainbow Chasers, A Story Of The Plains. Boston: Little, Brown and Company, 1904. 393p.

With Fremont The Pathfinder; Or, Winning The Empire Of Gold. Boston and Chicago: W. A. Wilde Company, 1903. 320p.

The Young Ditch Rider; A Story Of The Plains. Elgin, Il. and Chicago: D. C. Cook Publishing Co., 1899. 96p.

Appendix

Fictional Works Using
the World's Columbian Exposition as a Setting

Aiken, Albert W. *Joe Phenix In Chicago; Or, The Serio-Comic Detective*. New York: Beadle and Adams (Beadle's New York Dime Library, No. 954, February 3, 1897). 31p.

> Joe Phenix, a well-known New York detective, is called to action when a wealthy Englishman (Carroll Berkeley), while touring the U.S., finds that his brother (Marshall Berkeley) has disappeared somewhere in Chicago. Phenix and a female assistant eventually discover the truth of Marshall Berkeley's robbery and murder. The story is set during the time of the Columbian Exposition, and though the Fairgrounds are never actually described, the story does depict some of the economic and social developments resulting from the Exposition.

Bailey, Alice W. *Mark Heffron: A Novel*. New York: Harper & Brothers, 1896. 354p.

> Story deals with Christian Science, hypnotism, and other metaphysical questions. The Fair and its aftermath (including the Peristyle fire) are mentioned throughout the early chapters of the novel.

Bloch, Robert. *American Gothic*. New York: Simon and Schuster, 1974. 222p.

> G. Gordon Gregg, a psychopathic killer posing as a pharmacist/doctor, builds a guest hotel and pharmacy near the Fairgrounds

just prior to the opening of the Columbian Exposition. The building has a castle-like facade; its interior contains hidden stairways, passageways and trapdoors leading to secret rooms—rooms where Gregg murders guests, girlfriends and business associates. Crystal, a young female reporter, attempts to find evidence which will reveal Gregg's dastardly plans, and in doing so nearly becomes a victim herself. This story is based on the life of an actual person—Herman W. Mudgett. An interesting article on Herman Mudgett (entitled "Killer's Castle") can be found in *American Mercury*, Vol. 83 (October, 1956): pp. 116-124.

Burnett, Frances Hodgson. *Two Little Pilgrims' Progress: A Story Of The City Beautiful*. New York: Charles Scribner's Sons, 1895. 191p. [Children's fiction].

A boy and a girl take their small savings and leave home to seek adventure at the great World's Fair in Chicago in 1893.

Burnham, Clara Louise. *Sweet Clover: A Romance Of The White City*. Boston & New York: Houghton, Mifflin & Co., 1894. 411p.

Story of two love affairs set among the glory and grandeur of the Columbian Exposition. Main characters: Clover Bryant, Mildred Bryant, Jack Van Tassel, and Gorham Page. The story starts in 1889 and ends with the Peristyle fire, January 8, 1894. A very accurate and descriptive account of the Exposition in fictional form.

Butterworth, Hezekiah. *Zigzag Journeys In The White City; With Visits To The Neighboring Metropolis*. Boston: Estes and Lauriat, 1894. 320p.

A man is sent to Chicago by his town to report on the World's Columbian Exposition and to attend the Folk-Lore Congress. His father wants to attend the Peace Conference to be held in conjunction with the Exposition, and decides to accompany his son. The story describes major sights of both the city of Chicago and the Fair, with major emphasis placed on the Folk-Lore Congress and the Peace Congress.

Butterworth, Hezekiah. *Zigzag Journeys On The Mississippi: From Chicago To The Islands Of The Discovery*. Boston: Estes and Lauriat, 1892. 319p.

A description of a hypothetical trip taken by a grade school Spanish class. The volume includes stories and articles covering three separate but related topics: 1) the discovery of America, 2) the city of Chicago, and 3) the Mississippi River Valley. This book was intended as an introduction to the theme, history, and planning of the World's Columbian Exposition.

Cobb, Weldon J. *A World's Fair Mystery*. Chicago: Melbourne Publishing, 1892. 369p.

Adrian Burgoyne, an escaped convict, is intent on avenging the two men responsible for unjustly sending him to prison. Besides revenging the wrong done to himself, Burgoyne is bent on restoring the fortune meant for Patrice Ringold (his deceased friend's daughter). The key to Patrice's fortune is in the hands of the same two swindlers responsible for putting Burgoyne behind bars. This fast-paced adventure story begins and ends on the Fairgrounds of the World's Columbian Exposition, with a treasure-seeking trip to Mexico sandwiched in between. This same novel was published in 1893 under the title *The Victim Of A Crime*.

Finley, Martha. *Elsie At The World's Fair*. New York: Dodd, Mead and Co., 1894. 259p. [Children's fiction].

Elsie Dinsmore, accompanied by family and friends, takes a yachting trip from her southern plantation home to the Columbian Exposition. Brief descriptions of buildings, grounds, and exhibits are given.

Flinn, John J. *The Mysterious Disappearance Of Helen St. Vincent: A Story Of The Vanished City*. Chicago: Geo. K. Hazlitt & Co., 1895. 304p.

Edmund Powers, a journalist, is in love with a beautiful and talented woman named Helen St. Vincent. Edmund asks

Helen to marry him but she refuses because she is engaged to another (Henry Bolton, an immoral and lawless man). The story contains a bogus marriage, a case of mistaken identity, and a few near murders. Besides suspense, the story provides ample descriptions of Chicago and the Columbian Exposition.

Harrison, Elizabeth. "The Fair White City; or, a Story of the Past, Present and Future." In Harrison, Elizabeth, *In Story-Land*. Chicago: Sigma Publishing Co., 1895. pp. 65-77.

A short story, written in allegorical form, about some of the lasting effects of Chicago's "White City." All the stories in *In Story-Land* were written to be used by teachers and parents of grade school children.

Hawthorne, Julian. *Humors Of The Fair*. Chicago: E. A. Weeks & Company, 1893. 205p.

An amusing account of the Exposition, giving Hawthorne's impressions of the "White City," of the notable features and scenes of the Fairgrounds, of the officials and visitors, and of the customs of some of the foreign nations represented.

Herrick, Robert. *The Web Of Life*. New York: Macmillan Company, 1900. 356p.

The Web Of Life is a story of Chicago life which takes place shortly after the closing of the Columbian Exposition. The abandoned Fairgrounds are referred to quite often, and the Peristyle fire is described in some detail in Chapter 19 (pp. 170-180).

Jenks, Tudor. *The Century World's Fair Book For Boys And Girls: Being The Adventures Of Harry And Philip With Their Tutor, Mr. Douglass, At The World's Columbian Exposition*. New York: Century Co., 1893. 246p.

Purports to relate the adventures of two boys who go to the

Exposition with their tutor. One boy makes sketches of the Fairgrounds and the other takes photographs—the story tells how they learn a good deal about history, industry, and art in the process.

Josiah Allen's Wife (real name Marietta Holley). *Samantha At The World's Fair*. New York: Funk & Wagnalls Co., 1893. 694p.

Samantha and Josiah Allen's, an elderly couple from rural New York state, experiences at the Fair. Samantha gives quite detailed descriptions of the buildings, exhibits and events at the Fair, but scattered among her descriptions are her views on politics, women's suffrage and temperance. *Samantha At The World's Fair* is considered one of the most accurate and detailed fictional accounts of the Columbian Exposition.

Judson, Clara Ingram. *The Lost Violin; They Came From Bohemia*. Boston: Houghton Mifflin, 1947. 204p. [Young adult fiction].

Anna Kovec, a young immigrant from Czechoslovakia, loses her prize possession—a Mittenwald violin—on the day she arrives in Chicago. The disappearance of the instrument leads to adventure. The Fairgrounds of the Columbian Exposition are never really described, but the Exposition and its hoopla figure prominently in the storyline.

Kelly, Regina Z. *Chicago: Big-Shoulder City*. Chicago: Reilly & Lee, 1962. 158p. [Children's fiction].

The story of four successive generations of a Chicago family (the Stuarts). Starts with the Fort Dearborn Massacre in 1812, and ends with the Columbian Exposition in 1893. The Exposition is covered on pages 125-146.

Ketzel, Patricia Anne. "A Fair To Remember: Using Fiction To Teach The History Of Chicago In The 1890's." Master's thesis, Lake Forest College, 1988. 98p.

The story revolves around Sean McGowan, his sister Kathleen, and his love, Ann Carberry. Sean and Kathleen are orphaned at a young age—Kathleen is placed in the home of a fine family, and Sean is sent to an orphanage and is eventually forced to eke out a living on the streets of Chicago. Sean meets and falls in love with Ann Carberry at the Columbian Exposition. Ann is a worker at the Children's Building at the Fair and one of the children under her care is Sean's sister, Kathleen. Sean and Kathleen are reunited—fleetingly, for Sean is force to flee Chicago because he fears of retaliation from Finnigan, a miscreant that Sean stopped from bombing the Women's Building at the Exposition. Sean goes to Seattle to make his fortune. He returns to Chicago in 1897 and has to devise a way to stymie Finnigan, as well as figure out a way to win back the heart of Ann from her fiance Clarence.

Kingsbury, Elizabeth. *Tale Of An Amateur Adventuress: The Autobiography Of Esther Gray*. Abridged And Edited By Elizabeth Kingsbury. Cincinnati: Editor Publishing Co., 1898. 199p.

The daughter of an Indiana editor and Congressman, describes her experiences as a journalist, bookkeeper, door-to-door magazine subscription salesperson, actress, and private secretary. A large portion of the novel (pp. 70-129) is devoted to her experience as a guide at the Columbian Exposition.

Kirk, Hyland C. *The Revolt Of The Brutes: A Fantasy Of The Chicago Fair*. New York: Charles T. Dillingham & Co., 1893. 123p.

An allegory protesting mankind's mistreatment of animals. The story is set in Chicago during the Columbian Exposition, and is descriptive of the natural history exhibits at the Fair.

Lawson, Robert. *The Great Wheel*. New York: Viking Press, 1957. 188p. [Children's fiction].

The story of Conn Kilroy, a young Irish boy who follows the prophecy of an old aunt. The prophecy stated that Conn's fortune lied to the West and that one day he would ride the greatest wheel in all the world. The prophecy is fulfilled six years later when Conn leaves Ireland and ventures to Chicago to work on the first Ferris Wheel.

Mackie, Pauline Bradford. "In Old Vienna." *New Peterson Magazine*, Vol. 3 (February, 1894): pp. 118-121.

Short story set in the cafe at Old Vienna on Midway Plaisance. A society woman, after overhearing a young girl talking to her lover, realizes that she has created a comfortable, but unhappy existence for her daughter.

Miller, Francesca Falk. *The Sands: The Story Of Chicago's Front Yard*. Chicago: Valentine-Newman Publishers, 1948. 215p.

This story describes the development of "the Sands," a stretch of lake front ranging from the Chicago River north to the Oak Street Beach. In the 1850's this area of land was inhabited by fishermen, prostitutes, gamblers, and criminals. Today the Sands is one of Chicago's finest areas, built up with apartment buildings, billion dollar hotels, and exclusive shops. The Columbian Exposition is mentioned briefly in Chapter 8 of this novel, pages 77-83.

Moody, Minnie Hite. *Once Again In Chicago*. New York: Alfred H. King, 1933. 268p.

An account of one woman's experience of the Century of Progress Exposition as well as her memories of the World's Columbian Exposition.

Moore, Bernard F. *The Girl From Midway: A Farce Comedy In One Act*. Clyde, Ohio: Ames, 1895. 19p.

James Bradford, a retired businessman, is infatuated with Clementine, a woman who works at the Midway Plaisance. Bradford has visited the World's Fair fifty times—five times with his wife, the other forty-five to see Clementine. A comical situation develops when Bradford, Bradford's wife, Clementine, and Frank Raymond (an old chum of Bradford, and Clemetine's husband) come together in Bradford's house.

Neely, Frank T. *Looking Forward: An Imaginary Visit To The World's Fair*. Chicago: F. T. Neely, 1889. 203p.

Consists of humorous articles containing outlandish predictions for the Chicago World's Fair (e.g. creation of a several mile high tower, Fair's ability to handle three million people hourly, and a sea serpent display).

Neely, Frank T. *A Tale Of The World's Fair. Giving The Experience Of An Underwriter Visiting The Fair At Chicago, 1893*. Chicago: F. T. Neely, 1890. [No pagination].

Very similar to Neely's *Looking Forward* in that it contains outlandish "predictions" for Chicago's Fair of 1893.

Pace, Barney. "An Experimental Novel About The Columbian Exposition Of 1893: The Fame And Fortune Of Jimmie Dawson." Ph.D. dissertation, University of Michigan, 1982. 326p.

Nineteen year old Jimmie Dawson leaves his hometown of Dexter, Michigan (population 673) to seek fame and fortune in Chicago. Within a week of arriving in Chicago Jimmie lands a job as a clerk with the publicity department of the World's Columbian Exposition. Ambition and dreams of wealth drive Jimmie into quitting his clerical job for a sales position with a Chicago lumber company. Jimmie does quite well for himself selling lumber, but when the recession of 1893 hits, Jimmie finds himself jobless, homeless, and wondering if Chicago is the land of plenty after all. This novel does a good job of providing the reader with a feeling for the economic and social climate of Chicago during the time of the Fair.

Payne, Will. *Mr. Salt: A Novel*. Boston: Houghton, Mifflin & Company, 1904. 330p.

A story of romance between Henry Salt, a captain of industry, and his stenographer Esther Ross. The Columbian Exposition is mentioned throughout the novel and a visit to the Fair is described in Chapter 6 (pp. 54-66).

Pollard, Percival. "The White City's Dream." In Pollard, Percival, *Dreams Of To-Day*. Chicago: Way and Williams, 1897. pp. 247-264.

A man's dreaming takes him back to the days of the Columbian Exposition, and to the splendor and glory of the Exposition's Court of Honor.

Quondam (real name Charles McClellan Stevens). *The Adventures Of Uncle Jeremiah And Family At The Great Fair; Their Observations And Triumphs*. Chicago: Laird & Lee, 1893. 237p.

A rural Illinois family's experience with a long lost family member, and a variety of Exposition events and scenes (e.g. Midway Plaisance, La Rabida, the ship "Illinois," the Cold Storage Building fire, and the question of Sunday openings). The book contains over sixty illustrations.

Rathbone, Cornelia Kane. "No. 58: An Episode of the Columbian Exposition." *Outing*, Vol. 26 (April, 1895): pp. 13-26.

John Bowman, a rolling chair pusher at the Columbian Exposition, falls in love with one of his customers—Miss Harriman, a beautiful, wealthy, and somewhat snobbish society woman.

Rathborne, St. George. *The Bachelor Of The Midway*. New York: Mascot Publishing Co., 1894. 314p.

Dorothy Cereal (the beautiful daughter of Samson Cereal, a Chicago grain king) is the object of a bizarre kidnapping plot incited by a revengeful Turk. Aleck Craig, a young Canadian athlete, and his friend, Claude Wycherley, come to Dorothy's aid. The novel is full of adventure, coincidences, and Samson

Cereal's "dirty laundry." Most of the story's action takes place on the Midway Plaisance.

St. Felix, Marie (real name Harriet Louise Lynch). *Two Bad Brown Eyes*. New York: Merriam Company, 1894. 245p.

Honora Herrick, the possessor of the eyes in the title of the book, is a respectable country girl who is seduced by a clergyman named Philip Allan. Full of self-righteous repentance, and filled with horror at Honora's immorality, Philip deserts her. Honora leaves her home in rural New York, and strays into a life of sin in Bohemian Paris. Fifteen years later she returns to the United States to visit the Columbian Exposition (the Fair is described quite extensively in the novel). While in Chicago she meets Philip's daughter Patricia—a beautiful and naive 18 year old. With Patricia as agent, Honora seeks her revenge against Philip in a wickedly cruel way.

Sims, A. K. (real name John Harvey Whitson). *Chicago Charlie's Diamond Dash: Or, Trapping The Tunnel Thieves. A Story Of The White City*. New York: Beadle and Adams (Beadle's New York Dime Library, No. 786, November 15, 1893). 31p.

Sidney Mayfield, the man assigned to guard a diamond exhibit at the Columbian Exposition, is found dead. The Chicago police decide the death is a suicide even though $100,000 worth of diamonds have been stolen. Chicago Charlie isn't convinced that the death is a suicide, and with the help of some assistants sets out to stalk the murderer. (Note: The cover page of this dime novel lists the title as *Chicago Charlie's Diamond Haul*).

Sinclair, Harold. *The Years Of Growth, 1861-1893*. New York: Doubleday, Doran and Co., 1940. 415p.

The Years Of Growth chronicles the development of a town—Everton, Illinois—from 1861 to 1893. The final chapter, entitled "1893," makes mention to the Columbian Exposition.

Slimmens, Ebenezer (Real name A. J. Dockarty). *The Midway Plaisance. The Experience Of An Innocent Boy From Vermont In The Famous Midway.* Chicago: Chicago World Book Co., 1894. 260p.

A detailed look at the Midway Plaisance through the eyes of Ebenezer Slimmens—the innocent boy from Vermont. The story provides good descriptions of the Streets of Cairo, Blarney Castle, the Beauty Show, Hagenbeck's Circus, Old Vienna, the Ferris Wheel, and much more. Illustrated.

Statham, Frances P. *The Roswell Legacy.* New York: Fawcett Columbine, 1988. 379p.

Allison Forsyth has made a new life for herself after her husband Dr. Charles "Coin" Forsyth died in a battle during the Civil War. She has remarried and borne a son named Jonathan. Jonathan has grown up and fallen in love with a beautiful young woman named Ginna. Allison is excited about meeting Ginna and her family—but her elation is to be short-lived. For she soon discovered that Coin has not died at all, that he too has remarried and begun a new life—and that his daughter is none other than the beautiful Ginna. The novel is set against the backdrop of Grover Cleveland's Washington, and events such as the Columbian Exposition (mentioned throughout the book; Chapter 28, pp. 259-269, devoted to it) and the Pullman uprising permeate the story.

Stead, William T. *From The Old World To The New; Or, A Christmas Story Of The World's Fair, 1893.* [Published as the Christmas issue of the *Review of Reviews* for 1892]. 123p.

Walter Wynne and Rose Thorne fall in love in England in the Spring of 1886. Due to circumstances, and the meddling of others, the two lovers become separated for seven years, but are reunited on the Fairgrounds of the Columbian Exposition. Clairvoyance, telepathy, and spiritualism figure prominently in the story.

Street, Ada Hilt and Street, Julian Leonard. *Tides*. Garden City, NY: Doubleday, Page & Co., 1926. 412p.

> *Tides* is a picturesque and haunting chronicle of Chicago. References to the World's Columbian Exposition can be found throughout the novel.

Talbot, Jack. *The Lake Front Strangler; Or, The World's Fair Horror*. New York: Street & Smith (Log Cabin Library, No. 219). 32p.

> A burst of strangulation murders are threatening the success of the Columbian Exposition. Ned Harley (a tall, athletic, and handsome detective) is set on catching the strangler, but the case is complicated because his friend, Frank Lowell, appears to be mixed-up in the crimes.

Vynne, Harold R. *The Woman That's Good: A Story Of The Undoing Of A Dreamer*. Chicago and New York: Rand McNally & Co., 1900. 473p.

> A romance using the Columbian Exposition for backdrop. The novel centers on Eustace Gaunt, a young poet, novelist and journalist, who becomes involved in an affair of the heart with a woman other than his wife. The story describes Gaunt's change from heavy drinking to total abstinence, as well as his divorces and moral maturation.

Walker, Mildred. *Light From Arcturus*. New York: Harcourt, Brace & Co., 1935. 343p.

> The story of the development of Julia Hauser (wife of a businessman and a mother of four) built around three World's Fairs: the Centennial Exposition in Philadelphia in 1876, the World's Columbian Exposition in Chicago in 1893, and the Century of Progress Exposition in Chicago in 1933.

Ward, A. B. "A Medley of the Midway Plaisance." In *Short Stories From Outing*. New York & London: Outing Publishing Co., 1895. pp. 91-114.

Short story dealing with some successful and unsuccessful romances of the crew of the "Captive Balloon," a restaurant located on the Midway Plaisance (the restaurant was so named because it was adjacent to a hot air balloon ride).

Winslow, Helen M. "Met on the Midway." *Frank Leslie's Popular Monthly*, Vol. 36 (October, 1893): pp. 501-504.

Melinda Maybury, a 37 year old woman from Pottstown Corners, faints while riding the Ferris Wheel. She is rescued by Enos Fairchild—her long lost lover. Enos is now a husband and father. Neither one recognizes the other and they part.

Wood, Edith Elmer. "Martha Ellen at the Chicago Exposition." In Wood, Edith Elmer, *Shoulder-Straps And Sun-Bonnets*. New York: Henry Holt and Co., 1901. pp. 41-57.

Martha Ellen Powers is a maid for a wealthy, good-hearted, autocratic woman named Mrs. Robinson. Martha Ellen is a widow who will sacrifice anything for her three indolent children. Mrs. Robinson is appalled when she finds out that Martha Ellen has spent her life's savings on sending all three of her shiftless offspring to Chicago to see the wonders of the Columbian Exposition. Feeling sorry that Martha has no pleasures because she spends all the fruits of her toil on the pleasures of her unappreciative children, Mrs. Robinson decides that she will finance a trip to the Fair for Martha Ellen. Mrs. Robinson personally drives her protegee to the station, and sees her board the Chicago train to make sure Martha Ellen does not sell her ticket back at the last moment, and give the proceeds to her children. On her return home, Mrs. Robinson questions Martha Ellen about the Fair and discovers that Martha Ellen never actually entered the Fairgrounds because, in Martha's own words, "half a dollar seemed sech a sight o' money ter pay jest ter walk through a turnstile! Yes, I know ye give me five dollars, but feather boas was a-sellin' at four dollars an' eighty-nine cents—an' Ellie (her daughter) did want one so bad!" [This short story was first published in *Century Magazine*, Vol. 38 (May, 1900): pp. 46-50].

Yandell, Enid, Loughborough, Jean and Hayes, Laura. *Three Girls In A Flat*. Chicago: Knight, Leonard & Co., 1892. 154p.

> Chronicles the trials and triumphs of three women sharing an apartment in Chicago in the early 1890's. Talk of the Columbian Exposition, especially of the Woman's Building and the Board of Lady Managers, permeate the story. [Note: Ms. Yandell was a sculptor at the Fair].

Additional copies of *Fairground Fiction* may be obtained from the publisher.

Price: $15.95 per book (New York State residents please add 8% sales tax.)

Shipping and handling: Book rate: $2.75 for the first book and $1.00 for each additional book. (Surface shipping may take three to four weeks.) Air mail: $4.00 per book.

Please do not send cash. Make checks or money orders payable to:

EPOCH BOOKS
22 Byron Avenue
Kenmore, NY 14223

Please send _____ copies of *Fairground Fiction* to:

Name:_____

Address:_____

City:_____ State:_____ Zip:_____

Make checks or money orders payable to:
EPOCH BOOKS, 22 Byron Avenue, Buffalo, NY 14223